THE CLASSIC VEGETABLE COOKBOOK

BY THE AUTHOR OF

Cooking Fish and Shellfish

The Classic Vegetable Cookbook

by Ruth Spear

Illustrated by Grambs Miller

PERENNIAL LIBRARY

Harper & Row, Publishers, New York
Grand Rapids, Philadelphia, St. Louis, San Francisco
London, Singapore, Sydney, Tokyo, Toronto

To James Beard, mentor and friend

A hardcover edition of this book was published in 1985 by Harper & Row, Publishers.

Copyright acknowledgments appear on page 425.

First PERENNIAL LIBRARY edition published 1989.

LIBRARY OF CONGRESS CATALOG CARD NUMBER 84-48195
ISBN 0-06-091628-1

Contents

"One of the greatest luxuries in dining
is to be able to command plenty of good vegetables
well served up."

Thomas Walker,
The Art of Good Dining (1835)

Preface

The vegetables served in my childhood were cooked until dead, usually accomplished by boiling the life out of them. I never knew that vegetables could please, could really satisfy, until my first trip to France and Italy as a student. Even then I didn't understand that it was not just rewarding flavor, but also texture and color that contributed to the satisfaction.

There are certain meals from my early European travels that I still remember and think of as personal vegetable epiphanies: in France, a plate of *haricots verts,* thin as soda straws, green, tender, and beanless, each slender wand glistening with sweet Normandy butter. They were served as a first and separate course, and each mouthful was a revelation. Following was a *poulet de Bresse* and spinach, bright green and buttery, with no bitter aftertaste. That same year, in a quite ordinary trattoria in Rome, I had a simple plate of fresh sweet peas cooked with bits of prosciutto and mushrooms, a dish that played second fiddle to nothing but was served properly on its own. It was so incredibly good I went back and ordered it every day for a week. That summer I ate my first zucchini, lightly battered and fried, or sweetened with fresh basil in a frittata, which became my favorite summer lunch. None of these things was served with any particular fanfare and certainly not touted for nutritional reasons. Eventually I did, however, find myself eating less flesh of all kinds and having those wonderful vegetable dishes as courses on their own. I also wondered why such good things were not available at home; surely it was more than distance that lent such enchantment.

I became quite shameless about asking to be let into kitchens, private and professional, to observe the preparation of an admired dish. I began to collect vegetable recipes, thinking to share my excitement in a cookbook, but marriage and children somehow kept my project on the back burner. This seems an especially good time for that sharing. Americans have never taken such a long, hard look at the way they eat or weighed so carefully the implications of diet in relation to health and well-being. According to the latest nutritional theory, we don't need half as much protein as we were brought up to believe we did. The government's newest official dietary guidelines urge the daily consumption of deep yellow and dark green leafy vegetables such as carrots, spinach, and broccoli, plus members of the cabbage family like cauliflower, kale, and brussels sprouts, which are thought to contain certain natural cancer-inhibiting substances.

These considerations are bringing about sweeping changes in the way we eat, both in content and combination. For me, the change has been a redefining of the concept of the main course, with meat, poultry, or fish often playing a minor, flavoring role. And we are all quite content to have an occasional nonmeat meal. Many people I speak to have fallen into similar patterns; though they eat meat, they're eating less of it. Vegetables and grains are part of a new life-style that is quite outside the strictures of vegetarianism.

I find, however, that most cooks do not have the repertoire they would like or a broad understanding of how vegetables should be prepared, which means that the commitment is there without a secure background in how to choose, cook, and serve them. That is why I would like to share what I've learned, along with the dishes my family most enjoy.

How to Use This Book

My intention in compiling this book was to gather together in one place everything you need to know about buying, cooking and serving vegetables, to provide not only a varied selection of tempting, reasonably foolproof recipes but also the kind of background information that the reader could apply to any recipe from any source.

The section Vegetable Basics at the front of the book explains the most often-used cooking techniques and includes a few words on canned and frozen vegetables. Part One, literally the A to Z of vegetables, contains a mini–chapter on every common vegetable from artichoke to zucchini. Each contains information on buying, storing, and preliminary preparation and anything else I felt was useful or just fun to know. There are often a number of informal recipes, simple ways of cooking that are really just the practical application of the methods given in Vegetable Basics, followed by recipes featuring that particular vegetable. Where appropriate, a soup or a dish involving pasta is included.

Part Two includes recipes for mixed vegetable dishes and for rice and other grains that are used like vegetables. You will also find here recipes for basic stocks and useful sauces and dips, and information on preparing attractive vegetable garnishes and using culinary herbs.

General information related to vegetable cookery is grouped in the Appendix. This includes sections on how to cook pasta and plan vegetarian meals, a glossary of the terms used in my recipes and a source list for buying specialty food items by mail.

Acknowledgments

I would like to thank a number of people for their help and support. My agent, Susan Lescher, believed in what I wanted to do and was more generous with time and encouragement than any writer could hope for. Robert Lescher stepped in as the voice of reason and moderation just when he was needed most.

I shall be forever grateful to Virginia Slifka, at whose tasteful table the idea for this book was born, and to my husband, Harvey Spear, who said it first. Without proselytizing, Ginny helped me to think like a vegetarian and understand the meal planning problems, inherent in being one. Harvey, of course, was the number-one guinea pig in every case.

Thanks are due to the restaurateurs who let me be underfoot in their kitchens and pester them with questions—Jean-Pierre Coffe, of the sadly defunct La Ciboulette restaurant in Paris, and Nicola Civetta of La Primavera in New York—and to friends and family who contributed recipes, ideas, thoughts, observations, and put me on the trail of some extraordinary dishes—especially Paula Wolfert, Joy Ubina, Jacqueline Simon, Monique Eastman, Suzanne Hamlin, and my daughter Jessica. Finally I thank Betty Publicker, who patiently shopped for, peeled, cut, and chopped a staggering amount of vegetables as we tested, tasted, argued about, changed, accepted, and rejected recipes for this book, and Joan Whitman, whose editorial instincts and good sense made it all come together.

Vegetable Basics

Cooking Techniques

I n order to keep the recipes in this book as simple as possible, the vegetable cooking techniques I refer to are explained here, along with some general information I feel might come in handy.

The cooking times given in this book pertain if vegetables are of equal size. They allow for the fact that foods will continue to cook for a minute or two in their own internal heat after being removed from the source of heat. Whenever possible, have vegetables at room temperature just prior to cooking. If they are mature and fibrous, increase the cooking times accordingly. In general, the younger the vegetable, the more tender it is and the faster it will cook.

Many vegetables are affected adversely by aluminum and cast iron, and are best cooked in glass, stainless steel, or enamel-lined saucepans. I have tried to mention this in each recipe where it applies.

Boiling is cooking in a liquid kept at 212°F, the method most often used (and abused) in cooking vegetables. A *rolling* or *hard boil* is a full, seething boil, with lots of large surface bubbles. By reducing the heat slightly you get a *slow boil,* with just occasional small bubbles on the surface.

Bring water to the boil, add salt (about 1 tablespoon to 4 quarts), and add the vegetables in small batches so the temperature of the liquid doesn't drop. The cooking time is calculated from the time the water returns to the boil after the food is added. The more water used in proportion to the vegetable, the more rapidly the second boil will be reached; thus the shorter time spent by the vegetable in water. Liberally salting the water helps set the color and does not make the food salty, since the water is discarded. The old trick of adding baking soda to keep green vegetables green is never necessary with proper cooking and actually should be avoided, because it destroys valuable nutrients. Cook green vegetables uncovered because covering them dulls their color. Root vegetables, which are denser and have less fragile colors, are usually cooked covered.

Blanching means to drop food into boiling water and boil it until it has softened and is partly or completely cooked. It indicates the shortest possible time spent in boiling water and is the preferred French method for cooking green vegetables. Blanching is often the preliminary step to further cooking or flavoring. You can also use a brief blanching to remove a strong or slightly bitter flavor from mature vegetables, such as cabbage or kale.

Refreshing entails plunging vegetables that have just been blanched into cold water to stop the cooking. With green vegetables, refreshing sets the color. Vegetables can be blanched and refreshed ahead of time —even hours—and finished in butter just before serving.

Parboiling is boiling a dense vegetable, such as a potato, for a short time to soften it prior to some additional cooking treatment, for example, roasting with meat or adding to a stew. To parboil a vegetable, shorten its regular boiling time by a third.

Simmering means to cook in a liquid just below the boiling point, with relatively little surface movement in the liquid other than tiny bubbles.

Reducing a cooking liquid, stock, or cream means to boil it down to concentrate the flavor. The result is called a reduction. Most recipes will specify that you reduce by one half, a third, and so forth.

Braising

Braising is cooking slowly with relatively little liquid in a covered vessel. It may be done on top of the stove or in the oven. Cabbage, endive, celery, onions, and carrots are frequently braised.

Sweating,

Sweating, a useful preliminary procedure for vegetables that are going to be braised for soups and stews, is a combination of stewing in butter and steam-frying. Sweating softens vegetables and releases their juices and flavor without actually frying them, which would change their taste.

To sweat vegetables, melt the appropriate amount of butter in a skillet or saucepan. Add the vegetables, cover with a round of wax paper, put the lid on and cook over low to medium heat for 5 to 7 minutes, shaking the pan once or twice, until natural juices begin to exude. The timing is approximate; use your eye to judge softness. The vegetables should not brown.

Steaming

Steaming is cooking over, rather than in, water. Because green vegetables lose color in covered cooking, I steam only young ones that will cook quickly.

Vegetables should be arranged with as little overlap as possible, so use stacked baskets if necessary or steam in several batches if quantity warrants.

There are many kinds of steaming vessels, ranging from simple pots with interior racks to Chinese stacked bamboo baskets, which allow you to steam several foods at once. All you really need is a pot with a lid that fits snugly (but not so tightly that dangerous pressure could build up) and a rack inside. The rack can be a proper vegetable steaming basket or simply a cake rack or an ovenproof pie plate sitting on upside-down demitasse cups—anything that is shallow and heatproof and will keep the food above the level of the boiling water.

Put enough water in the pot or bottom pan so that it will not boil away during the cooking time, but little enough so there is about an inch between the water level and the food being cooked. Bring the water to the boil, put the prepared vegetables on a plate, uncover the steamer carefully to avoid being scalded, and slide them onto the rack in a single layer. Cover and begin timing from this point. Check the water level occasionally to make sure it is not in danger of boiling away. When the vegetables are finished, remove the lid and let the steam dissipate for a few seconds (don't have your face right over the pot when you uncover it). Remove the vegetables with a slotted spoon from the rack or lift the baskets off using oven mitts. Finish as desired.

Frying is a simple technique, but there are several important factors for achieving a good result.

The temperature and purity of the oil are critical. The oil must be heated to the required temperature, usually 365° to 375°F, and then *maintained* at that level. Develop a discriminating eye; oil heated to proper frying temperature gets a little wrinkle on the top and a special smell at the right moment. Another test: a cube of bread will brown in 2 to 3 seconds. The vegetables to be fried must be small and of uniform size and added a few at a time, as the temperature of the oil drops with each piece of food that is added. If too many pieces are added at once, the oil will not be hot enough to sear them instantly; they will absorb fat, with a greasy, soggy result. Never crowd the pan; the food should be able to float freely.

Remove each piece as it is done and immediately add another until all are finished. Removing too many pieces at once raises the temperature of the oil, and the outside of the food will become dark brown before it has a chance to cook. Should the oil reach its smoking point, it will begin to decompose chemically, which adversely affects food flavor and is unhealthy. If this happens, discard it.

The oil you choose has a lot to do with a successful outcome. The higher the smoking point, the less tricky it is to handle. Soybean oil has the highest smoking point of any cooking oil, but you may not like the taste. Corn oil and peanut oil are good choices. Olive oil begins to smoke at 385°—too low for frying.

The amount of oil you use is another critical factor. There must be enough to surround the food completely and cook it quickly. Maintaining the temperature is also easier with a large amount of oil.

Frying oil may be strained, stored, and reused to cook similar foods, but keep track of the number of times you use it; each subsequent use lowers the smoking point. Store in a tightly sealed jar in the refrigerator if possible. It will look cloudy but come back to normal at room temperature. Discard any oil that is dark and has a strong smell.

A word of warning to those who are inexperienced with frying: *oil is highly flammable when very hot,* so use a deep-frying thermometer to gauge the heat. Very hot oil does not boil and so can be deceptive. Should you find yourself with an oil fire, put the pot lid on quickly. If burning oil has spilled, douse flames with a couple of good handfuls of salt or baking soda. Do not douse with water, which just spreads the fire. Don't lift or move the pot, which may also spread the flames.

Sautéing means to cook a food in a small quantity of fat to soften it, brown it, or completely cook it through. The vegetables must be cut in small, uniform pieces that are quite dry so they will not steam. The fat must be hot so the juices are quickly sealed in. Butter contributes the best flavor, but because it cannot be heated to the necessary temperature without burning, it must be clarified (see p. 404) or mixed half and half with oil. You can, of course, sauté in oil alone. The sauté pan must be neither so small that the food is crowded nor so big that there are bare spots that may overheat.

Stir-frying, a kind of quick sautéing, is a technique that keeps the food in constant motion in a greased pan so everything cooks evenly without sticking. (An interesting side benefit only recently discovered is that stir-frying actually increases the fiber content of food, which scientists believe helps control cholesterol in the blood.) The rounded bottom and sides of a wok facilitate the scooping-tossing motion (a long-handled spatula especially designed for wok cookery is best for this) and keep the vegetables well coated with a relatively small amount of oil. But a large sauté pan with sloping sides can also be used.

Vegetables should be washed, drained, cut (and parboiled if necessary), then dried well before beginning.

To stir-fry, always start with a dry pan or wok. Place over high heat until the pan is hot enough to make a drop of water sizzle. Then add the oil (peanut or vegetable) and heat it until it is bubbling but not smoking. If the oil is not hot enough, the food will stick and become limp rather than crisp. Very high heat also seals the vegetable so that it does not absorb grease.

Broiling and grilling: Broiling takes place under and close to a source of intense heat—two to four inches from the source is ideal.

Slices of eggplant or tomato brushed with oil, mushroom caps, and skewered peppers and onions are some of the vegetables I broil regularly. Make sure the broiler is thoroughly preheated and keep the food basted so it doesn't dry out.

If you are grilling over charcoal, let your coals burn for a good thirty to forty-five minutes, until they are covered with a fine white ash. Cook the vegetables, turning with tongs or a large spatula so the skin is not pierced. Or wrap vegetables in heavy-duty foil packets firmly sealed at the ends. Use one kind or an assortment of vegetables. A favorite summer combination includes baby eggplant, peppers, tomatoes, and green and yellow squash. These vegetable packets will take about half an hour.

Canned and Frozen Vegetables

Mushrooms are best done in a hinged grill to make turning easier. Paint them with oil first. Use large caps and barbecue them along with steaks, other meat, or poultry. Serve plain or filled with warm béarnaise sauce.

Canned vegetables: Other than for extreme situations—like stocking a larder in the Australian outback—I find little to recommend in canned vegetables because their taste and texture are so altered by the long canning process. There are a few exceptions: I buy canned tomatoes, because I use tomatoes for lots of dishes and good ones are simply not always available. I use canned cannelini and kidney beans when I don't have the time for dried ones. I always have beets in jars on hand because fresh small beets are hard to find and the older ones require such long cooking. Canned corn (one of the few foods minimally altered by canning) is another of my pantry staples because we love corn pancakes with maple syrup on Sunday mornings in winter. Jarred artichoke hearts and olives make a substantial main course salad out of leftover rice, so they're on hand, too. Beyond that, my personal predilection is to follow seasonal availabilities and rejoice in them.

My home canning is limited to pickles and chutneys. For precise instructions for putting these up, consult one of the books on the subject. There is an excellent one offered to the public by the Ball Corporation (see Appendix).

Frozen vegetables: When fresh vegetables are not available, are too dear, or time presses, frozen vegetables are my next choice. Depending on the season, some commercially frozen vegetables (like peas, for example) actually cost less than a comparable amount of fresh (unless, of course, you buy them frozen in a fancy sauce of some sort). Because of the blanching given vegetables preliminary to their freezing, the cooking times suggested on the package will be shorter than that for fresh vegetables. Nonetheless, these times often result in vegetables that are overcooked by today's standards. Use the smallest amount of water possible, and check frequently.

To take advantage of a seasonal glut or the abundance of your own garden, you can also freeze your own vegetables—some much more successfully than others. The only raw vegetables I myself freeze are sliced green peppers (seeds and ribs removed) and onions for emergencies. They are flabby when they defrost but perfectly fine for cooked dishes.

When mushrooms begin to turn brown, I chop them and make duxelles (p. 173), which freezes well. I also freeze pureed vegetables, fresh tomato sauce, and some completed dishes, such as ratatouille.

CUTTING TERMS

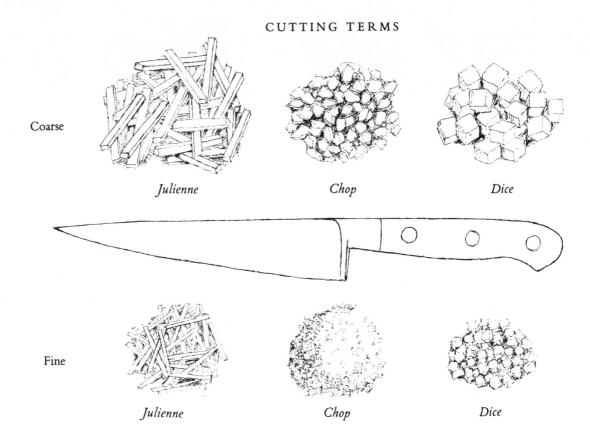

Coarse

Julienne

Chop

Dice

Fine

Julienne

Chop

Dice

Part One

Artichokes

(Cynara scolymus)

The thorny leaves of the globe artichoke conceal a delicious sweet heart that has been prized for centuries. Sicily seems to have been its early home, and the name, from the Arabic *al-khurshūf,* may indicate that it was brought there from Asia by the Saracens. References in Greek and Roman writings pinpoint it for some scholars as a Mediterranean food, while others think what they described was not the globe artichoke at all but another thistle, the cardoon. Their introduction into France, like so many other gastronomic pleasures, is credited to Catherine de Médicis of Florence, who, if one would believe everything one reads, must have astounded Henry II with the culinary diversity of her nuptial baggage.

In the last twenty-five years in the United States, artichoke cultivation has boomed in California's Salinas Valley, making artichokes abundant now year-round and, if not exactly cheap, eminently within reason.

There are other varieties of artichoke besides the globe we know. Provence has a spindle-shape purple variety. The Italians have several, each with a distinctive look and taste: the *Mamme,* like our globe; the tiny *vert de Florence,* about 5 inches long and so young and tender it is eaten whole (and sometimes raw); and a small egg-shape variety that is usually put up in jars in oil.

Artichokes contain a substance called cynarine that causes food taken immediately afterward to taste sweetish. Because of this I prefer whole artichokes to be served as a course by themselves. They also queer the flavor of wine, so I avoid serving it until the following course.

The tender meaty bottom, or heart, of the artichoke is a delicacy when served on its own. The preparation is rather lengthy, beginning with trimming away the leaves from the globe. I prefer hearts served as a separate course, either warm, filled with duxelles, or cold, stuffed with crabmeat or small shrimp bound with homemade mayonnaise.

To Buy

Look for firm, compact, solid heads of medium size, 3 to 3½ inches in diameter. While the very large ones are spectacular, they can be fibrous. A few small brown spots are not serious (they occur from frost); but pass up those with brown, withered stems and cracked leaves (an indication of age). Allow 1 whole artichoke per serving and 1 or 2 hearts.

Occasionally you may come across a French or Italian recipe calling for "young artichokes," meaning those whose choke has not begun to form. These are rare in American markets, although they are beginning to make a tentative appearance in fancier ones.

Artichoke hearts are also available frozen and in jars and cans. I keep a jar or two on hand for a last-minute antipasto, with tomatoes, olives, salami, and crusty bread.

To Store

Keep in a closed plastic bag in the refrigerator. Use within 2 days.

To Prepare for Cooking Whole

Hold the artichoke by the stem and let cold water run

over and into the head to dislodge any dirt in the scales. Remove the stem by bending it at the base until it snaps off. If it is too soft to do this, use a sharp knife to cut it even with the base, so that the artichoke can stand upright (drawing 1). Break off any small outer leaves. If the stem is not very thick and fibrous, it may be peeled, trimmed, and then steamed or boiled along with the artichoke.

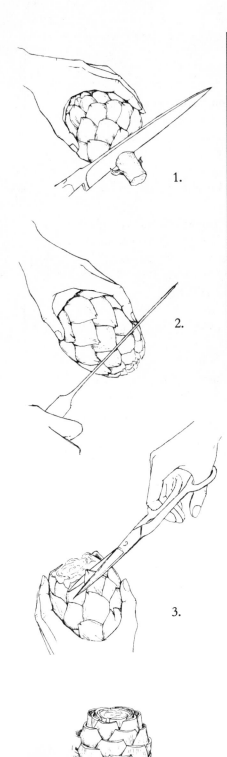

Place the artichoke on its side and cut off approximately 1 inch from the top (drawing 2). Immediately rub the cut stem end and top with a lemon half to prevent discoloration. Squeeze the rest of the lemon half into a bowl of water so you can drop the artichokes into the water as you work.

Using a pair of sharp kitchen shears, cut off and discard the sharp thorny tip of each leaf (drawings 3, 4). Rinse the artichoke briefly under cold water and drop into the acidulated water. The artichoke is now ready to be cooked.

Note: The choke, which is the tight cone of soft curling leaves with prickly tips surrounding a layer of inedible hairy fuzz, can be removed before or after cooking. I find it easier to do it after the artichoke has been cooked. Or the diner can remove it at table.

To Boil Whole

Place the prepared artichokes in an enamel-lined or stainless steel pot and add cold water to cover. Add the juice of 1 lemon and 2 teaspoons of salt. (Since artichokes float no matter how much water you use, a piece of rinsed cheesecloth will keep the protruding tops from discoloring while they cook, but I rarely bother.) Bring to a boil, adjust heat, and simmer uncovered for 30 to 40 minutes, depending on size, until the bottoms are easily pierced with the tip of a sharp knife or a leaf pulled out is tender. Do not overcook, as this makes them flaccid and quite tasteless. Remove artichokes and let them drain upside down on a rack until cool enough to handle.

To Steam Whole

Place prepared artichokes on a rack over 1 inch of boiling water. Cover and cook for 30 to 40 minutes, checking to make sure that the water has not boiled away.

To Remove the Choke

Part the center leaves and, taking hold of the tightly wrapped center cone of leaves, pull the choke out in one piece. Scrape away the hairy part underneath (which covers the heart) with a teaspoon or a melon baller until clean and smooth. Turn the removed cone of leaves upside down and set in the hollow in the center of the artichoke as a message to the diner that the choke is out.

Serve warm with plain melted butter or melted butter mixed with lemon juice, hollandaise, maltaise or mousseline sauce. A thick sauce like hollandaise can be spooned into the center hollow and served that way.

My favorite way to eat artichokes is at room temperature (chilling impairs the flavor and texture), dipping the leaves and the heart in herbed vinaigrette (p. 375).

How to Eat an Artichoke

Pull off a leaf, hold it by the tip, and dip the fleshy end into the accompanying sauce; scrape the flesh and sauce together off the leaf with your teeth. (Place discarded leaves around the rim of your plate or in a separate bowl if one is provided.) When all the leaves are eaten, use a knife and fork to scrape off and remove the hairy choke (if it has not been removed by the cook). Then eat the now clean heart.

To Prepare for Stuffing

Prepare whole artichokes for cooking and parboil them, partly covered, for 10 minutes. Remove choke, then turn artichoke upside down on the kitchen counter and press down on it with the flat of the hand to open the center. Turn right side up, place the stuffing in the center and between the leaves as well, and cook according to recipe.

To Prepare Hearts or Bottoms

Buy the largest artichokes you can find.

Have a bowl of acidulated water ready, about 2 tablespoons lemon juice or vinegar to 1 quart of water.

Cut off and discard the stem of the artichoke. Rub this and subsequent cut surfaces with lemon juice to prevent discoloration. Hold the artichoke upside down and bend a lower leaf back on itself until it snaps off. Proceed in this manner until you have gone past the curve of the heart and see leaves turning inward. Slice off the remaining leaf cone, leaving a base about 1½ inches thick. Pare away the leaves at the base. Turn the heart on its side and, working as rapidly as you can, pare away all green parts to end up with a smooth, flattened, greenish-white disk. As each heart is finished, drop into the acidulated water. After cooking, scoop out and scrape away the fuzzy choke.

Because artichoke bottoms discolor easily, they are frequently cooked in a *blanc-légume,* a combination of flour and a dash of oil mixed into acidulated water. If the color is not of paramount importance, however, I suggest you not bother cooking them *à blanc;* not only is it messy, but it seems to leach out the flavor. Simply rub with lemon and boil in salted water for 30 to 35 minutes, or until easily pierced with the tip of a sharp knife.

To cook à blanc: Put ¼ cup flour in an

enamel-lined or stainless steel saucepan. Beat in enough cold water to make a paste. Then add a quart more water, 2 tablespoons lemon juice, and 1 teaspoon salt. Bring to a boil and cook for 5 minutes. Add the artichoke hearts, bring back to the boil, and simmer 30 minutes, or until the hearts are tender. They should be covered with liquid at all times, so add more water if needed. Let cool in the blanc-légume. (If done a day ahead, cool in the cooking liquid, film it with oil, and refrigerate.) Just before using, remove from liquid and wash under cold water. Remove any remaining hairs, taking care not to damage the meat. Then use as recipe indicates.

Hot artichoke hearts with poached eggs:
For a rich and impressive dish that is not at all hard to prepare, make hollandaise sauce (p. 377) and keep it tepid; poach 4 eggs and keep them warm. Heat 4 serving dishes and reheat 4 cooked artichoke hearts by a brief immersion in boiling water. Put 1 heart on each plate, top each with an egg, and mask with the sauce. Sprinkle with finely snipped chives and serve at once with French bread as a light lunch.

Chilled artichoke hearts with céleri rémoulade:
This makes a nice first course at lunch or dinner. Pile céleri rémoulade (p. 102) onto cooked artichoke hearts that have been chilled.

This is my husband's favorite way to eat artichokes, so we often have it for lunch. Served with crusty bread to sop up the savory braising juices, it is a meal in itself, but it could also be a hearty first course.

Artichokes Braised with Mushrooms and Pork

4 medium artichokes, prepared for cooking whole	½ pound mushrooms, chopped
5 tablespoons olive oil	Pinch dried thyme
1 medium onion, chopped (about ¾ cup)	Salt and freshly ground pepper
½ cup finely chopped pork (see note)	4 strips lean bacon
	½ cup white wine
	½ cup chicken broth

Preheat the oven to 350°.

Parboil the artichokes for 10 minutes. Drain and, when cool enough to handle, scoop out the choke.

While the artichokes cook, prepare the stuffing. Heat 3 tablespoons of the olive oil in a 10-inch skillet. Add the onion and pork and sauté over low heat just until the pork loses its raw color. The mixture should not brown. Add the mushrooms and thyme and cook, stirring, about 5 minutes longer. Season with a little salt and liberal grindings of pepper, but do not taste because the pork is still raw. Spoon this stuffing into the centers of the artichokes.

Wrap a piece of bacon around each artichoke vertically and secure at the top with a toothpick. Heat the remaining 2 tablespoons olive oil in a heavy pot that will hold the artichokes snugly. Add them and cook uncovered over moderate heat for 3 minutes. Pour in the wine and broth, bring to a simmer, cover, and put in the oven for 45 to 50 minutes. Remove the artichokes to heated shallow soup dishes and spoon the braising juice over each. If a large quantity of juice remains, you may boil it down until it becomes a bit syrupy. Serves 4.

Note: Two half-inch-thick pork chops, totaling about ½ pound, will give you this amount of meat. Chop it in the food processor. Or use an equal amount of pork shoulder.

The bacon strips will be cooked but not brown. They can be served with the artichokes, or removed and saved to skillet-brown for breakfast.

Artichokes alla Romana

Hearty and garlicky, this Italian dish is a fine opener for any meal.

4 medium artichokes, prepared for cooking whole	¾ cup olive oil
	¾ cup chopped parsley
	2 teaspoons minced garlic
1½ cups chicken or vegetable broth	Salt and freshly ground pepper

Preheat the oven to 400°.
Parboil the artichokes for 10 minutes. Remove with

a slotted spoon and drain upside down. When cool enough to handle, remove the center leaves and choke.

Combine the broth, oil, parsley, garlic, salt to taste, and a liberal grinding of black pepper. Place the artichokes upright side by side in a baking dish and pour the broth mixture evenly over and around them. Bake for about 25 minutes, or until the outer leaves begin to turn a coppery color. Remove from the oven, spoon pan liquid over the artichokes, and broil until the tops brown—about 3 minutes. Serve in soup bowls with the remaining liquid divided among them. Serves 4.

Souffléed Artichokes

This impressive first course—baked artichokes used as containers for tiny cheese soufflés—is adapted from a recipe of Nathalie Hambro. It is quite filling and can also easily serve as the main course for a luncheon. The soufflé takes on the flavor of the artichoke as it cooks, and is then used as the dip for the individual leaves.

6 large artichokes, prepared for cooking whole	1 tablespoon chopped parsley
4 tablespoons butter	1½ cups (loosely packed) grated Swiss cheese, preferably Gruyère (about 6 ounces)
4 tablespoons flour	
2 cups milk	
Salt	5 medium eggs, separated, at room temperature
Cayenne	
Several gratings of nutmeg	1 additional egg white
	3 tablespoons grated Parmesan cheese

Simmer the artichokes, covered, in salted water for 20 minutes. Drain upside down and carefully and completely remove the center leaves and choke. Dry the inside of each artichoke with a paper towel. (This may be done early in the day.)

Preheat the oven to 425°.

Oil the bottom of a baking dish that will hold all the artichokes. Melt the butter in a heavy saucepan, blend in the flour, and cook slowly, stirring, for 2 minutes. Add the milk all at once and whisk rapidly until smooth. Beat in the salt, cayenne, nutmeg, and parsley and add the Gruyère cheese. Stir with a spoon until the cheese is melted. Let cool for a few minutes, then add the egg yolks one by one, beating well after each addition.

Beat the egg whites with a pinch of salt until stiff but not dry. Stir a couple of large spoonfuls into the cheese sauce to lighten it, then carefully fold in the balance.

Make the center opening of the artichokes as wide as possible. Spoon some of the soufflé mixture into the center of each and sprinkle the top with the Parmesan cheese. Place in the baking dish and bake in the center of the oven for 40 minutes, or until the soufflé is puffed and the top is golden. Serve at once. Serves 6.

Note: Because of the variation in artichoke size, you may find yourself with some soufflé mixture left over. Bake it separately in a small cup and have it for a snack.

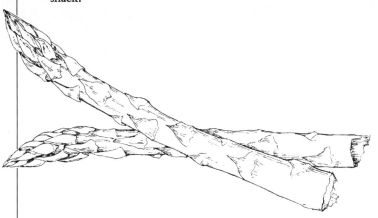

Asparagus
(Asparagus officinalis)

The origin of these prized cultivated spears is something of a historical puzzlement. They have been frequently and enthusiastically mentioned down through the centuries, almost always as an indulgence and an extravagence, but information on their source is curiously absent. We know the ancient Egyptians cultivated them and offered them to their gods; the Romans, from Pliny through Julius Caesar and Augustus, adored them; they are mentioned in seventeenth-century cookbooks in France. Asparagus also grows wild, a form thought tastier by some, Juvenal and the sixteenth-century herbalist John Girard among them.

Asparagus is a delicacy whose flavor I like to experience totally, so you will never find it served as a side dish in my house. Unless a recipe calls for asparagus tips or stir-fried asparagus, these superb stalks are best appreciated as a solo act. And be sure to eat them with the fingers, the way they are most delectable. Serve with a very dry white wine; the sulphur in asparagus makes wine taste sweeter than it is.

To Buy

Asparagus used to be strictly a spring crop, the eagerly awaited harbinger of the season. Though it can now be found off-season, when it is invariably more costly and less flavorsome, it is still at its best from late February to early June, with the peak in April. Virtually the entire supply is domestic.

Most American asparagus is green, with slender to medium-thick stalks. In Europe one sees purple-streaked thickish stalks and the prized soft white asparagus, which is grown under the earth to prevent the development of the chlorophyll that turns it green. In America white asparagus is usually available only in tins or jars, which I find disappointingly tasteless.

Whether you buy fat spears or skinny ones is just a matter of taste and how you plan to use them; the large ones can be just as tender as the small. Condition is much more important. Look for tightly closed tips and stalks that are firm, straight, and not limp or dry at the cut end. Ridges in the stem mean they have been around longer than qualifies for freshness.

It is critical to calculate the cooking time accurately with asparagus, and the calculation is made easier if they are of uniform thickness. Buy spears loose rather than bundled so you can choose ones that are all of a size. Allow a minimum of 6 to 8 per person—about ½ pound.

To Store

Very fresh asparagus keeps well in the refrigerator for about two days. Treat borderline cases like flowers: trim a bit off the bottom and stand them in a jar with about an inch of water in it. Cover with a loose plastic bag and refrigerate.

To Prepare for Cooking

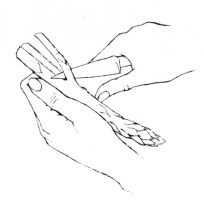

Snap off the base of the stalks at the point at which they break naturally. Rinse quickly under cold running water. It isn't necessary to peel the stalks unless they are tough and the small triangular scales very obvious; use a small sharp knife or a swivel-bladed peeler. Hold the asparagus flat on your work surface or in your hand and peel from about 2 inches below the tip down to the end of the stalks, turning until the whole is done.

To Cook

"As quick as cooking asparagus" was an old Roman saying meaning something accomplished rapidly; evidently even then the succulent spears were considered best when briefly cooked.

Asparagus should be cooked only until they are tender-crisp and bright green. Some cooks bundle the asparagus and stand them upright in about 3 inches of boiling water, cover, and cook for about 8 minutes, or until the tips are tender. Thus the stems are boiled at the same time the tips are steamed. I have never felt a need to use this method and personally prefer to blanch asparagus.

To blanch: Fill an enamel or stainless-steel pot (an

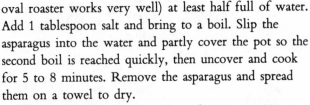

oval roaster works very well) at least half full of water. Add 1 tablespoon salt and bring to a boil. Slip the asparagus into the water and partly cover the pot so the second boil is reached quickly, then uncover and cook for 5 to 8 minutes. Remove the asparagus and spread them on a towel to dry.

When cooking a large number of asparagus, it is a good idea to bundle and tie them, so they can all be retrieved from the water at the same time. Leave one loose so you can fish it out from time to time and take a bite to see if it's done. Ideally, it should be slightly resistant to the tooth and not limp. Practice makes perfect in asparagus cookery.

To bundle asparagus: Wrap one end of a
piece of kitchen string around your middle finger; make a neat bunch of 10 or 12 asparagus; wrap the other end of the string tightly around the lower ends of the stalks, pull taut, then bring the string across and up to a point under the tips. Wrap and tie securely with a double knot (see drawing).

Pan-steamed: This method produces a delicious
result but is to be used only for very young asparagus. Put ½ pound washed and trimmed very slender asparagus in a covered skillet with 2 tablespoons butter, cut up, and only the water that clings from washing. Cover and cook over a medium heat for 7 minutes. The spears will emerge perfectly cooked, bright green and attractively slicked with butter.

Asparagus may be served warm or at room temperature—refrigeration dulls the flavor. For warm asparagus, the simplest sauce is butter that is barely melted, spiked with a bit of lemon juice, salt, and pepper. Hollandaise sauce and mousseline sauce are two other delicious, classic accompaniments. Maltaise sauce is perhaps best of all. A simple vinaigrette or herbed vinaigrette (with hard-cooked egg) is also excellent. For a dinner party, serve two sauces—a hollandaise and a vinaigrette, for example. Cold asparagus may also be served with a plain mayonnaise, preferably homemade.

(Recipes for all these sauces appear elsewhere in the book.)

Asparagus with Eggs Milanese

Eggs are one of the few foods that can accompany asparagus without detracting from their unique flavor, which is one reason an egg-based sauce like hollandaise is such a good foil. The eggs make this dish a whole meal—perfect for vegetarians, delicious for anyone, and very easy. Have it for lunch or a light supper.

1–1½ pounds medium asparagus, trimmed
4 poached eggs
4 tablespoons butter, melted
⅓ cup grated Parmesan cheese
Salt and freshly ground pepper

Arrange an oven rack in the highest position and preheat the oven to 450°.

Lavishly butter a shallow baking dish that will hold the asparagus and the eggs.

Blanch the asparagus, refresh, and drain very well. Place the eggs in the center of the baking dish and arrange the asparagus around them. Drizzle the melted butter over the asparagus and sprinkle them with Parmesan. Season lightly with salt and pepper and place in the upper third of the preheated oven for 4 minutes, until the cheese takes on some color. Serve on hot plates. Serves 4.

Asparagus parmigiana: Follow the preceding recipe, but increase the asparagus to 2 pounds and omit the eggs.

Asparagus with fried eggs: Prepare asparagus parmigiana and keep it warm while you fry 4 eggs lightly in butter. Divide the asparagus among 4 heated serving plates and top each with a fried egg.

Stir-fried Asparagus

Since quick cooking is best for asparagus, Chinese preparations are a natural. Here is a recipe I turn to when I am over the first spring hunger for asparagus served with its usual sauces. Try this on shredded lettuce leaves as a first course or as part of a Chinese meal.

1 pound slender asparagus, trimmed
1 teaspoon cornstarch
1 tablespoon cold water
2 tablespoons peanut or vegetable oil

¼ cup thinly sliced scallions, white and half of the green
½ cup chicken broth
1 tablespoon light soy sauce

Cut the asparagus into 1½-inch lengths.

Combine the cornstarch and water in a small bowl and stir into a smooth paste. Set aside.

Heat the oil in a large heavy skillet or wok and, when very hot, add the asparagus and scallions and stir-fry for 1 minute. Add the chicken broth, bring to a boil, and cook, stirring, for 2 or 3 minutes.

Make a well in the center of the asparagus and add the cornstarch mixture and the soy sauce. Cook, stirring, for 30 seconds or more, until sauce is smooth and thickened. Serve immediately. Serves 4 as part of a Chinese meal, 3 as a first course.

Chinese Asparagus Salad

Here is another easy Chinese treatment for asparagus. Serve this as a pleasant first course.

1 pound small to medium asparagus, trimmed
1 tablespoon soy sauce
1 tablespoon sesame oil

1 teaspoon red wine vinegar
1½ teaspoons sugar

Slice the asparagus on the diagonal into 2-inch lengths, keeping the tips and the stems separate.

Combine the soy sauce, oil, vinegar, and sugar in a small saucepan. Stir over moderate heat just until the sugar dissolves. There will be a small amount of sauce. Set aside.

Several years ago I bought seeds from France for the true *haricots verts,* or *mangetout,* and now I deliberately leave some on the vine to go to seed every year. These my daughter and I patiently shell to be saved for planting again the following year. Imported thin French string beans now appear in fancy markets at astronomical prices, and seedsmen specializing in imports often carry the French bean (see Appendix). Next best is to pick the smallest string beans at the market, one by one, or grow an American variety and pick when they are still pencil-slim.

To Buy

Select crisp, blemish-free pods and avoid very large, lumpy ones with big seeds. Tender green and yellow wax beans will snap when bent. Count on 1 pound to serve 4.

To Store

Refrigerate unwashed in a perforated plastic bag.

To Prepare for Cooking

Wash, tip, and tail them and leave whole or, if you're making a soup, cut into 1½-inch pieces. If beans are very slender, I like them with the ends left on. Never "french" them, a pointless mutilation to make overgrown beans appear slender, a procedure quite unknown in France.

Should you need to string your beans, which is rare today, break off the tips and just pull downward like a zipper. The string will come away.

To Cook

The way to keep green beans truly green is to blanch them, the only cooking method I recommend. I don't like steaming them because it does something odd to the

Bring a pot of lightly salted water to a bo
the stems and cook 1 minute. Add the tips a
minute more. Drain and run under cold wa
asparagus in a bowl, add the soy mixture, a
Serve at room temperature on lettuce leave

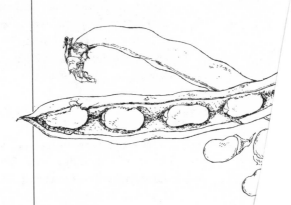

Beans

tring beans, shell beans,
different stages of devel
plant. String beans are
immature state; their s
Shell beans are the next stage
seeds become beans like favas
mature to the point at which
have dried beans, of which
specific varieties grown for

String Beans

tring beans are probab
likes without reservat
they were also one of th
abused. Early cookbook
anywhere from half an
green beans or snap be
improved varieties on
Wax beans, which ar
the purple string bea
be treated exactly li

flavor and can impair the color. I also blanch wax and purple beans.

Blanched:
Bring a great deal of water to the boil, much more than you think you will need—6 or 7 quarts. The greater the amount of water, the shorter the time returning to the boil after the beans are added; as a result, the beans will cook more quickly, thus preserving their color and flavor. Salt the water (1 teaspoon to 1 quart) and add the trimmed beans a small handful at a time. Cook at a rolling boil, uncovered, the length of time to be determined by their age, your tooth, and your eye. Generally, 7 to 10 minutes after the water returns to the boil is about right.

Green beans will turn deep green and have a slight translucence. Bite one to test; it should be tender and crisp but not crunchy and should have none of the raw, starchy taste of undercooked beans.

Spread a dry clean towel on counter. Place the beans in a colander, shake, then dump onto the waiting towel and spread out to dry. (This may be done far in advance of serving.) I don't refresh beans in cold water if I am going to finish the recipe right away, but I do refresh them if I am blanching in advance or if I have accidentally overcooked them and they seem very limp, in which case the cold water firms them somewhat. Finish them simply in butter, which I like best, with butter and herbs, or in any of the other ways suggested here.

Buttered beans:
Shake blanched beans in a dry sauté pan over heat to evaporate any residual moisture that would prevent the butter from coating them evenly. Using about 2 tablespoons per pound of beans, add the butter, cut into small fragments, and toss until it has melted and the beans are coated. Do not let the beans or butter brown. Season to taste with salt and pepper and serve at once.

Herbed beans:
Finish with butter as described and sprinkle with a tablespoon or so of finely minced

parsley, tarragon, and chervil, or just parsley. Top with an additional pat of butter and serve.

Lemon beans: Toss beans with butter as described and add a good sprinkling of lemon juice along with salt and pepper.

Beans with mushrooms: Slice ¼ pound of mushrooms for each pound of beans and sauté in 3 tablespoons butter until they give up some of their moisture. Add the blanched beans and cook another minute or two, until beans are heated through and coated with butter. Season to taste with salt and pepper.

Green beans vinaigrette: Blanch 1½ pounds trimmed green beans. Mix ½ cup finely minced red onion into 1 cup vinaigrette dressing with mustard (p. 375) and pour over the slightly warm beans. Add a handful of chopped parsley if desired. Serve at room temperature. Serves 6.

Dry Sautéed String Beans

This is one of my favorite Chinese dishes, and very simple to make. The beans are so good this way, you'll want to make them your main course.

1½ cups vegetable oil for deep frying	1 tablespoon sugar
2 pounds string beans, trimmed	1 tablespoon Chinese hot sauce (see note), or 8 dried hot peppers, crumbled
1 scallion, finely chopped	
3 tablespoons soy sauce	

Heat the oil in a wok or heavy skillet until it smokes. Fry the beans just until they wrinkle and are lightly browned—about 8 minutes. Remove beans and drain in a colander.

Pour off all but 2 tablespoons of the oil. Add the scallion and stir-fry for 1 minute. Add the beans, soy sauce, sugar, and hot sauce, and stir rapidly over high heat until the beans have soaked up the sauce—about 1 minute. Serves 6–8 as part of a Chinese meal, 4 as a separate course.

Note: Chinese hot sauce can be found in Oriental markets.

String Beans Basque Style

When I first tested this dish and tried it out on my family, the reception was so enthusiastic they wouldn't eat string beans any other way for a long time. Made with really slender fresh young beans, it merits being a course by itself.

1 pound string beans, trimmed	**Westphalian ham in 2 slices, diced**
¼ cup olive oil	**Salt and freshly ground pepper**
1 medium onion, minced	
1 garlic clove, minced	**2 tablespoons chopped parsley**
¼ pound prosciutto or	

Blanch and drain the beans. Refresh in cold water and let sit in a colander.

Heat the oil in a skillet and sauté the onion until it is transparent; add the garlic and cook until the onion is golden. Add the ham and beans and cook until the beans are heated through. Season to taste with salt and pepper and stir in the parsley. Serves 4–6.

Green Beans, New Potatoes, and Pesto

When I'm in the mood to eat just vegetables (something I find happening more and more), I can be very happy with a big plate of this. I think it is the pesto that makes such humble ingredients so satisfying.

12 small new potatoes (about 1¼ pounds)	**trimmed**
1 pound string beans,	**1 recipe pesto sauce (p. 382)**

Scrub potatoes but do not peel them. Place in a saucepan with water to cover and bring to a boil, covered. Cool for about 20 minutes. Drain but do not peel.

Blanch and refresh the beans. Drain and dry.

Heap the beans on a serving platter, cut the potatoes into quarters and arrange around the perimeter. Make a well in the center of the beans and spoon the pesto into it. Toss everything together just before serving. Serve slightly warm. Serves 4.

Haricots Panachés

This mixture of pale green flageolets with brighter green string beans is a wonderful dish to pair with lamb or veal. Because it combines a starch and a green vegetable, no additional vegetable is required at a meat meal, and the mixture is hearty enough to serve as a vegetarian meal. If you can find them, use the tiny, slender *haricots verts* in this dish (they are expensive, but you get so many to a pound you can buy fewer). Otherwise, choose small string beans.

1 pound dried flageolets	**preferably the**
7 tablespoons butter, cut	**flat-leaved kind**
into 14 pats	**Salt and freshly ground**
2 pounds green beans, or	**pepper to taste**
1¼ pounds *haricot verts,*	**2 tablespoons olive oil**
trimmed	**4 shallots, chopped**
¾ cup chopped parsley,	**2 garlic cloves, minced**

Wash, sort, and soak the flageolets overnight. Drain, place in a heavy pot with fresh water to cover, bring to a boil, partly cover, reduce heat, and simmer for about 1 hour, or until tender. Drain, toss briefly with 2 pats of the butter, and cover with foil.

Blanch and drain the string beans. Immediately spread them on a towel to dry and let cool. Return the beans to the pot, set over medium-high heat, and add 8 pats of butter a couple at a time. Shake or stir with a wooden spoon until the butter melts and the beans are coated. Add a good handful of chopped parsley, salt, and pepper and stir again. Keep warm while you finish the flageolets.

Melt the remaining butter and olive oil in a skillet and sauté the shallots and garlic until wilted but not brown. Add the flageolets and turn them gently in the mixture until coated and warmed through. Add the remaining parsley, toss and cook 30 seconds more.

Mound the flageolets in the center of a shallow oval serving platter and surround with the string beans. Or mix the beans together and arrange them around a platter of sliced lamb or veal. Serves 10 to 12.

Note: Because this is a good company dish, the recipe is deliberately large. It can easily be halved.

Haricots panachés with cherry tomatoes: A friend serves this colorful combination with roast lamb.

Wash two boxes of ripe cherry tomatoes and dry well. Melt 4 tablespoons butter in a skillet and roll the tomatoes in it, then sprinkle them with coarse salt. Mound the flageolets in a serving platter, surround with the string beans, and scatter the cherry tomatoes among the string beans.

Jimmy Weldon's Chinese Bean Salad with Coriander

This salad looks and tastes wonderful. It makes a good first course or a lovely light lunch, served alone or with cold fish or cold chicken.

¾ pound young string beans, trimmed and cut on the diagonal into ½-inch pieces	chick-peas, drained
	⅓ cup minced Spanish onion
4 tablespoons finely chopped fresh coriander (see note)	White pepper
	½ head iceberg lettuce
1 recipe mustard vinaigrette (p. 375)	3–4 scallions, white and part of the green, finely chopped
1 15-ounce can cooked	1 hard-cooked egg, finely chopped

Blanch the beans for 3 to 4 minutes. Drain and run cold water over beans briefly so they lose some heat but remain warm. Stir 2 tablespoons of the coriander into the vinaigrette; toss ⅓ cup of it with the beans and set aside for 15 minutes.

One-half hour before serving, add the chick-peas, Spanish onion, and remaining coriander to the string beans and toss to mix. Season with white pepper. Moisten with another ¼ cup of vinaigrette.

To serve: Arrange a border of whole lettuce leaves on a platter. Shred the remaining leaves and make a bed of these in the middle. Pile the bean mixture on this bed.

In a small bowl, mix together the scallions and chopped egg and spoon over the top of the beans. Serve at once, and pass the remaining vinaigrette separately. Serves 8 as a first course, 5–6 as lunch.

Note: The fresh coriander flavor is an important aspect of this salad, but fresh dill or parsley can be substituted if coriander is unavailable.

Fresh Shell Beans

These include the large, meaty fava or broad bean; the lima bean, and the red-streaked cranberry bean. Very young and tender (bite one) fava beans without a developed skin can be eaten raw, dipped in coarse salt, as an hors d'oeuvre. Old or young ones can also be braised or blanched and stir-fried with other vegetables. Or dress them as you would pasta, with tomato or pesto sauce and grated cheese.

To Buy

Fava beans are available fresh in summer, though they are hard to find. Look for fresh green pods without brown marks or very large seeds. The same applies to lima beans. Cranberry beans, also available fresh in summer, should have unwrinkled pods.

Favas are also available in cans, already skinned and cooked; look for them in Middle Eastern markets. All can be bought dried, but they taste mealy when cooked. Frozen limas are available year-round and are excellent.

To Store

Keep pods in a plastic bag in the refrigerator and do not wash. Shell just prior to cooking. Because of the variation in number of beans to the pod and pod sizes, quantities are difficult to give. A general rule for all shell beans: buy 1 pound of pods to get 1 cup, enough for 1 serving.

To Prepare

In addition to shelling, fava beans need to be skinned (unless they are very young and tender), a process that can take hours. This is more easily done if you boil the shelled beans in lightly salted water for about 10 minutes. Let beans cool and, if time permits, chill, which makes the skin slip off more easily. Peel and use beans in any of the recipes given here.

To Cook

For lima and cranberry beans, simple boiling is best. Cover with cold water, add a bit of salt if desired, cover, and simmer until tender. Cranberry beans will be tender after 10 or 12 minutes. Lima beans should be simmered for 20 to 30 minutes, depending on size. Finish by seasoning and dressing with melted butter and any desired herbs.

Herbed fresh shell beans: Cook as described with a favorite herb (savory is the traditional bean companion) and a piece of bacon or salt pork, if you wish. Finish in butter, salt, pepper, and a handful of finely minced parsley.

Braised fresh shell beans: Very small beans can be cooked without a preliminary blanching. Wilt some finely chopped onion in melted butter, add shelled fresh beans, cover, and let steam gently in the butter

until tender—5 to 10 minutes depending on size. Season with salt and pepper.

Stewed fava beans, Roman style:

Shell 2 pounds fresh fava beans; skin if required. Sauté a finely chopped medium onion in olive oil until golden, add ½ cup diced prosciutto, fat and lean, and let cook gently for 2 minutes. Add the beans, several good grinds of pepper, and a roughly chopped lettuce heart. Cover and cook about 15 minutes, adding a bit of water or chicken broth if necessary. Add salt only if needed. Serves 4.

Succotash

There are a dozen "authentic" recipes for succotash, which comes from the Narragansett *msickquatash,* a stick-to-the-ribs dish made with cranberry or kidney beans, corn, and bear grease. The Indians often added other vegetables as they were available and the later colonials added celery. This version is the kind I ate as a child, occasionally enlived with green peppers.

2 tablespoons butter
2 tablespoons minced
   onion
10-ounce package whole
   kernel corn, or fresh
   corn from 2 ears
Salt to taste
½ cup heavy cream

10-ounce package frozen
   baby lima beans,
   cooked according to
   package directions
Freshly ground pepper
1 tablespoon minced
   parsley, optional

Melt the butter in a heavy saucepan and sauté the onion until soft. Add the corn, salt, and cream. Let simmer for 3 minutes, or until most of the liquid has been absorbed. Add the lima beans, cover, and simmer gently until beans are heated through—about 4 minutes. Season with a liberal amount of pepper and sprinkle with parsley. Serves 4.

Dried Beans and Peas

Dried beans are so versatile it is not surprising that they are an important food staple for a large part of the world's population. They are inexpensive, pose no storage problem, and can be turned into a staggering variety of nourishing soups, casseroles, salads, and dips. Moreover, when they are paired with grains, nuts, seeds, or a small amount of a dairy product, they become a source of protein equal to that from animal sources. Beans were an important foodstuff for America's early settlers; in fact Boston baked beans can be traced back to the Penobscot and Narrangansett Indians, who mixed maple syrup with beans and cooked them for hours in a coal-lined bean pit dug especially for this purpose. As each newly arrived ethnic group brought along its own bean tradition, we became enriched by a dizzying variety of beans and ways to eat them.

Apart from their value as a source of protein, beans are particularly attractive in light of current dietary recommendations because they contain little fat and no cholesterol and are low in sodium and high in dietary fiber, iron, and the B vitamins.

Beans are legumes, which, along with peas and lentils, are called pulses. Among the pulses both popular and easily available in this country are:

Azuki (or aduki) beans: A small red Oriental bean that is sweet and quite easy to digest. Can be cooked with rice or stewed simply with herbs, as a side dish. They may be mashed into a paste and sweetened for use in Oriental desserts.

Black (or turtle) beans: Black-skinned, these are often used in Caribbean and South American soups and stews. Frequently they are combined with rice.

Black-eyed and yellow-eyed peas: Really beans, but so called because their flavor is reminiscent of peas. Use in Southern recipes like Hopping John (black-eyed peas and rice) or cook Carolina-style, slow-simmered with salt pork until

soft-tender and served with the "pot likker" and cornbread.

Cannellini: White kidney beans, the *fagioli* of *pasta e fagioli*. Good with sautéed onion, garlic, and tomato, or as a salad. Also available in cans, ready for use.

Chick-peas (also called *garbanzos* or *ceci*): Very popular in Spain, Italy, Greece, and the Middle East. They may be salted and spiced for a savory snack, pureed, used in soups and stews. Also bake or sauté in butter with garlic.

Flageolets: The French name for a pale green kidney bean taken from the mature pods of French or string beans. Available cooked in cans and jars.

Great Northern beans: Large plump bean of the group known as white beans; substitute for cannellini in Italian recipes, use for cassoulet and instead of flageolets in French dishes. *Navy* or *yankee beans* are a smaller variety; *pea beans,* smaller still. Bake, boil, puree; use in soups and salads.

Kidney beans: Reddish-brown beans whose shape is suggested by their name. Boil, bake with sausages, or with onions and bacon smothered in tomato sauce, or add to a salad as with cannelini beans. Available in cans, ready to use.

Pink beans, red beans: Southwestern favorites, used interchangeably in Mexican recipes.

Pinto beans: A richly flavored variety of pink bean with brown flecks that takes well to spices and chilies, very popular in the Southwest. Use as you would pink or red beans, or in any baked bean recipe, or mix with rice, garlic, and tomatoes.

To make frijoles refritos (refried beans), mash leftover pinto beans and fry in bacon fat or vegetable oil until hot. Sprinkle with grated Cheddar or longhorn cheese. Serve alone or as a filling for tacos or burritos.

Pigeon peas (called *gandules* on Spanish-speaking Caribbean islands):

Like black-eyed peas, pigeon peas are treated like dried beans. They originated in Africa and are popular in West Indian kitchens, where they are made into a soup or stew with ham hocks, beef cubes, and rice. They are available dried and canned in Spanish markets.

Split peas, green or yellow, are treated like dried beans. They are used mostly to make split pea soup, but they make a delightful, hearty pureed vegetable to accompany boiled or braised tongue, pork chops, or game.

To make a puree of split peas, soak and drain 1½ cups dried green or yellow peas. Add chicken broth or water to cover, about 3 cups, and a medium peeled onion stuck with 2 cloves, 1 bay leaf, 2 teaspoons salt, and several grinds of fresh black pepper. Bring to the boil, cover, and simmer over very low heat, stirring occasionally, until peas are soft,—about 40 minutes. If the liquid has cooked away before peas are tender, stir in ¼ cup water. Drain, reserving the broth and discarding the onion. Puree in a blender or food processor and add 3 to 4 tablespoons softened butter and enough of the broth to give a pleasing consistency. Adjust seasoning and serve hot. Serves 6.

To Buy

Most dried beans and peas are boxed or plastic-bagged. If you are buying them loose from a sack, as they are often sold in Oriental markets, check that they are clean, insect-free, and unwrinkled. Store in a cool dry place in a covered jar. Try not to mix fresher beans with older ones.

Though they are dried, beans do not last indefinitely. Ideally they should be from the current year's crop; old stale beans have a grainy flesh that bursts when cooked.

One cup of dried beans will yield 2 to 2½ cups of beans after soaking and cooking. Allow ½ cup per person as a side dish (more if beans are the main course). One pound of dried beans will serve 4 to 6.

To Prepare for Cooking

Most dried beans and peas must be soaked; otherwise they will burst their skins in cooking. Many varieties are sold presoaked and redried, a process that shortens their cooking time. I find them to have less flavor and texture, but they are handy in a pinch.

Sort over, removing bits of gravel and broken pieces; place in a colander, rinse with cool water, and put to soak, adding about 6 cups water for each pound of beans. Let stand at room temperature, covered with a cloth. If the weather is very warm, refrigerate the beans while they soak so they don't sour.

As a general guideline, beans should be soaked 6 to 8 hours, but the actual time depends on how old and dry they are. When delicate beans like flageolets are old, they will be tough even after a prolonged soak.

To check if beans are completely soaked, cut one in half with a small sharp knife; if it is the same color all the way through, its moisture is completely restored. A whiter, harder center indicates the need for longer soaking. Discard any beans that float.

Quick soak: When you do not have time for the conventional soak, try this 2-hour method. Place sorted and washed beans and cold water in a pot (about 6 cups for each pound of beans), cover, bring to a boil, reduce heat, and simmer gently for 2–5 minutes. Remove from heat and let sit for 2 hours. Drain.

To Cook

As with soaking, cooking times vary with the variety and age of the bean, so the following are general guides. Chick-peas, Great Northern beans, and pink beans will be done in about 1 hour. Kidney and navy beans take about 1½ hours, black beans and pinto beans about 2 hours. Black and yellow-eyed peas can be tender in 45 minutes.

Method 1: Place beans in a large heavy pot (I use a Dutch oven), cover with fresh cold water by 2 inches, bring to a boil, and simmer very gently until tender. If there is any question about the heaviness of your pot, use an asbestos pad or Flame Tamer so the heat can be really low. Keep the pot partly covered and check occasionally to see if more water is needed. The beans should be covered with liquid at all times. Stir occasionally with a wooden spoon to keep them from sticking on the bottom. To check if beans are done, remove a spoonful and bite one; if skins break, they are done. Don't worry if more cooking time is needed. As long as you cook them at a gentle simmer, they will not get mushy.

If beans are to be used in a salad, undercook them slightly and leave them in their liquid until you use them.

Don't salt beans until after they are cooked; salt toughens them.

Fresh savory has a special affinity for beans; if it is available, add it to the pot when simmering. A bay leaf is nice, too.

To finish beans, drain, add salt and pepper to taste and 2 tablespoons or so of butter. Let it melt through, toss, sprinkle with some chopped parsley, and serve.

Method 2: This slightly different cooking method may be used for most beans, especially white ones. It involves an extra change of water that reduces the tendency of beans to produce flatulence.

Soak beans for 2 hours and drain. Cover well with lukewarm water and bring slowly to a boil. At the same time bring a kettle of water to the boil. Boil the beans, uncovered, for about 5 minutes, then drain, cover with boiling water, bring to a second boil, cover, lower heat, and simmer until beans are tender.

Method 3: Place soaked beans in a heavy pot and cover with fresh cold water. Bring to the boil on top of the stove, then bake in a 300° oven. Add about a quarter again as much cooking time to those given.

To Freeze

Cool cooked beans, then pack in a freezer box or bag for future use. Thaw at room temperature for 2 hours.

Cuban Black Beans

Elisabeth Lambert Ortiz, an authority on Caribbean cooking, is the source for this immensely popular Cuban dish. When served with rice, it is called *Moros y Cristianos*—"Moors and Christians."

1 pound black beans, washed and picked over
1 quart cold water
3 tablespoons olive oil
2 ounces salt pork, diced
1 medium onion, finely chopped
2 garlic cloves, minced
1 sweet green pepper, seeded, deribbed, and chopped
1 bay leaf
Salt and freshly ground pepper to taste

Do not soak the beans. Put them in a large saucepan, cover with cold water, cover, bring to a boil, lower heat, and simmer gently, partly covered, until tender— 1½ to 2 hours. Add more hot water as necessary.

Heat the oil in a heavy skillet and render the fat from the salt pork. Add the onion, garlic, green pepper, and bay leaf, and sauté until the onion is transparent. Add this mixture to the bean pot, which should still have quite a bit of liquid, and continue simmering ½ hour longer. Stir once or twice. The beans should be tender and neither too soupy nor too dry.

Remove 2 spoonfuls of the beans, mash, and add to thicken the sauce. Correct seasonings and serve. Serves 6 to 8.

Flageolets Bretonne

In France, where flageolets are taken very seriously, good purveyors proudly advertise the arrival of flageolets *demi-sec,* meaning freshly dried from that year's harvest and not requiring soaking. Flageolets are the traditional accompaniment to roast leg of lamb, and there are few happier combinations in the food world. They are also superb with a roast of veal.

2 cups dried flageolets, soaked
3 tablespoons butter
½ cup chopped onion
2 cloves garlic, minced

Salt and freshly ground pepper
1 tablespoon finely chopped parsley

Drain and rinse the flageolets.

Melt the butter in a heavy medium saucepan, add the onion and garlic and let cook until just wilted—about 2 minutes. Stir in the drained beans and cook over gentle heat for about 3 minutes; then add enough hot water to just cover the beans. Bring to the boil, cover, lower heat, and simmer for about 1 hour over gentle heat. Check from time to time to see that the liquid has not cooked away; if the beans look dry, add a cautious additional amount of hot water. Cook until the beans are tender and the liquid is absorbed. Season to taste with salt and pepper, toss with the parsley, and serve. Serves 6 to 8.

Note: If the beans seem dry, toss with additional melted butter or, if they are to accompany roasted meat, with several spoonfuls of the fatty meat juices.

For extra flavor, cook the beans in chicken broth instead of water. In another variation, a coarsely chopped, peeled, and seeded ripe tomato can be tossed with the beans at the end for a nice color and flavor touch.

White Bean Salad

One of our favorite summer lunches revolves around leftover grilled chicken, this salad, and sliced tomatoes.

1 pound dried white pea beans, soaked	2 teaspoons salt
	Freshly ground pepper
1 medium onion	4 scallions, white and part
5 cloves	of the green, chopped
½ cup olive oil	¼ cup minced parsley
¼ cup lemon juice	¼ cup minced dill

Drain the beans, cover with fresh water by 2 inches, and add the onion studded with the cloves. Bring to a boil, cover, lower heat, and simmer for 1½ hours, or until tender. Drain.

Combine the oil, lemon juice, salt, and pepper and mix with the beans. Add the scallions, parsley, and dill and marinate in the refrigerator for 3 hours. Serve as part of an hors d'oeuvre tray or as a side dish. Serves 4–6 as a side dish.

Note: Two crushed garlic cloves may be added to the marinade for a heartier flavor, but be sure to fish them out before serving.

Turkish Beans

This tastes even better made early in the day or the day before.

1 cup dried large white beans (great northern) or one 20-ounce can cannellini beans, well drained	½ cup diced green pepper
	1 medium rib celery, diced (about 1 cup)
	2 medium garlic cloves, finely chopped
3 tablespoons olive oil	3 tablespoons finely chopped parsley
2 medium carrots, sliced into ¼-inch rounds (about 1 cup)	2 medium tomatoes, peeled, seeded, and

chopped   cayenne pepper to taste
Salt and ground black or

If you are using dried beans, soak them. Drain and rinse. Combine them with 3 cups boiling water in a heavy saucepan and simmer, partly covered, for 15 minutes. Drain, cover again with 3 cups boiling water, and cook for 1 hour. If using canned beans, omit this step.

Heat the olive oil in a heavy skillet. Sauté the carrots, green pepper, celery, garlic, parsley, and tomatoes until softened but still firm and not browned. Add the drained beans, salt, and pepper. Stir together carefully, cover, and simmer gently for 25 minutes, until vegetables are tender, adding a little more water if necessary to prevent sticking. Serves 4.

Serving suggestion: As an appetizer, serve at room temperature or cold on lettuce leaves, garnished with lemon slices and black olives. As a side dish, serve in the casserole as an accompaniment for lamb. This recipe can easily be doubled or tripled and is an attractive and economical choice for a buffet, as there is almost nothing it cannot accompany.

Tuscan Beans

The Tuscans, whose food is regarded as very elegant and simple, have so many bean dishes that they are known as bean eaters by other Italians. Here is a classic preparation that makes a marvelous accompaniment to meat of any kind, especially roast pork.

1½ cups navy or pea   Salt and freshly ground
   beans, soaked   pepper to taste
2 tablespoons butter   ½ cup chopped Italian
3 tablespoons olive oil   plum tomatoes
1 teaspoon ground sage

Place the drained beans in a heavy kettle with fresh water to cover and bring to a boil over moderate heat. Partly cover, reduce heat, and simmer for about 45 minutes, or until the beans are just tender. Do not salt while beans are cooking and do not overcook or the beans will split open. Drain.

Heat the butter and olive oil in a large skillet. Add the beans, sage, salt, and pepper and cook, stirring with a fork, for 3 to 5 minutes. Add the chopped tomatoes and toss lightly to blend. Cook 2 or 3 minutes more and serve. Serves 6.

Boston Baked Beans

Of course you can buy these in cans, but they don't have that long-cooked taste or make your house smell so wonderful! Serve these beans with ham or homemade meat loaf on a buffet and watch how fast everything disappears.

2 cups (1 pound) dried navy or pea beans, soaked	2 teaspoons salt
	8-ounce can tomato puree (see note)
3 tablespoons molasses	1 medium onion, peeled
3 tablespoons brown sugar	½ pound salt pork, the rind scored
½ teaspoon dried mustard	

Put the drained beans in a soup pot. Add water to twice the depth of the beans, cover pot, and simmer for 1 hour. Drain and reserve 2 cups of the water.

Preheat the oven to 250°.

Combine the molasses, sugar, mustard, salt, and tomato puree with the reserved water. Put the beans and this mixture in an ungreased bean pot or Dutch oven. Push the onion down into the beans and push the salt pork into the top. Cover and bake 4 to 6 hours, or until the beans are tender. Take a peek occasionally to stir and see if more water is needed. Remove the lid for the last hour of cooking so a crust develops. Serve very hot. Serves 6.

Note: The tomato puree is not authentic, but I like it.

Hummus Bi Tahini

This savory salad makes an excellent appetizer served with warmed pita bread. Use it also as a dip for crudités, as a sauce for fried or roasted eggplant, or broiled or baked fish.

1 cup (about 6 ounces) dried chick-peas, soaked, or 1¼ cups canned
½ cup lemon juice, or to taste
2–3 garlic cloves
4 tablespoons tahini paste (see note)
Salt

Garnish

1 tablespoon olive oil
Paprika

1 tablespoon chopped parsley

Cook the dried peas in fresh water until soft—about 1 hour. Drain either dried or canned peas and set aside a few whole ones for garnishing.

Puree the drained peas in a food processor or blender. Add the lemon juice and blend again. Put the garlic through a press and add, along with the tahini and salt to taste. Blend again until thick and creamy. If too thick, add a little water and blend again; mixture should have the consistency of thick mayonnaise. Taste and add lemon juice, garlic, or salt as necessary. Spoon into a serving bowl.

Mix the oil and paprika together and drizzle over the top. Sprinkle with chopped parsley and garnish with a few whole chick-peas. Makes about 1¾ cups.

Note: Tahini, or sesame paste, can be purchased in Middle Eastern food shops.

Black Bean Soup

This American favorite is a perennial in the dining room of the U.S. Senate. It can be eaten hot or cold.

1 pound dried black (or turtle) beans, soaked	1 bay leaf
3 tablespoons butter	3 cloves
2 large onions, coarsely chopped (about 1½ cups)	8–10 peppercorns
	1 lemon, quartered
1 celery rib, coarsely chopped	1 tablespoon salt, or to taste
3 garlic cloves, minced	½ cup dry sherry
1 veal or beef knuckle, optional	Thin lemon slices
	Chopped hard-cooked egg for garnish

Put the drained beans in a soup pot.

Melt the butter in a skillet and sauté the onion, celery, and garlic just until onion is soft. Add to the soup pot with 3 quarts of water and the veal or beef bone. Tie the bay leaf, cloves, and peppercorns in a cheesecloth bag and add. Add the lemon quarters and salt to taste. Bring to a boil and simmer until beans are very soft—about 3 hours. Remove and discard the bone, lemon quarters, and cheesecloth bag.

Puree the beans with their liquid in batches in a food processor or blender. Return to the pot, taste for seasoning, stir in sherry and heat. If too thick, thin with a little hot water to the consistency of heavy cream. Serve hot, garnished with lemon slices and hard-cooked egg. Serves 8.

Serving suggestion: Hearty enough to make a light but filling supper served with garlic bread and a salad and cheese following.

Split Pea Soup

1 package (16 ounces) green split peas, soaked	1 bay leaf
	1½–2 quarts water
1 onion stuck with 2 cloves	Ham bone (see note)
	Freshly ground pepper
2 celery ribs	

Drain the peas, rinse, and put in a large soup kettle with the onion, celery, bay leaf, water, and ham bone. Bring to a boil, lower heat, and simmer gently for about 1 hour, or until the peas are completely soft. Remove the bone and put the soup through a food mill. If soup seems too thick, add more water to obtain the desired consistency. Taste for seasoning, add salt only if needed, and a liberal amount of black pepper. Serve steaming hot. Serves 4–6.

Note: If a ham bone is difficult to come by, use a small smoked pork butt, in which case you can cut up the meat and add it to the soup afterward; either lends a superb flavor. Or eliminate the bone for a vegetarian version and add ½ cup heavy cream and some croutons fried in butter.

This soup becomes a hearty meal with the addition of sliced frankfurters or knockwurst cooked in it while it heats.

Lentils

Lentils, the seed of a grass, are a legume, a relative of beans, and supposed to be the "mess of pottage" mentioned in the Bible. Brown or gray lentils are sold in packages and are usually processed for quick cooking. Red lentils, sometimes called Egyptian lentils, are split and cook more quickly. They both need the zest of herbs and spices to make them interesting— cumin is one in particular that goes very well.

Besides making a splendid soup, lentils make a particularly good salad for buffets and picnics. Lentil puree is good with roasted game birds or a pork roast. Combine them with rice for complete protein in a meatless meal.

Be sure not to overcook lentils; they become mushy. Allow 1 pound for 4 to 6 servings.

Lentil salad:

Follow the recipe for white bean salad (p. 44), substituting 2½ cups lentils (about 1 pound) for the beans. Cover with 6 cups water, add 1 teaspoon salt, and bring to a boil. Cover and simmer gently for 25 minutes. Drain and add the salad ingredients. Check for seasoning. This is best made a day ahead.

Lentil puree: Cover 2½ to 3 cups dried lentils with water, add a tablespoon salt and an onion stuck with 2 cloves, and simmer until lentils are tender—about 25 minutes. Puree in a food processor or blender, then mix with 4 to 6 tablespoons butter, ½ teaspoon ground cumin or to taste, and up to ½ cup heavy cream as needed to make the puree smooth. Correct seasoning and serve very hot.

Egyptian Lentil Soup

I was so intrigued with the hearty flavor of this soup when I first ate it in Cairo at the Nile Hilton that I ordered it at every meal, despite the heat. The management kindly shared the recipe, which I have adapted to the home kitchen.

5 tablespoons butter
1 large onion, chopped
2 small carrots, peeled and diced
1½ cups (about 10 ounces) lentils, preferably red, sorted and washed

6 cups homemade beef broth or chicken stock (see note)
1 large potato, peeled and diced
Salt and freshly ground pepper

Garnish

1 tablespoon chopped onion
1 large garlic clove, finely

minced
1 teaspoon ground cumin
Croutons

Melt 4 tablespoons of the butter in a large heavy soup pot, add the onion and carrots, and cook over moderate heat until the onion is limp. Add the lentils and the broth, bring to the boil, cover, lower heat, and let cook for ½ hour. Add the potato and continue to cook for another half hour, or until the lentils are very soft.

Drain in a colander set over a bowl. Return the

liquid to the pot. Puree the soup through a food mill and return to the pot. Season to taste with salt and pepper if needed. Bring to a gentle simmer again while you prepare the garnish.

Melt the remaining tablespoon of butter in a small skillet. Add the onion and garlic and sauté just until soft but not brown. Add the cumin, stir to blend, and add this mixture to the soup. Serve in earthenware bowls with croutons. Serves 8.

Note: Canned beef broth has too assertive and sweet a flavor for this soup. Of course you may also use water or vegetable stock.

Bean Curd

Called *tofu* by the Japanese and "meat without bones" by the Chinese, bean curd consists of soybean curd, drained and pressed into custardlike cakes about 1 inch thick and 3 inches square. It is highly nutritious, easily digested, and quite inexpensive. Bean curd is extremely versatile and can be boiled, steamed, stir-fried, deep-fried, marinated, or baked with other flavor-enhancing spices and ingredients. It is available fresh in soft, medium (regular), and hard textures, sold singly in cake form, in cans, and also as thin, flat, anise-flavored cakes called spicy bean curd or pressed, seasoned bean curd. This can be julienned and added to vegetable dishes, salads, and soups. There is also a watery bean curd, meant to be sweetened and served as a snack.

To Buy

Fresh bean curd is available in Oriental and health food stores, and, increasingly, in supermarkets. Don't buy canned bean curd—it is rubbery.

To Store

Put in a container with water to cover, and refrigerate. Use within 3 days and change water daily. To store seasoned bean curd: add 1 teaspoon salt and ¼ cup soy sauce to 1 quart water and store as directed. Will last about 2 weeks.

Bean Curd, Zucchini, and Mushrooms

Chinese recipes often sound more complicated than they are because of the preparation each ingredient requires. This rather unusual and hearty dish is both attractive and tasty, and goes quite fast once everything is lined up.

½ ounce tree ear mushrooms	Dash sesame oil
4 cultivated mushrooms	1 teaspoon light soy sauce
½ cup vegetable or chicken broth	½ teaspoon sugar
	½ teaspoon salt
1 package (2 ounces) dried spicy bean curd, or 3 pieces fresh spicy bean curd	2 tablespoons peanut oil
	2 quarter-size slices fresh ginger, peeled and lightly mashed
10 ounces very fresh young zucchini	1 large shallot, sliced
15 thin slices peeled carrot	6 whole water chestnuts, sliced
½ teaspoon cornstarch	1 tablespoon white wine
	1 teaspoon dark soy sauce

Rinse the tree ears and soak in 2 cups boiling water for ½ hour. Drain, rinse, and cut out hard "eyes." Combine the tree ears with the regular mushrooms, add the broth, bring to a boil, cover, lower heat, and simmer for 3 minutes. Uncover and let cool for about 1 hour. Drain and reserve the broth. Slice the cultivated mushrooms.

While mushrooms cool, simmer the dried spicy bean curd in water for 15 to 20 minutes, until most of the pieces separate. Drain and set aside. If using fresh spicy bean curd, eliminate this step and merely cut the slices in half and set aside.

Wash the zucchini, trim ends, and peel in alternating lengthwise strips. Cut each piece into triangle sections about 1½ inches long at the base. Set aside.

Blanch the carrot slices for 3 minutes in a small pot

of boiling water. Drain and refresh in cold water. Set aside.

Combine the cornstarch, reserved broth, sesame oil, soy sauce, sugar, and salt. Blend until smooth, and set aside.

Heat a wok or pan, add the oil in a circular motion around sides, heat 30 seconds, and stir-fry the ginger and shallot for 15 seconds. Stir in tree ear and cultivated mushrooms, the zucchini, and water chestnuts, and stir-fry for 1 minute. Add the bean curd, and sprinkle wine over. Add the cornstarch mixture, and turn heat to low. Stir in dark soy, cover, and cook for 1 minute. Serve immediately with rice. Serves 4.

Bean Sprouts

Bean sprouts with their tiny white tails and green hoods are actually the sprouts of mung peas. They add texture and a delicate taste to Oriental dishes. My children love their crunch in green salads and omelets. They can also be included in any mixed vegetable salad. Called "teeth vegetable" in Chinese, they should be cooked only briefly to retain their crunchiness.

Sprouts are sold fresh by weight and are also available in cans. Fresh sprouts should be white and silky. Store in an uncovered container of water in the refrigerator. Change the water every day and use as soon as possible; they turn brown after 3 or 4 days.

Because the water content varies, a pound of fresh sprouts will yield anywhere from 2 to 3½ cups.

One occasionally sees a larger, coarser sprout in Chinese food shops; this is the sprouted yellow soybean, which has a more pronounced flavor.

Beets

(Beta vulgaris)

Small baby beets, straight from the garden, steamed or boiled and rolled in butter and coarse salt, are a joy to eat. A bunch of old, limp-leaved storage beets that need to be boiled for an hour or baked for three might as well be different vegetables. When I can't get reasonably young beets, I opt for the kind that come in jars or cans. They seem to do just fine for the way I use them, which is pickled, sweet-and-sour, or in salads. Borscht, however, does require fresh beets, so I use storage beets for that. The natural sweetness of beets makes them a good bet for sweet-and-sour preparations such as borscht, Harvard beets, and the two salad recipes that follow.

To Buy

Look for unblemished, uncracked small beets that have fresh and fairly small leaves and firm stems. Choose bunches of similar-size beets so they will cook in the same length of time. One pound of trimmed beets (or a 15-ounce can) will give you about 2 cups sliced.

To Store

Remove the green tops, leaving an inch or so of stem, and refrigerate. Do not wash until ready to cook.

To Prepare for Cooking

Wash gently, being careful not to tear the skin. Don't peel the beets or remove the root ends or stems at this time because the beets will bleed.

To Cook

Boiled: Cover with cold water and bring to a boil, covered. Arrange the lid so the beets are partly covered and simmer until tender; the cooking time will range from 20 minutes for baby beets to 1 hour for mature ones. Test with a fork for tenderness, but not too frequently because the beets will bleed. Let cool in the cooking liquid, drain, and slip off the skins under running water. The beets are then ready to use in any recipe calling for cooked beets.

Hot Sweet-and-Sour Borscht

Hot borscht is served all over Russia in countless variations, usually with cabbage and meat, or at least made with meat stock. The beef from which the stock is made can be served sliced or diced in the soup, as in my recipe, or as a separate course, to be eaten with stingingly hot horseradish, pickles, and slabs of buttered black bread or fresh rye.

The beef stock

3–4 pounds beef knuckle or marrow bones, or a mixture, cracked
1½ pounds brisket or shin beef (see note)
1 onion, quartered
1 carrot, peeled and quartered
1 parsley root, peeled and quartered, optional (see note)
2 celery ribs
Bouquet garni: celery leaves, several parsley stems, 2 bay leaves
1 tablespoon salt
8–10 peppercorns

Wash the bones in several changes of cold water and put in a large, heavy soup kettle. Add the beef and 4 quarts of cold water and bring to a boil over high heat.

Cook for 5 minutes, constantly skimming off the grayish foam that rises to the surface. Add the onion, carrot, parsley root, celery, bouquet garni, salt, and peppercorns. Set cover on slightly askew and lower heat. Simmer until the meat is tender, adding water as needed if more than half boils away. If you are using brisket, remove after about 1½ hours and continue to simmer the stock 1½ hours longer. Shin beef will take the full 3 hours to become tender.

Set a large sieve over a bowl and strain the stock. Discard the bones and vegetables. Let cool and skim as much fat as possible from the surface.

This step may be done the day before or early in the day. Keep the meat wrapped in foil until ready to use.

The soup

3 tablespoons vegetable oil	¼ cup wine vinegar
1 cup finely chopped onion	8 cups strained beef stock
2 cloves garlic, minced	Half a small green cabbage, about 1 pound, cored and coarsely shredded
4–5 large fresh beets, about 1½ pounds after trimming, peeled and coarsely grated	Reserved brisket or shin beef
1 pound potatoes, peeled and cut into large chunks	Salt and freshly ground pepper
1 can (8 ounces) tomato puree	Finely chopped dill, optional
1 teaspoon sugar, or more to taste	½ cup sour cream, optional

Heat the oil in a heavy 6- to 7-quart soup kettle. Add the onion and cook for 3 minutes. Add the garlic and cook 2 minutes more, stirring, until onion is lightly browned.

Add the beets, potatoes, tomato puree, sugar, vinegar, and 4 cups of the beef stock. Bring to a boil, partly cover, lower the heat slightly, and simmer for 20 minutes.

Add the cabbage and the balance of the beef stock

and continue simmering until potatoes are tender—
another 20 minutes. If the meat is to be served in the
soup, cut into large dice and add 5 minutes after the
cabbage.

Correct seasoning with salt and many liberal grinds
of pepper, and add more sugar if the sweet-sour balance
is not to your liking. Serve very hot from the pot or a
heated tureen, sprinkled with dill. Pass the sour cream
separately. Serves 6–8.

Note: Shin beef, from the shank, is the traditional cut
used in borscht. It is extremely tasty but not
particularly attractive and requires long cooking to
tenderize. Brisket is preferable if you are going to serve
the meat as a separate course.

Parsley root is not to be confused with parsnip or the
tiny roots that normally appear on leaf parsley. This is
the Hamburg or turnip-rooted parsley widely used in
Russian soups and stews. It is often found in packages
of combination vegetables labeled soup greens, and has a
flavor somewhat like celery root. Russians often add it,
grated, to the borscht along with the beets.

Beets in Butter and Coarse Salt

This is the best way to prepare young beets.

8 medium or 12 small beets, cooked and peeled	**3 tablespoons butter** **Coarse salt** **Freshly ground pepper**

Quarter medium-size beets, leave small ones whole.
Put them in a pot and shake over heat for a moment to
dry them. Add the butter to the pot and stir to coat the
beets. Season with salt and pepper. Serves 4–6.

Harvard Beets

I think I've known Harvard beets since shortly after
learning my own name. They are a quintessential
American dish, yet no one seems to know exactly how
they got their name. One notion says it has to do with
their crimson color.

Harvard Beets, continued

10–12 small beets, cooked and peeled	**2 teaspoons cornstarch**
Scant ½ cup sugar	**½ cup vinegar**
½ teaspoon salt	**2 tablespoons butter**

Slice the beets and return to the pot.

Mix the sugar, salt, and cornstarch together in a small saucepan and stir in the vinegar. Set over heat, bring to a boil, and simmer until glossy, about 3 minutes. Pour over the beets and heat gently, shaking the pan several times. Just before serving, swirl the butter into the sauce. Serves 4–5.

Scandinavian Pickled Beets

The Danes like the sharpness of pickled beets to set off meat loaf or meatballs. The Swedes wouldn't consider a smorgasbord complete without them. Serve as you would any relish.

1 pound small beets, cooked and peeled	**½ cup sugar**
½ cup mild vinegar	**1 teaspoon salt**
½ cup water	**Freshly ground pepper**

Cut the beets into ¼-inch slices. You will have about 2 cups. Combine the vinegar, water, sugar, salt, and pepper in an small enamel or stainless steel saucepan. Bring to a boil and cook for 2 minutes, or until sugar dissolves.

Put the sliced beets in a glass bowl, pour the hot vinegar mixture over them and let cool, uncovered, to room temperature. Cover the bowl and refrigerate for at least 12 hours, stirring once or twice during this time. Makes 2 cups.

To make Swedish-style pickled beets, cut beets into ½-inch dice instead of slicing them. To serve, drain and decorate with slices of hard-cooked egg.

Pickled Beets and Onions

This variation is good on an hors d'oeuvre tray, as a meat accompaniment, or just as a snack. They keep for at least a week in the refrigerator.

1½ pounds small beets,
   cooked and peeled
Salt and freshly ground
   pepper

2 teaspoons sugar
1½ teaspoons wine vinegar
1 small purple onion,
   thinly sliced

Cut the beets into ¼-inch slices. You will have about 2¾ cups. Put the beets in a mixing bowl and add the salt and several grinds of pepper. Put the sugar and vinegar in a cup and stir until the sugar is dissolved. Add to the beets. Taste and correct seasoning balance if necessary. Add the onion and mix well. Refrigerate for several hours before serving. Makes 3 to 4 cups.

Broccoli

(Brassica oleracea botrytis)

Broccoli is the most elegant member of the cabbage family, more flavorsome than cauliflower and less pungent than head cabbage. Though it originated in Asia Minor, it was called Italian asparagus when it reached England in the seventeenth century. First brought to America by Italian immigrants from Calabria, it did not really catch on until the early 1930s.

One of the most versatile of vegetables, broccoli lends itself to almost all cooking methods: it can be boiled or steamed and served plain or sauced, stir-fried, deep-fried (with or without batter), gratinéed, or made into a soufflé. It is delightful cooked and served as a salad with vinaigrette dressing. Bonus: raw broccoli, popular as a *crudité,* is packed with calcium and vitamins A and C.

Information on broccoli di rape, a turniplike green, will be found in the section on Greens.

To Buy

Look for tightly closed buds. The head may have a bluish or purplish cast. Pass it up if the buds are open and yellowing, if it is limp, or if the stalks are thick or woody or have dry, open cores. One bunch averages 1½ pounds and will serve 4 people.

To Store

Refrigerate, unwashed, in a perforated plastic bag for no more than 3 days.

To Prepare for Cooking

Rinse in cool water. (Garden or farm-stand broccoli may need soaking in salted water to get rid of bugs.) Cut off and discard the woody bottom. Remove the tough skin of the stalk by peeling up from the base to the flowerets with a sharp paring knife, using the thumb as a guide so the cut is not too deep (see drawing). Separate flowerets at the point where small stems end— about 2½ inches below the head. Peel as close to cooking time as practical.

Unpeeled broccoli stems may be kept aside for another meal and then blanched or fried. The way you cut them—into disks or sticks—is up to you as long as the pieces are uniform.

To Cook

Blanched: Bring a large pot of salted water to the boil and add the trimmed and peeled broccoli. If the stems are unusually thick, add them one or two minutes before the flowerets. Boil uncovered until tender but still crisp—about 5 minutes after the water returns to the boil. Drain, handling gently. If you are serving immediately, you may plunge them briefly into a basin of cold water to set the color and stop the cooking. Otherwise, spread pieces on a towel to cool. I try to cook broccoli a little ahead, as I prefer not to refresh it. The cold water seems to deplete the flavor and can make the head soggy.

If you are using the broccoli later in the day, refrigerate it, covered by a damp paper towel, until ready to use.

Finish with melted butter, lemon butter, garlic and oil, as in broccoli with garlic Italian style, or serve with hollandaise sauce. Dieters will like lemon juice, salt and pepper, plus red pepper flakes. Peeled stems can be blanched alone and served at room temperature with oil, vinegar, and salt.

Steamed:
Put an inch of water in the bottom of the steamer and bring to a boil. Place trimmed and peeled broccoli in the steamer basket set over the water, cover, and steam until tender. Broccoli separated into flowerets with stems about half an inch thick will be tender in 5 to 7 minutes. Thick stems may take an additional minute. Finish in any of the ways suggested for blanched broccoli.

Whole branches of broccoli steamed with the stems intact are a special treat; they taste very much like asparagus, especially when served with lemon butter.

Steamed broccoli and cauliflower flowerets:
Trim and separate a pound each of broccoli and cauliflower but leave the stems quite long. Arrange the two vegetables in two 10-inch bamboo steaming baskets in a pleasing color pattern, overlapping them slightly so just the tops show. Steam over 3 inches of boiling water for 10 minutes. Using oven mitts, remove the baskets to a large plate or dish, let cool, and serve with Consuelo's green sauce (p. 379) and taramasalata (p. 380).

Broccoli with Garlic, Italian Style

It seems we have broccoli this way at least once a week; it is my family's favorite, and it goes with everything.

3 tablespoons olive oil
2–3 cloves garlic, or more to taste (see note)
1 bunch broccoli, trimmed, peeled, and
blanched
2–3 tablespoons water
Salt and freshly ground pepper
Lemon wedges

In a large skillet, heat the olive oil and brown the garlic. Discard the garlic, add the broccoli, and turn to coat in the oil. Add the water, bring to a boil, season with salt and pepper, and let cook for 3 to 5 minutes. Try not to let the delicate heads crumble. Serve hot with lemon wedges. Serves 4.

Note: If you want a stronger garlic flavor, push the garlic through a press into the hot oil to cook, and do not remove it. Be careful not to let it burn, however.

Cold Broccoli Vinaigrette

Word of Mouth is a Manhattan take-out food shop where everything is of the highest quality and delicious. Ilene Weinberg, one of the owners, has generously shared this recipe for one of their most popular salads.

1 head very fresh broccoli
Salt
1 tablespoon red wine vinegar
¼ cup Dijon mustard
Freshly ground pepper
1 tablespoon chopped fresh dill
1 cup oil, a blend of olive and vegetable

Cut off and discard the bottom 2 inches of the broccoli head, unless it is very young and fresh.

Separate the broccoli into flowerets with stems attached. Bring a pot of salted water to the boil, add the broccoli, and cook for 4 minutes. Immediately drain in a colander and spread the pieces on a kitchen towel to cool and dry.

In the bowl of a food processor combine the vinegar, mustard, pepper, salt to taste, and the dill. With the motor running, add the oil. The sauce will be very thick, almost like mayonnaise.

Arrange broccoli in a shallow serving bowl and pour the dressing over. Let stand at least an hour before serving. Serve at room temperature. Serves 4–5.

Broccoli Soufflé

Follow the recipe for spinach soufflé (p. 279), substituting 1 cup chopped cooked broccoli for the spinach.

Fried Broccoli Stems

My youngest daughter, who believes she hates vegetables, can always be wooed with this dish.

Stems from one broccoli head	**½ teaspoon salt, or to taste**
¾ cup flour	**¾ cup water**
¼ cup cornstarch	**Oil for frying**
1½ teaspoons baking powder	

Peel the stems and slice slightly on the diagonal into ¼-inch rounds, or cut into 2 × ½-inch sticks. Steam or blanch about 5 minutes until crisp-tender. Refresh with cold water.

Make a batter of the flour, cornstarch, baking powder, salt, and water. It will be quite thick.

Heat the oil in a wok or a deep fryer. When it reaches 375°, carefully dip out a spoonful of oil and add to the batter. Using tongs, dip the broccoli pieces in the batter to coat, let excess drip off, and lower into the hot oil about 5 pieces at a time. When the pieces are browned and puffy, remove with a slotted spoon and drain on paper towels. Serves 3–4.

Broccoli-Mushroom Quiche with Chicken

Really more of a pie than a quiche, this is a dish I rely on a great deal for Sunday-night dinners. With a salad it is elegant enough for company because it is tasty,

Broccoli-Mushroom Quiche with Chicken, continued
filling, and extremely attractive, especially when served in a white porcelain quiche dish. Since we frequently have roast chicken on Friday, I try to squirrel away enough for this dish, but in a pinch one can poach a couple of chicken breasts.

1 recipe savory pâte brisée (p. 177)
¾ pound broccoli, trimmed and blanched (see note)
1 tablespoon butter
1 small onion, peeled and coarsely chopped
½ pound mushrooms, chopped
¼ pound imported Swiss or Gruyère cheese, shredded
6 ounces boneless cooked chicken coarsely chopped
4 large eggs
1½ cups heavy cream or cream and milk mixed
Salt to taste
¼ teaspoon lightly crushed dried tarragon, optional

Place an oven rack about one-third up from the bottom and preheat oven to 450°. Roll out the dough and with it line a 9-inch quiche dish. Refrigerate while preparing the filling.

Chop the broccoli and set aside.

Melt the butter in a medium skillet and sauté the onion until it wilts; add the mushrooms and cook until they give off their moisture and most of it evaporates.

To assemble: sprinkle half the cheese over the bottom of the prepared quiche pan. Add the broccoli and chicken in an even layer over the cheese. Scatter the mushroom-onion mixture over and sprinkle with the remaining cheese.

Combine and beat together the eggs, cream, salt, and tarragon. Pour slowly into the quiche pan. Bake in the preheated oven for 10 minutes; lower heat to 325° and bake for 20 to 25 minutes more, or until the filling is firm and browned. Let stand at least 10 minutes before cutting. Serve warm or at room temperature. Serves 4–6.

Note: You can use a package of frozen broccoli for this dish. Defrost and squeeze out excess water, then chop.

Chicken Cutlets with Broccoli-Leek Puree

I always have boned chicken breasts in the freezer, because they're low in calories and can be combined with vegetables in so many satisfying ways. This particular preparation is especially dependable and easy for last-minute company—and I love main courses that go from oven to table in the same dish! The puree is also delicious as a vegetable by itself. The sweetness of the leek makes the broccoli rather mysterious and interesting.

7½ tablespoons butter
1 bunch broccoli
¾ pound leeks, white and
   light green portions
2 tablespoons crème
   fraîche or heavy cream
Salt and freshly ground
   pepper

Nutmeg
2 whole boned chicken
   breasts, at room
   temperature
2 slender scallions, cut
   crosswise into ⅛-inch
   rings

Butter an 8×14×2-inch gratin dish with ½ tablespoon of the butter and set aside.

Separate the broccoli into stems and flowerets. Save the stems for another use. You should have about 3 cups of flowerets. Blanch, drain, and plunge into cold water. When cool, drain again.

Trim the leeks, cut crosswise into half-inch pieces, and wash well in a colander under running water. Boil for 8 minutes in salted water to cover. Drain, run cold water over, and press out as much liquid as possible.

Puree both vegetables together in a food processor, in two batches if necessary. Add 2 tablespoons of the butter and the crème fraîche and season with salt, pepper, and a grating of nutmeg. Spread in the baking dish and set aside.

Preheat the oven to 350°.

Cut the chicken breasts in half so you have four pieces; flatten them slightly. Sauté the cutlets for 4 to 5 minutes in 4 tablespoons of the butter, turning once. Do not overcrowd them in the pan. Season to taste and place in the baking dish on top of the puree.

Soften the scallions in the remaining butter in the same pan; sprinkle on top of the chicken along with any butter remaining in the pan. Place the dish in the preheated oven for about 10 minutes to heat the puree and gloss the chicken. Serves 4.

Note: This dish may be prepared ahead, kept covered with plastic wrap at room temperature for 2 hours, and heated as directed just before serving. It can also be refrigerated for a longer period but must be brought to room temperature before baking.

Cold Broccoli Soup

1½ pounds fresh broccoli
4 cups chicken broth
1 cup chopped onion
2 carrots, sliced
3 celery ribs (inside branches with leaves, if possible) cut into 3 or 4 pieces
5 sprigs parsley

1 teaspoon salt
1 tablespoon cornstarch
¼ cup water
½ cup heavy cream
½ cup milk
Salt and freshly ground pepper
Chopped chives, optional

Wash the broccoli and separate the flowerets from the stems. Divide the flowerets into two piles. Put one pile and the stems into a 5-quart soup pot and add the chicken broth, onion, carrots, celery, parsley, and salt. Bring to a boil, lower heat, and simmer uncovered for 15 minutes.

Bring 2 cups of salted water to a boil in another pot. Have a bowl of ice-cold water ready. Cut the remaining flowerets into slender flowers, drop into the boiling water, and cook uncovered for 5 minutes. Immediately drain and plunge into the cold water to stop the cooking and set the color. Reserve for garnish.

Put the cornstarch in a blender or the bowl of a food processor, add the ¼ cup water, and whirl until smooth. Add 3 or 4 ladlefuls of the hot broth and blend again. Pour this mixture into the soup pot and cook for 5 minutes more over moderate heat.

Let the soup cool slightly, then puree in two batches in the blender or food processor. Add the cream and milk and season to taste with salt and pepper. To achieve a very silky, smooth puree, put the soup through a *chinois,* food mill, or strainer; this is not absolutely necessary, but there may be an occasional bit of woody thread from a stalk or small bits of vegetable that missed the initial pureeing.

Refrigerate and check seasoning after chilling.

To serve, ladle into individual soup bowls and garnish each serving with one or two broccoli flowerets and a sprinkle of chopped chives. Serves 8.

Note: Depending on the strength of the chicken broth, the soup may thicken considerably as it chills. If you like it thinner, add a bit more milk or cream.

Penne with Broccoli and Pesto

Anna Theresa Callen, a friend and Manhattan cooking teacher, made this for me for lunch one day. She calls it Summer Pasta and uses it frequently for hot-weather buffets because it is meant to be eaten at room temperature. I find it equally delicious warm.

1 bunch fresh broccoli, trimmed and separated into bite-size pieces	2–3 garlic cloves, lightly smashed
1 pound penne (or fusilli, rotelle, or bow ties)	¼–⅓ cup pesto sauce (p. 382) without cheese
5 tablespoons olive oil	Freshly ground pepper and salt, if desired

Blanch the broccoli for 4 minutes and drain, reserving the cooking water. Pour the broccoli water into the pot in which you will cook the pasta, adding additional water as required. Bring to a boil and add the penne and cook until al dente, or according to package instructions.

While the pasta is cooking, heat the oil in a large heavy skillet. Add the garlic and, as soon as it starts to fry, add the broccoli and sauté briefly until it is tender and heated through. Do not overcook.

Drain the pasta and reserve 1 cup of the cooking water. Add the pasta to the skillet with the broccoli and cook for 5 minutes over low heat, tossing gently. Put in a warm bowl. Add half the reserved pasta water to the pesto, stir to blend, and add to the broccoli–pasta mixture. Toss. If pasta seems too dry, cautiously add a little more water. Season with fresh black pepper and salt and toss again. Serves 4–5.

Note: Serve with grated Parmesan cheese *only* if serving as a warm dish. Cherry tomatoes or sliced ripe tomatoes make a nice garnish when served at room temperature.

Brussels Sprouts

(Brassica oleracea gemmifera)

This winter vegetable is really a miniature form of cabbage with a delicate, nutty flavor all its own. Served alone or combined with chestnuts (the size, colors, and textures complement each other), sprouts are a holiday table staple and make a lovely festive accompaniment to game. Their flavor also balances nicely with pork dishes.

To Buy

Sprouts are generally sold in 10-ounce containers that sometimes contain widely varying sizes (if so, cook the

larger ones first and add the smaller ones 2 or 3 minutes
later). Look for firm green closely curled heads with no
brown spots, yellow leaves, or signs of wilt. They
should be weighty for their size, and the core end
should be white. Generally, the smaller they are, the
sweeter; large sprouts tend to be coarse. One box will
feed 3 people.

To Store

Do not wash; refrigerate covered with plastic wrap and
use within 3 days.

To Prepare for Cooking

Remove any yellow or withered leaves and stem ends if
any. If sprouts are large, pierce a shallow "X" with the
tip of a sharp knife in the stem end for even cooking.
Soak in lightly salted water to rid them of dirt or small
insects.

To Cook

Boiled: This method actually half-steams them. Put
sprouts in a saucepan with an inch or so of lightly
salted water, bring to a boil, and cook, tightly covered,
for 10 or 15 minutes, depending on size. Drain. Melt 1
or 2 tablespoons of butter in a skillet and add the
sprouts. Roll about to coat and cook for about 4
minutes, shaking the pan once or twice. Season with a
little grinding of fresh black pepper and serve
immediately as is, or with a knob of maître d'hôtel
butter (p. 395) or additional browned butter. Or simply
squeeze a little lemon juice on them before serving.

Steamed: Steam over ¾ inch boiling water until
tender—10 or 12 minutes for medium sprouts. Finish in
any way given for boiled sprouts.

Blanched: Cook uncovered in rapidly boiling
salted water—4 to 5 minutes for small sprouts, 7 to 8

minutes for medium to large. Drain and refresh in cold water. Braise or cook with chestnuts.

Oven–braised: Blanch and refresh 2 boxes of sprouts. Arrange in a well-buttered baking dish in one or two layers, season with salt and pepper, and drizzle with 3 tablespoons melted butter. Cover with foil and cook over low heat until you hear the butter begin to sizzle. Place in a preheated 350° oven for 20 minutes. Serves 6.

Braised: Blanch and refresh 2 boxes of sprouts. Melt 4 tablespoons of butter in a skillet, add the sprouts, and cook for 2 minutes, shaking the pan almost constantly. Add ½ cup chicken or vegetable broth, bring to a simmer, cover, and cook over low heat for 8 to 10 minutes, or until tender but not mushy. Most of the broth should be absorbed. If not, cook uncovered an additional 2 minutes over brisk heat. Season to taste with salt and pepper. Serves 6.

Brussels Sprouts with Chestnuts

This combination makes an excellent companion for roasted game birds or the Thanksgiving turkey.

2 ten-ounce containers brussels sprouts	braised chestnuts (see following recipe)
4 tablespoons butter	Salt and freshly ground pepper
1 pound peeled and	

Trim, blanch, and refresh the sprouts. Let cool. (Sprouts may be prepared ahead up to this point.)

Melt the butter in a saucepan, add sprouts and chestnuts, and shake gently over medium heat until coated and heated through. Season with salt and pepper and serve. Serves 6–8.

Braised Chestnuts

2 cups peeled chestnuts	2 tablespoons butter
1 cup chicken broth	

Combine all the ingredients in a saucepan and bring to a boil. Cover, reduce heat, and simmer for 20 minutes, or until chestnuts are tender. Serve as is or combine with other vegetables, such as brussels sprouts. Cut braising time in half if the chestnuts are to be used in a dish to be cooked further, such as stuffing.

Cabbage
(Brassica oleracea)

We eat quite a lot of cabbage in the course of a year. In winter we enjoy it cut into wedges, steamed, and seasoned with just pepper and a little butter. Stuffed cabbage is frequently in the freezer for Sunday-night suppers, and the first snowy day almost automatically means a steaming borscht. Sweet-and-sour red cabbage is a must when we have paprikash chicken, duck, or a goose at holiday time. And homemade coleslaw is in the refrigerator on weekends, as it makes a meal out of any leftover or a sandwich and is easy for children to help themselves to. A couple of times a year, after our begging becomes tiresome, my friend Mia Solow invites us for her fabulous whole stuffed cabbage, surely one of the premier glories of the French kitchen. And then, of course, there is sauerkraut, embellishing the good old

frankfurter and starring in choucroute garni. Here is a vegetable you can count on!

Cato held raw cabbage in high esteem as an antidote for a hangover, and Hungarian housewives make a cabbage soup, called drunkard's soup, to be consumed after New Year revelries.

Cabbages fall basically into two categories: the round heads that form hearts, and the tall, nonhearting types. Round cabbages include *green cabbage,* the most common, which is quite mild in flavor, with smooth outer leaves and inner leaves that can be eaten raw in salads; *Savoy cabbage,* also a green cabbage and used interchangeably but distinguished by its pretty, loose, deeply veined and ruffled leaves; and *red cabbage,* sometimes called purple cabbage.

Nonhearting types include *Chinese cabbage,* called *bok choy* by the Cantonese, which has a yellow flower and is dark green and leafy, like chard. It can be stir-fried with any meat, poultry, or seafood. *Celery cabbage* (also called *Tiensin* or *Napa* cabbage or *Chinese lettuce*) is a very mild, slightly tart cabbage of the nonhearting type. It has a white stalk and elongated, pale yellow leaves and looks somewhat like romaine. Steam, stir-fry, or use it in salads, raw and finely cut. Or use the stalks and save the leaves for soup. A variation, confusingly called *Shanghai bok choy* by the northern Chinese, has a pale green stalk and light green leaves and is frequently blanched, sauced, and served as a side dish.

The vast *Brassica* family also includes broccoli, brussels sprouts, cauliflower, kale, and kohlrabi, discussed under their own headings.

Long cooking of cabbage releases an enzyme that breaks down to release hydrogen sulfide, the characteristic odor of rotten eggs. It is a rank smell that lingers, is unpleasant, and for many has connotations of boarding houses and improverished homes. The best way to avoid it is speedy cooking in a large quantity of already boiling water. Covered cooking inhibits the smell, too. There are, of course, dishes in which cabbage is paired with some other food and lengthy cooking time is required for the exchange of flavors, but

somehow those smells are not offensive. Red cabbage, which is tougher and needs longer cooking, is usually cooked with enough spices to make the smell quite pleasant.

To Buy

Round cabbage: look for firm, heavy, brightly colored leaves with no blemishes. Savoy cabbage leaves should not be limp; the core should be white. Avoid wilted, yellowed, blemished specimens. In general it is not at its best in winter. Chinese cabbage: look for crisp leaves.

Cabbage yield varies with the type and preparation. A firm 2-pound head, trimmed, yields approximately 9 cups sliced and 5 to 6 cups cooked. Red cabbage, because it is coarser and hence must be cooked longer, yields less—about 4 cups cooked. A trimmed Chinese cabbage yields about 6 cups sliced.

To Store

Do not wash any cabbage before storing. Head and Savoy cabbage keeps a week to 10 days in the refrigerator. Once it is cut, wrap it tightly in plastic and use promptly. Chinese cabbage keeps up to a week in tight plastic wrap in the crisper drawer of the refrigerator.

To Prepare for Cooking

Trim off any tough or bruised outer leaves. For wedges, cut head in quarters. Cut away most of the core, but leave enough to hold the leaves together. For shredding, cut head in quarters and remove the core entirely. Shred with a large, heavy knife or the slicing disk of a food processor. To prepare a whole cabbage for stuffing, consult the recipe for chou farci (p. 78). To prepare individual leaves for stuffing, cut around the core of the cabbage and carefully remove the leaves intact. Parboil

for 10 minutes, and pare away any thick ribs without tearing the leaf.

To Cook

Boiled: Bring a large pot of salted water to the boil, add cabbage wedges gradually so water does not stop boiling, and cook, covered, for 12 to 15 minutes. Drain. Season with pepper and a little butter. If it is to be used further in a recipe, squeeze out excess moisture with the hands.

Steamed: Cook over 1 inch of boiling water in a covered steamer. Cored quarters of a 1½-pound cabbage will take 15 minutes; smaller wedges, 9 minutes. Shredded cabbage will take 8 minutes and whole leaves will be tender in 3 or 4 minutes. Finish with butter, salt, and pepper to taste.

Stir-fried Chinese cabbage: Remove and discard any tough outer leaves. Separate the stalks and leaves. Split lower stalks lengthwise and then cut into 2-inch strips. Cut leaves into 2-inch pieces. Heat oil in a wok, add 3 slices fresh ginger root the thickness of a quarter, and stir-fry a few seconds. Add stalks and stir-fry to coat with oil and soften slightly. Mix together about ½ cup chicken or vegetable broth and 1 tablespoon soy sauce and add to the wok by pouring down the sides. Raise heat, then cook covered until stalks are tender—about 3 minutes. Add leaves, cover again, and simmer just until they soften—1 to 2 minutes more.

Steamed Cabbage with Bacon

I have had cabbage prepared this way by an excellent Barbadian cook and several good Southern cooks as well. It is utterly simple and very delicious. Accompanied by a baked potato, it makes a whole meal.

1 head green cabbage   **Freshly ground pepper**
3–4 strips bacon

Trim and shred the cabbage coarsely. Cut the bacon into 8 crosswise pieces, and put everything into a heavy pot. Cover and cook over low heat until tender—about 15 minutes. The combination of moisture from the cabbage and fat from the bacon is enough to cook the cabbage with no additional liquid. Add a generous amount of freshly milled pepper at the end, and salt, if desired, although you should not need it because of the bacon. Note that the bacon will not be crisp, but is very delicious. Serves 8.

Steamed Cabbage and Ham Supper

This is a good Saturday night meal that is quite complete—an assortment of mustards, rye bread, sweet butter, and beer are the only other accompaniments needed. Leftover ham can be used for Sunday morning ham and eggs.

2 pounds green cabbage   3–4 medium potatoes,
2 pounds precooked   peeled and cut into
    boneless ham   quarters
2 medium onions, cut in   6–8 carrots, scraped and
    half   cut into 1½-inch pieces

Cut the cabbage into wedges and remove the bulk of the core, leaving just enough to hold the leaves together. Arrange the cabbage, ham, and onion halves in a steamer basket. Place the potatoes in a second steamer basket and the carrots in a third. Place 2 inches of water in the bottom of the steamer, cover, and bring to a boil. Uncover, stack the baskets on top, cover, and steam for 25 to 30 minutes, or until potatoes are tender. Serves 4.

Alsatian Cabbage and Potatoes

The first time I was served these roughly mashed potatoes studded with nuggets of cabbage and golden onion, I found the dish so good I elected to eat it

without the hot sausages it accompanied—which tells you something about how well it might do at an all-vegetable meal. Besides sausages, it is equally good with hot tongue or corned beef.

4–5 medium boiling potatoes, peeled and quartered	2–3 tablespoons vegetable oil or rendered chicken or goose fat
1 large head green cabbage, trimmed and quartered	1 large onion, chopped Salt and freshly ground pepper

Put the potatoes in a heavy pot with salted water to cover. Place the cabbage quarters on top. Bring to the boil, cover, and cook until the potatoes are just tender —about 20 minutes. Do not overcook.

Remove the cabbage and drain. Chop coarsely and set aside. Drain the potatoes and mash with a potato masher. (Do not puree because they will not have the proper texture.) Set aside. Dry the cooking pot and add the oil. When hot, sauté the onion until golden brown. Add the mashed potatoes and cabbage to the onion and blend thoroughly. Season to taste with salt and pepper. Reheat briefly and serve. Serves 6.

Kulebiaka of Cabbage

Kulebiaka, or coulibiac as it is sometimes spelled, is a Russian savory pastry roll most often enclosing a complex mixture of salmon and mushrooms. In France it is made with puff pastry or brioche dough. The pastry here is more like the Russian. The whole thing can be assembled a day ahead and refrigerated. The finished result is so attractive it could be the star of any buffet, especially a vegetarian one.

The pastry

4 cups all-purpose flour	butter
½ teaspoon salt	16 ounces cream cheese at room temperature
2 teaspoons sugar	
½ pound (2 sticks) sweet	½ cup sour cream

The filling

1 head green cabbage, 2½–3 pounds, trimmed and coarsely shredded	1 bay leaf
	3 hard-cooked eggs, chopped
4 tablespoons butter or chicken fat	¼ cup finely chopped dill
	½ teaspoon sugar
2 medium onions, finely chopped (about 1½ cups)	1½ teaspoons salt
	Freshly ground pepper

The assembly

1 egg yolk   1 tablespoon cream

For the pastry, sift the flour, salt, and sugar into a mixing bowl. Cream the butter and cream cheese together. Add and blend in the sour cream. Blend in the flour mixture, one cup at a time. Form into a ball, wrap, and chill for an hour or overnight. Let come to room temperature and divide into two parts before using.

For the filling, bring a gallon of salted water to a boil in a large pot, and add the cabbage by the handful. Simmer, uncovered, for 5 minutes from the second boil. Drain and set aside.

Melt the butter in a large, heavy skillet or 4-quart saucepan, add the onions, and sauté over medium heat until soft and pale gold. Add the cabbage (which will seem not to fit but will quickly reduce in volume as it cooks). Add the bay leaf and cook, covered, over low heat for 20 minutes, or until tender. If any liquid accumulates in the pan, raise the heat and cook until it has evaporated. Drain the cabbage, remove and discard the bay leaf. Combine the chopped egg and dill with the cabbage. Add the sugar and season rather highly with salt and pepper. Let cool slightly.

To assemble, butter a heavy cookie sheet. Roll half the dough into a rectangular shape on a floured surface. Lightly flour the dough and continue rolling until it is about 6 by 14 inches and ⅛ inch thick. Transfer to the

cookie sheet and trim to a neat rectangle. Save the pastry scraps.

Mix the egg yolk and cream in a small bowl and have handy, along with a pastry brush.

Spread the filling down the center of the pastry, leaving a 1-inch border of pastry all around. Mound and pat the filling into a loaf shape.

Roll the second half of the dough into a rectangle about 2 inches wider and longer than the first. Brush the exposed border of the filled half with the egg yolk mixture. Lay the second piece of dough over it, edges matching. Brush the top of the border. Trim the corners so they are rounded. Starting with the long ends, roll up the border all around and crimp firmly with the dull side of a knife blade. Cut a quarter-size hole in the center to allow steam to escape.

If you have the patience, gather the pastry scraps, roll them out, and with a small sharp knife cut out leaves or other decorative shapes for the top of the kulebiaka. Brush the top and decorations with the egg yolk mixture. Refrigerate the loaf for half an hour.

Preheat the oven to 400°.

Bake the pastry for 1 hour, or until golden. Slice and serve at once. Pass a bowl of sour cream, if desired. Serves 8.

Chou Farci

Mia Solow's friends adore her whole stuffed cabbage, which was always prepared for guests on hunt weekends at the chateau of friends in Belgium. Disdaining blood sports, Mia spent her time observing in the kitchen. She always demurred when asked for the recipe, saying, "You have to see it done." I thought this was the classic put-off until one day she invited me to watch. Every French housewife has her version of this heavenly dish. Though Mia's recipe is long, it is not at all difficult, and the Lucullan result more than justifies the effort.

The cabbage and stuffing

1 very large unblemished head green cabbage
3 sweet Italian sausages, casings removed
⅓ pound ground pork
¼ pound boiled or baked ham
¾ pound ground beef top round
¾ pound ground veal
5 tablespoons butter
1 fat leek, trimmed, washed, and sliced crosswise into ½-inch pieces

1 large onion, chopped
3 cloves garlic, finely chopped
⅓ cup chopped parsley
Salt and freshly ground pepper
¼ teaspoon thyme
¼ teaspoon sage
¼ teaspoon allspice
2 carrots, coarsely grated
16-ounce can plum tomatoes, undrained
¾ cup fresh bread crumbs
1 egg

The bouillon

2–3 strips bacon
1 medium onion, chopped
3 cups red wine

2 cups beef broth
⅓ cup chopped parsley

Blanch the whole cabbage in a large heavy pot of boiling salted water for 15 to 25 minutes, depending on its size, until the leaves are supple. Lift out with two wooden spoons or sturdy spatulas and, when cool enough to handle, begin gently nudging the leaves back one at a time with a gentle rolling, peeling motion, taking great care not to tear them. Lay them back as you go, as if opening a rose. When you reach the central white knot of leaves that resists opening, stop. Cut this core out, chop finely, and reserve.

Combine the sausage meat, pork, and ham in a heavy skillet. Stir over moderate heat for about 10 minutes, breaking up meat with a wooden spoon, until all pink has disappeared. Set aside.

Combine the beef and veal in a bowl and set aside.

Melt 3 tablespoons of the butter in another skillet and sauté the leek, stirring, for about 5 minutes. Add the onion and continue cooking until it is limp; add the

garlic, parsley, and reserved chopped cabbage and cook, stirring, for another 5 minutes. Season to taste with salt and pepper.

Transfer about three-quarters of the onion-leek mixture to the pan with the pork mixture. Add the remaining 2 tablespoons of the butter to the remaining mixture and stir to blend. Add and sauté the beef-veal mixture until it loses color. Season with salt, pepper, thyme, sage, and allspice.

In a large bowl combine the contents of both skillets. Add half the grated carrots and 3 of the canned tomatoes, and mix well with your hands. Add the bread crumbs, egg, and liberal grinds of black pepper and mix again. Sauté a spoonful of the mixture in a skillet and check for seasoning.

For the bouillon, choose a large pot that will hold the whole cabbage comfortably with some space around it. In it fry the bacon until almost crisp. Sauté the onion in the fat until limp, adding a bit of butter if necessary. Add the balance of the grated carrot, 2 cups of the wine, the broth, and the balance of the tomatoes and their juice. Cook for 10 minutes, breaking up the tomatoes with the side of a wooden spoon.

To assemble the cabbage, begin inserting the stuffing in and around the leaves; using one hand to bring each cabbage leaf up and back into shape and keeping the nonworking hand positioned on top of the cabbage to hold the works together. (The moistness of the leaves and filling makes this easier than it sounds.)

Using string or dental floss, begin tying the cabbage, making your first knot on top and then winding the string or thread around, up, and over and tying at critical junctures. Can be prepared ahead to this point (see note).

Preheat the oven to 300°.

Carefully place the tied cabbage in the broth. Slowly pour the remaining cup of wine over the cabbage so it penetrates the leaves. Cover and bake for 2½ to 3½ hours, depending on size. If there is a great deal of liquid in the pot, uncover during the last 45 minutes of cooking time and baste cabbage often.

Carefully transfer to a serving platter, using a wooden spoon and a sturdy fork. Sprinkle with lots of chopped parsley. To serve, cut into pielike wedges. Serves 8.

Preparation notes: Mia advises "garlic with abandon," so if you love it, add more. She prefers dental floss to kitchen string for tying the cabbage. You can prepare the cabbage up to the point of baking the day before and refrigerate it in the liquid. Bring to room temperature 2 hours before you plan to bake it.

Serving suggestion: Precede with potage crécy (p. 91). Accompany with buttered, parsleyed new potatoes, and pass a bowl of sour cream, if desired. Follow with a mixed green salad, cheese, and a warm fruit dessert like apple tart or apple crisp.

Sweet and Sour Stuffed Cabbage

These are best made the day before and allowed to mellow. They also freeze very well.

The cabbage:

1 large head green cabbage	1 teaspoon ground coriander
2 tablespoons vegetable oil	1 egg
⅓ cup chopped onion	Salt and freshly ground pepper to taste
1 pound ground beef	
2 tablespoons raw rice	

The sauce:

3 tablespoons vegetable oil	juice, or to taste
1 large onion, sliced	¼ cup brown sugar
2 eight-ounce cans tomato sauce	¼ cup golden raisins
1 pint water	6 small gingersnaps, crumbled
2–3 tablespoons lemon	

Prepare and parboil the individual cabbage leaves. Heat the oil in a skillet and sauté the chopped onion

until golden. Combine the onion, ground beef, rice, coriander, egg, salt, and pepper in a large bowl. Place one or two tablespoons of the mixture (depending on size of leaf) at the bottom of each leaf; fold up bottom, fold in each side, and roll up securely. Stack on a plate until all are made. Shred any extra leaves and set aside.

Select a heavy pot large enough to accommodate all the cabbage rolls and sauce. Heat the oil for the sauce and sauté the onion until soft. Add 8 ounces (1 can) of the tomato sauce, 8 ounces (1 can) of the water, the lemon juice, brown sugar, raisins, and gingersnaps. Bring to the boil, lower heat, and simmer, covered, for 1 hour. Season with salt and pepper to taste, and add more lemon juice if a more pronounced sweet-sour flavor is desired.

Add the remaining 8 ounces of tomato sauce, remaining water, and any shredded cabbage. Place the cabbage rolls in the sauce side by side as tightly as possible. Bring to the simmer, cover, and cook for 2 hours. Check the pot from time to time to see that the simmer is gentle enough not to break open the rolls and that the sauce does not burn.

Makes 10 to 14 rolls, depending on size. Allow 1 roll per person as an appetizer; 3 as a main course.

Note: May be refrigerated or frozen in aluminum baking pans and reheated, covered, in a 350° oven for 45 minutes. If frozen, defrost first in the refrigerator.

Choucroute Garni

I can't think of another dish that involves so little cooking with which you can feed so many people heartily. Try to find the very best pork products you can; German or Polish pork stores usually have what is needed here, and they often sell fresh sauerkraut as well. Of course you can also make your own, or buy the kind sold in plastic bags in the supermarket. Just remember to rinse it well.

3 tablespoons goose fat or butter	**2 pounds fresh sauerkraut, drained, then rinsed**
1 onion, thinly sliced	**1 cup dry white wine**

1 tart apple, coarsely chopped	1 tablespoon kirsch
1 teaspoon juniper berries, tied in cheesecloth	4 smoked pork loin chops
2 cups or more chicken stock	4 white veal sausages, optional
1 pound smoked lean bacon in one piece	4 bratwurst or frankfurters
	8 potatoes, boiled in their jackets, then drained

Melt the fat in a heavy flameproof casserole and cook the onion for 7 minutes, until soft and transparent. Squeeze the sauerkraut by handfuls to remove all the water; add to the casserole and simmer for 5 minutes, stirring. Add the wine, apple, juniper berries, and enough stock to barely cover. Cover and cook over very low heat for 2 to 2½ hours.

In another saucepan, cover the bacon with cold water, bring to boil, and boil for 10 minutes. Drain and rainse in cold water.

One hour before the choucroute is done, add the bacon, burying it in the sauerkraut. Forty-five minutes before it is done, add the kirsch and the pork chops.

Prick the sausages and frankfurters and poach separately in hot water for 10 minutes without letting water boil.

Remove the juniper berries and discard. Remove the bacon and slice it thickly. Stir the sauerkraut with a fork and transfer to the center of a large platter. Surround it with the bacon, the chops, sausages, frankfurters, and potatoes. (Mashed potatoes may be served in place of the boiled potatoes.) Serve with an assortment of mustards—Dusseldorf, hot Dijon, and Moutarde de Meaux. Serves 4–5.

Chinese Mustard Cabbage

1 large head Chinese cabbage, about 1½ pounds	taste
	2 tablespoons soy sauce
2 teaspoons dry mustard	2 teaspoons rice or wine vinegar
¼ teaspoon sugar, or to	

Discard any tough outer leaves of the cabbage. Cut the head crosswise into 1-inch slices. Bring a large pot

of salted water to the boil and add the cabbage in small batches; push down with a wooden spoon. Cook for just 1 minute after water returns to the boil. Drain well.

Whisk together the mustard, sugar, soy sauce, and vinegar in a large bowl. Add the cabbage, toss to coat, and let cool. Cover and chill before serving. Serves 4–5.

Sweet and Sour Red Cabbage

This is an indispensable accompaniment to roast goose, duck, and paprikash chicken.

3 tablespoons vegetable oil	¼ cup brown sugar, or more to taste
2 tablespoons butter	½ teaspoon cinnamon
2 medium onions, finely chopped (about 1 cup)	5 cloves
1 large apple, peeled and chopped	1 bay leaf
1 medium head red cabbage (about 2½ pounds), trimmed and shredded	1 teaspoon salt
	Several good grindings of fresh pepper
2 tablespoons lemon juice	1 cup white wine, or an equal amount wine vinegar

Heat the oil in a heavy enamel-lined pot, add the butter and melt it. Sauté the onions until wilted—5 to 8 minutes. Stir in the apple. Add the cabbage and cook over moderate heat, stirring frequently, for 10 minutes, or until the cabbage appears glossy. Add the lemon juice, sugar, cinnamon, cloves, bay leaf, salt, pepper, and half the wine. Cover tightly and cook over low heat for 2½ hours. The cabbage should be glossy and dry and not watery. Stir in the balance of the wine and add more sugar or seasoning to taste as needed. Remove the bay leaf and place cabbage in a heated serving dish. Serves 6.

Preparation notes: This dish improves with age and, like many spiced dishes, is better cooked a day ahead. To prepare ahead, cook the cabbage for 1½ hours, let cool, and refrigerate. Add the balance of the wine and

cook for the remaining hour the next day. Keep leftover cabbage refrigerated; it may be reheated frequently.

When you first cut the cabbage it will seem like an enormous amount, but it will shrink to about half its volume in the cooking.

Stir-fried Chinese Cabbage with Pork

This is a good winter dish as part of an Oriental meal or on its own. The pork makes it very hearty.

1½ pounds Chinese cabbage	oil
1½ pound lean pork, such as boneless pork loin	2 slices fresh ginger, about the size of a quarter
2 tablespoons soy sauce	1 teaspoon sugar
3–4 dried hot red peppers	½ teaspoon salt
½ cup peanut or vegetable	Sesame oil, optional

Separate the cabbage leaves and cut crosswise into thirds, one leaf at a time. Stack the pieces and slice lengthwise into fine shreds. Cut the pork into thin slices and shred into strips the same length as the cabbage. Combine the pork and the soy sauce in a small bowl and stir to coat. Cut the peppers into half-inch dice.

Heat ¼ cup of the oil in a wok or large skillet until almost smoking. Add the pork and stir-fry quickly until it begins to brown. Remove with a slotted spoon and set in a sieve over a bowl. Reserve juices.

Heat the remaining oil and stir-fry the ginger for 30 seconds. Add the cabbage and hot peppers and stir-fry until the cabbage is wilted—about 1½ minutes. Add the pork juices, sugar, and salt and cook, stirring, for 3 minutes more. Cover and cook another 3 minutes. Add the pork and toss and stir over high heat. Season with a few drops of sesame oil, if desired. Serves 8 as part of an Oriental meal, 4 as a main course.

Note: This is one of the few Chinese dishes that can be made slightly ahead and kept warm in a slow oven or on an asbestos pad.

Coleslaw

1 medium head green
  cabbage
1 small onion
2 carrots, peeled
½ green pepper
6 tablespoons mayonnaise
3 tablespoons cider
  vinegar

1 tablespoon Dijon
  mustard
2 teaspoons sugar
1 tablespoon salt
2 teaspoons celery seeds,
  optional
Heavy cream, optional

Trim and shred the cabbage. Grate the onion, carrots, and green pepper over the cabbage and mix thoroughly with the hands.

Combine the mayonnaise, vinegar, mustard, sugar, salt, and celery seeds. Thin with a little cream, if desired. Pour over the cabbage, toss thoroughly, and refrigerate for several hours before serving. Serves 8.

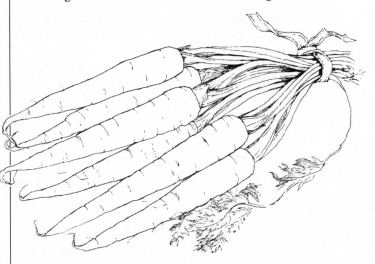

Carrots

(Daucus carota sativa)

Carrots are a vegetable one takes for granted, used so frequently they cease being noticed as a separate entity. So, having added a carrot to almost every stock and soup I'd ever made, I was pleasantly astonished to learn how incredibly good plain carrot soup could be. One of my favorite accompaniments is carrots and celery flavored with caraway. Glazed carrots alone or in combination with turnips are wonderful with meats or poultry. Pureed, carrots lend their color and sweetness to a number of otherwise pallid vegetables, such as parnips, turnips, and potatoes.

Carrots contain more sugar than any other vegetable except beets, which also qualifies them for desserts. The Irish make a pudding of them, as do the Hindus, who then decorate it with edible silverleaf. There is also carrot jam, carrot wine, and our own beloved carrot cake.

To Buy

Try to buy small carrots, since very large ones tend to have woody cores and are not as sweet. Packaged carrots with a small green remnant of stalk on the top were fresh when shipped and will be sweeter than storage carrots, which have flat, dry tops. Avoid crooked carrots, which are hard to peel, and those that are split or sprouted. Allow 1 pound of carrots, after tops are removed, for 3 or 4 persons. (Belgian baby carrots in jars are tasteless.)

To Store

Break off the leafy green tops of bunched fresh carrots; they sap the roots of moisture.

Carrots may be stored in a plastic bag in the crisper drawer of the refrigerator for several weeks, but eventually they become shriveled and limp. Don't store near apples; the ethylene gas exuded by the fruit as it ripens makes carrots bitter.

To Prepare

Baby carrots do not need to be scraped, only rinsed. Scrub fairly young carrots with a vegetable brush. Older carrots do need scraping; use a peeler rather than a knife. Older carrots (unless they're being used for stock) should also have their cores cut out before using; quarter them lengthwise and pry out the core with the tip of a small sharp knife. Cut into 1½-inch logs,

¼-inch round disks, or disks on the diagonal, or
julienne (p. 354).

To Cook

Waterless: I like this method for young carrots
because they steam in their own sweet juices. Thinly
slice rinsed carrots on the diagonal and cook over very
low heat in a heavy, covered pot for 8 to 10 minutes,
depending on thickness. Finish by melting a little butter
in the pot and stirring the carrots around.

Steamed: Bring 1 inch of water to the boil in the
bottom of a steamer. Place carrots cut into 2-inch logs
in the basket, cover, and steam 5 minutes. Roll in
melted butter.

In stews or pot roast: Add quartered carrots
30 to 45 minutes, depending on thickness, before the
meat is done.

Blanched: Bring a large pot of salted water to the
boil. Add julienned carrots and cook for 2 minutes.
Drain. Melt butter in a skillet, add the carrots, season to
taste, and cook over moderate heat for 2 minutes,
stirring and tossing or shaking the pan almost
constantly. Serve at once.

Carrot bundles: This is a pretty way to garnish
a company plate. Blanch julienned carrots as described.
Drop several long green pieces of scallion in salted
boiling water for 10 to 15 seconds, drain, and
immediately refresh in cold water. You will now have
limp, bright green strings. Make a bundle of carrot
sticks and tie each with a piece of scallion.

Miniature carrots: These are fun to make and
serve when real baby carrots are not available but fresh
carrots with tops are. Cut off the feathery part, leaving
a good 2 inches or so of stem. Scrape the carrots and

cut off the smaller ends (save for nibbles or soup) so you have miniature whole carrots, 3 or 4 inches long. Drop into boiling salted water and cook until just tender—6 to 8 minutes. Refresh in cold water. They may now be kept to reheat in butter to garnish a hot dish, alone or with other vegetables, or used as is to garnish cold seafood.

Puree of carrots and parsnips: See page 204.

Glazed Carrots

This dish is one of the best all-around accompaniments to meat, poultry, and fish. The buttery sugar syrup gives the carrots a lustrous glaze.

2–3 tablespoons butter	water
1½ pounds carrots, cut	Salt and freshly ground
into 1½-inch logs	pepper to taste
1 cup chicken broth or	2 teaspoons sugar

If you have the patience, "turn" the carrots (p. 386), though this is not critical.

Melt the butter in a heavy-bottomed enamel-lined saucepan. Add the carrots and stir or shake to coat with butter. Add the broth and cook, covered, over gentle heat for 18 to 20 minutes, or until carrots are tender. Halfway through the cooking, season with salt and pepper and stir to redistribute the carrots.

If the liquid is not reduced, cook uncovered over brisk heat for a minute or two. Add the sugar, cover the pan, and shake back and forth for a minute. Cook another minute with pot uncovered until carrots are nicely glazed but not brown. Serves 6.

Glazed Carrots and Turnips

This is a good companion to roast meat, fowl or game, when turnips are in season.

Glazed Carrots and Turnips, continued

1 pound carrots, cut into 1½-inch logs	3 tablespoons butter
1 pound small white turnips, cut into 1½-inch lengths	2 tablespoons sugar
	Salt and freshly ground pepper

"Turn" the carrots and turnips into ovals (p. 386). Save the scraps and parings for use in soup.

Blanch the carrots, covered, for about 12 minutes, or until crisp-tender. Drain and immediately plunge into cold water. Drain and set aside. Do the same with the turnips, cooking them for about 10 minutes. (May be prepared several hours ahead to this point.)

Just before serving, melt the butter in a skillet large enough to hold the vegetables in one layer. Stir in the sugar, add the vegetables and salt and pepper to taste, and cook just long enough to heat through and glaze the vegetables slightly. Shake pan frequently. Serves 4.

Scalloped Carrots and Celery with Caraway Seeds

This was an anonymous contribution to a regional cookbook I once compiled, and it has gotten me out of countless last-minute difficulties ever since. It is utterly simple yet oddly festive, and there is almost nothing it cannot accompany; it is especially nice to cheer up broiled fish. And carrots and celery are almost always on hand.

4 tablespoons butter	¼ cup chicken broth
¼ cup chopped onion	½ teaspoon salt
3 cups celery, thinly sliced on the diagonal	Freshly ground pepper to taste
3 cups carrots, thinly sliced on the diagonal	1 teaspoon caraway seeds

Melt the butter in a medium-size saucepan and sauté the onion, but do not let it brown. Add the celery, carrots, broth, salt, and pepper. Cover and bring to the boil. Lower the heat and cook for 10 to 15 minutes, or until the vegetables are tender but still slightly crisp.

Uncover, raise the heat slightly, and cook for 2 to 3 minutes more to evaporate any excess liquid. Add the caraway seeds and toss just before serving. Serves 6–8.

Moroccan Carrot Salad

A very tasty and useful dish to know, this is wonderful with grilled food of all kinds, nice to set out on a cold buffet. It keeps for several days.

6–7 large carrots, scraped
2 shallots, finely chopped
2–3 tablespoons sugar
½ teaspoon salt
½ teaspoon ground cumin

Freshly ground pepper
Dash cayenne, optional
3 tablespoons lemon juice
½ cup finely minced parsley

Grate or julienne the carrots with the appropriate disk of a food processor. Add the shallots and toss. Combine the sugar, salt, and cumin and toss with the carrots. Season with liberal grindings of pepper and the cayenne. Add the lemon juice and toss again. Let marinate for 1 hour. Sprinkle with parsley and serve at room temperature. Serves 4–6.

Potage Crécy

This is one of my favorite soups. You won't believe how delicious such a simple concoction can be.

3 tablespoons butter
¾ cup finely chopped onion
6–8 carrots, thinly sliced (about 3 cups)
4 cups chicken broth

2 tablespoons raw rice
1 cup hot water
2 teaspoons sugar
Salt
White pepper
½ cup heavy cream

Melt 2 tablespoons of the butter in a heavy 3-quart pot, add the onion, and cook, stirring occasionally, until soft but not brown—3 to 5 minutes. Add the carrots, broth, and rice. Cover and simmer gently for about 25 minutes, or until the carrots are very soft. Put through a food mill or puree well in a food processor or blender.

Return the puree to the pot and add the hot water, using a little more if the puree is very thick. Add the sugar, salt, and pepper. (May be prepared ahead to this point.)

At serving time add the cream to the soup and bring just to the simmer. Correct seasoning and swirl in the remaining tablespoon of butter. Serve plain, garnished with chopped parsley or chives, a single feather of dill, or a carrot curl sprinkled with parsley. Serves 4–6.

Carrot Tzimmes

Tzimmes is a Yiddish word meaning "stew." It may be made with sweet or white potatoes and prunes, with carrots as here, and with or without meat. It is a traditional dish for the Jewish New Year, when, to ensure that it be sweet, honey is often used symbolically in place of brown sugar.

3 tablespoons rendered chicken fat or vegetable oil
2 medium onions, diced
4 medium sweet potatoes, peeled and cut into ½-inch slices
4–5 carrots, scraped and cut into 1-inch slices
3 cups boiling water

¼ teaspoon cinnamon
Salt and freshly ground pepper to taste
Several gratings nutmeg
⅓ cup firmly packed brown sugar
1 tablespoon butter or vegetable shortening
2 tablespoons flour

Melt the fat in a heavy casserole or Dutch oven and slowly brown the onions. Add the potatoes, carrots, water, cinnamon, salt, pepper, nutmeg, and brown sugar. Stir to mix, partly cover, and simmer for 45 minutes. Shake the pot to prevent scorching but do not stir.

Melt the butter in a small skillet over medium heat. Blend in the flour and let the mixture take on some color. Stir in 1 cup of the kettle liquid, then return the mixture to the pot. Shake but do not stir to distribute it. The stew should be thick but not soupy. Heat for 2 minutes. Correct seasoning. Serves 4.

Tzimmes with meat: Cut 1½ to 2 pounds boned beef chuck into 1-inch cubes. Brown these in chicken or other fat in a heavy soup pot. Scoop out with a slotted spoon and reserve. Brown the onions in the pot drippings and proceed as given, adding the meat with the potatoes and carrots. Serves 4–6.

Old-fashioned Carrot Cake

Carrot cake became wildly popular a few years back, and recipes for it proliferate. This is the best I've tasted.

2 cups sugar
1½ cups corn oil
4 eggs
2 cups all-purpose flour
1 teaspoon salt
2 teaspoons baking soda
2 teaspoons cinnamon

½ teaspoon nutmeg
½ teaspoon allspice
6–8 carrots, grated (about 3 cups)
½ cup chopped walnuts or pecans (about 3 ounces whole)

Preheat the oven to 300°. Butter a 13×9×2-inch baking dish.

With an electric mixer or by hand, beat together the sugar, oil, and eggs. (If working by hand, beat eggs well first.) Sift the flour, salt, soda, and spices together. Add the flour mixture to the egg mixture in four equal parts, blending well after each addition. Fold in the carrots and nuts. Bake in the center of the oven for 60 to 70 minutes or until a tester comes out dry. Serve with butter cream sauce. Serves 12–15.

Note: Cake may be made in a buttered bundt pan; bake at 350° for 55 to 60 minutes.

Butter Cream Sauce

4 tablespoons sweet butter, cut up
8-ounce package cream cheese, cut up

4 tablespoons confectioner's sugar
2 teaspoons pure vanilla extract

In the bowl of a food processor or an electric mixer, whirl the butter for 2 or 3 seconds; add the cream cheese and whirl again briefly. Add the powdered sugar and the vanilla and blend for a few seconds more. Makes enough sauce or frosting for one carrot cake.

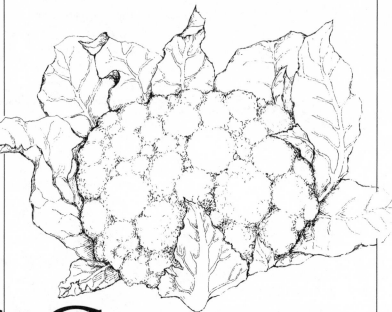

Cauliflower

(Brassica oleracea botrytis)

Cauliflower is a type of cabbage that is encouraged to flower rather than produce leaves. The compact mass of unopened flowers that form the head is sometimes called the curd. Mark Twain called it "a cabbage with a college education." Because it is often overcooked and hence waterlogged, many people find it uninspiring, though they will eat it raw with a dip. When it is combined with some other flavorings, as in the cauliflower and tomato gratin, it is really surprisingly tasty.

To Buy

Fresh cauliflower is snowy white, has no dark spots, and smells sweet—not cabbagy. Any green leaves should not be tinged with yellow. There is also a purple variety that is a cross between cauliflower and broccoli. Cauliflower is usually sold by the head rather than by weight. A medium head with a diameter of 6 to 7 inches will yield about 1½ pounds after trimming, which will serve 6.

To Store

Like other cabbages, do not wash before storing; moisture results in brown spots. Put the whole cauliflower in a plastic bag with a hole in it and refrigerate for up to a week.

To Prepare

Remove any green outer leaves except small ones firmly attached to the flowerets. Cut off any protruding stem, rinse head, and, if using whole, remove the tough central core by cutting around it with a sharp knife. Otherwise, separate into flowerets and trim tough stems.

To Cook

Boiled: Drop flowerets into a large pot of boiling salted water and cook, covered, for about 8 minutes. Drain and finish with browned (noisette) butter or finish with noisette butter and half a cup of fresh bread crumbs browned in butter to which a tablespoon of capers has been added.

Steamed whole: Steaming keeps the head intact and cooks it through. Set a steamer basket in about 2 inches of salted water in a pot large enough to hold the whole head. Set the head firmly upright on the basket and cover the pot, or, if the head protrudes, cover with a piece of foil. Bring the water to a rolling boil and steam until the stem part is tender—17 to 20 minutes for a medium head. Put in a colander lined with wax paper and let drain, upside down. Salt to taste, if desired, and serve drizzled with melted butter.

Whole with cheese: Steam as directed. Grate

a mild Cheddar or colby cheese on top and set in a preheated 400° oven until the cheese melts.

À la greque:
Follow the recipe for mushrooms à la greque on page 178, substituting half a head of cauliflower, separated into flowerets.

Curried:
Follow the recipe for curried mixed vegetables on page 345, substituting 1 head cauliflower, separated into flowerets, for the vegetables.

Cauliflower à la Polonaise

This is a classic dish to serve with meat. The egg yolks make it good in a vegetarian meal, too.

1 medium head cauliflower, trimmed and separated into flowerets	pepper
	2 hard-cooked egg yolks
	3 tablespoons chopped parsley
6 tablespoons butter	2 tablespoons coarse fresh
Salt and fresh white	bread crumbs

Blanch the cauliflower in salted water for 5 minutes, or until crisp-tender, and drain.

Melt 2 tablespoons of the butter in a skillet and sauté the cauliflower, turning frequently, until a few golden flecks appear. Season with salt and pepper and arrange in a serving bowl, more or less reassembled as a head. Keep warm.

Rub the egg yolks through a coarse sieve or chop finely and mix with 1 tablespoon of the parsley. Sprinkle the mixture over the top of the cauliflower, concentrating it in the center. Melt the remaining butter in a skillet and sauté the bread crumbs until golden brown. Pour the crumbs and pan butter over the cauliflower and sprinkle with the remaining parsley. Serve at once. Serves 4–6.

Cauliflower with Three Peppers

My children call this Christmas cauliflower because of the pretty colors. The sweet and hot peppers do very nice things to a vegetable that can be rather bland.

1 medium head
    cauliflower, trimmed
    and separated into
    flowerets
⅓ cup olive oil,
    approximately
1 sweet red pepper, seeded,
    deribbed, and coarsely

chopped
1 green pepper, seeded,
    deribbed, and coarsely
    chopped
2 dried red chilies,
    chopped
Salt and freshly ground
    pepper to taste

Boil the cauliflower until crisp-tender and drain.

Heat the olive oil in a large heavy skillet and add the red and green peppers and dried chilies. Cook over gentle heat for about 5 minutes. Raise the heat slightly and add the cauliflower. Cook, stirring frequently, for 5 minutes more. The cauliflower must not take on any color. Season to taste and place in a hot serving dish. Serves 4–6.

Cauliflower and Potato au Gratin

1 head cauliflower,
    trimmed and separated
    into flowerets
Approximately 1 cup
    mashed potatoes (about
    ½ pound potatoes)
¼ cup heavy cream

2 tablespoons butter
Salt and white pepper to
    taste
2 tablespoons grated
    Gruyère cheese
2 tablespoons butter, cut
    into tiny pieces

Preheat the oven to 425°.

Boil the cauliflower until quite tender—about 15 minutes. Drain well and puree in a blender. Mix the potatoes and cauliflower puree together, add cream, butter, salt, and pepper. Pile into an ovenproof casserole or gratin dish. Sprinkle with the cheese and dot with the butter. Bake in the upper third of the oven for 15 minutes, or until top is brown. Serves 6.

Celery

(Apium graveolens)

Celery is a cultivated plant, developed by sixteenth-century Italians from a wild plant of much sharper flavor enjoyed by the ancient Romans. The latter believed wearing a wreath of its leaves protected against hangovers. Though we speak of a single rib as a stalk, properly speaking, the whole bunch is a stalk, a single piece is a rib.

To Buy

Choose firm, compact stalks without blemishes, cracks, or porous brown ends, which means they've been trimmed a long time ago. The leaves should be fresh and green.

Most celery we see is Pascal, a large-bunched variety. Celery hearts are the tender centers of the celery stalk after the outer ribs and upper leaves have been removed. These can be bought packaged or can be made from stalks (see following). Allow 1 heart per serving.

To Store

Celery will keep refrigerated in the crisper drawer, for 7 to 10 days. Check the root end; if it is very brown, cut a thin slice off before storing. Celery can freeze in a too-cold refrigerator and turn brown and mushy, so don't put it on a bottom shelf.

To Prepare

Wash the inner surfaces of the ribs, where black soil collects. Large ribs can be fibrous and requires stringing if they are to be eaten raw. Scratch along the side of a rib to check. (Don't throw away celery leaves. They give wonderful flavor to soups of all kinds. They are the "secret" ingredient in my meat loaf and in the cucumber soup on p. 117.)

To string: Snap off a small piece from the narrow end of a rib and pull backward toward the broad end. The strings will come away.

To crisp: Wash, trim to desired size, and put in a bowl of ice water in the refrigerator for a couple of hours.

To make celery hearts: Remove all but the inner 4 or 5 ribs of as many bunches of celery as required. Halve lengthwise and trim to about 5 inches. (Save discards for soup and stocks.) Cut off the discolored base, but not so deeply that inner ribs separate. Soak in ice water for 30 minutes.

Braised Celery

Celery is usually eaten raw and gets near heat only when a soup or stock is in the making. But it is quite tasty on its own braised with aromatic vegetables, and makes a fine accompaniment to roast fowl or pork.

6 whole celery hearts	1 bay leaf
2 tablespoons olive oil or butter	1 cup beef or veal stock
1 carrot, thinly sliced	Salt and freshly ground pepper to taste
1 onion, thinly sliced	Chopped parsley
1 garlic clove, sliced	

Preheat the oven to 375°.
Blanch the celery in boiling water for 5 minutes. Drain and refresh.

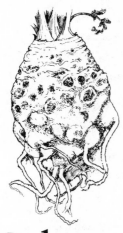

Celery Root

(Apium graveolens rapaceum)

Heat the oil in an ovenproof casserole; add the carrot, onion, garlic, and bay leaf. Cook, stirring, for 4 or 5 minutes, until the onion is lightly golden. Stir in the stock and season with salt and pepper. Add the celery.

Cover and bake for 20 to 30 minutes, or until the hearts are very tender. Remove the celery from the casserole and cut lengthwise into halves. Arrange on a heated serving dish.

Remove and discard the bay leaf. If the cooking juices have not reduced to a consistency that will coat the celery, boil them down uncovered over brisk heat for a few minutes, then pour over the celery. Sprinkle with chopped parsley. Serves 6.

The brown, gnarled celery root or celeriac, sometimes known as knob celery or turnip-rooted celery, is not the root of stalk celery, although it is of the same family. It has a similar though more pronounced flavor. Cooked and pureed, alone or with potatoes or, more unusually, apples, it is an excellent accompaniment to roast pork and game. Raw or lightly blanched and dressed in a mustardy mayonnaise, it becomes that most reliable of first courses, céleri rémoulade.

To Buy

Select smooth, small specimens, which are easier to peel and will have less woody cores. Avoid any that seem soft or have a soft spot on top. A pound of celery root, grated or julienned, yields about 3½ cups, which serves 4 or 5. The same amount, trimmed and cooked, yields about 1 cup of puree.

To Store

Trim off any little roots or leaves, but don't cut into the flesh. Refrigerate unwashed in the crisper drawer for up to a week.

To Prepare

Since celeriac oxidizes quickly when cut, drop into bowl of acidulated water after peeling. Remove the root end, scrub in cool water, and peel deeply with a medium-size knife, making ⅛-inch circular peelings and cutting deeper where there are pits. (A paring knife works better than a swivel-bladed peeler.) Cut in half through the root and remove the spongy portion of the flesh in the center near the stem end, then cut in slices, chunks, or julienne.

To Cook

Creamed: Make a bouillon *à blanc* (p. 17). Cut celery root into half-inch slices and boil for 8 minutes in the bouillon. Drain and fold into a béchamel sauce (p. 376).

Celery root and potato gratin: Cut celery root into ⅛-inch slices. Follow the recipe for gratin dauphinois (p. 238), but omit the garlic and use chicken broth in place of the milk. Make alternate layers of potatoes and celery root slices.

Puree of Celery Root and Potatoes

I serve this silky and mysterious mixture with roast loin of pork stuffed with prunes. It is at once hearty and delicate and always gets raves.

2½–3 pounds celery root, peeled and cut into ½-inch slices	2 cups warm mashed potatoes (about 1 pound potatoes)
3–4 tablespoons butter	Freshly ground white pepper
Coarse salt	

Put the celery root in a saucepan with 2 tablespoons of the butter, coarse salt to taste, and enough water to barely cover. Bring to a boil, cover, and simmer slowly for 25 to 30 minutes, or until tender. If any liquid remains, uncover the pot and cook over high heat until it evaporates.

Puree the celery root in a food processor or blender and combine well with the mashed potatoes. Warm the puree briefly, season with pepper to taste, and stir in the remaining butter. Serves 8.

Céleri Rémoulade

This classic French salad makes a delightful and reliable first course during the winter months, by itself or as part of an hors d'oeuvre selection. I also like it with leftover ham or other cold meats. The sauce, which is like a supermustardy mayonnaise, has nothing whatever to do with the classic rémoulade sauce.

½ lemon
1 or 2 celery roots, 1–1¼
    pounds total weight
2 tablespoons Dijon
    mustard
1 tablespoon wine vinegar

Pinch salt
Freshly ground white
    pepper
½ cup peanut or corn oil
Chopped parsley, optional

Squeeze some of the lemon into a bowl of water. Squeeze the rest into a pot of water and bring it to a boil.

Peel the celery roots, cut into halves or quarters and then into medium julienne with the appropriate disk of a food processor or by hand (p. 354). You should have 3½ to 4 cups. Keep the uncut pieces in the water as you work, and return the julienned pieces to it.

Drain the julienne and plunge it into the boiling water. When the water returns to the boil, drain celery root in a colander, run cold water over, place on a kitchen towel, and pat dry.

Whisk together in a large bowl the mustard, vinegar, salt, and pepper; add about 2 tablespoons of the oil, beating vigorously, then add the rest in droplets, beating all the time. Fold the celery root into the sauce. Let sit several hours before serving. Dress with chopped parsley if desired. Serves 4–6 as a first course.

Puree of Celery Root and Apples

Use 1 pound of celery root for every ¾ pound of tart cooking apples. Peel the root, cut into pieces, cover with milk and simmer, uncovered, for 20 minutes. Peel the apples, cut into chunks, and add to the celery root; cook until both are tender—another 5 or 10 minutes. Drain and reserve the milk. Puree both vegetables in a food processor, add some of the milk to get the desired consistency, and season with salt and pepper. For a really silky consistency, put through a food mill, using the finest disk. Enrich with a bit of cream if desired. This is excellent with roast pork or braised pork chops.

Celery Root Bisque

If you like that elusive celery taste, you'll love this soup. So will your guests, though they may have trouble identifying it.

1½ pounds celery root, peeled and cut into cubes
2 small boiling potatoes, peeled and cubed
2 medium leeks
2 tablespoons butter
6 cups chicken broth, heated
Salt and freshly ground pepper to taste
½ cup heavy cream
2 tablespoons finely snipped chives

Put the celery root and potatoes into acidulated water. Trim off the roots and dark green portion of the leeks, wash well, and slice into half-inch rounds.

Melt the butter in a saucepan large enough to hold all the soup ingredients; add the leeks and cook until softened—about 5 minutes. Add the chicken broth, celery root, potatoes, salt, and pepper. Bring to a boil, cover, lower heat, and simmer until the potatoes are tender—about 25 minutes.

Let cool for 5 minutes, then puree in batches in a food processor fitted with the steel blade. Rub through a coarse-meshed sieve or a chinois.

Rinse out the saucepan, return the puree to it, bring to a simmer, and stir in enough cream to give a pleasing consistency. Taste for seasoning. Serve in heated soup bowls or cups, garnished with chives. Serves 6–8.

Salade Beauçoise

This interesting mix of colors and textures illustrates the French gift for taking a small amount of a leftover and making something quite regal out of it.

3 new potatoes, unpeeled
¼ cup wine vinegar
Salt and freshly ground
    pepper to taste
¾ cup oil—walnut, olive,
    vegetable, or a mixture
1 small celery root, peeled
    and julienned (about 1
    cup)
1 teaspoon lemon juice
1 rib celery, julienned
½ tart apple, julienned

1 small endive, thinly
    sliced crosswise
3 mushrooms, thinly sliced
¾ cup julienne of leftover
    cooked chicken or ham
Mayonnaise, preferably
    homemade
½ cup chopped herbs:
    parsley, chives, tarragon
    —any or all
4–5 ounces boiled beets,
    sliced (may be canned)

Cover the potatoes with cold water, bring to a boil, and cook until tender when pierced with a knife tip—about 25 minutes. Drain.

Prepare a vinaigrette with the vinegar, salt, pepper, and oil. Peel and slice the potatoes, dress with some of the vinaigrette, and set aside.

Toss the celery root with the lemon juice and salt to taste in a bowl and let stand 20 minutes or so.

Combine the celery, apple, and endive with the celery root, dress with enough vinaigrette to moisten, stir, and let stand 1 hour.

Just before serving, add the mushrooms, chicken or ham, and enough mayonnaise to bind the ingredients. Mound on a serving plate and sprinkle with the herbs. Surround with alternating slices of potato and boiled beet. Serves 3–4 at lunch, 5–6 as a first course.

Note: Tongue, smoked chicken breast, or leftover turkey, may also be used. Or you may omit the meat entirely.

If chives are not available, add a finely minced shallot or two to the vinaigrette.

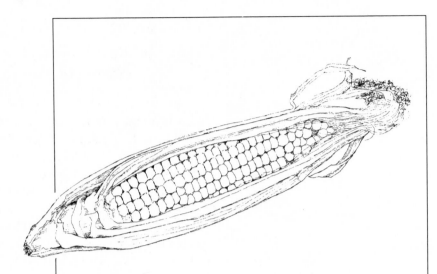

Corn

(Lea mays)

There is an old recipe for corn that goes like this. Put a pot of water on to boil. Pick your corn and run back to the kitchen. If you drop it on the way, feed it to the pigs and pick some more.

The point obviously is that corn is best when picked as near to cooking time as possible, and certainly it should be consumed the day it is picked. Connoisseurs with access to farm stands often try to get the first picking of the day, because that is the coolest time and hence when corn is sweetest. Once an ear is off the stalk, its sugars begin to convert to starch (new hybrids are being developed to retain sugar longer, but these have not reached market yet). Refrigeration of very fresh corn may also help retard the change until you are ready to cook that evening.

Corn is one of the few vegetables with a decent (sometimes superior) canned version. Along with frozen kernels, it is preferable to out-of-season corn.

To Buy

Look at the stem ends first; they should be moist, closed and pale green. (After a day the cut end turns whitish and then becomes brown.) Husks should be tight, tassels silky and without signs of decay. If the market allows, strip a bit of husk from the tip end and look at the kernels. If they are wrinkled, the corn is old. There should be no worm holes, barren ends, or signs of mushiness at the cob tip. If you are still in doubt, press a few kernels—there should be a slight resistance, and if one kernel is popped with your fingernail, a milky juice should spurt out. If the juice is thick, the corn is old; if it is thin and watery, the corn is immature.

There are a number of varieties of corn on the market. Most common is the golden yellow corn, the size varying with the variety. Also look for late summer white corn with small kernels, as sweet as sugar, and then several bicolored types that have both yellow and white kernels, one called Butter and Sugar, another called Sweet Sue. The corn season runs from June to late September at the outside.

Allow 2 ears per person for eating on the cob. Four plump ears yield approximately 2 cups of kernels.

To Store

Refrigerate unhusked if it is not to be cooked immediately.

To Prepare

Don't shuck until just prior to cooking. Pull strips of husk back to stem, discard, and snap off stem and any underdeveloped tip. Remove silk; a soft vegetable brush is helpful with stray hairs.

To cut the kernels off the cob, stand ear on end and cut straight down with a sharp knife, cutting off 3 or 4 rows at a time.

For cream-style corn, cut down center of each row of kernels; then scrape into a bowl with back of knife.

To Cook

Boiled: Bring a pot of unsalted water to the boil (salt toughens the kernels), add the ears, and when the water returns to the boil, cover the pot and remove from heat. The corn can be eaten in 5 minutes or remain in the water for 20 minutes without becoming tough.

An easy way to butter corn: Serve little ramekins of melted butter with an inexpensive flat paintbrush from the hardware store for each person.

Grilled in the husk: This has a delightful nutty flavor. Pull back husks carefully but do not detach. Remove the silk, pull husks back up, and twist or tie closed at the tips. Let the corn soak in a large pot or tub of water, husks on and closed, for at least 20 minutes. Then cook them over moderately hot barbecue coals, about 4 inches from the heat, for 15 to 20 minutes, depending on corn size. Serve with butter, salt, and pepper.

Roasted: Prepare as for grilled. Place on a rack in a 400° oven. Roast for 20 to 25 minutes, depending on size.

Cumin butter: This makes a nice change, especially for those on salt-free diets. Melt 4 tablespoons unsalted butter over low heat and stir in 1 tablespoon ground cumin. Add salt only if desired. Let steep for 5 minutes or so before serving. Serve with lime wedges, if desired. Makes enough for 6 to 8 ears of corn.

Corn Pudding

This is one of those essence-of-summer dishes that everyone loves. I find it particularly good with fish, and even make it off season with canned corn.

4 eggs	Salt and freshly ground
2 cups corn kernels	pepper to taste
3 tablespoons flour	1 cup milk or light cream
1 tablespoon sugar	1 tablespoon melted butter

Preheat the oven to 325°.

Butter a 1½-quart casserole. Beat the eggs until thick and add the corn. Combine the flour, sugar, salt, and pepper. Slowly stir in the milk, then the butter. Combine with the corn and blend well. Pour into the prepared casserole and bake about 1 hour and 20 minutes, or until a knife inserted in the center comes out clean. Serves 4–6.

Corn pudding with peppers: Sauté a small finely chopped onion in butter for 4 or 5 minutes, add ½ cup chopped sweet red pepper and 2 small jalapeño peppers, seeded and very finely minced. Combine with the corn in the recipe given.

Serving suggestion: For an easy, well-balanced meatless meal, precede with cold cucumber soup. Serve with buttered baby beets and sliced tomatoes with purple onion.

Curried Fresh Corn and Green Peppers

After you satisfy that first hunger for corn on the cob, try this for a change. It is marvelous with any grilled poultry or meat and great for a vegetarian dinner.

6–8 tablespoons butter	2 large green peppers,
1 medium onion, chopped	seeded, deribbed, and
2 cloves garlic, minced	coarsely chopped
2 tablespoons curry	3½–4 cups corn kernels
powder or to taste	1 cup heavy cream
½ teaspoon salt	

Melt the butter in a heavy skillet and add the onion, garlic, curry powder, and salt. Cook over low heat for 5 minutes, or until onion is transparent. Add the green peppers and sauté 5 minutes longer.

Add the corn to the skillet. Add the cream and cook, stirring, until mixture just begins to simmer. Cover the skillet loosely and gently simmer over low heat for 15 to 20 minutes, without allowing the cream to boil. Serves 6.

Corn "Oysters"

These corn fritters are a delicious accompaniment to roast chicken and make a great brunch, too. They were once tea fare, served with maple syrup.

½ cup sifted flour	¼ cup milk
Salt to taste	1 egg, lightly beaten
½ teaspoon baking powder	2 cups corn kernels
	Vegetable oil

Preheat the oven to 200°.

Sift the dry ingredients together into a bowl. Slowly pour in the milk and beat until smooth. Beat in the egg and mix in the corn.

Add the oil to a large heavy skillet to a depth of ¼ inch. Drop 2 or 3 tablespoons of the batter for each fritter into the pan and fry a few at a time, 3 to 4 minutes per side, until golden and crisp. As they are done, put them in a slow oven to keep warm until all are cooked. Makes about 12.

Corn Pancakes

These make a hearty Sunday breakfast with bacon or sausages. They differ from corn oysters in being more like pancakes and less like fritters. Try both.

¾ cup flour	½ teaspoon pepper
1 tablespoon baking powder	1 egg
1 teaspoon salt	1 can (10½ ounces) creamed corn

Mix the flour, baking powder, salt, and pepper together. Beat the egg and add. Add corn and mix well. Drop the mixture into a hot, greased skillet by tablespoons, a few at a time. Cook until golden; turn with a spatula and cook second side. Keep warm in a slow oven until all are cooked. Serves 4.

Corn and Pepper Salad

Although corn is a singularly American food, this salad is very popular on the Continent, probably because it is so good and easy to make with canned corn and because it adds such a tasty and colorful note to

Corn and Pepper Salad, continued
informal cold buffets. It is also good with cold leftover meats and broiled chicken.

2 one-pound cans whole-kernel corn, well drained	1 whole canned pimiento, diced
1 medium green pepper	½ cup lemon vinaigrette (p. 375)
2 ripe tomatoes, peeled, seeded, juiced lightly, and diced	Freshly ground black pepper
	Several dashes cayenne

Put the corn in a serving bowl.

Seed, core, and derib the green pepper and cut into ½-inch strips. Blanch the strips in boiling salted water for 3 minutes. Refresh under cold water, then dice. Add the pepper, tomatoes, and pimiento to the corn, dress with the vinaigrette, and add the black and cayenne peppers. Taste for seasoning. Let sit an hour before serving. Serves 6.

Corn and Steamed Peppers

Another pleasant departure from corn on the cob and a joy to make in summer when both vegetables are abundant. It goes well with all kinds of barbecued food, and is very pretty if you have access to all three colors of peppers.

4–6 green, red, or yellow peppers, or any combination	2 cups corn kernels
⅓ cup olive oil	Salt and freshly ground pepper to taste
1 large garlic clove, thinly sliced	Dash cayenne
	1 tablespoon butter

Seed and derib the peppers and cut into ½-inch-long strips.

Heat the oil in a heavy skillet, add the garlic, and let it soften for a minute or two. Add the peppers, stir to coat, and cover the pan. Let steam over low heat until soft—12 to 15 minutes. Shake the pan from time to time. Add the corn, salt, pepper, and cayenne. Add the butter, let it melt, mix in gently, and cook uncovered over low heat for 5 minutes. Shake rather than stir the pan to avoid breaking up the kernels. Correct seasoning and serve hot. Serves 4.

Corn Chowder

3 medium potatoes, peeled and cut into 1-inch dice (about 3 cups)	1 medium onion, chopped
	2 cups corn kernels
	3 cups milk
4 slices bacon, cut into small pieces	Salt and freshly ground pepper

Put the potatoes in a pot large enough to hold all the ingredients; add enough boiling water to cover (about 1 cup) and a dash of salt. Cover and bring to the boil.

Meanwhile, fry the bacon slowly until crisp. Remove and drain on paper.

Add the onion to the skillet and sauté until lightly browned. Add the onion and about 2 tablespoons of the bacon fat to the potatoes; add the corn and continue cooking until potatoes are just tender. Add the milk and heat to just below boiling. Season to taste. Ladle into heated bowls, crumble the bacon, and garnish each with it. Serves 6.

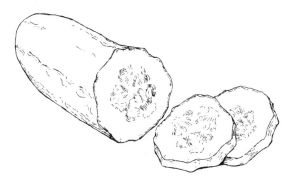

Cucumbers
(Cucumis sativus)

While not particularly noted for its vitamin content, the cucumber is one of the most pleasant, universally liked, and enduring of vegetables. The cucumber that usually appears at market today is fairly hefty; its skin is often waxed to preserve moisture. The smaller, paler green edible-skinned Kirbys, called pickling cucumbers, make tasty eating and have negligible seeds. A long variety, called hothouse, available at a premium price, is virtually seedless or "burpless," making it worth the extra cost to those with sensitive digestions. For most uses the three types are interchangeable. I use Kirbys for salad needs in winter, when small cukes are hard to find.

To Buy

Cucumbers are available all year, though summer is the peak season. Look for medium-size, firm cucumbers with firm ends; they become bitter as they get larger. A medium cucumber is 6 or 7 inches long and about 1¾ inches in diameter. Two medium cucumbers will yield about 3½ cups sliced.

To Store

Put in a sealed plastic bag in the refrigerator crisper drawer. They will keep in peak condition only for 3 to 5 days; being mainly water, they lose their moisture quickly and become mushy and spotty.

To Prepare

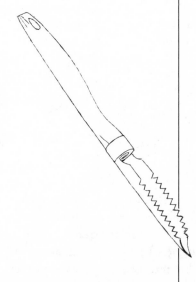

Scrub with a vegetable brush; peel with a swivel-bladed peeler for salad use or if old or very waxy. (The wax, used to help retain the moisture content, is harmless, however.) Simple slices may be enhanced by scoring unpeeled cucumber with the tines of a fork. Or remove alternate lengthwise strips of skin for a striped effect. For paper-thin slices, cut on a mandoline or with the thin slicing disk of a food processor. Additional decorations will be found under Garnishes.

To seed, cut in half crosswise through the middle and use a melon baller or apple corer to remove seeds. Or run a sharp thin knife around the seeds. Cucumbers are often salted and weighted to rid them of excess bitter juices.

Cucumber boats:
Cut crisp cucumbers in half lengthwise and remove seeds. Sprinkle the hollows with salt and set upside down on a plate lined with paper towels. Let drain for 20 minutes, then chill well. Fill with salade russe (p. 344) or any fish mousse. Serve as a garnish or a first course.

Creamed cucumber:
This is a pleasant accompaniment to fish or shellfish and should be made just before serving. Peel and seed 2 medium cucumbers (about 1 pound). Cut into ½-inch slices. Melt 3 tablespoons of butter in a skillet, add 1 cup water, salt and pepper to taste, and the cucumber slices. Cook uncovered over gentle heat for several minutes. They should not brown. Add ¾ cup cream and shake the pan over the heat until the cream thickens. Add several gratings of nutmeg and serve sprinkled with paprika. Serves 3–4.

Tea sandwiches:
Use small cucumbers with tiny seeds if possible; larger ones will have to be seeded. Peel, slice thinly, and soak in water seasoned with salt for an hour. Drain and dry thoroughly. Put cucumber slices on thin, crustless, well-buttered bread. Season with salt and pepper and cut into finger-size sandwiches.

To obtain thin slices of bread, either buy an unsliced loaf, partially freeze it, and cut slices the long way with a serrated knife, or halve bread slices by pressing them flat with the hand and working a serrated knife back and forth with a sawing motion.

The following five cucumber recipes are all delicious, all slightly different, each with a definite application. I use and enjoy them at different times and I hope you will, too!

Braised Cucumbers with Lemon

I found this unusual recipe in a lovely little book called *Leaves from Our Tuscan Kitchen.* It is a perfect foil for any meat cooked with fruit, such as apricot glazed ham or pork stuffed with prunes.

2 medium cucumbers
4 tablespoons butter
¾ cup chicken broth or
   water
Pinch dried thyme or

fresh chervil
2 lemons
Salt and freshly ground
   pepper

Cut alternating strips of peel from the cucumbers, cut into 2-inch lengths, and then into thick wedges. Put into a heavy skillet with 2 tablespoons of the butter, the broth, and thyme. Cover and cook over gentle heat for 15 minutes.

With a sharp knife, remove the peel and white pith from the lemons. Slice thickly and cut out the segments from the dividing skins. Add these to the cucumber and shake the pan over gentle heat. Add the remaining 2 tablespoons butter and shake pan again until butter is melted. Season to taste with salt and pepper. Serves 4.

Cucumbers in Sour Cream with Dill

This is good with smoked fish of all kinds.

4 medium cucumbers
1 tablespoon plus 2
   teaspoons salt
1½ cups sour cream
¼ cup cider vinegar

1½ teaspoons sugar
4 tablespoons chopped
   chives
½ cup chopped fresh dill
Paprika

Peel and thinly slice the cucumbers. Toss the slices in a bowl with 1 tablespoon of the salt. Cover with a plate and weight; refrigerate for 2 to 3 hours.

Mix the sour cream, vinegar, remaining salt, sugar, and chopped chives.

Drain the cucumber and place in a serving bowl. Reserving a good handful of the chopped dill, add the rest and toss with the cucumbers. Pour the sauce over and toss again. Sprinkle the top with paprika and the reserved dill. Chill before serving. Serves 6–8.

Danish Cucumber Salad

(Agurkesalat)

This classic cucumber salad appears with slight variations throughout Scandinavia. It accompanies meat, chicken, or cold cuts, and is indispensable in a smorgasbord. In Norway it is almost always served with freshly caught fish.

3 medium cucumbers
1 tablespoon plus 1
    teaspoon salt
1 teaspoon sugar

White pepper to taste
¾ cup white vinegar
Chopped dill or parsley

Peel the cucumbers or lightly score the skin with a fork. Slice paper-thin. Sprinkle with 1 tablespoon salt, arrange in a thin layer, weight down with a plate and something heavy, and let stand for 2 or 3 hours or overnight.

Drain and squeeze out liquid with the hands. Lay out on paper towels, pat dry, and put in a bowl. Mix the sugar, remaining salt, pepper, and vinegar and pour over. Sprinkle with dill or parsley. Chill for 2 hours. Drain off most of the liquid before serving. Serves 4.

Cucumber and Onion Salad

One often sees this salad as part of a mixed hors d'oeuvre tray in a French restaurant, and for good reason—it goes with just about everything.

5 medium cucumbers
2 medium onions, or ½
    Bermuda onion, sliced
    paper thin
1 tablespoon salt
¼ cup white vinegar

2 teaspoons sugar, or to
    taste
2 tablespoons vegetable oil
Chopped parsley or dill,
    optional

Peel, cut in half lengthwise, and seed the cucumbers. Cut into thin slices and combine with the onions and salt in a bowl. Set in a sieve over a bowl to drain for ½ hour.

Rinse under cold water, then press in the sieve to get rid of most of the water. Combine the vinegar, sugar, and oil in a salad bowl and add the cucumber slices.

Add a little salt if desired. Let sit for an hour before serving. Sprinkle with the parsley or dill. Serves 6.

Armenian Cucumber and Yogurt Salad

(Jajik)

This makes a nice warm weather accompaniment to any lamb dish and a fine light lunch when stuffed into a warmed pita.

2 medium cucumbers
1 small garlic clove, mashed
¼ teaspoon salt
2 tablespoons finely chopped fresh mint

leaves, or an equal amount chopped fresh basil, or 1 teaspoon dried mint
2 cups unflavored yogurt

Peel, seed, and chop the cucumbers coarsely. In the bowl of a mortar, combine the garlic and salt and work together with the pestle to a smooth paste. Combine the mint and yogurt, add the cucumbers and garlic paste, taste for seasoning, and refrigerate for an hour before using. Serves 4.

Variation: Add 3 tablespoons each chopped walnuts and golden raisins.

Cucumber Raita

A proper Indian meal is accompanied by a chutney, a pickle, and a raita, which is a vegetable in yogurt, to cool the mouth. Cucumber raita is probably the most popular.

1 tablespoon fresh coriander leaves, optional
2 medium cucumbers, peeled and seeded

2 teaspoons salt
2 cups unflavored yogurt
½ teaspoon ground cumin
1 garlic clove, pressed
Cayenne pepper

Chop the coriander in a food processor with the steel blade and remove. Insert the grating disk and grate the cucumbers. Add the salt to the cucumbers, put into a colander and let drain for 15 minutes. Rinse and press out water with hands.

Combine the yogurt, cumin, and garlic. Add the cucumbers, put into a serving bowl, and decorate the top with a sprinkling of cayenne and the chopped coriander. Refrigerate for a few hours to allow the flavors to ripen. Makes 2 cups.

Preparation notes: The traditional decoration is alternating spokes of cayenne and coriander leaves, which is very pretty if you have the patience. Though it may not be authentic, I once mixed the coriander with the cucumber, with delicious results. You may also omit the garlic and add ½ teaspoon ground coriander.

Cold Cucumber Soup

This is my "best" summer soup, and it helps me to use up the cucumbers that proliferate in my garden. The base can be made a day ahead (a food processor makes it a snap) and the soup finished and chilled the next morning.

2 medium cucumbers
1 handful celery leaves
1 small bunch chives
1 large handful parsley leaves (no stems)
2 tablespoons butter
2 tablespoons flour
1½ cups chicken broth, homemade or canned, heated
1 cup cream, half-and-half, or milk
Salt and freshly ground pepper to taste
½ teaspoon cumin
Dash cayenne
Chopped dill or grated lemon rind for garnish

Peel and seed the cucumbers. Cut into chunks; you should have about 2 cups. Set aside.

In a food processor, finely chop the celery leaves, chives, and parsley. Add the cucumbers and process until smooth.

In a heavy 1½-quart saucepan, melt the butter, stir in the flour, and cook for 2 minutes without letting the mixture take on color. Remove the pan from the heat and whisk in the chicken broth. Return to heat and simmer for 5 minutes. Add the cucumber mixture, return to a simmer, and cook 5 minutes more. (May be made to this point and refrigerated for up to 3 days.) Remove from the heat, add the cream, and season with salt, pepper, cumin, and cayenne. Chill. Correct the seasoning and serve garnished with a sprinkling of chopped dill or grated lemon rind. Serves 4.

Serving suggestion: For a wonderful summer lunch, follow with the zucchini frittata on page 328, accompanied by sliced tomatoes. I frequently serve this soup with wedges of pita bread that have been spread with herbed butter and crisped in the oven.

Cucumber Sauce

This is superb served with barbecued salmon or cold poached salmon or trout. Vegetarians like it over fried eggplant.

3 medium cucumbers	1 teaspoon grated onion
1 teaspoon salt	1 tablespoon white wine
1 cup sour cream	vinegar
1 cup mayonnaise	Salt and freshly ground
1 tablespoon commercial	pepper to taste
horseradish	

Peel the cucumbers and slice them to almost transparent thinness. Dissolve the salt in 2 cups of water, add the cucumbers, stir well, and let them sit for 30 minutes. Drain and dry on paper towels.

In a 2-quart bowl, combine the sour cream, mayonnaise, horseradish, onion, and vinegar. Fold in the cucumbers and season with salt and pepper. Cover with plastic wrap and refrigerate for several hours. Makes about 2½ cups.

Old-Fashioned Bread-and-Butter Pickles

I make a big batch of these in July when my cucumbers are at their peak. We have them all year long with just about everything that is nice with a tart-sweet pickle.

20 medium cucumbers, enough to make 6 quarts when sliced
20 small white onions, peeled, enough to make
2 quarts when sliced
2½ green peppers, seeded
½ cup coarse salt
1 quart cracked ice

Marinade:

4½–5 cups sugar
1½ teaspoons turmeric
½ teaspoon ground cloves
2 tablespoons yellow
mustard seeds
1 tablespoon celery seeds
4½–5 cups cider vinegar

Scrub the cucumbers, remove ends, and cut into ¼-inch slices. Slice the onions thinly, and slice green peppers into thin rings. Put in one or several large bowls and mix with salt and ice. Cover with a plate that will sit right on the cucumbers and weight with cans or other heavy objects.

Combine the marinade ingredients in a large kettle and simmer until the sugar is dissolved—about 8 minutes. Drain the cucumber mixture, add to the pot, bring again to just under a boil, and simmer until the cucumber skins turn slightly brown—about 10 minutes. Stir gently and frequently with a wooden spoon so everything is immersed in the marinade.

Cool slightly, fill sterilized pint jars according to the manufacturer's directions, and seal. Makes about 10 pints.

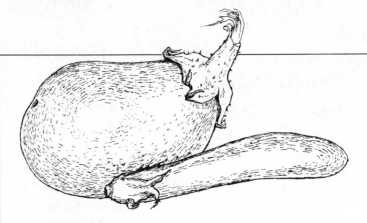

Eggplant
(Solanum melongena)

Though its name seems to reflect no particular physical characteristic of this purple-skinned vegetable, there are varieties that are small and white and could be said to resemble eggs. These, by the way, are the sweetest. There are many other types—long, round, squat, in colors ranging from whitish green to purple-black. In England and France eggplant is called *aubergine*.

Italian eggplant is a small, slender variety not unlike a purple zucchini, which can be rather sharp in flavor. Japanese eggplant is another slender variety recently introduced at market in summer. It looks like a fat amethyst-color banana with an almost translucent skin. It is delightfully sweet, cooks rapidly, and does not require purging because of its fine-textured flesh. Use in any recipe calling for eggplant, especially the Japanese eggplant salad or the Philippine fried eggplant. Baby eggplants are simply miniatures of the standard kind.

Eggplant is essentially rather bland, but becomes so flavor-rich when married with onions, garlic, tomatoes, herbs, and cheese that dishes based on eggplant are, of all the vegetables, the most satisfying taste substitutes for meat. Sautéed with olive oil, garlic, and parsley, it takes on a taste similar to mushrooms. Eggplant is particularly good fried, but tends to absorb great quantities of oil. This can be avoided by draining its excess moisture and frying it in very hot oil.

To Buy

Eggplants should be firm and heavy in relation to their size. Look for taut, glossy skins without blemishes or breaks. In eggplants, as with humans, wrinkled, lusterless skin is a sign of old age. Allow about 1½ pounds of eggplant for 4 persons. There are about 4 baby eggplants in a pound.

To Store

Because of its high moisture content, eggplant keeps poorly. It shrivels easily, becoming bitter when it does. Keep in a cool, dry place for a day or two, or, if that is not practical, in the refrigerator crisper drawer. Try to use within 3 days.

To Prepare for Cooking

If your recipe calls for peeled eggplant, do not do this until just prior to cooking, as the flesh discolors easily. Remove the calyx, then the skin in long strips.

When a recipe calls for lengthwise slices, cut a thin strip from one side to allow a flat base on which to rest the eggplant, then slice. (This is a useful maneuver to keep any rounded vegetable from rolling during cutting.)

To purge: Salting eggplant slices or cubes, weighting them, and letting them drain degorges the sharp, sometimes bitter juices. This is called purging. I do this when the eggplant is to be sautéed or fried, as salting inhibits the vegetable's tendency to soak up oil.

Cut eggplant in slices or cubes as required and sprinkle liberally with salt (about 1 tablespoon for each 2 pounds). Cubes may be put in a colander set in a bowl and weighted with a plate and something heavy on top; slices do best in one layer on a rimmed cookie sheet lined with paper towels, weighted with a second cookie sheet and something heavy. Let sit at least an hour. Drain, rinse, and dry slices with additional paper towels. For cubes, scoop them up a few at a time, rinse, and gently twist dry in a kitchen towel.

I do not purge baby eggplant or Japanese eggplant.

Eggplant must always be prepared in glass, enameled cast iron, or stainless steel pots. A metal like aluminum will cause the flesh to darken.

To Cook

Broiled: Slice eggplant into ½-inch rounds, brush each with olive oil, and put in a preheated broiler about 6 inches from the heat. Cook for about 5 minutes, until surface is flecked with brown. Turn, brush second side again with oil, and complete cooking —about 5 minutes more.

Serve sprinkled with salt, fresh pepper, and chopped parsley, or salt, pepper, olive oil, lemon juice, and a mince of onion and parsley.

Charcoal grilled: Split the eggplant lengthwise; make a series of cross-hatched incisions on the flesh side, taking care not to pierce the skin. Let marinate in a fruity olive oil for 15 minutes or so, then put over hot coals flesh side down. Eggplant is done when flesh is golden brown and tender near the stem end.

Alternatively, you can simply oil the skin of whole, medium-size eggplants and put them directly on the coals until they are charred and tender. To serve, split in half (the inside will be white), season with salt, pepper, and a drizzle of olive oil.

Fried: Cut eggplant into slices about ⅜ inch thick. Salt, drain, and dry slices on paper towels. Dip into flour and gently shake off excess. Pour oil into a skillet to a depth of about ¼ inch, heat until almost smoking, add slices in one layer, and fry about 2 minutes on each side. Season with fresh black pepper and serve at once.

Grilled Japanese Eggplant with Miso and Sesame

I go to a Japanese restaurant just to have eggplant done this way. It is deliciously different from the many eggplant-garlic-onion-tomato combinations. The recipe comes from my favorite book on charcoal cookery, Maggie Waldron's *Fire and Smoke.* I serve it as a separate course, or as part of a mixed grill of vegetables, or as an accompaniment to grilled chicken.

1 medium eggplant	2 tablespoons honey
2 tablespoons each red and white miso paste (see note)	2–3 tablespoons sesame seeds, toasted (p. 406)

Cut the eggplant into ½-inch-thick rounds. Grill over very hot coals, turning once, until it is quite soft and brown and nicely marked by the grill. While the eggplant is cooking, combine the two misos in a small pan and heat very gently on the stove or at the side of the grill—just enough to soften the paste. Stir in the honey and sesame seeds. Spread thickly on the eggplant slices and serve. Serves 4.

Note: Miso, a salty paste made from fermented soybeans, can be found in vacuum-packed plastic bags in Japanese and Korean markets. Miso is also excellent stirred into soups.

Eggplant Caviar

1 large or 2 medium eggplants (about 2 pounds)	2 large ripe tomatoes, peeled, seeded, and finely chopped
1 cup finely chopped onion	½ teaspoon sugar
6 tablespoons olive oil	2 teaspoons salt, or to taste
½ cup finely chopped green pepper	Freshly ground pepper
1 teaspoon finely chopped garlic	Dash cayenne, optional
	2–3 tablespoons lemon juice

Preheat the oven to 425°.

Bake the eggplant on a rack in the center of the oven for about 45 minutes, turning it once or twice until the skin is soft and darkened. (Place a cookie sheet underneath to catch any drips.)

Meanwhile, cook the onion in 4 tablespoons of the oil over moderate heat for 6 to 8 minutes, until it is soft but not brown. Stir in the green pepper and garlic and cook, stirring occasionally, 5 minutes longer. With a rubber spatula, scrape the mixture into a mixing bowl.

Cut the eggplants in half and scrape the flesh into another bowl, or simply strip the skin off. Chop finely by hand or process briefly in a food processor, then drain any accumulated liquid in a strainer. Add eggplant to the onion mixture and stir in the tomatoes, sugar, salt, several grindings of pepper, and the cayenne. Blend thoroughly.

Heat the remaining 2 tablespoons of oil in a 10-inch skillet over moderate heat and add the eggplant mixture. Bring to a simmer, stirring constantly, then cover the skillet and continue simmering over very low heat for 45 to 50 minutes. Remove the cover and cook an additional 10 to 15 minutes, stirring from time to time, until all the moisture in the pan has evaporated and the puree is thick enough to hold its shape in a spoon. Stir in the lemon juice, and taste for seasoning, adding more lemon juice, salt, or pepper if needed. Chill in a bowl covered with plastic wrap for several hours. Makes about 2½ cups.

Serving suggestions: As an hors d'oeuvre, serve with slices of black bread or pumpernickel. For a light lunch or supper, serve with a salad and cheese or some slices of leftover meat loaf or any other meat you have. Also good as a filling in an omelet.

Preparation notes: Can be frozen—a wonderful way to use end-of-summer garden bounty. Can also be made in double quantity, in which case increase final cooking time to evaporate liquid.

Caponata

An eggplant appetizer of Sicilian origin, this makes a nice first course on lettuce leaves or a splendid drink accompaniment. It keeps for ages in the refrigerator or indefinitely in sterilized jars. For that reason the recipe is for a large quantity. Let it "ripen" for a couple of days before serving.

3 medium eggplants (about 3 pounds)
4 celery ribs
4 medium onions
1 cup olive oil
1 teaspoon chopped garlic
Salt and freshly ground pepper
1 can (2 pounds 3 ounces) Italian plum tomatoes, drained

2 tablespoons drained capers, lightly crushed
36 pitted small green or black olives, or a mixture of both, coarsely chopped
Several dashes hot red pepper flakes
½ cup wine vinegar
1 teaspoon sugar

Cut the eggplants into ¾-inch cubes without removing the skin. Purge with salt, rinse, and dry.

While the eggplant degorges, cut the celery into ½-inch dice and peel and slice the onions. Preheat the oven to 350°.

Heat ½ cup of the olive oil in a large heavy pot until almost smoking; sauté the eggplant, lightly seasoned with salt and pepper, until golden on all sides. Remove with a slotted spoon and reserve.

Add the rest of the olive oil and sauté the celery, garlic, and onions just until wilted. Cover and let simmer together for a few minutes to gather flavor. Add the tomatoes, bring to the simmer, and cook for about 10 minutes, stirring often. Add the capers, olives, and pepper flakes.

Heat the vinegar in a small saucepan, add the sugar, and stir until dissolved. Add to the pot.

Continue cooking gently, covered, until the celery is very tender—about 15 minutes. Add the reserved eggplant, cook for a few more minutes, and adjust seasoning. Allow to cool. Makes about 2 quarts.

Baba Ghannoush

(Eggplant and Tahini Dip)

Two strong flavors—smoky eggplant and lemon-sharpened tahini or sesame paste—make an exciting marriage of taste in this Middle-Eastern favorite. Play around with the proportions according to your taste, as the size and therefore the flavor intensity of eggplant are not always the same.

Baba Ghannoush, continued

1 large or 2 small
  eggplants
¼ cup tahini, or a little
  less, depending on size
  of eggplant
¼ cup water
3 tablespoons lemon juice,
  or more to taste
¼ cup olive oil
1–2 garlic cloves, crushed

Salt and freshly ground
  pepper to taste
¼–½ teaspoon ground
  cumin, optional
2 tablespoons finely
  chopped parsley
A few black Greek olives
  or thinly sliced tomato
  for garnish, optional

Pierce the eggplant in several places and broil for 15 to 20 minutes, turning two or three times until the skin blackens and blisters. (This can also be done on a charcoal grill.) When cool enough to handle, peel the eggplant and squeeze out the bitter juices with your hands.

In a food processor or bowl, combine the tahini, water, lemon juice, olive oil, and garlic, and process or beat until a smooth, creamy puree is formed.

Mash the eggplant with a potato masher or fork and add to the puree. The mixture should have some texture. Season with salt and pepper and add more lemon juice, garlic, or tahini if you think necessary. Stir in the cumin.

Transfer the puree to a serving bowl and garnish with the chopped parsley, black olives, or sliced tomatoes, and serve as a dip with pita bread, or as a salad. Makes 1½ cups.

Note: Here is an attractive way to serve baba ghannoush that never fails to elicit comments: Choose a beautiful, glossy, well-shaped, rather large eggplant. Slice off about a quarter of it lengthwise, rub with lemon juice, and set that piece aside. Scoop out the insides of the larger piece by running a knife around the perimeter, leaving a good quarter-inch of flesh. Be careful not to pierce the skin. Make a series of shallow cross-hatched cuts with the knife tip, then scoop out the flesh with a spoon and discard. Immediately rub the inside of the eggplant shell with half a cut lemon. Pile the baba ghannoush in the eggplant and set the lid on at an angle. Put on a large round tray with curls of blanched red pepper, decorative greens, even some crudités if you like, and serve with small warmed triangles of pita.

Japanese Eggplant Salad

This elegant salad presents the unusual combination of Oriental flavorings with the Western concept of the hearty composed salad. It is ravishingly attractive and intensely delicious. Use it as a luncheon main course or for dinner with a light entree to follow. As in much of Oriental cooking, the ingredients are quickly combined, so do have all the components for the eggplant preparation measured and at hand before you proceed.

Half a large head of romaine lettuce (about ½ pound)
¼ pound fresh snow peas
½ large sweet red pepper
3 tablespoons vinaigrette dressing
1 medium eggplant or 4–5 Japanese eggplants (about 1 pound)
3 tablespoons vegetable oil
1 tablespoon Oriental sesame oil
½ small dried red pepper, seeds removed, finely crushed
1 cup chicken stock
2 tablespoons dark or Japanese soy sauce
2 tablespoons dry sherry
1 tablespoon plus 1½ teaspoons sugar
¼ teaspoon cornstarch mixed with 1 tablespoon water
1 scant teaspoon grated fresh ginger
1 teaspoon rice vinegar
1 medium garlic clove, minced

Wash and dry the lettuce; cut crosswise into 1-inch strips and put in a bowl. Blanch the snow peas in boiling salted water to cover for 1 minute. Cut the red pepper into julienne (about ⅛ by 2 inches). Set these aside in separate dishes, along with the vinaigrette dressing.

Trim the stem ends of the eggplant and cut lengthwise into ½-inch slices. Stack the slices and cut lengthwise into 1-inch strips, then crosswise into 3-inch lengths.

Heat the vegetable and sesame oils in a large, heavy skillet over medium-high heat. Select a heatproof dinner plate of a diameter slightly smaller than the top of the skillet and have it at hand. Add the eggplant and dried pepper to the skillet. Stir-fry for about 5 minutes, until the eggplant is lightly browned on both sides. The oil will vanish almost immediately, but if you keep the eggplant moving, it should not stick. Try not to add more oil. Some seeds may detach from the eggplant; this is not important. Add the stock, soy sauce, sherry, and sugar.

Place the dinner plate directly on top of the eggplant, inner side down.

Reduce the heat to medium and cook until the eggplant is tender but still retains its shape—about 8 minutes for mature eggplant, 6 for the baby. Remove the plate carefully and wipe it clean. Using a slotted spoon, transfer the eggplant to the plate. Set aside.

Strain the liquid that accumulated in the pan. You should have about ¾ cup. Return liquid to the skillet and cook until reduced to ½ cup. Stir in the cornstarch mixture and continue cooking, stirring constantly, until liquid is thickened—about 20 seconds.

Pour the sauce into a small bowl. Add the ginger, vinegar, garlic, and any juices that have accumulated around the eggplant. Correct seasoning if necessary, and let cool to lukewarm. (May be made ahead to this point.)

In a bowl, toss the lettuce with the vinaigrette and divide among 4 large salad or dinner plates. In another bowl, toss 3 tablespoons of the ginger sauce with the snow peas and julienne of pepper. Spoon an equal amount of this mixture onto the center of each lettuce bed. Arrange the eggplant in a spoke pattern radiating from the center of each salad and spoon the remaining ginger sauce over them. Serve immediately. Serves 4.

Ratatouille

There are many ways to make this summer favorite, and the vegetables may be used in almost any proportion that pleases. There is one pitfall to ratatouille: if it is undercooked, the flavors do not marry well; if fully cooked, it has a tendency to get soupy. One way to solve the problem is to remove and reduce the liquid, then return it, which makes the whole dish very tasty as well.

2 medium eggplants
4 medium zucchini
2 teaspoons salt
6 tablespoons olive oil or more
4 medium onions, thinly sliced
2 small green peppers, seeded and thinly sliced
3 garlic cloves, minced
4–6 tomatoes, peeled, seeded, and juiced
Salt and freshly ground pepper
1 bouquet garni, composed of a bay leaf, some thyme, and a few parsley sprigs
¼ cup chopped parsley

Peel and slice the eggplants into ½-inch rounds, then cut into large cubes. Cut the zucchini into ¼-inch rounds. Toss both vegetables with the salt in a bowl and let stand for about ½ hour. Drain and pat dry with paper towels.

Lightly and quickly sauté the eggplant and zucchini pieces in 2 or 3 tablespoons of the oil. Do not have more than a single layer of the vegetables in the pan at any one time. Remove sautéed pieces to a warm dish.

Heat the remaining oil in a heavy enameled cast-iron pot with a lid. Sauté the onions, peppers, and garlic until the onions are softened. Add the tomatoes, cover, and cook for 5 minutes. Season to taste with salt and pepper.

Put three-quarters of the tomato-onion mixture in a bowl and spread the remainder over the bottom of the pot. Over this put about a third of the zucchini and eggplant pieces. Keep layering in this manner, seasoning the vegetables lightly as you go, and ending with the tomatoes. Tuck the bouquet garni on top. Cover and simmer for ½ hour.

Tilt the pot and pour the excess liquid into a small pan. Boil over high heat until reduced to about ¼ cup. Pour this liquid back over the vegetables and cook over medium-high heat, uncovered, for about 10 minutes. The vegetables should be soft, but still retain their identity, and there should be relatively little liquid left.

Remove the bouquet garni before serving and sprinkle the ratatouille with fresh parsley. May be served hot, warm, or at room temperature. Serves 6–8.

Note: Ratatouille may be prepared well in advance and will keep under refrigeration for several days. Leftovers are wonderful with cold meat or chicken.

Ratatouille with eggs: For an easy yet complete lunch or light supper dish, place the ratatouille in a medium-size baking dish. With the back of a soup spoon, make as many indentations in the ratatouille as you have diners and break an egg into each. Sprinkle ¼ cup grated Parmesan cheese over the top and bake in a preheated 400° oven for 10 minutes, or until the eggs are set but not hard. Serve immediately with crusty bread and a salad.

Serving suggestion: As the main dish of a vegetarian meal, accompany with baked summer squash casserole (p. 289) and steamed rice.

Fried Eggplant Fans

There is something complexly satisfying about the flavor of properly fried vegetables that makes them a wonderful bet for nonmeat meals. If you can find them, use small Japanese or Italian eggplants for these pretty eggplant fans.

6 small eggplants, or 2 medium eggplants, halved, about 2 pounds	1 recipe tempura batter (p. 346)
Oil for frying	Salt

Line a cookie sheet with paper toweling or brown paper and place in an oven set on warm.

Wipe the eggplants with a damp towel. With a sharp knife make 7 or 8 lengthwise slits in each, leaving them intact at the stem end. With the flat of your hand press down gently on each eggplant to fan out the slices.

Pour oil into a large heavy skillet to a depth of ½ inch. Heat to almost smoking. Holding by the stem end, dip each fan into the batter; let excess run off, then lay in the hot oil and cook for about 4 minutes on each side, or until browned and tender. Remove and keep warm on the cookie sheet. You will have to cook the fans in three or four batches; keep adjusting the heat so they brown evenly. When all are cooked, sprinkle with salt, if desired. Serve immediately. Serves 2–4.

French-fried Eggplant

2 medium-size firm
    eggplants, about 2
    pounds total weight
Oil for frying
½ cup flour

¼ cup fine fresh bread
    crumbs
2 eggs, beaten in a bowl
    with a pinch of salt
Freshly ground pepper

Peel the eggplants and cut into ½-inch lengthwise slices. Cut the slices into 1-inch lengthwise strips, then crosswise into 3-inch fingers. Purge with salt and dry.

Heat the oil in a deep-fat fryer to 375°.

Combine the flour and bread crumbs in a brown paper bag. Soak the eggplant slices in the egg, then shake in the paper bag, a handful at a time. Fry in small batches in the hot oil for about 8 minutes, or until golden. Do not let them get too dark or they will be bitter. Place on a paper-lined cookie sheet to drain in a slow oven until all are done.

Season with pepper to taste. Serves 4–6.

Preparation note: Any amount of fried eggplant may be prepared this way; just keep in mind the double flour-to-crumb ratio.

Serving suggestion: As a separate course or main course, serve with skordalia (p. 200). As a main vegetarian course, serve with yogurt. Also a delicious accompaniment to any unsauced meat or chicken.

Philippine Fried Eggplant

Select firm, glossy Japanese eggplants, allowing at least 3 per person. Buy as many with caps and stems as are available. Heat the broiler, wash and dry each eggplant, and prick each in two or three places with a fork. Place in one layer in the broiler pan. Broil for 10 to 15 minutes, depending on size, turning once, until the skins have become opaque and dusty brown. Remove from the oven and, using a sharp knife, make one single lengthwise slit in the skin, then flick off the skin in strips with a fork.

In a shallow bowl, beat an egg or two with a little water and season with salt, pepper, and several dashes of cayenne. Set the oven on warm. Heat about ⅛ inch of cooking oil in a heavy skillet.

Holding an eggplant by the stem, gently flatten (do not mash) the flesh with the back of a fork. Dip both sides in the egg and place in the hot oil. Repeat until the pan is full but not crowded. Fry for about 3 minutes on each side, turning with a spatula. Drain on brown paper and keep warm until all are cooked. Season with several grinds of pepper; splash lightly with a mild, fruity vinegar; and serve at once.

Gratin of Eggplant

This is high on my list of favorite dishes around which to build a meatless meal. It is tasty, attractive, and filling, and the house smells wonderful while it is baking. I especially recommend it for the first time you try a meatless meal on your family.

2 medium eggplants, 2–2½ pounds total weight
Salt
½ cup flour, more or less
Vegetable oil, or a mixture of vegetable and olive oil
2 medium onions, thinly sliced, about 1½ cups
¼ cup olive oil
15-ounce can whole tomatoes, undrained
8-ounce can tomato sauce, or 1 cup homemade
2 tablespoons chopped parsley
1 bay leaf, broken in half
2 garlic cloves
Salt and freshly ground pepper to taste
1 cup freshly grated Parmesan cheese

Peel the eggplants and slice into ½-inch rounds. Purge with salt and dry.

Preheat the oven to 350°. Have ready a cookie sheet lined with brown paper.

Spread flour in a pie plate or dish. Pour vegetable oil into a heavy skillet to a depth of ¼ inch; heat until almost smoking. Dip the eggplant slices in flour on both sides, shake off excess, and fry briefly on both sides without letting them take on too much color. Drain the slices on the cookie sheet as they are done. Set aside.

In a heavy enamel-lined or stainless steel saucepan, sauté the onions in the olive oil until wilted. Add the whole tomatoes, breaking them up with the side of a wooden spoon, then the tomato sauce, parsley, and bay leaf. Put the garlic through a press and add. Cover, bring to the boil, lower heat, and simmer for 12 minutes, then uncover and cook 5 minutes more, letting the sauce reduce slightly. Correct seasoning.

Grease a baking dish large enough to hold all the ingredients (an oval gratin dish, 14 × 8 × 2, works well). Put enough tomato sauce in to cover the bottom, then arrange a single layer of eggplant slices and sprinkle with some of the grated cheese. Continue layering in this manner, ending with the rest of the sauce and cheese. Bake in the preheated oven for 30 minutes, or until the top is golden. For a deeper burnishing, run under the broiler for 8 to 10 seconds. Serves 4 to 6 as the main course of a meatless meal, 6 to 8 as an accompaniment.

Note: The sauce may be prepared ahead.

The exact amounts of the ingredients in this recipe are not critical and are pretty much determined by the amount of eggplant you have and how many you wish to feed.

Baked Baby Eggplant with Dill

This is a nice room-temperature dish that can go with absolutely anything, and it's a wonderful way to take advantage of baby eggplants when they appear at market. The vinegar does something very interesting to the flavor.

2–2½ pounds baby eggplants, halved
2 large onions, thinly sliced, separated into rings
⅓–½ cup olive or salad oil

Salt and freshly ground pepper
Red wine vinegar
Handful of roughly chopped dill

Salt the eggplant halves and let them drain facedown for 30 minutes.

Preheat the oven to 400°. Oil a shallow baking pan or rimmed cookie sheet and arrange eggplant halves on it, faceup. Cover with onion rings, drizzle oil over, and season with salt and liberal grindings of pepper. Bake for about 35 minutes—until skins are crisp and flesh and onions browned and tender. Turn frequently while baking so vegetables are constantly baked in oil.

Put in a bowl, let cool slightly, then splash with vinegar, more salt and pepper if needed, and a good sprinkling of dill. Serve at room temperature. Serves 8.

Note: If baby eggplants are not available, this dish can be made with 2 or 3 medium-size eggplants cut into ½-inch slices, purged, then baked as directed. Two finely minced garlic cloves may also be added along with the onion.

Eggplant Orientale

Prepare the baked baby eggplant using rounds of regular eggplant. Put in a chilled serving bowl, chop finely, and garnish lavishly with dill. Splash with vinegar. Serve with thin, well-buttered slices of black bread. Serves 8–10 as a drink accompaniment.

Stuffed Eggplant

I first ate eggplant stuffed with lamb in Spain, and I thought I'd never tasted anything so delicious. I tried several versions before I felt I had recreated that memorable dish. Another thing I like is that this recipe makes a pound of lamb go a long way.

6 small or 3 large eggplants, about 2½ pounds total weight
2 tablespoons olive oil
¾ cup finely chopped onion
1 garlic clove, finely minced
1 pound ground lean lamb
Several gratings fresh
nutmeg
Salt and freshly ground pepper to taste
3 tablespoons butter
2 tablespoons flour
1½ cups half-and-half
1 egg yolk
½ cup grated Swiss or Gruyère cheese (about 3 ounces)

Preheat the oven to 425°.

Trim and discard the stem ends of the eggplants. Split them in half lengthwise. Run a sharp knife around the inside rim of each half about 1 inch in from the skin, making an incision about 1 inch deep. Score the eggplant all over the cut the surface in a diamond pattern.

Place the eggplants, skin side down, on a baking sheet and bake for 25 minutes if they are large, 15 if small. Turn the eggplants cut side down and continue baking about 10 minutes longer, or until the flesh is tender.

While the eggplants bake, prepare the filling. Heat the olive oil in a large, heavy skillet and add the onion and garlic. Cook 4 or 5 minutes, until the onion is wilted. Add the lamb and cook, stirring and cutting down with the side of a spoon to break up any lumps. Sprinkle with the nutmeg and continue cooking until the lamb loses its pinkness. Season to taste with salt and pepper.

Melt the butter in a heavy saucepan and add the flour, stirring with a wire whisk. When bubbling stops, add the half-and-half, stirring rapidly. Return to heat and cook for 2 minutes. Season to taste with salt, pepper, and nutmeg. Spoon half the sauce into the lamb mixture and blend.

Using a spoon, scoop out the flesh of each eggplant half, leaving a shell about ½ inch thick. Chop the flesh (there should be about 2 cups), add to the lamb mixture, and blend well. Spoon equal portions into the eggplant shells. Put the stuffed shells in an oiled baking dish.

Add the egg yolk to the remaining cream sauce, beating vigorously. Bring just to the boil but do not let it boil. Spoon equal portions of this mixture over the stuffed eggplants and sprinkle with the cheese.

Return the stuffed shells to the oven and bake for about 15 minutes or until they are piping hot throughout and nicely glazed. Serves 6 to 12.

Serving suggestion: Precede with cold cucumber soup (p. 117) and serve with rice pilaf (p. 363) and a tossed green salad.

Eggplant Parmigiana

Filling and rich in flavor, this needs only a soup to precede it and perhaps garlic bread with salad to follow. It makes an excellent lunch or light meatless dinner. The tomato sauce may be made ahead and the whole dish assembled early in the day or even the day before, covered tightly with plastic wrap, and refrigerated.

1 medium to large
  eggplant, about 1½
  pounds
Salt
1½ cups bread crumbs,
  approximately
2 eggs
1 cup freshly grated
  Parmesan cheese

⅓ cup vegetable oil,
  approximately
2–2½ cups quick tomato
  sauce (p. 309), or an
  equal amount of good
  canned sauce (see note)
¾ pound mozzarella
  cheese in thin slices

Cut eggplant lengthwise into ½-inch slices. Purge with salt, rinse, and dry.

Preheat the oven to 350°. Oil a 9 × 12-inch baking

dish or oval casserole. Spread the bread crumbs on a piece of wax paper. Beat the eggs with 2 tablespoons of the Parmesan cheese. Let the vegetable oil get very hot in a heavy skillet. Dip each slice in the egg, then the crumbs, and fry, one or two at a time, until lightly brown on each side. Drain on brown paper as each is cooked. (Large slices may be cut in half first.)

Lightly cover the bottom of the baking dish with tomato sauce. Make a layer of eggplant slices, sauce, a sprinkling of Parmesan, and a layer of mozzarella. Repeat these layers, ending with mozzarella. Bake for about 30 minutes, until the eggplant is tender and the sauce hot and bubbly. Let stand 10 minutes to firm before serving. Serves 4–6.

Preparation note: If you are using canned sauce, heat it and flavor with some crumbled oregano, salt, pepper, and a clove of garlic put through a press. Cook for a few minutes to bring up the flavor.

Escalivada:

Catalan grilled eggplant, pepper, and onions, page 213.

Baked Ziti with Eggplant

This is a good Saturday night dish that often waits for us in a slow oven, covered with foil, while we go to an early movie.

2 pounds eggplant
Salt
Flour for dredging
¾–1 cup olive oil
½ pound ziti
4 cups well-seasoned

tomato sauce
Red pepper flakes to taste
1 pound mozzarella cheese, shredded
½–¾ cup freshly grated Parmesan cheese

Preheat the oven to 375°.

Peel the eggplant and cut into ¾-inch rounds. Purge with salt, rinse, and dry. Dredge with flour.

Put a large pot of salted water on to boil for the pasta.

Heat the oil in a large heavy skillet and, when it is

quite hot, fry the eggplant on both sides until golden brown—about 10 minutes. Drain on brown paper.

Boil the ziti until tender. Drain thoroughly in a colander, put in a bowl, and mix with 1½ cups of the sauce and the red pepper flakes. Put half the ziti in a 9 × 13 × 2-inch baking dish, then half the eggplant. Make another layer of ziti and eggplant, and pour the remaining sauce over all. Cover with the mozzarella and sprinkle on the Parmesan. Bake for 15 minutes, or until the cheese is melted and the top golden. Run under the broiler for a few seconds if the top needs gilding. Serves 6.

Serving suggestion: A mixed green salad with a good garlicky vinaigrette is all that's needed to complete a light meal. For a more filling one, start with sweet peppers parma (p. 215).

Imam Bayeldi

The origin of this dish is a Turkish legend with many versions. The name means "the Imam fainted." A revered imam, a Muslim religious dignitary, was inordinately fond of eggplant. His wife, who always took great pains to find new ways to prepare it, came up with a dish that made him swoon when he tasted it. Whether he was overwhelmed by its richness or the pleasure of eating it you will have to decide for yourself.

3 small eggplants, about ¾ pound each
½ cup olive oil
3 medium onions, about ¾ pound, finely chopped
3–4 garlic cloves, chopped
4 ripe tomatoes, peeled, seeded, and chopped
1 tablespoon chopped

parsley
3 tablespoons pine nuts, optional
Salt and freshly ground pepper
1 teaspoon sugar
Juice of ½ lemon
1½ cups hot chicken broth or water

Preheat the oven to 350°. Oil a baking dish that will hold the eggplants, and set aside.

Rinse the eggplants and cut in half lengthwise. Carefully scoop out the flesh, leaving a good ½-inch margin. Chop the flesh and set aside. Oil the skins and the insides of the shells lightly.

Heat half the oil in a skillet and sauté the onions until softened but not colored. Add the garlic, cook a minute more, then add the reserved eggplant flesh and half the tomatoes. Simmer over low heat for 15 minutes, until soft. Add the parsley and pine nuts and season to taste with salt and pepper.

Spoon this mixture into the eggplant halves, dividing it equally, and arrange them side by side in the baking dish. Spread the remaining tomatoes on top. Add the sugar and lemon juice to the broth, taste for a pleasant sweet-sour balance, adding more sugar if necessary, and pour over. Drizzle balance of oil over eggplant. Cover the dish with heavy foil and bake until the eggplants are quite soft—about 30 minutes. Allow to cool and serve cold. Serves 6.

Serving suggestion: For lunch or a light supper, accompany with tabbouleh (p. 370).

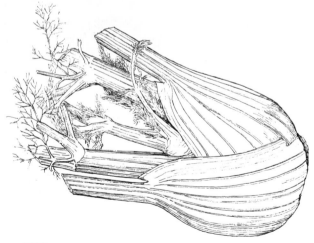

Fennel
(Foeniculum vulgare)

What looks like celery, tastes like licorice, and can be eaten as a first course, a salad, or a dessert? The crisp, beautifully formed fennel with its feathery, bright green leaves atop a fat, globelike base. It is such a favorite in Italy, where it is known as finocchio, that it can appear anywhere in the meal, though most frequently it is served raw as part of an antipasto. It is also served *in pinzimonio,* "to be eaten with the fingers," dipped in very good olive oil seasoned with salt and pepper. Braising or baking mellows the anise flavor somewhat and makes fennel a wonderful companion to fish, a combination used throughout Europe for centuries. (It is said that fish with fennel was a popular Lenten dish among aristocrats, while the common people ate fennel alone.)

The seeds, which are the dried fruit of the plant, are used to flavor court bouillons and stuffings. The ancient Romans, who gave the plant its name, used them to make perfume as well.

Cultivated garden fennel is called Florence fennel. There is also a stalk fennel that grows wild; the stalks are dried and used to lend their aromatic smoke to grilled foods, particularly fish.

To Buy

Usually found from October to April, fresh fennel should have crisp white stalks with leaves attached. Stay away from brown bottoms, cracked bulbs, and dried, porous tips. Fennel ranges in diameter from 4 to 7 inches at the widest part. One pound will yield ¾ pound after trimming.

To Store

Remove leaves if not using right away, and keep the fennel in a plastic bag in the refrigerator. It will keep for 4 or 5 days, but be careful not to let it get too cold or it will turn mushy.

To Prepare

Wash, dry, and trim stalks level with the bulb tops. (Use chopped fennel leaves in tossed green or seafood salads.) Trim the root end, leaving enough to hold the bulb intact. Cut off and discard any tough outer leaves. Older fennel will occasionally require stringing, like celery: Insert the tip of a paring knife just under the flesh at the tip and pull backward toward the base. A thin layer of skin will come away, the strings with it.

If serving fennel raw, cut vertically into halves and then wedges. For cooked fennel, cut into halves or quarters.

To Cook

Fennel varies widely in cooking time, depending on size. When it is properly cooked, the bulb part will be crisper than the rest. This is correct—don't try to make it uniformly soft or it will turn mushy.

Blanched: Drop halves into boiling salted water for 12 to 15 minutes. Drain.

Braised: Cut 2 pounds of prepared fennel into ½-inch-thick lengthwise slices (see drawing). Rinse in cool water. Heat 4 tablespoons olive oil in a sauté pan and add the fennel and ½ cup water or broth. Cook, covered, for about ½ hour, or until tender, checking after 20 minutes. Uncover and turn up heat. Cook a few minutes more over high heat to evaporate any remaining liquid, turning the slices until pale gold. Season with salt and pepper.

Fried: Cut fennel into ½-inch-thick lengthwise slices, blanch for 8 to 10 minutes, and drain. Dip in beaten egg and then in fine dry bread crumbs. Fry in ½ inch of hot vegetable oil until golden on both sides. Salt to taste. Serve with meats or as a separate course.

Fennel salad: Cut washed fennel into strips or slivers about 2 inches long. Dress with a good olive oil, lemon juice, salt, and pepper. Let sit at room temperature about 3 hours before serving.

Fennel au Gratin

Fennel baked this way makes an unusual and delicious accompaniment to broiled fish.

6 small fennel bulbs (about 2 pounds), halved	1 cup chicken broth
	½ cup grated Parmesan cheese
Salt and freshly ground pepper	3 tablespoons butter

Preheat the oven to 400°. Butter a 9 × 12-inch baking dish. Blanch the fennel for 12 to 15 minutes and drain. Arrange cut side up in the baking dish. Season to taste and pour the chicken broth over. Sprinkle with the cheese, dot with butter, and bake in the upper third of the oven for half an hour, or until the top is golden. Serves 6–8.

Fennel and Tomato Soup

Sally Scoville has made fennel a personal cause, because she feels Americans are for some reason put off by it. No one who tastes this excellent soup served at Sally's *Le Cherche Midi* restaurant in New York could entertain such a prejudice for long!

1½ to 2 pounds fresh fennel bulbs, trimmed	seeded, and quartered
Salt to taste	2 quarts chicken stock
4 tablespoons olive oil	Bouquet garni of thyme, ½ bay leaf, and parsley
1½ cups sliced yellow onions (about 3 medium onions)	Freshly ground black pepper
1 can (2 pounds 3 ounces) tomatoes, drained and chopped, or 2 pounds ripe tomatoes, peeled,	5–6 tablespoons tapioca
	2 tablespoons butter
	1 tablespoon chopped fresh fennel tops or fresh dill

Wash, trim, and peel the fennel. Cut into halves if small, quarters if large. Blanch for 5 minutes in boiling salted water, then drain and refresh. Cut into slices.

Heat the olive oil in a 3-quart saucepan and in it sauté the onions until they are soft and golden. Add the fennel and cook until lightly browned. Add the tomatoes and simmer slowly, stirring occasionally, for 20 to 25 minutes or until the vegetables are tender. Puree them in a food processor, then pass the puree through a food mill or fine sieve. (May be done ahead to this point.)

Put the puree back in a saucepan, add the stock and the bouquet garni, salt if desired, and fresh pepper and simmer uncovered for 15 minutes.

Remove and discard the bouquet garni. Pour the tapioca into the soup very slowly, stirring all the while until the soup thickens. Taste, correct seasoning, and remove from heat. Stir in the butter and pour into a heated tureen or heated plates. Serve sprinkled with snipped fennel tops or dill weed. Serves 8.

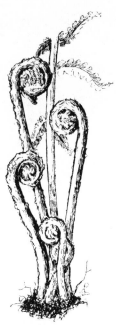

Fiddlehead Ferns

(Matteucia struthiopteris)

The tightly coiled crosiers, or green tips, of young fern fronds look somewhat like a violin seen from the side, hence the name. Until recently fiddleheads were available mostly to those willing to gather them; now they are just making a cautious appearance in Eastern specialty food markets for a few brief weeks in early May. Their devotees are such that perhaps the supply will increase.

They have a woodsy taste something like a cross between asparagus and spinach.

Not all fern tips are edible; fiddleheads are the sprouts of the ostrich fern, found along river and stream banks chiefly in New England and Canada and as far south as the Virginia uplands. In the most northerly spots they may be gathered as late as July, but in New England their season is brief—two or three weeks in May. In the south they may be found early in April.

To Store

Fiddleheads will keep well for up to a week, covered and refrigerated, and in the freezer, properly blanched, wrapped, and kept at 0°, for a year. If you are picking them far from home, they keep well on ice. I'm told fiddleheads are sometimes available frozen. Tinned ones are not recommended.

To Prepare

If the tips have been freshly gathered and are still attached to the fern, snap them off so that you have a top with about 2 inches of stem attached. Rub off any dry casings by hand. Soak in several changes of cold water, and drain on kitchen toweling. There will be lots of little brown bits and pieces; don't worry if some remain.

To Cook

Bring salted water to the boil, add ferns (allow 2 cups for 4 persons) and simmer for 12 or 15 minutes, or until just crisp-tender. Season and eat plain or with some melted butter or butter and lemon juice. Alternatively, fiddleheads may be steamed for the same amount of time or sautéed until crisp-tender. An unusual contemporary treatment is to sauté them in olive oil and toss with lemon juice and pignolis.

Fiddleheads may also be enjoyed cooked and sauced with hollandaise, or cold, in a mustard vinaigrette sprinkled with finely chopped hard-cooked eggs. Serve as a first course or light lunch.

To blanch for the freezer: Have a bowl of ice water handy. Immerse cleaned fern heads in a pot of boiling salted water, bring to the boil again over high heat, and cook for exactly 1 minute from that time. Drain ferns immediately and immerse in the ice water. When they are cool, drain them, seal well in an airtight package or container, label, and freeze.

Greens

This category of vegetable includes leafy greens ranging from the mild tops of beets to the more pungent collard, dandelion, and broccoli di rape and the sharper turnip and mustard greens. Technically, mild greens like spinach, kale, and Swiss chard belong here, too, but as they are usually cooked differently and have broader applications, they are treated as separate vegetables.

All greens, except those of the beet and any very young leaves, are best cooked in broth rather than water, as it mellows their bite. The greens mentioned here may be used interchangeably in recipes for any specific one, provided they are not bitter (bite one). Baby greens of the milder types may be used as you would kale, swiss chard, or escarole. Very young greens may also be sautéed in garlic or onion-flavored oil without a preliminary blanching. The more pungent greens and mature greens should be given a preliminary blanching before cooking to rid them of some bitterness.

The old custom was to cook greens to death to tenderize them and remove the bitterness, and also to get the bonus of "side meat" (from the pork hock they were cooked with) and "pot likker" (the delectable juices that accumulated during the long cooking). To conserve the considerable vitamin and mineral content and still obtain good flavor, it is preferable to simmer the side meat first, then add the blanched greens and cook only until tender.

To Store and Prepare

Keep refrigerated, unwashed, in a damp towel. Wash very well before cooking. Because greens cook down to one-quarter their volume, allow 1 pound for 2 servings. Cook greens in an enamel-lined or stainless steel saucepan.

Beet greens: Rinse stems and leaves of 3 bunches of beets; pull stems off and snap them in two to pull away any strings. Boil the stems in at least 3 quarts of boiling salted water for about 10 minutes; add the leaves and cook until tender—about 5 minutes. Drain and dress with butter, salt, and pepper.

Beet green salad: Prepare as directed, and dress while still warm with vinaigrette dressing (p. 374).

Broccoli di rape, or broccolirab as it is called in the southern Italian dialect, is a turnip green that appears frequently in the cuisine of Tuscany. It is mildly bitter, has a slight bite and an elusive broccoli flavor, and is my favorite of the greens. It is also used in Chinese cooking and can be found in markets dealing with those cuisines in late fall and winter. Both the leaves and stalks are used; the stalks require peeling. Blanch for about 5 minutes in boiling salted water and then simmer in chicken broth. This green is delicious coarsely chopped and finished as for broccoli with garlic Italian style (p. 62). Omit the water called for in the second cooking, and make sure the greens have excess moisture pressed out.

Collards: A leafy cabbage that is part of the soul-food tradition of the South. It is a popular green in Africa today and, cooked with buttermilk curds, the national dish of Ethiopia. The flavor is milder than turnip or mustard greens. Blanch mature collards for about 10 minutes, then simmer for an hour in a vegetable or ham broth.

Dandelion greens: A tart, sometimes bitter green whose serrated leaf edge suggests lion's teeth to the French, who call them *dents de lion,* source of our name. In a preparation, though, they are referred to as *pissenlit,* a reflection of their mild diuretic quality. April and May are the height of their season, but don't gather them indiscriminately on suburban lawns where weed killer may have been used. Use the small green leaves that surround the heart of the plant and discard the large tough leaves. To prepare, pull clusters apart, cut off root end, and wash very well, as these are usually quite dirty. Use as a salad green or braise in butter.

Mustard greens: These are quite sharp in flavor. Blanch for 5 minutes (a few minutes longer for more mature greens) to remove bitterness, then boil in broth until tender.

Turnip greens: These have a sharp taste like mustard greens. Remove fibrous stems, and wash leaves well. They may be steamed for about 10 minutes and dressed with butter, or prepared like collards, though the long cooking does destroy the vitamin content.

Dandelion Salad

This is a popular salad in France, where the mild bitterness of dandelion greens is much favored. Any of

Dandelion Salad, continued
the tougher salad greens like escarole and curly endive
may also be prepared this way.

1½ pounds dandelion greens	**1 garlic clove, minced**
½ tablespoon butter	**3 tablespoons wine vinegar**
3 slices thick-cut bacon, diced	**2 hard-cooked eggs, chopped**
	Fresh black pepper

Pull the dandelion clusters apart; cut off the root ends
and any large tough leaves. If the leaf hearts are large,
halve them. Wash and dry well and put in a salad
bowl.

Melt the butter in a skillet and fry the bacon until
lightly browned. Add the garlic and cook until the
bacon is brown and crisp. Remove the bacon with a
slotted spoon, add to the greens, and pour off most of
the fat in the pan. Add the vinegar to the pan and heat,
scraping the bottom to dissolve any brown particles,
then pour over the greens. Add the egg quarters and
pepper to taste, and toss. Serves 4.

Note: The salt in the bacon is usually sufficient for this
salad.

Dandelion salad with croutons: Fry a

cup of stale bread cubes in vegetable oil, drain, salt
lightly, add to the salad, and toss.

Southern Mixed Greens

The pork produces a marvelously flavored bouillon that
enhances the flavor and cuts the bite of the greens. Be
sure to serve with good bread, preferably cornbread, to
dunk up the "pot likker."

5 pounds mixed greens (any combination of collards, kale, turnip or beet greens or chard)	**2 quarts cold water**
	Salt to taste if desired
	1 teaspoon red pepper flakes
4 ham hocks, about ¾ pound each	**Freshly ground pepper to taste**

½ pound streaky bacon or
 salt pork, cut into cubes
1 cup finely chopped
 onions

½ cup finely chopped
 green pepper
2 tablespoons red wine
 vinegar or to taste

Pick over the greens; discard roots and damaged leaves, remove and discard tough midribs and stems. Wash well in cold water, drain, and dry. Cut or tear into bite-sized pieces. Set aside.

Put the ham hocks in a very large heavy kettle or casserole, cover with the water, add the two peppers and salt to taste and bring to the boil. Adjust heat and let simmer for about 45 minutes.

In a separate pot, render the bacon or salt pork, add the onions and green pepper and cook until soft and browned. Scoop out the pork and vegetables with a slotted spoon and add to the hock pot. Simmer about half an hour more, or until the meat is so soft it begins to fall from the bones.

Add and stir in the greens. Cover pot closely and cook for about 30 minutes, stirring and lifting the greens occasionally.

Correct seasoning and add the vinegar. To serve, put the meat and greens on a serving plate and serve the pot liquor in separate small bowls, along with hot cornbread. Serves 4.

Jerusalem Artichokes
(Helianthus tuberosus)

Jerusalem artichokes are not artichokes, nor do they come from Jerusalem. They are a knobby edible tuber of the sunflower family, *girasole* in Italian, which is probably the origin of the name. They look more like round, fat ginger roots than artichokes. They are native to this continent and were much appreciated by the American Indians, though few Americans now know them. Commercial growers propose to change that and have recently introduced them on the market as "sunchokes." When raw, they have a nutty taste and a crunchy texture like water chestnuts. When cooked, they become sweetly mealy. They may be steamed or boiled and then dressed with butter. I liked them included in a mixture of curried vegetables.

Jerusalem artichokes have two qualities that make them loved by some and despised by others. Inulin, the form of carbohydrate they contain, is not metabolized as starch and does not turn into sugar; therefore it is ideal for dieters and diabetics. The negative quality is a tendency to cause flatulence.

To Buy

Jerusalem artichokes, or sunchokes, are usually sold in 1-pound plastic bags, so it is a little hard to tell what you're getting. Try to select the smoothest small ones, which will be easier to clean and peel. The knobbier they are, the more waste. Allow 1 pound for 4 persons.

To Store

Place the bag in the refrigerator, where they should keep for at least a week.

To Prepare

Scrub well with a brush and cut away any stringy roots or tip. The skin is edible and contrasts pleasantly with the flesh, especially when cooked. Or peel after cooking by running under cold water; the skin will slip off like beet skin.

To Cook

Boiled: Drop whole chokes into boiling water and cook for 12 to 15 minutes after the water returns to the boil. Watch carefully, test with a fork, and remove and drain when there is still a tiny bit of resistance. They will continue to cook with their own internal heat for a bit, and overcooking makes them mushy.

If whiteness is important, cook *à blanc* (p. 17) in an enamel-lined or stainless steel saucepan.

Steamed: Bring 1 inch of water to the boil in the bottom of a steamer, add chokes, and steam for 15 to 20 minutes, depending on size. Peel or not after steaming and serve with hollandaise sauce.

Baked: This is one of the most delicious ways to do chokes, and very easy. Put chokes in a single layer in the pan in which you have just roasted a chicken or leg of lamb. While the roast rests, bake the chokes at 400° for about 20 minutes. Use a long-handled spoon to roll them around in the fat (if it is on the meager side, add some butter or vegetable oil to augment it). If chokes vary in size, put the larger ones in first, and adjust timing according to size. Season and serve with the meat.

Deep-fried: Peel chokes with a swivel-bladed vegetable peeler and drop in acidulated water as you work. Slice or julienne with the appropriate disk of a food processor or by hand. Dry well in a salad spinner, then deep-fry for about 5 minutes, following the instructions for french-fried potatoes (p. 234), but using only a single frying. Season with salt and pepper and serve immediately.

Pureed: Cook Jerusalem artichokes *à blanc*. Put through a food mill into a bowl containing an equal amount of sieved cooked potato. Beat in 2 tablespoons each butter and cream, and season with salt and white pepper. Reheat in a double boiler.

In cream sauce with peas: Boil 1 pound Jersalem artichokes and peel. Combine with a package of cooked frozen peas, or 1½ cups cooked fresh peas,

and mix into béchamel sauce (p. 376) that has been thinned with a bit of the cooking liquid.

Marinated: Prepare a double amount of basic vinaigrette sauce (p. 374) and add to it 2 tablespoons finely chopped shallots and a large pinch of thyme rubbed well between the hands. Slice 2 pounds raw, scrubbed chokes (peeled or unpeeled) into the marinade cover, and refrigerate overnight. For a nice touch of color, add some chopped sweet red pepper and a small handful of chopped parsley and toss before serving. Serves 4–6.

Kale

(Brassica oleracea acephala)

I rarely saw kale at market until recently, yet this coarse-leaved green, a nonheading cabbage, is full of vitamins and minerals and is a wonderful winter vegetable because it can survive frosts and snow—in fact, kale lovers say it mellows after a frost.

The Scots are particularly fond of kale; at one time every country family had its own patch, called a kailyard. When a Scotsman asks you to kail, he's asking you to dinner, though kale may not actually be served.

To Buy

Look for crisp, unwilted, dark green leaves and firm stems and midribs. Small young leaves can be eaten stems and all; larger leaves will need stems removed, making them not as good a buy. Frozen kale is also available in supermarkets and may be used in any recipe calling for fresh kale. Allow ½ pound fresh kale per person, as kale will reduce to about one-fourth its volume in cooking.

To Store

Refrigerate, unwashed, in a sealed plastic bag. Though it is tough-looking, kale wilts easily and should be used within 2 or 3 days.

To Prepare

Kale can be quite gritty. Just prior to cooking, wash leaves thoroughly in two or three changes of cold water. Lift and swish them with the hands; merely putting them in a colander will just move the grit from one leaf to another. Tough stems should be stripped before washing, as you would sorrel and spinach: fold the leaf in half, grasp the bottom of the stem, and pull back toward the tip.

To Cook

Blanched: Bring a large amount of salted water to the boil in a stainless steel or porcelain-lined pot, add kale, and boil uncovered for about 8 minutes, or a little more if leaves are large. Drain and squeeze out moisture, chop, and dress with butter, salt, and pepper or crumbled bacon.

Steamed: Bring an inch of salted water to the boil in the bottom of a steamer. Add kale, cover, and steam for about 5 minutes, or until limp. Finish as for blanched kale.

Kale can also be cooked like spinach, with just the water that clings to its leaves. This method conserves the maximum amount of vitamins and minerals. Kale may be substituted in almost any recipe calling for spinach, allowing the appropriately longer cooking time.

Caldo Verde

This is a traditional soup of the early Portuguese settlers of New England. There are many versions, all made with kale. This is one I like best, from George and Nancy Marcus's delightful little book called *Forbidden Fruits and Forgotten Vegetables*. It is simple to do and makes a light but filling supper.

4 potatoes, peeled and diced	2 teaspoons salt
1 pound kale, well washed and very finely shredded	Freshly ground pepper
	3 tablespoons olive oil
	Slightly stale French or Italian bread

Bring 2½ quarts water to a boil in a heavy soup pot. Add the potatoes and cook partly covered for 20 minutes, or until tender enough to mash. Remove from the liquid with a slotted spoon, mash in a bowl and return to the cooking liquid. Bring again to the boil and add the kale. Cover and cook over moderate heat for 30 minutes, or until tender. Add salt and pepper to taste and stir in the oil.

Put several slices of bread in each soup bowl and pour the hot soup over. Serves 6.

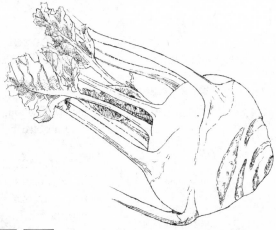

Kohlrabi

(Brassica oleracea gongylodes)

Kohlrabi has two edible portions—the leaves, which can be used like turnip greens, and the spectacularly shaped globular stem. It enjoys great popularity among Middle Europeans and, though it is available here, it has a relatively small following.

Kohlrabi may be sliced and served raw as a part of a crudité platter (it tastes like a radish), or shredded into a salad. It may be steamed, which seems to intensify its delicate flavor, or boiled. Substitute in any of the recipes for celery root or turnip.

To Buy

Available in late spring through early fall, the small ones (under 2½ inches in diameter) are the sweet ones; large kohlrabi can be fibrous and tough. The leaves (usually removed at market) should be green. Pass over ones with soft spots or a yellow cast. One pound will serve 3 or 4 people.

To Store

Refrigerate, unwashed, in an open plastic bag. Separate stems and leaves. Like other roots, kohlrabi may be kept in a cool, dark cellar.

To Prepare

Wash just before cooking. Unless kohlrabis are very young and small, they will need to be peeled, which may be done after cooking. Cut a thin slice off one end, lift the skin, and pull away.

To Cook

Boiled:
Place trimmed, unpeeled kohlrabis in a pot, cover with water, bring to a boil, add salt, cover, and cook until tender, about 30 minutes. Drain, peel, slice or cube, and turn in melted butter. Season with salt, pepper, and a dash of lemon juice.

Steamed:
Bring 1 inch of water to a boil in the bottom of a steamer. Place trimmed, unpeeled kohlrabis

in the basket, cover, and steam until tender—about 40 minutes. Peel and finish as for boiled kohlrabi.

Vinaigrette:
Cut fresh kohlrabi in julienne, blanch in boiling water for 5 minutes, and drain. While still warm, combine and toss with mustard vinaigrette (p. 375). Refrigerate at least an hour, then let come to room temperature before serving.

Kohlrabi, fennel, carrot, and endive salad:
Peel and grate 3 kohlrabi with the grating disk of a food processor or by hand. Peel and grate 1 carrot. Combine with 1 thinly sliced fennel bulb and 2 pieces of endive cut into ¼-inch rounds. Dress with mustard vinaigrette (p. 375) and let steep for 30 minutes before serving. Serves 4.

Kohlrabi rémoulade:
Substitute peeled, raw, julienned kohlrabi for celery root in the recipe for céleri rémoulade (p. 102).

Creamed Kohlrabi with Dill and Caraway

8 kohlrabis
4 tablespoons butter
½–¾ cup cream
Salt

Fresh lemon juice to taste, optional
1 tablespoon chopped dill
1 teaspoon caraway

Peel and grate or julienne kohlrabis, using the grating disk of a food processor or the largest holes of a hand grater. Blanch in a large pot of boiling salted water for 3 minutes. Drain and press out moisture with the hands.

Melt the butter in a skillet, add the kohlrabis and toss well. Blend in the cream, raise heat slightly, and cook for a few minutes, stirring, until vegetable is well coated with cream. Season with salt and lemon juice and stir in the dill and caraway. Serves 6.

Serving suggestion: As an accompaniment to veal cutlets or veal scallops.

Leeks
(Allium porrum)

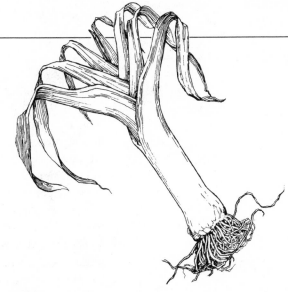

Sometimes called the poor man's asparagus, the leek is perhaps the most delicious and underutilized member of the onion family. It was not until nouvelle cuisine chefs made them fashionable that Americans thought of leeks as anything but a soup green or an ingredient of vichyssoise. Their flavor is subtle and gentle but distinctive, without some of the spirited effects of the other culinary *alliums*.

Leeks have been cultivated as long as history has been recorded. Juvenal wrote in his *Satires* that "leeks are gods" in Egypt. They were among the rations given to the laborers on the pyramids, and the Old Testament mentions that "cucumbers, melons and leeks" were the foods most sorely missed by the Jews during their desert wanderings after the Exodus from Egypt. Nero believed they promoted eloquence and clarity of voice and ate leek soup every day, earning for himself the sobriquet "Porrophagus."

Certainly leeks found a happy home when Casear's armies carried them to the British Isles, where they became the Welsh national emblem.

To Buy

Leeks vary from ½ inch in diameter to 2 inches or more. Those that are 1½ inches or smaller are best;

very large ones can be fibrous. If leeks are to be used whole, try to choose those of uniform size.

They should be crisp, not soft, limp, or mushy. The tops, if present, should be unwithered and green (some greengrocers trim off the superfluous green; the roots are usually left on). Avoid very fat or bulbous bottoms; this is a sign of age and may indicate a woody core. Most recipes specify leeks by number, though they are sold by weight. The part you use, unless otherwise specified, is the white and about two inches of the green. Discarded green may be used for soups and stocks. You can get maximum use of the green portion by reverse trimming (see drawing). For eating whole, allow 2 medium leeks per person. Two pounds after trimming will yield about 2 cups chopped cooked leeks.

To Store

Leeks keep for 2 to 3 weeks in the crisper drawer of the refrigerator. Trim off the roots and excess foliage, but do not wash until ready to use. Brush off visible soil before storing.

To Prepare

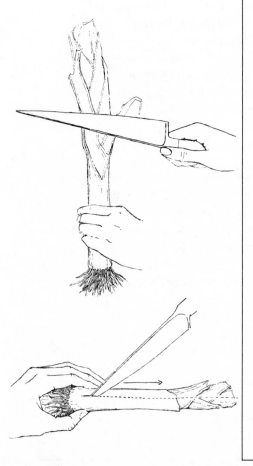

As leeks grow, the earth is hilled up around them to blanch the bulb. For this reason they tend to be gritty and have to be well washed. Remove any yellow or withered leaves, cut off the roots from the white end, and cut off the coarser part of the green so that leeks are about 7 inches long. If using whole, make a lengthwise slit through the leaves to within 1 inch of the bulbous base (see drawing). Soak for about 10 minutes, then wash well several times under running water, spreading out the leaves as you do.

If your recipe calls for sliced leeks, do the slicing first, then wash in a colander under running water, giving special attention to those pieces with visible dirt. Press with your hand to get out as much water as possible, and dry on a towel before proceeding with the cooking.

To Cook

Boiled Whole: Split large leeks in half
lengthwise; leave small ones whole. A large quantity of
small leeks may be bundled as you would asparagus,
tying 4 or 5 together with two lengths of string. Layer
them in a large pot (a 5-quart oval roaster works
particularly well) and add enough cold water to come
halfway up the sides. Add salt, bring to the boil, and
cook at a fairly brisk boil with the cover slightly askew
for 15 to 18 minutes, or until the white part is tender
when pierced with the tip of a sharp knife. Start testing
at 15 minutes; do not overcook or leeks will become
slimy. Drain and refresh under running cold water.

Butter-braised: Use 8 leeks, about 1-inch in
diameter, or 12 smaller ones. Arrange them in an oval
Dutch oven or other heavy pot in a double layer. Add
4 tablespoons butter and salt to taste. Cover and cook
over low heat for 12 to 15 minutes, turning gently
once or twice with wooden spoons. When just tender,
uncover, turn up heat, and let liquid evaporate almost
completely. Leeks will brown slightly. Then sprinkle
with ¼ cup grated Parmesan cheese, turn leeks to coat,
remove to a heated platter and serve at once. Serves 4.

Puree of Leeks

A rich accompaniment to chicken, veal, or shrimp.

4 pounds leeks	**Nutmeg**
4 tablespoons butter	**3 tablespoons heavy cream**
Salt and freshly ground	**or crème fraîche**
pepper	

Slice the leeks in half lengthwise, then cut crosswise
into 1-inch pieces. Wash thoroughly and dry.

Bring to the boil enough salted water to cover the
leeks, add them, bring again to the boil, cover, and
simmer for 20 minutes, or until tender. Drain off the
liquid and puree the leeks in a food processor. Some
liquid may separate from the leeks; do not discard it.

Return the pureed leeks and any liquid that has accumulated to the saucepan and cook, uncovered, over medium heat, stirring constantly, until all the liquid has disappeared and the puree is on the verge of sticking.

Over low heat, swirl in the butter piece by piece, beating with a wooden spoon until absorbed. Then season to taste with salt, pepper, and a grating or two of nutmeg. Add enough cream to give a smooth, not too loose consistency. Taste and adjust seasonings. Serves 4.

Note: Leeks take longer than most vegetables to become a smooth puree. The puree may be made ahead and reheated in a double boiler.

Julienne of Leek

Sheer green leek threads make an attractive garnish for poached or sautéed fish fillets, or poached oysters.

2 medium leeks, trimmed to within 1 inch of green	**2 teaspoons water or dry vermouth**
2 tablespoons butter	**Salt and freshly ground pepper to taste**

Cut the leeks in half lengthwise, then crosswise into 2-inch pieces. Wash thoroughly and dry. Stack two or three lengths together and cut with a shredding motion into very fine julienne.

Melt the butter in a saucepan. Add the julienned leeks and salt and pepper to taste, and stir to coat. Sprinkle with the water and cook, stirring, over moderate heat about 5 minutes, until the leeks wilt. Makes about ¾ cup.

Leeks Provençal

A few very ordinary ingredients are given extraordinary dimensions by the two forms of lemon in this recipe. The colors, too, are extremely pleasing. Domestic black olives can't compare in flavor to the niçoise or Greek kind, so they are worth going out of your way to obtain.

12 fresh leeks of uniform
    size, about 3 pounds
    before trimming
¼ cup olive oil
Freshly ground pepper
    and salt, if desired
2 small ripe tomatoes,
    skinned and cut into

eighths (see note)
12–16 pitted black olives,
    preferably the niçoise
    kind
Juice of ½ lemon
1 teaspoon grated lemon
    peel

Cut the leeks crosswise into inch-long pieces. Wash
thoroughly and dry.

In a heavy stainless-steel or porcelain-lined casserole
that can be used on top of the stove (and perhaps go to
the table as well), heat the oil and add the leeks,
pepper, and salt. Cover and simmer gently for 7 to 10
minutes, depending on thickness. Add the tomatoes,
olives, lemon juice, and grated peel, and cook slowly,
covered, for another 10 minutes. Serve warm, as an
accompaniment to grilled chicken or fish, or chill and
serve as a salad or first course. Serves 4–5.

Note: If you have time, skinning the tomatoes makes
the dish a bit more refined; if fresh ripe tomatoes are
not available, use 8 ripe cherry tomatoes, cut in half.
Canned tomatoes are a last choice.

Sweet-and-Sour Leeks

The play of sweet and sour against the subtle leek
flavor makes this easily prepared dish very delicious.

2 pounds small leeks of
    uniform size
3 tablespoons vegetable oil
2–3 garlic cloves, peeled
    and crushed

1 tablespoon sugar
¼ cup lemon juice (1–2
    lemons)
Freshly ground pepper
Salt to taste

Cut the leeks crosswise on the diagonal into pieces
about 2 inches long. Wash thoroughly and dry.

Heat the oil in a heavy 4- or 5-quart porcelain-lined
or stainless-steel pot. Add the garlic, cook about 3
minutes, then sprinkle in the sugar and cook over
moderate heat another 2 or 3 minutes, until the sugar

melts and takes on a suggestion of color. Add the leeks and cook, turning gently with a wooden spoon, until they take on a bit of color—3 to 5 minutes. Add the lemon juice, cover, and let stew gently for 12 to 15 minutes, or until tender. Toward the end, watch that the sugar does not burn. Season with several good grinds of pepper and a light sprinkling of salt, if desired. Serve warm or at room temperature. Serves 3–4.

Serving suggestion: Excellent with broiled herbed chicken and bulgur pilaf.

Leek Toasts

This is a nice first course before a fish dinner.

3 fat or 4 small leeks	4 slices homestyle bread,
5 tablespoons butter	crusts removed, cut in
½ teaspoon flour	diagonal halves
Salt and freshly ground	1 egg yolk
pepper	Lemon juice
⅓ cup heavy cream	Chopped parsley

Cut the leeks in half lengthwise, then crosswise into ½-inch dice. Wash thoroughly and dry. Blanch about 10 minutes, until tender. Refresh in cold water and press out excess water in a colander.

Melt 3 tablespoons of the butter in a saucepan over medium heat. Add the leeks, turn to coat, and sprinkle with the flour, salt, and pepper. Blend in the cream, cover, and simmer over low heat for 10 minutes. Let cool slightly. (May be prepared ahead to this point.)

Melt the remaining 2 tablespoons of butter in a large skillet and fry the bread triangles on both sides until golden—about 3 minutes per side. Set aside.

Stir the egg yolk into the cooled leeks, return to gentle heat briefly until slightly thickened. Season with a small squeeze of lemon.

Arrange two toast halves on each of four hot plates, spoon leeks over, sprinkle with parsley, and serve. Serves 4.

Gratin of Leeks and Mussels

Fresh briny mussels and sweet leeks mellowed with cream make an unusual main course combination for lunch or a light supper.

4 fat leeks, white and part of the green (about 1¼ pounds before trimming)	4½ pounds mussels, scrubbed and debearded
	½ cup water
	Salt
6 tablespoons butter, cut into 8 pieces	1 small pinch powdered saffron
4 shallots, minced	1 cup heavy cream
1 cup white wine	White pepper
4–5 whole black peppercorns	Chopped parsley

Cut the leeks in half lengthwise, then crosswise into ½-inch pieces. Wash thoroughly and dry.

Melt 3 pieces of the butter in a large heavy pot and gently sauté the shallots until softened. Add the white wine and peppercorns, bring to a boil, and simmer for 3 minutes, until slightly reduced. Add the mussels, cover, bring to a boil, and cook over brisk heat until the mussels are opened—about 5 minutes. Shake the pot once or twice during this time to redistribute the mussels.

Remove the mussels with a slotted spoon, take them out of their shells, put in a small dish, cover with foil, and keep warm. Discard the shells. Strain the broth through a double thickness of cheesecloth into a small saucepan. Add to the pan any liquid that accumulates around the mussels.

Warm six individual gratin dishes or one oval 8 × 14-inch dish.

Melt 3 more pieces of the butter in a skillet and lightly sauté the leeks for 5 minutes. Add the water, salt very lightly, and cook, covered, for about 20 minutes over low heat, until the water has evaporated and the leeks are tender. Stir occasionally and make sure the leeks do not scorch. Set aside, covered, and keep warm.

Add to the reserved mussel broth any liquid that accumulates around the leeks. Add the saffron and cook over high heat until reduced by half. Blend in the cream and, over low heat, add the remaining 2 pieces of butter, one at a time, blending well to make a smooth, velvety sauce. Season to taste with white pepper.

Divide the leeks among the serving dishes, or put in one serving dish, spread the reserved mussels among them, and nap with the sauce. Heat briefly in the oven, sprinkle with chopped parsley, and serve very hot. Serves 6.

Serving suggestion: A white Sancerre goes very well with this. For a pleasant nonmeat dinner, add a casserole of baked rice and serve as a main course.

Soupe Bonne Femme

Recalling his childhood in the Bourbonnais, chef Louis Diat of New York's old Ritz-Carlton wrote that a steaming bowl of thick, hearty leek and potato soup was the way the family started the day, much better than the "American's strange meal of orange juice, ham and eggs." It was this soup that inspired him to create the chilled version, crème vichyssoise, that follows.

2 fat or 4 medium leeks, about 1 pound partly trimmed	(about 3 cups) Salt
3 tablespoons butter	3 cups boiling water
½ cup coarsely chopped onion	2 cups hot milk
2 medium potatoes, diced	Chopped parsley or snipped chives

Cut the leeks in half lengthwise, then slice crosswise and cut into ½-inch dice. You should have about 2 cups. Wash thoroughly and dry.

Melt 2 tablespoons of the butter in a heavy saucepan, add the leeks and onion, and cook over low heat, covered, for about 6 minutes. Stir frequently with a wooden spoon so they do not take on color. Add the potatoes, salt, if desired, and the boiling water. Bring to the boil, cover, lower heat, and simmer for 25 minutes, or until the potatoes are soft.

Add the hot milk and the remaining tablespoon of butter and serve hot, sprinkled with parsley or chives. Serves 6.

Crème Vichyssoise

4–6 leeks, about 1½ pounds after trimming, white part only
4 tablespoons butter
4 cups coarsely chopped potatoes (about 1½ pounds)

3 cups boiling water
3 cups chicken broth
Salt and white pepper
1 cup heavy cream
Milk
Chopped chives

Cut the leeks crosswise into thin slices. Wash thoroughly and dry. Melt the butter in a 5-quart saucepan, stir in the leeks, cover, and let cook slowly without browning for 5 minutes. Add the potatoes, water, broth, and 1 teaspoon salt. Bring again to the boil, partly cover, lower heat, and simmer for about 30 minutes, or until potatoes and leeks are tender.

Let cool slightly, then puree through a food mill or in a blender or food processor. Add the cream and season to taste with salt and white pepper (be slightly heavy-handed here, as chilled soups need more). Chill for at least 8 hours, or overnight. If soup seems too thick, thin slightly with milk. Check seasoning again. Serve in chilled bouillon cups, garnished with snipped chives. Serves 8.

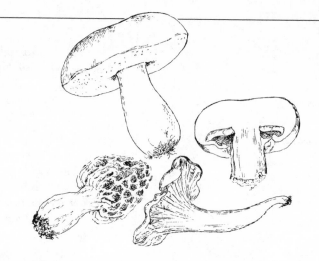

Mush-rooms

(Agaricus)

Cultivated Mushrooms

The early Egyptian pharaohs thought mushrooms much too exquisite for the proletarian palate and reserved them by edict for royal use only. Today anyone can eat them, and current interest in such that we are seeing new kinds at market all the time.

There are so many kinds of mushrooms it would be impossible to do them all justice. So I'll tell you about those most commonly available and some of the ones I like best.

The cultivated *Agaricus* is the mushroom you see most at market. It can be white, tan, or light brown and range from 1 to 3 inches in diameter. It is pleasant but bland compared with a wild mushroom. Most plentiful in midwinter, these mushrooms may be stuffed, baked, sliced and sautéed, used whole in stews, deep-fried in batter, or turned into the delectable sauce known as duxelles. Raw, they are good sliced and dressed with garlic vinaigrette (p. 375) and a sprinkling of parsley.

Button mushrooms are a young, domestic white mushroom (not a variety). They're available in cans but are too bland to be used in any but dire emergencies. Better to change the menu.

Wild Mushrooms

Wild mushrooms are no longer imported exotica; gathering them is a burgeoning cottage industry in the forests of Oregon, Michigan, and Washington. They are also being farmed in Vermont, Maine, and Virginia. Menus now list "Michigan morels" as proudly as they used to say "imported French."

When wild mushrooms are not available fresh, they are always in abundance dried. Though they are costly, just a few, reconstituted, can lend their incomparable aroma and depth of flavor to a sauce. Virtually all wild mushrooms can be used interchangeably (though you would not be likely to make a soup out of expensive ones like morels). Cultivated mushrooms lack the earthiness and character of wild ones and are a poor substitute in recipes in which mushroom flavor is the whole point, but for economy's sake you can combine domestic and wild mushrooms (dried or fresh) to extend the more intense flavor of the latter with very good results.

Here are some of the most common domestic and imported wild mushrooms:

Cèpe:

A *Boletus* mushroom, *cèpes* grow in oak, chestnut, and beech forests. Domestic cèpes are now available, as well as those imported from France, in fresh, canned, and dried forms. Cèpes have a great deal of character; use them to make sauces when you want a rich, deep mushroom flavor. They are most abundant in late summer.

The dried Polish, Yugoslavian, or Italian mushrooms commonly sold by weight from large jars or in cellophane bags with no further identification are usually cèpes.

Chanterelles:

Delicate, multileaved, spongy fall mushrooms with a pale apricot color. They have a delicate flavor when sautéed in butter with a bit of parsley and garlic, and are best enjoyed on their own as a first course.

Enoki: Unlike any other mushroom, the enoki-dake has a long, slender stalk and a tiny button cap that adds an artful Oriental note to food. It has a delicate flavor and is the only wild mushroom that cannot be used interchangeably in recipes. Enoki come in a solid bunch in 3-ounce packages; once you remove the hard end that holds them together and separate them, there are a lot. Gently wash and dry. Use raw in salads or sauté very briefly in butter and serve with chicken or Cornish game hen.

Girolles: A golden mushroom found in deciduous forests. Sauté them as you would chanterelles. These are naturally chewy; don't overcook or they will become tough.

Morels: Brown and spongelike, these are my favorite mushrooms, with an intense, earthy flavor that has been variously compared to sweetbreads, buttery eggplant, and steak. Use them simply sautéed in butter, served on toast points or in a light cream sauce topping a chicken cutlet or veal scallops. If large, cut into halves or quarters. Because of their intensity, a few go a long way. The pointed, convoluted top holds a lot of sand; wash and/or soak well. Available fresh, dried, and canned, domestic and imported.

Oyster mushrooms: *Pleurotus ostreatus* is a very rich tasting mushroom, hence its name. Use as you would morels. These also mix well with cultivated mushrooms, sautéed and served on toast.

Pied de mouton, also called lamb's foot or hedgehog, is a pale orange and, when cooked, has a deep, woodsy flavor. Use as recommended for morels.

Porcini: The Italian *Boletus*. Porcini are rich and buttery and can reach dinner-plate size. One of the large ones, brushed with olive oil, grilled and seasoned, is a stunning course. Available both fresh and dried. The smaller ones can be sautéed with garlic, parsley, and a little white wine. Abundant in late summer.

Shiitake

: A distinctively flavored, rather chewy mushroom also called oak mushroom. Probably the first mushroom to be cultivated (the Japanese have been growing them for 2,000 years), they are now farmed in Virginia. Their size ranges from 3 to 10 inches in diameter. The best have a deep tan tortoiseshell pattern. These keep better than others and can be refrigerated, well sealed in plastic, for a week, though stems will shrivel. Grill or broil after brushing with oil, use in sauces, sauté with garlic and parsley or as follows.

Sautéed shiitake:

Cut ½ pound shiitake into halves or quarters and sauté in 4 tablespoons melted butter for 6 to 8 minutes. Stir in 1 tablespoon soy sauce.

Steamed shiitake:

Bring ¾ inch water to a boil in the bottom of a covered steamer, add mushrooms, cover, and steam for 5 minutes. Serve with soy sauce.

To Buy

A fresh mushroom shows no space between the cap rim and the stem. As it ages, its moisture evaporates and the cap opens, exposing a brown, velvety ring of accordionlike pleats called gills. Buy mushrooms with slightly open caps only if they can be used at once. Pass up those with wide open caps, blackish gills, or shriveled stems. (They are still edible but have a musty overtone and turn quite dark on cooking.)

Buy mushrooms loose so you can pick the best. Factory-packaged mushrooms often carry a much higher price tag, are less flavorsome because they are often treated with a chemical preservative that alters their taste, and are often well past prime. The size of a mushroom cap has nothing to do with quality.

One-half pound will give you 2 cups sliced. Three ounces dried mushrooms equal 1 pound fresh.

To Store

Fresh and wild mushrooms are very perishable and need air circulation, coolness, and humidity. Use them within a day or two of purchase. Refrigerate in a basket or other open container covered by damp paper toweling, never in a plastic bag. If they do turn dark, chop them and use promptly in a sauce.

Dried mushrooms should be kept unrefrigerated in a screw-top jar with a good seal.

To Prepare

Fresh mushrooms absorb water and therefore should not be washed. A gentle wipe with a dampened paper towel is all they need. I never peel them unless they are to be fluted.

I clean fresh wild mushrooms with a special mushroom brush that looks like a very soft nail brush. It is available in shops dedicated to specialty kitchenware.

Mushroom stems are edible but are not as tender as the caps. If they are shriveled, discard them, as they will be rubbery. If they are very pulpy, remove and use for soup or sauce making. To remove stems, hold the cap in one hand and bend the stem back with the other until it snaps off.

To Reconstitute Dried Mushrooms

Soak in tepid water for 20 minutes to an hour, depending on thickness. Save the soaking water for flavoring sauces or soups; pour off carefully, letting any sand settle at the bottom.

Dried shiitake require minimum soaking—about 20 minutes in warm water. Chinese dried black mushrooms, available in Oriental markets year-round, should be soaked in hot water for half an hour. Then cut off any hard inedible stems. Another Chinese mushroom is the tree ear, also called cloud ear, which looks like a round piece of paper with charred edges. There are two sizes: thick and thin. Buy the latter and soak for half an hour.

To Cook

Sautéed: The French call mushrooms *les assasins du beurre*—"the butter killers"—because they absorb so much butter in cooking. Being mostly water, they also give off a great deal of liquid and shrink a lot.

When sautéing, do not overcrowd the pan; they will steam instead. When cooking stems and caps together, slice stems and add them after the caps have given up some liquid so they can steam a bit.

Do not overcook mushrooms; they become dry and rubbery.

Broiled: Allow 4 to 6 large mushrooms per person. Clean and remove stems as directed. Preheat the broiler. With a pastry brush, coat the caps inside and out with melted butter. Broil about 4 inches from the heat for 2 minutes. Turn caps with tongs, brush upturned sides with a little more butter, and broil 2 to 3 minutes more. Do not overcook. Season with salt and pepper and serve.

Broiled with snail butter: Have 2 toast points for each diner ready on warmed plates. Broil caps as directed, but when they are on the second side, place ½ teaspoon of snail butter (p. 395) on each cap. As soon as it melts, remove mushroom carefully with a spatula to the toast and serve.

Risotto of Mushrooms

The risotto is unique among rice dishes; when perfect— each grain separate yet the whole bound by a delicious creamy emulsion of butter, broth, and cheese—it is one of the most pleasurable and satisfying foods I know. Just follow the instructions carefully and be sure to use

Italian rice; no other will give the proper result. You can add just about anything to risotto from apples to zucchini; this one, richly flavored with mushrooms, is one of my particular favorites.

2 ounces dried porcini
    mushrooms
6 cups chicken broth,
    heated
6 tablespoons butter
1 small onion, chopped,
    about ½ cup
1 tablespoon chopped
    parsley, preferably the
    flat Italian kind

½ cup dry white wine
1½ cups Italian Arborio
    rice
½ cup Parmesan cheese,
    freshly grated, plus
    additional cheese to
    pass
Salt and freshly ground
    black pepper

Soak the mushrooms in a small bowl of lukewarm water for 20 minutes; drain. Bring the broth to a boil and keep it simmering.

Melt 4 tablespoons of the butter in a heavy 2½- to 3-quart saucepan. Add the onion and sauté until lightly golden. Add the parsley and wine and simmer uncovered until the liquid almost cooks away.

Add the rice and stir rapidly over low heat so that each grain is coated and glistening. Add a large ladleful of hot broth to the mixture and bring to the boil. Lower the heat and cook uncovered, stirring frequently, until almost all the liquid is absorbed. (Watch so that at no time does all the liquid cook away or rice will burn.) Then add the drained mushrooms. Continue adding and stirring in broth by the ladleful until rice reaches the desired doneness, which ideally is chewy, yet not hard, moist, yet not too soupy. This will take 20 to 25 minutes.

Shortly before you judge the rice to be fully cooked, add and stir in the Parmesan cheese. At the very last stir in the balance of the butter. Taste and add salt and several good grinds of pepper. Mix well and serve immediately. Additional cheese may be passed separately. Serves 4 to 6.

Serving suggestion: Risotto is almost always a first course and can be followed by any meat or fish that does not contain cream or cheese. The only risotto served as an accompaniment is the plain saffron version that accompanies osso buco.

Duxelles

La Varenne, *chef de cuisine* to the marquis d'Uxelle, gets the credit for the simplest yet most versatile of mushroom preparations. Duxelles is nothing more than a hash of finely minced mushrooms combined with shallots or onions and cooked slowly in butter until the moisture is evaporated; yet its uses and applications are endless. Added to sauces, duxelles imparts an intense mushroom presence without diluting them. It can be mixed into stuffings without making them soggy, or used on its own to stuff fish or chicken. For a classic garniture, use it to stuff tomato shells or artichoke bottoms.

½ **pound cultivated mushrooms**
2 **tablespoons butter**
3 **tablespoons very finely chopped shallots, or 2 tablespoons chopped**
onion
Salt and freshly ground pepper
2 **teaspoons finely chopped parsley**

Chop the mushrooms as fine as possible; you should have about 2 cups. Melt the butter in a 10-inch sauté pan and, just before the foam dies down, add the shallots or onions and cook, stirring, for 3 minutes over moderate heat. Add the mushrooms, stir until well distributed, then let cook over moderate heat for several minutes until they begin to give up liquid. Lower the heat and cook, stirring from time to time, until most of the moisture is evaporated but the mushrooms are not brown, about 10 minutes (a well-made duxelles is quite dry). Season to taste and stir in the parsley. Makes about ¾ cup.

Notes: All the chopping can be done in a food

processor. Duxelles can be stored in the refrigerator for at least a week covered with buttered paper, or in the freezer indefinitely.

Creamed duxelles:

Prepare duxelles as directed in the preceding recipe, but do not season or add the parsley. Just before all the moisture has evaporated from the pan, sprinkle 2 tablespoons flour over the mushrooms and cook for a minute or two until all traces have disappeared. Stir in $\frac{1}{3}$ to $\frac{1}{2}$ cup heavy cream, bring to a simmer, and cook a minute longer until there is no taste of raw flour. The mixture will be quite thick.

Remove from heat, add 1 tablespoon chopped parsley, and season with salt, fresh black pepper, a dash of cayenne, and lemon juice to taste. Let cool, then refrigerate if not using immediately. Stuff croustades or large mushroom caps with the creamed duxelles for the best hors d'oeuvre you ever ate. Makes about 1¼ cups.

Note: To make extra creamed duxelles for freezing, simply double the recipe. It freezes well and indefinitely. I freeze duxelles in a square container, and then knock the frozen duxelles block out of the plastic and wrap it well. Whenever I need some, I slice off the required amount and let it come to room temperature.

Mushrooms stuffed with creamed duxelles:

Preheat the oven to 350°. Remove the stems of 24 medium-size mushrooms and save for another use. Spoon and mound room-temperature creamed duxelles into each cap. Sprinkle with a few grains of grated Parmesan cheese and dot with a tiny bit of butter. Place on a buttered cookie sheet and bake for 10 minutes to heat through. Run under the broiler very briefly just to gild the top.

Croustades with creamed duxelles:

Make or buy 3-inch pastry croustades. Fill 24 of them

with the creamed duxelles and finish and bake as directed for mushroom caps.

Shirred eggs with duxelles: Lavishly butter an individual ovenproof gratin dish; make a bed of several tablespoons of plain or creamed duxelles in the bottom. Break 2 eggs carefully over the mushrooms, sprinkle with salt but no pepper and set over a medium heat for 1 minute. Drip a teaspoon of melted butter over each yolk and bake in a 350° oven for 10 to 12 minutes, or until the whites are set. The whites must be creamy and not too hard. Serve at once. Serves 1.

Low–cholesterol version: A great treat for those who may not eat eggs: Grease the gratin dish with margarine; heat several tablespoons of duxelles in the dish, cover with 2 or 3 egg whites (which you have stored in your freezer), then proceed as directed. A sprinkling of snipped chives before baking adds a nice flavor note.

Mushroom Puree Le Pavillon

This Lucullan essence of mushroom accompanied Poularde Pavillion—chicken baked in champagne—was one of the best loved dishes at Henri Soulé's legendary Pavillon restaurant. It is very concentrated, so serve only a small amount to garnish a roast chicken. Soulé frequently served this with braised celery stalks.

2 pounds cultivated mushrooms	2–3 scrapings fresh nutmeg
Salt and freshly ground pepper	1½ cups heavy cream

Chop the mushrooms finely by hand or with a food processor. Place in a fine strainer over a bowl and let any excess liquid drip off. Then place in a heavy saucepan over low heat, and cook, stirring constantly, for 8 to 10 minutes; remove from the heat as soon as mushrooms begin to stick. Season with salt, pepper, and nutmeg. Return to the heat, add the cream, and cook uncovered at a slow simmer for 15 minutes, stirring frequently. Correct seasoning. Serve very hot. Serves 6.

Note: This puree can be served in pastry shells.

Mushrooms with Garlic and Parsley

It is critical in this dish that the oil not be overheated at any time. I have specified cultivated mushrooms because they are the easiest to find, but cèpes and porcini are fabulous this way. I also use a mix of three-quarters cultivated and one-quarter oyster mushrooms. Either way, it makes a fabulous first course or light lunch.

1 pound medium cultivated mushrooms
½ cup olive oil
Salt and freshly ground pepper
⅓ cup fresh bread crumbs
made from home-style white bread
1 teaspoon minced garlic
2 tablespoons chopped parsley

Wipe the mushrooms clean; cut off the stems and reserve them. Thinly slice the caps.

Heat the olive oil in a heavy skillet. It should be very warm but not hot or smoking. Add the sliced caps and let them stew gently, rather than fry, for 10 minutes. Remove with a slotted spoon to a serving dish.

Raise the heat a bit and sauté the stems in the same oil. Scoop out and add to the cooked caps. Season to taste with salt and pepper.

Add the bread crumbs to the pan and sauté, stirring, for 1½ minutes until crumbs are lightly golden. Combine the garlic and parsley, press together with the back of a spoon or your fingers, and add to the crumbs. Pour the mixture and the hot oil over the mushrooms. Let cool and refrigerate for several hours. Stir and serve at room temperature. Serves 4–6.

Serving suggestion: Serve as a first course followed by chicken cutlets with broccoli-leek puree (p. 65) and blanched carrots (p. 88).

Mushroom Quiche

This is particularly satisfying and filling quiche that freezes well. Serve with a salad for an easy light meal.

3 tablespoons butter
2 tablespoons minced
  shallots
¾ pound cultivated
  mushrooms, thinly
  sliced
3 large eggs
1¾ cups heavy cream
Salt and freshly ground

pepper to taste
1 fully baked 8- or 9-inch
  pâte brisée shell,
  "waterproofed" (see
  following recipe)
2 tablespoons grated
  Parmesan cheese
2 tablespoons chopped
  parsley

Preheat the oven to 375°.

Melt 2 tablespoons of the butter in a large skillet. Sauté the shallots until they are transparent. Add the mushrooms, cover, and cook over moderately low heat for 8 minutes. Uncover and raise heat; cook off any moisture that has accumulated.

Beat the eggs, cream, salt, and pepper together in a large bowl. Gradually add and stir in the mushroom mixture. Pour into the prepared pastry. Sprinkle the cheese and parsley on top and dot with the remaining tablespoon of butter. Bake for 25 to 30 minutes. Serves 4–6.

Note: If you are preparing this quiche for the freezer, use a metal rather than a glass or porcelain pie plate. Wrap tightly and freeze on a level surface. To bake, unwrap and place directly in a 375° oven for about 55 minutes, or until the custard has set.

Pâte Brisée

This recipe makes enough for one 9- to 9½-inch quiche.

1 cup unbleached flour
1 teaspoon salt
6 tablespoons butter, cut

into small pats
3–4 tablespoons ice water

Combine the flour and salt in the bowl of a food processor. Process briefly. Add the butter and process briefly with on-off motions until mixture resembles coarse meal. Add the water cautiously in small amounts, and process with brief on-off motions just until the mixture forms small balls. Turn out onto wax paper, flatten into a disk, sprinkle with flour, wrap, and chill for at least 30 minutes before rolling out.

Note: Very moist fillings may leak through the pricked holes in the bottom of a pie or tart shell or make it soggy. To "waterproof" the pastry, brush the fully baked shell while it is still hot with beaten egg white.

Mushrooms à la Greque

Mushrooms are frequently served this way in French restaurants as a light first course or as part of a mixed hors d'oeuvre tray. I have always felt the flavor was interesting but that something was missing. For me it turned out to be the addition of a hot pepper, which seems to boost all the spices.

2 cups water
¾ cup olive oil
⅓ cup lemon juice (about
   1½ lemons)
6 sprigs parsley
2 garlic cloves, minced
½ teaspoon dried thyme
1 bay leaf, crumbled
1 tablespoon coriander
   seeds, crushed

10 peppercorns
½ crumbled dried hot red
   pepper
1½ pounds small
   cultivated mushrooms,
   whole, or medium
   mushrooms, quartered
Salt and freshly ground
   pepper to taste

Combine the water, oil, and lemon juice in an enamel-lined or stainless-steel saucepan and bring to the boil.

Put the parsley, garlic, thyme, bay leaf, coriander seeds, peppercorns, and hot pepper flakes in a cheesecloth bag and add. Add the mushrooms a handful at a time, reduce heat, and simmer uncovered for 5 minutes, stirring occasionally.

Drain the mushrooms, reserving the marinade. Boil marinade down by half. Discard spice bag and let marinade cool. Pour over mushrooms and refrigerate overnight. Scoop out and serve at room temperature moistened with a little of the marinade, a little additional oil, and salt and pepper if desired. Serves 4–6.

Note: You can do exactly the same thing with a medium head of cauliflower, cut into small flowerets. Cooking time is the same.

Serving suggestion: As a first course, as part of a selection of hors d'oeuvres, with drinks, or as a quick snack.

Barley Mushroom Soup

This is a hearty meal-in-a-pot that has nostalgic overtones for anyone of Middle European extraction. I grew up on it.

4–5 dried Polish
   mushrooms
2 pieces beef flanken,
   about 2½ pounds
Cracked beef bone,
   optional
Salt, if desired
2 quarts water,
   approximately
2 carrots, peeled, cut in
   half, and halved
   lengthwise

2 medium onions, peeled
   and halved
1 celery rib, cut in half
1 parsley root, optional
1 parsnip, scraped and
   halved, optional
¼ cup pearl barley, rinsed
   (or 1–2 tablespoons
   more if you like a
   thick soup)
Chopped parsley or dill
   for garnish

Soak the mushrooms in hot water to cover for 20 minutes.

While they soak, put the meat, the well-rinsed bone, and salt in a heavy soup kettle. Add water to cover, bring to a boil, and boil for 5 minutes. Skim any gray scum (wipe sides of pot with paper towel if necessary to remove it), cover, lower heat, and let simmer gently.

Line a sieve with a dampened paper towel, drain the liquid from the mushrooms, and add to the pot. Chop the mushrooms coarsely and add. Add the carrots, onions, celery rib, parsley root, and parsnip. Cover and simmer for 1 hour. Add the barley and simmer ½ to 1 hour more, or until the meat readily falls from the bones. Remove meat and bones; discard bones and set meat aside covered with foil. Remove carrots and reserve; remove and discard the other vegetables.

Let soup cool and remove fat, which will have risen to the surface. Dice reserved carrots or push through a strainer and return to the soup. Cut meat into spoon-size pieces and return to the soup. Reheat and taste for seasoning. Sprinkle with parsley or dill. Serve as a one-course meal with garlic bread. Serves 4–6.

Note: While the bone adds flavor to the broth, it also makes it greasy. If you have time, carefully chill and skim the fat from the top. The warmed meat may also be served as a separate course following the soup, accompanied by horseradish, good rye bread, and pickles.

Enoki Mushroom and Snow Pea Salad

½–¾ **pound fresh snow peas**

3 heads Bibb lettuce, or 1 head Boston

1 package (3 ounces) enoki mushrooms (see note)

1 recipe sesame vinaigrette (see p. 375).

Trim ends and string the snow peas. Bring a pot of salted water to the boil and blanch peas for 3 minutes. Rinse immediately under cold running water, drain, and pat dry.

Separate the leaves of the lettuce, wash well, and dry.

Trim and discard the rough end of the mushrooms. Rinse gently and pat dry.

Arrange the lettuce leaves in a fanlike pattern on four individual serving plates. Arrange the snow peas in the same way over the lettuce, and top each plate with a cluster of mushrooms. Drizzle with sesame vinaigrette. Serves 4.

Note: If enoki mushrooms are not available, substitute ¼ pound small white cultivated mushrooms, thinly sliced.

Okra

Hibiscus esculentus

The ridged and tapered okra was introduced into the western hemisphere by slaves from Africa, where it is an important vegetable in a number of dishes. It is quite popular in Egypt and Morocco, and from there, presumably, the taste spread to the Middle East and to India, where it is called ladyfinger.

The African word for okra, *ngombo,* was shortened to *gumbo.* Gumbo originally meant the vegetable, but became the name of a stew the American Indians had originally thickened with filé, a powder made from dried young sassafras leaves, until the mucilaginous quality of okra proved superior. Interestingly enough, gumbo is now the name of any Southern stew that contains filé, but not necessarily okra.

Okra remains quite popular in the South, where it is coated with cornmeal and deep-fried, or combined with corn and tomatoes. Though it has a fresh pleasant taste and a special affinity for tomatoes, onions, eggplant, and spices, the very mucilaginous quality for which it is prized by some also earns it the opprobrium of others.

To Buy

Select small, bright green okra, about 3 inches long. Pass over large pods, which can be stringy and tough, or those browned at the edges. Fresh okra is available from late spring through early fall. One pound will serve 3 to 4 people.

To Store

Refrigerate and use promptly. Okra molds easily.

To Prepare

If using whole, to keep the liquid contained, wash the okra in cold water, scrub lightly with a vegetable brush if light fuzz is present, and remove the stems and tips, but do not puncture the pods. When okra is older or its thickening property is desired, clean as directed and slice into rounds.

To Cook

Boiled: Simmer whole pods for 7 to 9 minutes. (Overcooked okra becomes slimy and disagreeable.) Dress with melted butter and a squeeze of lemon.

Fried: Prepare 1 pound of small whole okra and parboil for 5 minutes. Drain and pat dry. Sift 1 cup of flour with salt to taste, stir in 1 cup of milk, and add 1 beaten egg. Heat oil in a deep fryer to 375° and, with tongs, dip okra into the batter, letting excess drip back into the bowl. Fry, a few pieces at a time, for about 2 minutes, until golden. Drain on paper towelling and keep fried pieces warm until all are done. Serves 4.

Bamia

(Okra Stew)

Bamia is the Arabic name for okra and for this dish, which is eaten throughout the Middle East. It is important that the okra be young and uniformly sized.

2 tablespoons clarified
butter (p. 404), or 1
tablespoon butter and 1
tablespoon vegetable oil
2 garlic cloves, peeled and
crushed
2 tablespoons freshly
ground roasted
coriander seeds (p. 393),
or 1 teaspoon dried
ground coriander

2 medium onions, chopped
1½ pounds small okra,
washed and trimmed
14-ounce can Italian plum
tomatoes, drained and
chopped
1 cup chicken or vegetable
broth
Salt and freshly ground
pepper
3 tablespoons lemon juice

Heat the butter in a medium saucepan and add the
garlic. Cook for 1 to 2 minutes over moderate heat
until golden but not brown, then stir in the coriander
seeds. Cook for 2 minutes more, add the onions, and
continue cooking until the onions are golden. Add the
okra and tomatoes and cook 5 minutes more.

Add the broth, season to taste with salt and pepper,
bring to a boil, cover, and simmer gently for 30
minutes. Add the lemon juice and simmer for another
10 minutes. Serve with rice pilaf. Serves 4.

Southern Okra and Corn Stew

This dish is found all over the South, with slight
regional variations. Louisiana has the spiciest version,
made with a red chili pepper, seeds removed, and a
minced garlic clove or two.

3 tablespoons butter
1 medium onion, chopped
1 small green pepper,
seeded, deribbed, and
finely chopped
2 ripe tomatoes, peeled,
seeded, and coarsely
chopped, or a 14-ounce

can Italian tomatoes,
drained and chopped
½ pound small okra, cut
into ½-inch slices
2 cups corn kernels
Salt and freshly ground
pepper
Several dashes cayenne

Heat the butter in a flameproof casserole and sauté
the onion until wilted. Add the green pepper and sauté
until soft. Add the tomatoes and okra. Cover and cook
over gentle heat for about 15 minutes, or until the okra

is tender. Add the corn, salt, pepper, and cayenne to taste, cover and cook 5 minutes longer. Serves 4.

Serving suggestion: Serve with any kind of chicken cooked without a sauce, or with grilled shrimp. Precede with curried Cream of Zucchini Soup and follow with a tossed green salad and cheese. Vegetarians can have the stew over rice and use the same menu.

Onion Family
(Allium)

Whenever I am tempted to complain about the high cost of some food or other, I console myself with the notion that the *real* cooking indispensables, onions and family, are quite cheap. We take them for granted, but we certainly can't do without them. At the height of the Civil War, General Grant fired off an urgent message to the War Department: "I will not move my Army without onions." Grant's interest was not purely culinary; he believed they prevented dystentery and other ailments. Indeed, onions were thought to have medicinal powers as early as the time of Hippocrates, who thought they helped eyesight. But Robert Louis Stevenson didn't know his onions when he called one "a rose among roots"; the onion is a bulb, a member of the lily family that hybridizers have been working on for years to make it ideal: heavy, sweet, and uniformly sized. One such effort resulted not only in a brand-name onion but an onion war.

The hybrid yellow onion grown in Vidalia, Georgia, is so admired for its mild sweetness, it brings twice the price of most other onions. (Local people say it can be eaten like an apple.) When four Georgia counties each claimed to be the true home of the Vidalia onion, a judge had to be called in, who ruled that only an onion grown within thirty air miles of Vidalia could bear the name. Today Vidalia onions are shipped all over the world; they are available from May to mid-June.

Two members of the onion family, chives and leeks, are discussed separately—leeks in their own section and chives in the herb section.

Onions are divided into several distinct groups according to use:

Cooking onions: The all-purpose pungent yellow onions. Also called storage onions, standard onions, globe onions, boiling onions.

Sweet onions: Large, mild onions that are less pungent than yellow onions. They are also called Bermuda onions and Spanish onions; though the names are used interchangeably, the Bermuda is white and has flattened ends, while the Spanish onion, the largest of the sweet onions, is more spherical and may be yellow or white. They are good for eating raw and, because of their size, for making french-fried onion rings.

Red onions: Also called purple onions, these may be round or ovoid, depending on where they are grown, and are a variety of the standard onion. The Italian red onion, prized for its sweetness, was so called because it used to be imported in long braids from Italy. Now the term is used interchangeably for any red onion, though a true Italian variety does come to market from California and Mexico. Sweet red onions add color and a gentle onion flavor to salads of all kinds. Don't cook them, however; they bleed all over other food.

White onions: These are a variety of cooking onion sometimes called silverskins, and range from tiny pearl onions, the kind used in gibsons, to golf-ball size. The average size is 1 inch in diameter—ideal for pickling, creaming, or using in stews. The large ones tend to be less sweet.

Scallions: Also called green onions and spring onions, they can be simply immature onions, harvested while young, or a specific variety of the onion family called scallions or bunching onions. For culinary use they are pretty much interchangeable. The true scallion has a straight-sided white end, a finer texture, and a slightly less assertive flavor than the more bulbous bottomed spring onion. With either it is usually the white and pale green part that is used; the deep green leaves tend to be peppery.

In Oriental cookery scallions are preferred to onions because of the visual appeal they contribute. Stir-frying cooks them quickly and actually enhances their color.

In Louisiana scallions are called shallots. But they're not.

Shallots: Until rather recently shallots were the exotic member of the onion family, but today they are available in most supermarkets. Because they cook quickly, they are ideal for sauces, imparting a subtle mild onion presence when the standard onion might be too aggressive. It is hard to imagine a beurre blanc or a béarnaise sauce without them. They make many ordinary dishes special: a prosaic chicken salad, for example, is quite a different dish flavored with shallots instead of onion.

To Buy

Select onions individually rather than buying them bagged. The price is higher, but bad ones can be avoided this way. Look for clean, dry, shiny skins and firm, small necks. Size does not affect quality. Pass up those with sprouting green shoots or soft or wet spots, a sign of rot. One medium onion will give you about ½ cup chopped. Allow 4 to 6 small white onions per serving.

Dehydrated onions are a convenience food I have never found any need to use.

Scallions should have crisp green leaves and firm white stems that are long, not bulb-shaped.

Shallots should be firm, with dry, papery skins; avoid shriveled, sprouted shallots or those with gray mold spots.

To Store

Onions and shallots: Circulation of cool air is the key to good onion storage, which is best in a cool, dark place, and ideally in a single layer. Do not refrigerate onions or shallots except once they are cut. Then wrap them tightly in plastic and use as soon as possible. Scallions are quite perishable. Keep them in a plastic bag in the crisper drawer of the refrigerator, and do not wash them until just prior to use.

To Prepare

Peel and chop or slice onions just before cooking, because the flavor becomes strong and acrid when the flesh is exposed to air.

White onions: These can be difficult to peel because the outer skin is snug. Drop them in boiling water for 1 minute, then transfer to a bowl of cold water. Trim both ends, and the skin should slip off easily. Pierce a cross in the root end with the tip of a sharp knife to allow even cooking.

Yellow, sweet, and red onions: Cut a thin slice off both ends, then halve the onion, and the skin will peel away easily. Or leave whole and, after the thin slice is removed, lift strips of the outer layer and pull them away, using your paring knife.

Shallots: Cut off the tops and tails. Slit the thin outer skin with the tip of a sharp knife and pull. Slice or chop as you would onions, but on a smaller scale. Because they have less liquid than onions, they do not become mushy when quickly chopped in a food processor.

Chopping onions: Working quickly with a

good, sharp cook's knife is the best solution to avoid tears when cutting onions. To chop, lay a halved onion cut side down on the work surface. Make a series of parallel vertical cuts down through the onion (drawing 1). Next make horizontal cuts through the stem end (drawing 2). Then make several up-and-down cuts along the curved surface at cross angles to the first series of cuts, and the onion will be diced (drawing 3). If you wish finer pieces, hold the point of your blade down on the work surface and chop with the heel of the knife until you have the desired fineness. Minced onions are very finely chopped.

Chopping onions in the food processor is tricky; they turn to mush very quickly and then are too wet to sauté properly. If you're determined, cut onions in large cubes first and chop with 4 to 6 half-second pulses—no more.

To take the pungency out of chopped onions that will not be cooked, such as in tuna or chicken salad, put them in a strainer and pour boiling water over. Follow with cold, and press water out with your hand. If chopped raw onions are to be served raw, as for caviar or steak tartare, rinse after chopping under cold water and then press out the water by hand or in a towel. This will prevent them from darkening.

Slicing onions: I also start with onion halves—the flat surface makes a firm base against which to cut. Large Bermudas to be sliced for onion rings or hamburgers are an exception.

Grated onions: Because there are no big pieces,

this method gives you the gentlest onion flavor, desirable in stuffings, meat fillings, and meat loaf, when

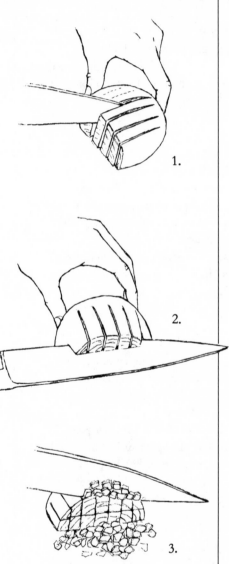

1.

2.

3.

the heat penetration isn't great enough to cook the onion. To grate in a food processor, cut a medium onion into cubes, add 3 tablespoons water, and process for 15 seconds. Or use the medium side of a four-sided grater.

To Cook

Baked whole: Use large, well-shaped yellow onions for this. Do not peel. Cut a narrow slice off the root end so they can stand firmly. Place in a shallow baking dish, add about ½ inch of water, and bake at 400° for 1 to 1½ hours, until soft. Peel away the outer skin and serve with butter and fresh pepper.

Charcoal-grilled: Peel Bermuda onions, remove stem ends, and cut into halves or thirds crosswise. Brush well with oil or a marinade and place in a hinged basket. Grill, turning as needed, until both sides are brown and crusty and the onion is quite soft.

Red onion and mayonnaise sandwiches: I first learned of this simple delight from James Beard. He used rye bread, I use homemade oatmeal bread; either way they are the best thing you can imagine on a picnic, along with roast chicken and deviled eggs. The onion should be sliced paper-thin, the mayonnaise freshly made, and whatever bread you use should be terrific.

Onion Soufflé

No, it is not a mistake; there is no flour in this incredibly light and elegant soufflé, the creation of an inventive and talented cook named Lauren Kaye, who is "not a vegetarian" but prefers not to eat meat. The onion base, thickened with a little cream and egg yolks, serves the function of the usual béchamel. There is almost no main course it could not precede with distinction.

Onion Soufflé, continued

5 large onions, about 1½ pounds
3 tablespoons butter
Salt and freshly ground pepper

3 tablespoons plus 1 teaspoon heavy cream
3 eggs at room temperature, separated
1 additional egg white

Select a heavy skillet with a lid in which to cook the onions, cut a circle of foil to fit, and butter the foil.

Slice the onions thinly and separate into rings. Melt 2 tablespoons of the butter in the skillet, add the onions, spread them out evenly, and season with salt and pepper. Cover with the buttered foil, pressing it down to cover them closely. Cover with the lid and gently simmer for 45 to 55 minutes, stirring occasionally. The onions are finished when they can be easily crushed between two fingers.

Preheat the oven to 425°. Butter a 5-cup soufflé dish with the remaining tablespoon of butter.

Puree the onions in a food processor or food mill. Put the puree in a small skillet and set over low heat. Cook, stirring constantly, to evaporate the excess liquid —about 5 minutes. Add the 3 tablespoons cream and continue cooking and stirring for another 5 minutes. Remove from heat.

Beat the egg yolks with the remaining teaspoon of cream. Stir in a tablespoon or so of the onion mixture, then combine with the rest of the onion puree, stirring constantly. The mixture will thicken. Add salt and pepper; it should taste rather highly seasoned.

Beat the egg whites until stiff but not dry. Add one-quarter of them to the onion mixture and stir in. Pour this on top of the remaining whites and fold in. Do not overblend.

Pour into the prepared dish and bake for 12 to 15 minutes, or until puffed and golden. Serve at once. Serves 4–6

Note: The onion base may be prepared 3 or 4 hours ahead. Reheat gently so the egg yolks do not curdle before proceeding.

Onion-Cinnamon Tart

This is an adaptation of the onion-cinnamon tart served at Mark's, a famous private supper club in London. It is an elegant and unusual first course.

1 recipe pâte brisée (p. 177)
3 tablespoons butter
2½ cups thinly sliced yellow onions, about ½ pound
½ teaspoon salt
2 eggs and 2 additional egg yolks
1 cup heavy cream
Pinch saffron
3 tablespoons currants, plumped in boiling water for 15 minutes
¼ teaspoon cinnamon
¼ teaspoon ground ginger
Dash nutmeg
1 tablespoon sugar
Several dashes cayenne
Fresh black pepper

Preheat the oven to 400°. Roll out the pastry as thin as possible and use it to line a 9-inch tart tin with a removable bottom, or a flan ring. Place on a foil-covered cookie sheet and bake blind for 10 minutes. Cool on a rack and lower oven heat to 350°.

Heat the butter in a skillet and sauté the onions until pale gold. Season with salt and set aside.

In a medium-size bowl, lightly beat the eggs and yolks. Put the cream in a small saucepan, stir in the saffron, and heat until scalding. Let cool slightly, add a bit to the eggs, then beat the eggs into the cream and pour back into the bowl.

To the onions add the currants, cinnamon, ginger, nutmeg, sugar, cayenne, and pepper. Blend well and stir into the egg mixture. Taste and check for salt.

Pour half the mixture into the prebaked shell and set it on the cookie sheet on the middle level of the oven. Pull out the shelf slightly and add the remainder. (This is to avoid spills.) Bake for 25 to 30 minutes, or until slightly puffed and firm. Serve hot or warm. Serves 6–8 as a first course.

Jane Salzfass Freiman's Braised Stuffed Onions

This is a perfect example of meat used as a condiment —a mere half-pound of inexpensive pork and veal is used to flavor a dish that will feed six. Try these tasty

Jane Freiman's Braised Stuffed Onions, continued
onions as a first course with a fish dinner, or with pasta, before or after. They are also a great buffet item.

6 medium (about 2½-inch diameter) yellow onions, peeled
1 tablespoon olive oil
1 medium garlic clove, peeled and minced
¼ pound ground veal
¼ pound ground pork
3 tablespoons dried bread

crumbs, or more, if necessary
1 teaspoon dried ground sage
1½ tablespoons minced parsley
Salt and freshly ground pepper
1 egg yolk

Braising Liquid

2 tablespoons unsalted butter
2 tablespoons olive oil
1 tablespoon sugar
¼ cup white wine vinegar

1 cup beef broth, or more as needed
Additional minced parsley for garnish

Plunge onions into 4 quarts of rapidly boiling water and blanch for 7 minutes. Remove and refresh under cold running water, then set aside to cool.

Heat the oil in a medium skillet, add the garlic, and cook until it softens. Add the meat, stirring to break up lumps, and cook until it loses color and is thoroughly cooked. Use a slotted spoon to remove mixture to a mixing bowl. Cool.

Add the bread crumbs, sage, parsley, salt, pepper, and egg yolk to the mixing bowl. Mix thoroughly.

Trim the bottoms of the onions so they stand upright. Cut off and discard the top quarter of each onion. With a grapefruit knife or spoon, carefully remove the center of each onion, leaving a shell 3 or 4 layers thick. Chop enough of the onion centers to make ⅓ cup and add to the stuffing mixture. Reserve remainder for another use. This stuffing should be crumbly, but you may add more bread crumbs if you like. Fill each onion with the meat and mound the top.

Heat the butter and oil for the braising liquid in a saucepan just large enough to hold all the onions. When bubbling, add the sugar and stir over low heat until it caramelizes. Remove the skillet from the heat and set it aside to cool for 5 minutes.

Stir in the vinegar and beef broth and bring to a boil, stirring to dissolve bits of caramelized sugar. Add the onions to the skillet and, if necessary, add additional beef broth to come two-thirds up the sides of the onions.

Bring liquid to a rapid simmer. Cover and simmer slowly until onions are tender when pierced with the tip of a small sharp knife—about 20 minutes. Remove and keep warm on a heated serving dish.

Reduce the braising liquid to about 1 cup by simmering rapidly until it becomes slightly thickened and shiny. Strain, adjust seasoning to taste, then spoon sauce over and around onions. Garnish with additional parsley and serve immediately. Serves 6.

Confiture d'Oignons

A distinct product of the nouvelle cuisine, onion marmalade is here to stay. It always elicits the pleasantest sounds of satisfaction and can be served in a variety of ways—in small croustades or on rounds of lightly toasted French bread or crackers as an hors d'oeuvre, or as a meat accompaniment.

Vegetable oil	**1 cup red wine**
1½ pounds yellow onions,	**⅓ cup sherry wine vinegar**
thinly sliced	**Salt and freshly ground**
¾ cup sugar	**pepper to taste**

Preheat the oven to 400° and place rack in lowest position.

Heat the oil in a heavy 12-inch skillet and lightly brown the onions, turning them frequently with a wooden spoon and breaking up the rings so they cook evenly. The onions should be light gold, not crisp and dark brown, so watch them carefully.

In a small, heavy stainless steel or enamel-lined saucepan, combine the sugar and the wine and cook over brisk heat until reduced to a thick syrup (230° on a candy thermometer). This will take about 10 minutes. Stir in the vinegar and add mixture to the onions. Mix the two well, and season to taste with salt and pepper.

Put the onion mixture in a 9 × 12-inch baking dish and bake on the lowest shelf for 1 hour. Stir occasionally. At the end the mixture should be deep amber and jamlike in consistency. Do not let it burn, however, or it will be bitter. Correct seasoning and serve at room temperature, spread on lightly toasted rounds of good French bread. Makes about 1½ cups.

Notes: If you use Spanish or Bermuda onions, reduce the amount of sugar somewhat, as they tend to be sweeter. The marmalade will keep for as long as three months in a closed jar in the refrigerator.

Onion Sauce

Brown onions lightly as for Confiture d'Oignons (p. 193), but do not preheat the oven. When sautéing is completed, puree in a food processor, return to the saucepan, and cook over very low heat for a few minutes, stirring constantly. Add 3 tablespoons fruit vinegar bit by bit, tasting frequently, just until sauce has a bite but is still oniony and gentle. Gradually add up to ½ cup of sugar, until a sweet-tart balance to your taste is achieved. Season with salt and pepper, if desired. Use as a bed for broiled or grilled fish. May be prepared ahead, refrigerated, and carefully reheated (watch for scorching).

John Clancy's Fried Onion Rings

Make lots of these—they are addictive!

1½ cups all-purpose flour	3 large Bermuda or
1½ cups beer, fresh or	Spanish onions
flat, any temperature	3–4 cups vegetable oil

Sift the flour into a large bowl. Gradually add the beer, blending with a wooden spoon. Cover and let sit at room temperature for about 3 hours.

Preheat the oven to 200°. Line jelly-roll tins with

paper towels or brown paper. Peel the onions and slice ¼ inch thick. Separate into rings and set aside.

Pour oil into a heavy frying pan to the depth of 2 inches, or add to a deep fryer. Heat to 375°.

Using tongs, dip the onion rings into the batter and lower carefully into the hot fat. Fry until evenly golden all over, turning once. Lift out and place on the paper-lined pan to keep warm until all are done. Serves 4.

Note: These rings will stay crisp for a couple of hours and may be reheated by placing in a 400° oven for several minutes.

Onion Soup Gratinée

This is the kind of onion soup that was ritualistically consumed at the old Les Halles market in Paris after a night on the town. For the workers there, it was an early breakfast. It is a wonderful thing to eat at any time.

4 tablespoons butter	4 cups water
2 tablespoon vegetable oil	Salt and freshly ground
4 cups thinly sliced yellow	pepper
onions (see note)	18 thin slices French bread
2 teaspoons flour	3 cups grated Gruyère
4 cups beef broth	cheese (about 1 pound)
½ cup sherry, optional	

Heat the butter and oil in a heavy soup pot and sauté the onions over low to medium heat until lightly browned—about 15 minutes. Sprinkle with the flour and cook 1 or 2 minutes more, or until it disappears. Add the broth, sherry and water, bring to a boil, cover, reduce heat, and simmer for 30 minutes. Season to taste. (May be prepared ahead to this point.)

Preheat the oven to 400°. Toast the bread slices on a rimmed cookie sheet in the oven. Put 3 slices each into 6 earthenware soup bowls. Put the bowls on the cookie sheet and fill halfway with the onion soup; let the bread soften, then fill to the top. (This is important to give a base to the cheese crust that follows.)

Sprinkle cheese on top of each bowl, pressing it around the edges so that the crust will adhere when it forms. Be generous with the cheese—use about ½ cup per bowl—but be careful not to push it under the liquid. Put the bowls in the preheated oven for about 30 minutes—until cheese is melted and a golden crust has formed. Serves 6.

Note: If your onions are very strong, try using a Bermuda onion for part of the requirement.

The soup itself is so tasty that you may use it as a simple onion soup, without the cheese or bread.

Garlic

All sorts of folklore is built around garlic, attributing to it powers of banishment ranging from germs to vampires. There are few cuisines in the world that do not use it and few regions that do not cultivate it.

Garlic is a bulb made up of a number of separate parts called *cloves.* The entire bulb is a *head.* Fresh garlic is so universally available and so easy to keep, it is a shame to ruin dishes with the various processed forms of garlic like garlic powder, made from ground dehydrated garlic; garlic salt, a blend of the powder and salt; or garlic extract, which is bitter.

To Buy

Look for firm, fat heads with well-developed cloves. Shriveled, yellowed garlic is old and will be bitter. I like to see what I buy and prefer loose garlic over the kind that comes in boxes, which invariably contain cloves too small to handle easily. Large heads mean large cloves and less peeling time.

To Store

I keep my garlic in a little open wire basket hung on a

hook near the window, but not in the sun. I try to break off only those cloves I will be using; once they are detached, individual cloves dry out after a week, while an intact head lasts many weeks. Don't refrigerate, as the moisture encourages sprouting.

To Prepare

Cut off any coarse peel at the root end and the tip. Then smack the clove lightly but firmly with the broad side of a heavy knife. This breaks the skin and gets you started. To peel a number of cloves, put them in a bowl and pour boiling water over them. Let sit for 5 minutes, then rinse under cold water. The skins will slip off easily.

If you are a purist, split a clove and, if there is a green line or shoot in the center, flick it out. It is bitter.

To chop or mince, use exactly the same cutting principles described for onions, but on a smaller scale, using a smaller sharp knife. The finer the mince, the stronger the garlic flavor will be.

Many serious cooks object to using a garlic press, saying they are hard to clean. This is true, though a strong brush does the job. Another objection is that garlic put through a press gives the most pungent result. I don't object, as I adore garlic, though I do confine its use this way to very hearty dishes—tomato sauces and the like, in which a definite garlic flavor is an asset. I also like the press because I believe it prevents garlic breath by holding back the woody fiber and the green pith, both hard-to-digest parts that remain in one's stomach for a long time, sending forth their heady odor.

If you find yourself with an unpleasant garlic aftertaste or you have eaten a lot and find people strangely distanced, chlorophyll is the antidote, and munching a handful of fresh parsley is the best way to obtain it quickly.

To Cook

The mildest garlic flavor is obtained by boiling whole cloves, unchopped, as in a soup or stew. Unpeeled cloves added to a roasting pan gently flavor the drippings and offer a delicious bonus: the softened cooked pulp, which is quite mild, may be squeezed and spread on toasted French bread. Using garlic in a marinade is another good way to instill its flavor gently in food.

Garlic should be sautéed very carefully, never to the point that it turns brownish-black, which makes it bitter and hard to digest.

Garlic in salad: I don't have the patience to rub a bowl with a cut clove, and I don't like the smell on my hands, so I simply let a crushed clove steep in fresh vinaigrette before using. Remove it before dressing the salad, lest someone eat it by mistake.

Elephant garlic: A giant garlic with cloves the size of orange sections that has appeared in specialty markets over the past few years. I find it a novelty for which I have no particular use, other than its ease of peeling.

The growers advise eating it raw or dicing it into salads. But my family certainly knew I was around for the next twelve hours after I once ate it raw. Other cooking possibilities include sautéing slices in parsley butter for 2 or 3 minutes to garnish meat, or tossing sautéed slices in olive oil and combining with cooked chard or spinach.

Baked Garlic

To the best of my knowledge, this now-famous dish was invented at Alice Waters's Chez Panisse Restaurant in California. It is not worth making it with anything less than firm, plump, young heads of white garlic.

6 whole heads white garlic	**Good fruity olive oil**
4 tablespoons unsalted butter in thin pats	**Salt and freshly ground pepper**

Preheat the oven to 250°.

With a sharp knife, make an incision in the outer skin of each garlic head around the middle, about ¾ inch above the base. Lift and discard the outer skin above this point, leaving it intact below, and leaving the inner skin covering each individual clove undisturbed.

Put the garlic heads base down in a baking dish just large enough to hold them. Top with the butter pats and drizzle each with olive oil. Season with salt and pepper.

Cover with heavy foil and bake the garlic for 30 minutes. Remove foil, baste, and bake an additional 1½ hours, basting every 15 minutes. Garlic should be very tender. Serve each person a whole head, accompanied by lightly toasted, crusty peasant bread and fresh goat cheese. Each clove can be picked up and the puree inside squeezed onto the bread. Serves 6.

Note: If you have fresh thyme, scatter 2 or 3 branches among the garlic before baking.

Sopa de Ajo

A classic soup from Castile. In Cuba, it used to be the traditional cure for the "morning after."

3 tablespoons olive oil	**bread**
5 garlic cloves, peeled	**5 cups hot water**
½ teaspoon paprika	**1 teaspoon salt**
4 slices Italian or French	**4 eggs**

Heat the oil in a heavy skillet and sauté the garlic to a golden brown (not too brown or it will turn bitter). Add the paprika and bread slices and sauté until lightly browned. Add the hot water and salt and bring to a boil. Cook over low heat for about 10 minutes.

Heat four ovenproof soup bowls. Divide the soup

among them and heat until the liquid bubbles. Break one egg into each bowl and serve. The eggs will cook in the liquid and may be consumed when done to the eater's taste. The egg should not be allowed to harden, however; the yolk should blend with the liquid and thicken it. Serves 4.

Herbed Garlic Bread

1 stick butter, softened
2 garlic cloves, put
   through a press
1 tablespoon lemon juice
¼ teaspoon dried oregano

2 tablespoons chopped
   parsley
Salt and freshly ground
   pepper

Preheated oven to 275°. Cream the butter with the garlic. Beat in the lemon juice drop by drop. Blend the oregano with the parsley and mix into the butter. Season to taste with salt and pepper. Slice Italian or French bread slightly on the diagonal and spread one side of each slice generously with the butter. Wrap in foil and bake for 10 minutes. Open the foil and bake 10 minutes longer. Enough for two 28-inch French baguettes or four smallish Italian loaves.

Preparation note: You may use almost any combination of herbs that strikes your fancy. These have a definite Italian cast. One of my favorite blends is 1 tablespoon chopped fresh tarragon leaves and 1 tablespoon or so of chopped chives, used as indicated, omitting the oregano.

Skordalia

An intensely garlicky sauce thickened with potatoes and bread, skordalia is indispensable in Greece to a variety of fried foods, in particular squash, eggplant, and fish. It can be served thick, as the recipe here will produce, or thinned with 1½ cups fish stock when used with fish. Walnuts are sometimes used instead of potatoes as the thickener, and vinegar may replace the lemon juice. In any form, it is not for the fainthearted.

5 slices home-style white bread, crusts removed	and boiled
	¼ teaspoon salt
3 fat garlic cloves, or more	¼ cup olive oil
	3 tablespoons lemon juice
1 medium potato, peeled	

Wet the bread with cold water, squeeze the moisture out with your hands, and crumble into the container of a food processor or blender. Add the garlic cloves and process until well blended. Drain and add the potato and salt, and process again. With the motor running, pour in the oil in a slow, steady stream and then add the lemon juice. Taste and add more salt or lemon juice if needed. The mixture should be quite stiff and rather shiny. Can be kept refrigerated in a covered jar for a week to ten days. Makes about 2 cups.

Parsnips
(Pastinaca sativa)

Long eclipsed by its cousin the carrot, this feathery-leaved végétable has had more than the usual ups and downs of popularity and in my opinion is ripe for rediscovery. Perhaps its medieval reputation as an aphrodisiac will provoke new interest. Then the special sweet, nutty flavor of the parsnip may gather fans even if its amatory performance proves negligible.

Though they are not outstanding in nutritive value, parsnips are inexpensive, filling, low in calories, and a good garden crop. There is a long-standing belief that a frost is needed to improve their flavor because cold temperatures change their starch to sugar, but it has recently been proved that near-freezing weather will do the same thing.

Parsnips may be boiled, steamed, or prepared au gratin. They have a special affinity for rich meats like beef, lamb, turkey, and ham, and are particularly good fried, which seems to intensify their sweetness.

To Buy

It is often difficult to find really good parsnips, perhaps because there is no steady demand for them. Though the big season is winter and early spring, they are often available all year, mostly in plastic packs, with likely as not a mix of fat and thin ones, which somewhat complicates the cooking times. If they are bagged, ask your dealer how long he's had them and if you may open several packs to choose uniformly sized ones. Allow about 1 pound for 3 persons.

Look for those that are unblemished, unwrinkled, and firm. Very large parsnips usually have a woody core and are fibrous and rather unpleasant on the tongue.

To Store

Refrigerate unwashed in a plastic bag. Parsnips will keep up to a month.

To Prepare

Wash in cool water and peel with a swivel-bladed peeler. If you are cooking whole small parsnips, slip off the skins after cooking. Core only if they are very large and pithy.

To Cook

Boiled: Cut peeled parsnips into 2-inch chunks. Cover with cold water, add salt, and bring to a boil.

Cover and cook over moderate heat until tender when pierced with a fork—10 to 12 minutes. Roll in melted butter. Season with salt and pepper.

Steamed: Put 1 inch of water in the bottom of a steamer, bring to a boil, and put either whole, unpeeled small parsnips or peeled 2-inch chunks in the basket. Steam for 7 to 10 minutes. Slip off skins under running water, if unpeeled.

Baked: Trim, scrub, and peel 1½ pounds medium parsnips. Cut in half, then halve lengthwise. (If very fat at one end, halve only that end and leave the slender end whole.) Melt 4 tablespoons butter in an ovenproof baking dish, add the parsnips, turn to coat, and bake uncovered in a preheated 400° oven for 30 to 45 minutes, until lightly browned and tender. Turn once or twice during cooking, so they color evenly. Season with salt and pepper, and serve. Chicken fat, beef drippings, or melted suet may be used instead of butter; drain excess fat before serving. Serves 4–5.

Parsnips and potatoes roasted with lamb or chicken:
Cut peeled parsnips so that the fatter end is about 2 inches in length and the skinny end is longer. Add to the roasting pan with cut-up potatoes. Baste and turn in the drippings, keeping in mind that they will be done in a far shorter time than the potatoes. Remove and keep warm, then mix the two vegetables when serving.

Pureed: Cut peeled parsnips into chunks and boil or steam for about 10 minutes or until tender. Put through a food mill and add your favorite enrichment—butter alone or butter and cream—enough to give the consistency of soft mashed potatoes. Season to taste with salt and pepper and, if you like, a dash of cinnamon. Chopped parsley is nice added at the end. This can be made ahead and kept warm or reheated; neither texture nor flavor suffers.

Fried: Peel parsnips and cut crosswise into 1½-inch pieces. Blanch in boiling water for 5 minutes. Drain and dry on a kitchen towel. Slice thin and add to a skillet in which you have melted 2 tablespoons butter. Sprinkle with 2 teaspoons sugar and sauté until golden brown.

Puree of Parsnips and Carrots

Even people who think they don't like parsnips eat this with gusto and usually take seconds. The taste is like carrots with oomph!

4 or 5 medium parsnips, about 1 pound	**Freshly ground pepper**
4 or 5 medium carrots, about ½ pound	**2 tablespoons butter at room temperature**
Salt, if desired	**½ cup cream or milk**
	Several gratings nutmeg

Trim off parsnip root ends and tops, scrape and cut in half crosswise. Cut each piece in half lengthwise and then into halves or quarters. Leave thin ends whole.

Scrape the carrots and cut into rounds about ¼-inch thick. This should give you about 3 cups. Combine both vegetables in a saucepan, cover with cold water, add a pinch of salt, bring to a boil and cook 10 to 13 minutes, depending on parsnip size.

Drain thoroughly and puree through a food mill. (You can use a food processor but the resulting puree will not be as silky). Put the puree back into the cooking pot (may be prepared ahead to this point).

Reheat gently, stirring in the butter, milk and seasonings to taste. Serve very hot. Serves 4 or 5.

Parsnip Fritters

These make a nice main dish at a nonmeat meal, especially when they're served with applesauce. Or use to accompany grilled chicken or fish.

2 pounds parsnips, peeled and cut into chunks	**Salt and freshly ground pepper to taste**
2 tablespoons cream	**1 cup fresh bread crumbs**
2 large eggs	**4 tablespoons butter**

Boil parsnips in salted water until tender, then puree. Stir in the cream and put in a skillet. Stir constantly over medium heat for a few minutes to dry. Let cool, blend in 1 egg, and season to taste with salt and pepper. Refrigerate mixture for at least 1 hour.

Beat the second egg in a shallow dish with a tablespoon of cold water. Put the bread crumbs on a piece of wax paper. Form 8 patties with the parsnip mixture, flatten, dip into the egg mixture, then into the bread crumbs. Lay on a cake rack and refrigerate for ½ hour.

Melt half the butter in a medium skillet and fry 4 of the patties until browned—about 2 minutes a side. Drain on absorbent paper and keep warm. Use the rest of the butter to do the second batch. Serves 4.

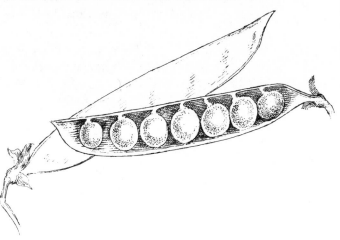

Peas
(Pisum sativum)

The French went crazy over *piselli novelli* when they were first sent from Genoa to the court of Louis XIV. According to the letters of Madame de Maintenon, the court ladies ate the delectable petits-pois at dinner and then snuck some more to their bedrooms to snack on before going to bed. Anyone eating garden-fresh peas for the first time might be tempted to do the same—the flavor bears little resemblance to the canned or frozen peas most of us have grown up with. Fresh peas appear at market in late spring and early summer, and the

pleasure of eating them is more than worth the effort of shelling.

I grow peas in my garden to nibble on while I weed; those that make it to the kitchen are cooked the way I learned from a French family I once lived with: with almost no liquid, in a saucepan lined with lettuce leaves, with small white onions, a pinch of sugar, and butter (p. 209). *That* is a dish fit for a king!

The pale green, flat snow pea (also called Chinese pea, pea pod, and mange-tout) is a Chinese variety with underdeveloped peas that are eaten pod and all. They are very tender and require little cooking to develop their crispness and subtle taste. Stir-frying suits them best. Sugar snap is another edible-podded variety that was developed recently. It has a plump, thick-fleshed pod that looks like a smaller standard pea, and contains fully developed peas. Sugar snaps are delicious raw, and can be eaten pod and all. They may also be blanched briefly or steamed.

To Buy

Regular peas: Look for crisp, shiny, well-filled, bright green pods. If you are in doubt about the age, open one. A white tail means the peas are old and beginning to sprout. Peas, like corn, begin converting their sugar to starch as soon as they are picked, and when they are too long off the vine they turn mealy. Old, large peas that are not sprouting can be quite edible braised the French way but without the onions. Never buy peas that are already shelled.

Sugar snaps should be plump and vivid green. Snow peas should be an even pale green. I have not had good luck with frozen snow peas, either commercially frozen ones or my own; they are rubbery and don't have that lovely green color.

One pound of podded peas yields 1 to 1¼ cups shelled peas. Allow 1 cup for two persons. One box of frozen peas will serve 3 or 4. One pound of snow peas serves 6 to 8, depending on whether they are used as a

single vegetable or in a Chinese dish. One pound of sugar snaps serves 4 to 6.

To Store

Peas will keep packed loosely in a plastic bag in the refrigerator, but in the interest of flavor, they should be used as soon as possible. Sugar snaps especially should be used within a day. Do not wash, shell, or string until ready to cook.

To Prepare

Shell regular peas just before cooking. My method is to press the seam near the stem end, run a fingernail down lightly, and squeeze the pod so the seam pops open, then run my thumb down the inside to free the peas. With sugar snaps, wash, dry, and remove both lateral strings by breaking off the tip and pulling downward. Snow peas need the stem tip removed and the string will come away with it. Leave these whole, if tender; if not, cut in two diagonally.

To Cook

Blanched shelled peas: Drop into a large quantity of boiling salted water, bring back to the boil, and cook uncovered for 5 to 8 minutes. Drain, return to the pot, and shake over moderate heat for a few seconds to evaporate the moisture. If not using immediately, refresh in cold water and put on a towel,

Blanched sugar snaps or snow peas:
Drop strung pods into boiling salted water for 45 seconds. Drain and refresh.

Stir-fried snow peas or sugar snaps:
Blanch as directed, dry, and stir-fry in oil or butter for 1 or 2 minutes—just until they turn bright green and are coated with fat.

Steamed sugar snaps: Steam for 5 minutes, then finish in melted butter.

Buttered peas: Blanch 2 cups of shelled peas, return to the pot to evaporate moisture, then roll in 4 tablespoons melted butter, 1 tablespoon sugar, and salt and pepper to taste. Cook over very low heat for 3 or 4 minutes to heat through, shaking the pot frequently.

Buttered peas with onions: Blanch 12 small white peeled onions and add to the peas for the final finish in butter.

Minted peas: Prepare buttered peas but add a tablespoon or two of finely chopped fresh mint leaves before the butter finish.

To add shelled peas to stews and soups: Add fresh raw peas during the final 10 minutes of cooking. If using frozen peas, partly defrost, put in a strainer, pour boiling water over them, then add in the final 5 minutes of cooking.

Rice and peas: Add 1 cup blanched fresh peas to 2 cups white rice that have been boiled in broth or water. Or try the slightly more elaborate recipe for rice and peas on page 209.

Frozen peas: This method takes away that odd starchy taste of frozen peas and is really quite good. Let the block partly defrost and break it up. Put the peas in a saucepan with ½ cup chicken broth, ½ teaspoon sugar, ¼ teaspoon thyme rubbed to powder between the palms of the hands, and a good knob of butter. Bring to a boil and simmer, covered, until the peas are tender and the liquid is almost gone—about 7 minutes. If a lot of liquid remains, cook uncovered over high heat 2 minutes longer. Serves 3–4.

Petits Pois à la Française

(Fresh Peas Braised with Lettuce and Onions)

The sweet liquid from the lettuce and onions mingles with the butter and makes these peas extraordinarily delicious. Sometimes I use two heads of lettuce, as I find it quite as delicious as the peas.

4–6 tablespoons butter, at room temperature
⅓ cup water
1 head Boston lettuce, separated into leaves
1 tablespoon sugar

Salt and freshly ground pepper to taste
3 pounds fresh green peas in the pod, shelled
8–12 small white onions, peeled and parboiled

In a heavy saucepan, bring the butter and water to a boil. Place the lettuce leaves around the sides and bottom of the pot. Add the sugar, salt, pepper, and peas. Bury the onions in the peas. Cover, bring again to the boil, lower heat, and cook slowly for 15 to 20 minutes, or until the peas are tender. Uncover and stir the peas and lettuce gently from time to time so everything cooks evenly.

Toss at the end, turn into a heated dish, and serve immediately. Serves 6.

Serving suggestion: This dish is so good it merits being a separate course. Or use it to accompany veal or fish, along with pan-roasted potatoes (p. 233).

Rice and Peas

(Risi e Bisi)

This is a much-loved dish in Italy, and a great way to serve fresh garden peas.

3 tablespoons olive oil
2 tablespoons diced salt pork, bacon, or ham fat
⅓ cup minced onion
3 tablespoons chopped parsley
2 cups fresh shelled peas (or 1½ boxes frozen,

see note)
½ cup water
Salt and freshly ground pepper to taste
3 cups hot boiled rice
¼ cup grated Parmesan cheese

Heat the oil in a heavy saucepan. Add the salt pork, onion, and parsley. Sauté until the onion is soft but not

brown—about 4 minutes. Add the peas and water, cover, bring to the boil, lower heat, and cook until the peas are tender. Season to taste with salt and pepper, and stir occasionally. Combine with the hot rice, toss with two forks, and top with the cheese. Serve very hot. Serves 4.

Note: If you use frozen peas, partly defrost them so they can be broken up, and eliminate the ½ cup water.

Serving suggestion: Serve as a first course and follow with broiled salmon or bass steaks, broccoli Italian style, and sliced tomatoes with basil.

Stir-fried Snow Peas

¼–½ cup chicken broth
1 tablespoon soy sauce
½ teaspoon sugar
2 tablespoons peanut oil
½ teaspoon salt

3 slices fresh ginger, minced
1 pound snow pea pods, blanched and refreshed

Combine the broth, soy sauce, and sugar.

Heat the oil in a large heavy skillet or wok. Add the salt and ginger and stir-fry a few times. Add the peas and stir-fry to coat with oil. Adjust heat if necessary to prevent scorching. Add the broth mixture and heat quickly. Cover and simmer for 1 to 2 minutes. Serves 4.

Snow peas and water chestnuts: Add 4 thinly sliced water chestnuts to the peas along with the broth mixture.

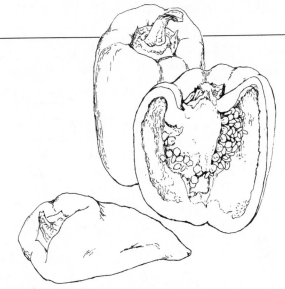

Peppers
(Capsicum frutescens)

The *Capsicums* are a hugely diverse group that for cooking purposes can be divided into two basic categories: hot and sweet. Like tomatoes, potatoes, and eggplants, peppers belong to the New World's premier vegetable family, the *Solanaceae* or nightshade. Neither sweet nor hot peppers are related to the everyday pepper, *Piper nigrum,* a vine whose berry gives us black and white peppercorns. The confusion can be laid to Columbus, who in his zeal mistook hot peppers, called *chillis* by the Nahautl Indians, for the peppercorns native to Asia. Brought to Europe by the early explorers, peppers quickly gained popularity in North Africa, Hungary, India, and eventually the Far East.

Sweet Peppers

The most familiar sweet pepper is the green pepper, also called the bell pepper. Red bell peppers are simply matured, fully ripened green peppers, and are at peak pepper flavor. Another sweet pepper is yellow when fully ripe. The narrow, elongated Italian peppers may be pale green, red, or yellow. They have a more delicate flavor and are good for frying.

Banana peppers are similar long, tapered sweet peppers, which can be green, yellow, or orange, and are good for salads and frying.

Pimentos are commercially packed sweet red peppers.

To Buy

Look for blocky bell peppers that are heavy for their size, with glossy, firm skins and no soft spots. Misshapen peppers can be hard to handle, and nooks and crannies make them hard to peel, if you are planning to roast them. Italian peppers should not have shriveled skins.

To Store

Keep sweet peppers, unwashed, in the crisper drawer of the refrigerator. After a week they begin to lose moisture and shrivel. Once they are cut, wrap the pieces in plastic and use quickly. Sweet red peppers are more perishable than green.

To Prepare

To seed and derib: Cut pepper in half
vertically along one of the crevices from base to stem. Pull the halves apart. The stem will remain with one side. Pull this out with your fingers, then cut away the whitish ribs with a paring knife. (For whole peppers, see to prepare for stuffing.)

To roast and peel: Use the thickest,
best-shaped peppers you can find. Lay on broiler rack 2 or 3 inches from the heat source and turn frequently with tongs or two wooden spoons as blisters form, until completely charred. This will take anywhere from 5 to 10 minutes. (When I char sweet red peppers I do not use tongs, because they can pierce the more tender skin, loosing the juices.) Or place a rack over the gas ring and grill peppers until charred. Immediately put peppers in a brown paper bag and twist tightly to seal. Put aside for 10 or 15 minutes (do not refrigerate). Then slip off the charred skin and pull out and discard the stem and seeds. Do not rinse the peppers, as they will get soggy. Patches of charred flesh are not important.

If peppers are to be marinated, work over a bowl to save the juices and add to the marinade. Cut peppers open and discard remaining ribs and seeds.

Sweet peppers may be seeded, deribbed, sliced or chopped, and frozen in plastic boxes. They are rather flabby when defrosted but fine for cooking.

To prepare for stuffing: Choose evenly
sized blocky peppers and, if necessary, slice a thin piece off the bottom to allow them to stand without toppling. Cut off a "lid" and scoop out the seeds and ribs with a teaspoon. Blanch the cases by dropping into a pot of boiling water. Remove when the water returns to the boil. Run under cold water and drain upside down. This preliminary tenderizing is not absolutely necessary, but I find it shortens the baking time, preserves the integrity of the pepper, and prevents the filling from being overcooked. The pepper may then be filled with the stuffing of your choice or any of those suggested for eggplant or tomatoes.

To Cook

Peppers are most frequently sautéed. Cut seeded, deribbed peppers into strips, or dice, and gently sauté in butter or olive oil until tender.

Escalivada

The Catalans of Spain are very fond of grilling food out-of-doors and will have a picnic at the drop of a hat just to eat their favorite foods. While the meat is cooking, they often pop eggplant, sweet peppers, and onions on the grill as well. When the vegetables are charred, then peel and chop them, add some garlic, and make this salad. Obviously you can use any number and proportion of vegetables you wish. It is a splendid accompaniment to grilled foods of all kinds, and can also be made in your broiler.

Escalivada, continued

2 small or 1 medium
  eggplant
2 large sweet green
  peppers
2 large sweet red peppers
½ cup thinly sliced red
  onion
2 garlic cloves, minced

2 small ripe tomatoes,
  peeled and lightly
  seeded
Salt and freshly ground
  pepper to taste
Fruity olive oil
Handful of fresh chopped
  parsley

Roast the eggplant and peppers on the gas ring, over charcoal, or in the broiler until the skins are blistered and charred, and peel. Cut the peppers into thickish julienne strips; cut the eggplant into 3-inch-long lengthwise strips (see Note). Place both in a salad bowl. Add the sliced onion and garlic. Cut the tomatoes into narrow wedges and add. Dress with salt, pepper, and olive oil. Refrigerate for 1 hour, then let come to room temperature and sprinkle with parsley before serving. Serves 4.

Note: In Spain, the eggplant is usually peeled, because the Spanish peel everything, but I think the salad is prettier with the skin left on.

Piperade

A specialty of the Basque country, this tasty concoction of tomatoes and sweet peppers is cooked down into a thickened, savory sauce, which is then incorporated with scrambled eggs.

15-ounce can Italian plum
  tomatoes, drained, or 4
  large ripe tomatoes,
  about 1½ pounds,
  peeled, cored, and
  seeded
2 tablespoons olive oil or
  butter
1 medium onion, thinly
  sliced
1 large sweet green
  pepper, seeded,

deribbed, and thinly
  sliced
1 small garlic clove, finely
  chopped
1 small hot green pepper,
  minced, or several
  dashes cayenne pepper
Salt and freshly ground
  pepper
Pinch dried thyme
8 large eggs
Chopped parsley

Slice the tomatoes into strips and set aside.

Heat the oil in a stainless steel skillet and add the onion and sweet pepper. Cover and cook slowly until they are both tender but not brown. Add the garlic, hot pepper or cayenne, salt, pepper, thyme, and tomatoes. Cover and cook for 5 minutes, shaking the skillet occasionally. Uncover, raise heat, and cook over high heat for a few minutes, stirring, to evaporate excess moisture.

Pour into a large gratin dish, reserving several tablespoonfuls. Prepare light, fluffy scrambled eggs, spread them over the piperade, and blend a bit of it into the eggs. Mound the reserved piperade on top and sprinkled with chopped parsley. Or use an appropriately smaller amount to garnish individual omelets. Makes 2¾–3 cups.

Serving suggestion: Piperade makes a wonderful Sunday brunch, served with flaky croissants. The sauce without the eggs can be served cold, on lettuce leaves as a first course for any meal, or as an accompaniment to cold meats or chicken.

Sweet Peppers Parma

(Roasted Marinated Sweet Peppers)

Almost every Italian restaurant offers peppers and anchovies, but at Parma, a favorite of mine in New York, the peppers do not come from a can or jar. They are scouted out diligently each day by the owner, John Piscina, roasted under the broiler, skinned, and dressed with nothing more than fine wine vinegar and the best olive oil. Anchovies and capers can be added when you are layering.

6–8 medium sweet peppers, roasted	Salt and pepper to taste
Wine vinegar	Olive oil

Peel the peppers right over the bowl in which you put them so you can catch and keep any liquid that accumulates at this time; it is the slightly caramelized juice of the peppers and very delicious. Cut or tear each pepper into manageable halves or quarters, and make a layer of them in a shallow glass or porcelain serving dish. Sprinkle, with a teaspoon or so of wine vinegar, the lightest dash of salt, if desired, and several good grinds of pepper. Repeat these layers until all the peppers are used; add enough olive oil to cover the top.

Cover with plastic wrap and refrigerate for 4 hours. Let come to room temperature before serving. Serves 4–6.

Serving suggestion: Roasted peppers are wonderful as a first course, served alone or with slices of fresh mozzarella, or as part of an antipasto.

Veal Chops with Peppers and Potatoes

This is a splendidly simple one-pan Italian dish. Slow braising blends the unique sweetness of the peppers and the savory meat juices into an unusually flavorsome dish.

4 veal loin chops, ¾–1 inch thick
6 tablespoons olive oil
1 medium onion, sliced
3 large sweet green peppers, seeded, and cut lengthwise into inch-wide strips

2 garlic cloves
4 medium potatoes, peeled and cut into ¼-inch slices
Salt and freshly ground pepper
Chopped parsley

Brown the veal chops lightly in 3 tablespoons of the oil in a large, heavy skillet that can hold them in one layer. Remove chops; set aside and keep warm. Add the remaining oil to the skillet and sauté the onion, peppers, garlic, and potatoes. Season with salt and pepper. When peppers and potatoes are lightly browned and soft, lay the chops on top, season with salt and pepper to taste, and cover. Cook over low heat for about 30 minutes, or until the veal is tender and well done. Sprinkle with chopped parsley and serve. Serves 4.

Red Pepper Quiche

This savory quiche is particularly pretty when made in a white porcelain dish.

3 tablespoons butter
¾ cup thinly sliced onion (1 medium onion)
2 sweet red peppers, cut into ½-inch strips
1⅓ cups grated Swiss or Gruyère cheese
9½-inch pastry shell (p. 177)

4 eggs
1 cup heavy cream
½ cup milk
Handful chopped fresh herbs: tarragon-parsley, parsley-dill, etc.
1 teaspoon salt
Several dashes cayenne

Preheat the oven to 350° and put a cookie sheet on the middle shelf.

Heat 1 tablespoon of the butter in a small skillet and sauté the onion until softened and faintly golden. Put in a bowl. In the same skillet, melt the remaining 2 tablespoons butter and sauté the peppers until faint brown edges appear—about 5 minutes.

Arrange the cheese over the bottom of the pastry shell; make a layer of the onions and then the peppers. Reserve the sweet orange liquid that collects in the pepper pan. Beat together the eggs, cream, milk, pepper liquid, herbs, and seasonings, and pour half of it over the onion-pepper mixture. Set on the cookie sheet in the oven and carefully add the balance of the liquid. Bake for 45 minutes or until golden and puffed. The quiche will sink somewhat as it cools. Serves 6–8.

Serving suggestion: With a green salad, this quiche makes a perfect light lunch or supper. I also use it as a first course when the main course is going to be a hearty vegetable soup that does not contain peppers, like soupe au pistou (p. 359). It can also be a first course before any light fish or chicken that is not in a rich sauce.

Italian Fried Peppers with Onions

It seems every southern Italian restaurant I ever went to had this on the menu, usually served with meatballs. It still is a good idea! My daughter invented the meatless Sloppy Joes that follow, using fried peppers because she tries to stay away from meat.

3 tablespoons olive oil
6–8 Italian frying peppers, cut lengthwise into 1-inch strips
2 medium yellow onions, sliced
1 garlic clove, minced
Salt and freshly ground pepper
Lemon juice

Heat the oil in a heavy skillet and sauté the peppers, onions, and garlic until the onion is pale gold—about 5 minutes. Stir, cover, and cook over low heat for about 10 minutes, shaking the pan from time to time. Uncover and cook 2 minutes more. Season to taste with salt and pepper and a squeeze of lemon juice. Serves 4.

Jessica's Vegetable Sloppy Joe

Prepare Italian fried peppers and onions using double the amount of garlic. After the covered cooking time, add ½ cup tomato or marinara sauce and cook over low heat, covered, for 5 minutes more. Season with a dash or two or Worcestershire sauce and one of cayenne. Serve on a hamburger bun or a toasted English muffin half. Serves 4.

Conchiglie with Pesto, Red Peppers, and Peas

This is one of my favorite starch-and-vegetable dishes in one. It is very pretty on a buffet and tastes marvelous. The addition of tuna turns it into a lunch dish that needs only a green salad as accompaniment.

1½ pounds pasta shells, preferably conchiglie
10-ounce package frozen small peas
1 large or 2 small sweet red peppers
Salt and freshly ground pepper to taste
7-ounce can Italian tuna fish in oil, optional
¾ cup pesto sauce (p. 382) (See note)

For the pasta, put a large pot of water on to boil, to which you have added a dollop of cooking oil and some salt.

While the water is heating, cook the peas in ½ cup boiling salted water for 5 minutes, drain, and run under cold water. Cut the pepper into ½-inch strips, blanch for 1 minute, refresh under cold water, pat dry, and cut into ½-inch pieces. (You should have about 1 cup, although exact amounts are not critical.) Set aside.

Slightly undercook the shells in boiling water, stirring them up from the bottom occasionally. This should take about 10 minutes, but will vary according to their size. Drain, shaking vigorously, and dry on kitchen toweling. Place in a large mixing bowl and season with salt and pepper.

If you are using tuna, drain, flake with a fork, and add to the pesto. Add the pesto to the shells and toss to coat. Add the peas and peppers and toss again. Season to taste with salt and pepper. Serve at room temperature. Serves at least 10.

Note: For this dish only, make the pesto sauce with 2 additional garlic cloves, omit the butter, and use double the amount of olive oil, to ensure coating the pasta well.

Serving suggestion: For a buffet, make without the tuna and serve with a cold poached fish, Consuelo's green sauce (p. 379), and a salad of cherry tomatoes and scallions in lemon vinaigrette (p. 375). This also goes well with baked ham.

Peperoni Tricolore with Pasta

This dish would have been possible only for a few home gardeners before yellow peppers from Holland began appearing at market. It is a perfect way to celebrate late summer, when ripe sweet peppers and fresh basil are abundant. If yellow peppers are not available, use all red. It is essential that the basil be fresh, the perfect counterpoint for the meaty sweetness of the peppers.

3 large sweet red peppers
2 yellow peppers
3 tablespoons olive oil
4 garlic cloves, sliced
Salt and freshly ground
   pepper to taste
¾ pound fresh fettuccine

4 tablespoons butter
¾ cup basil leaves,
   washed, dried, and torn
   into pieces
½–⅔ cup freshly grated
   Parmesan cheese

Wash the peppers, dry, and cut lengthwise into quarters, discarding the stem and seeds. Holding each piece in your hand, peel the skin with a potato peeler. Cut into strips about ¼ inch wide. Stack the strips and cut these in half.

Heat the olive oil in a large heavy skillet; add the garlic, cook quickly until it is golden, then remove and discard. Add the peppers and cook over medium heat, uncovered, for about 15 minutes. Season with salt and pepper.

Cook the pasta until al dente. Put the butter in the bowl in which you will serve the pasta and place the bowl in a slow oven to heat. The butter should melt.

When the pasta is done, drain and add to the bowl. Add the peppers, all the pan liquid, and the basil. Toss, add the grated cheese, and toss again. Serve immediately. Serves 4.

Serving Suggestion: As a first course preceding a whole baked fish or veal scallops, accompanied by steamed zucchini (page 324).

Chili Peppers

With over 200 varieties, chili, or hot, peppers account for about 90 percent of the *Capsicums.* A great number of them are the most characteristic seasoning in Mexican and Tex-Mex cooking. Each has its own characteristics, but it is generally the degree of heat rather than the flavor that dictates which one is used.

Hot chilies, whether fresh or dried, contribute a subtle taste as well as heat, and must be cooked into a dish, never dumped in at the last moment.

Hot peppers are available fresh, dried, and in cans. In a pinch, cayenne, red pepper flakes, or hot pepper sauce may be substituted. But fresh or dried chilies are interchangeable for most purposes.

Chilies are cross-pollinated by the wind and can be quirky. I have grown hot peppers that were disappointingly mild, and I have collected both hot *and* mild peppers from the same plant. So according to the pepper, you may have to adjust the amount called for in a particular recipe.

The heat in hot peppers comes from a substance called capsaicin, concentrated in the veins and seeds. For milder heat, remove the seeds (wearing rubber gloves when you do). For the mildest, yet still definite hot effect, sauté the seeded peppers in hot oil before using.

Should you eat too much hot pepper, resist the instinct to gulp water, which may spread the capsaicin. A big mouthful of bread, rice, or yogurt works better.

The following are the most commonly available fresh chilies:

California or Anaheim chili: Mild, long and green. Available fresh and canned, whole or chopped.

Poblano or pasilla: A large, dark green chili, mild to medium hot, the one most frequently stuffed. In Mexico, poblanos are called anchos when dried, but in California, poblanos are also called anchos when fresh.

Jalapeño: Small, dark green, with a smooth skin and rounded tip. Varies from hot to very hot. Available fresh, canned, and pickled *(en escabeche)*.

Serrano: Smaller and hotter than jalapeños, with absolutely incendiary seeds, these are usually canned.

Dried chilies are available in packages and occasionally loose. Many look alike, so pay attention to the name and, if possible, their origin. Chilies from New Mexico are hotter than those from California.

Other Forms of Hot Pepper

In Mexican and Tex-Mex cooking, the most frequently used dried chilies are the ancho, mulato, and pasilla. They are regarded as medium-hot. Among the really incendiary dried chilies are the serrano, cascabel, guajillos, and the tiny chilies pequins. Chipotle chilies have an unusual smoky flavor.

Oriental dried red chilies, usually sold in cellophane packages, are not particularly flavorful but are extremely hot. One will nicely heat a dish for two people. These are frequently sautéed in oil before incorporating them into food.

Cayenne or red pepper is ground from the dried ripe fruit of the *Capsicum frutescens, var, longum.* It is very hot, though not as hot as chili pepper.

Paprika is a dried pulverized form of the *Capsicum annuum* that is especially popular in Hungary. The best paprika comes from that country in three strengths: sweet, half-sweet or moderately hot, and hot. It has a unique flavor, and if you are making a paprikash dish, this is what you must use. Standard paprika, which comes from Spain, is harsh and relatively flavorless.

Condiments based on hot peppers include Tabasco sauce; crushed red pepper flakes; chili oil, used in Oriental cooking; and harissa, a paste used in North African cooking, usually sold in tubes.

Chili powder is a commercial blend of ground chili peppers with other seasonings added. In making chili it is preferable to use pure chili powder and add the other seasonings (cumin, salt, etc.) to your taste. This way the seasonings will be fresher, and you can control the degree of hotness.

To Store

Keep fresh chilies in a perforated bag in the refrigerator. They may also be strung and dried, then reconstituted as needed. Pass heavy-duty thread through the stems of ripe hot peppers, then hang in a cool dry place. Once the peppers are dried, put them in a screw-top jar and store in a cool dry place.

To Prepare

Wear rubber gloves when handling fresh chilies. They can cause the fingertips, particularly under the nails, to sting for hours. *Do not touch the face, particularly the eyes and lips, when handling chilies.* If you do touch your eye, irrigate immediately with cool water.

For fresh chili peppers, cut off the tips and chop, using or discarding the seeds depending on the recipe. To roast, use the same broiling or grilling method described for sweet peppers. Then cut a small slit on one side of the pepper and rinse under running water to remove seeds. Pat dry.

For dried chilies, put them in a saucepan, cover with boiling water, and bring to the boil. Remove from heat and let sit until softened. Remove stems and seeds, then chop or puree in a food processor or blender with just enough liquid to make a paste.

To Freeze

Wrap peeled, seeded fresh chilies individually in plastic wrap, put in a plastic bag, seal, and freeze.

Albuquerque Stuffed Green Chilies

These make a deliciously satisfying meatless meal accompanied by Spanish rice and refried beans.

8 fresh green chilies	½ teaspoon salt
1 cup Monterey Jack cheese, cubed	2 eggs, beaten
½ cup flour	Cooking oil

Roast and peel the chilies and remove seeds.

Divide the cheese and fill each chili with it. Sift together the flour and salt. Roll each chili in it, then in the beaten eggs. Fry in moderately hot oil until golden brown on all sides—about 8 minutes total. Serves 4.

Craig Claiborne's Jalapeño Cornbread

8½-ounce can cream-style corn
1 cup yellow cornmeal
3 large eggs
1 teaspoon salt
½ teaspoon baking soda
¼ cup milk
⅓ cup corn oil
1 cup grated sharp cheddar cheese
¼ cup chopped jalapeño peppers
2 tablespoons butter

Preheat oven to 400°.

In a mixing bowl combine the corn, cornmeal, eggs, salt, baking soda, milk, oil, half the cheese and the peppers. Blend well.

Put the butter in a 1½ quart casserole or a 9-inch skillet. Place the casserole in the oven until the butter is melted and hot but not brown. Tip the dish around to distribute the butter; immediately pour in the cornbread mixture. Sprinkle with the remaining cheese and bake for 40 minutes. Makes 1 loaf serving 8.

Jalapeño Jelly

Cunningly sweet *and* hot, this Tex-Mex favorite is addictive! Spoon onto cream cheese atop crackers or tostadas (see page 225) as a drink accompaniment, or serve with roast lamb or cold meats.

6 fresh jalapeño chilies, trimmed and seeded
2 green bell peppers, seeded
1½ cups cider vinegar
5½ cups sugar
6 ounces liquid pectin

Cut each chili and green pepper into 3 or 4 pieces. Drop through the feed tube of a food processor (see note) with the motor running and process until finely minced. Alternatively, finely chop by hand.

Place chilies, peppers, vinegar, and sugar in a 3-quart saucepan and bring to a boil, stirring to dissolve the sugar. Lower heat and simmer for 10 minutes, skimming foam from top as needed. Stir in the pectin and boil for 1 minute. Remove from heat and let stand for 15 minutes, then pour into sterilized jars and seal with paraffin according to manufacturer's directions. Makes 6 cups.

Note: Do not breathe the fumes while processing.

Variation: If desired, a few drops of green food coloring may be added with the pectin. Or substitute red bell peppers for the green ones, and/or any fresh hot red pepper for the green jalapeños.

Nachos

I am simply crazy about nachos; the more I eat the more I want. I love them for anything from a full-fledged meal to a quick snack. They are that rarity, a really high class snack food, because the combination of the cheese with the grain (corn) in the tostadas yields complete protein. For the best result, make your own tostadas from packaged tortillas. Sometimes you can buy miniature tostadas in a bag, but don't use Frito chips, because of their small size and excessive salt.

48 tostadas (see following recipe)
48 similar-size squares of Cheddar or Monterey
Jack cheese
4 jalapeño chilies, seeds removed, sliced into thin rings

Heat the oven to 425°. Place a baking sheet in the oven to heat. Remove sheet, arrange the tostadas on it, top each with a piece of cheese and one or more slices of jalapeño. Bake for about 7 minutes, or until the cheese melts. Makes 48 nachos.

Variations: You can put a spoonful of *salsa* or taco sauce (available in cans) on top of the cheese before adding the chilies. You can do the same with a spoonful of refried beans.

Tostadas

Oil or lard for deep-frying
12 corn tortillas
Salt, if desired

Heat 2 inches of oil or lard in a heavy pan. If you have a deep fryer, heat it to 375°.

With kitchen shears, cut the tortillas into quarters, but don't cut through completely at the center (this facilitates turning). Fry one at a time until crisp, turning once. Drain on absorbent paper, then break into quarters. Salt lightly if desired. Makes 48 tostadas.

Salsa Mexicana Cruda

Mexicans put a dish of sauce on the table much the same way that we might put out ketchup or mustard. This sauce, used with eggs, poached chicken, grilled or broiled meats, mixed into beans or simply dipped up with freshly made tortillas, is also called *salsa fresca* or "fresh sauce." Fresh is the operative word: it is best made at the last minute and no more than three hours before serving. This is the version made in Sinaloa; another uses onions in place of the scallions and omits the lime. Unless you can get really flavorful, ripe tomatoes, use good quality canned ones.

2 large ripe tomatoes or 4 medium unskinned, seeded and finely chopped, or 15-ounce can Italian plum tomatoes, drained, seeded, liquid reserved
¼ cup finely minced scallions, white and part of the green
2 jalapeño or serrano chilies, finely minced (see Note)
1 garlic clove, finely minced
¼ cup finely minced coriander leaves (about 10 sprigs)
1 teaspoon oregano
Juice of 1 lime
½ cup water or the reserved liquid from tomato can
Salt to taste

Mix all ingredients together in a bowl and season with salt to taste. Refrigerate if not using immediately. Makes about 1½ cups.

Note: In Mexico the chilies are used unseeded in this sauce. If you desire a very mild sauce, however, seed them, wearing rubber gloves.

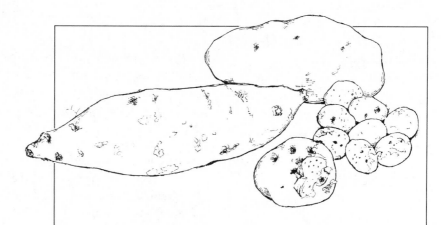

Potatoes

(Solanum tuberosum)

Though most histories credit Sir Walter Raleigh with having introduced "Virginia" potatoes to Europe by growing them on his Irish estate, the more likely story is that they arrived in Ireland as a result of a Spanish Armada ship that foundered on those shores in the mid sixteenth-century. The Spanish *conquistadores* had been carrying the tuber from its original habitat, Peru, where it was used for food since prehistoric times. In fact, the Spanish name for potato, *papa,* is its Peruvian name. Our word is a corruption of *batata,* the West Indian name for the botanically distinct sweet potato, with which the white potato was often confused.

The potato came to North American in 1719 with some Irish immigrants, and the "Murphy" or "Irish Potato" soon spread to the other colonies, whose inhabitants tended to think of it as animal fodder. The early field crops were sold to slavers as cheap food, and a mid-nineteenth-century American cookery book offered a grand total of four potato recipes.

Contrary to popular notion, potatoes are not fattening. When you eat meat and potatoes, it is the fat in the meat that makes the potatoes fattening. By itself, a potato, because of its high fiber content and good quality complex carbohydrates, fills you without fattening you. Of course, a potato drenched with butter or gravy is another story. But on its own, a 5-ounce

baked potato, which is a respectable size, has about 90 calories—about the same as a medium apple or a cup of orange juice. Nutritionally, it has almost no salt or fat and delivers more potassium than a banana, plus B vitamins, vitamin C, and important trace minerals. The skin, loved by some to the exclusion of the rest of the potato, is especially rich in minerals. One buff I know saves potato peelings and fries them as snack food.

You can prepare a potato in just about any way, but not all ways suit all potatoes. The confusing potato nomenclature and lack of widespread information about how specific kinds cook up are complicated by the fact that potatoes are marketed and known both by varietal names and places of origin. And, regardless of origin and variety, they are also known as old and new—old meaning those stored from the previous year's crop.

New or early potatoes can be any potato of the current year's crop. New is not a variety but a stage of growth. There is a common misconception that the small, round, thin-skinned red potatoes are new potatoes. Actually these are a variety, and can be new or old, depending on their age. Because new potatoes are tender and quick cooking, they are best cooked with their skins left on. Buy in small quantities, as they do not store well.

In this country potatoes known by source include pink potatoes from Bermuda and Florida and potatoes from California, Virginia, Maine, Long Island, and Idaho. From these sources come varieties that include Katahdins, Chippewa, Cobblers, Kennebec, Ontario, Pontiac, Sebago, and Vikings, each with a particular shape and quality.

Alas, there are no truly waxy potatoes available commercially here, though they certainly exist in small gardens. They make the best souffléed and roesti potatoes, and presumably would be marketed if consumers demanded them.

I would like to see potatoes identified according to their starch content, because this is what tells you how to use them. Old potatoes, which have more starch, are mature storage potatoes from the previous year's crop.

Having lost some moisture along the way, they absorb other flavors easily and so are ideal for making potato pancakes, stews, scalloped dishes, and potato salad. They are also good for frying, as the starch acts as a sealant, preventing the absorption of grease.

Low-starch potatoes have a moister, crisper flesh that holds its shape better in boiling and salad-making. To check starch content; rub two cut halves together; if they stick, the starch content is high.

To Buy

Look for potatoes that are free of soft spots and bad blemishes. Do not buy potatoes with green spots, which result from exposure to light. The green contains solanine, a toxic substance with a bitter taste that, if eaten in quantity, can cause illness. Eyes don't mean a thing, nor does an irregular surface, though both increase peeling time and waste. Choose potatoes with the starch content that suits your cooking purpose.

Three medium-size boiling potatoes weigh about 1 pound. One Idaho russet baking potato weighs about ¾ pound. There are 8 to 10 small new potatoes in a pound. One pound of all-purpose potatoes will yield about 2 cups mashed. This will feed 2–4 persons, depending on appetites.

High-starch: Russet Burbanks, the most popular potato in the United States, are also sold as Idaho bakers or baking potatoes. They have a dry, mealy quality that keeps them light and fluffy when baked and produces good mashed and french-fried potatoes. But the mealiness makes them fall apart when boiled.

Medium-starch: Maine potatoes, Katahdins from Maine, New Jersey, or Long Island, sometimes marketed as eastern or all-purpose potatoes. These are a little waxier than russets and can be used for boiling, mashing, and roasting. They may be baked, though they will be somewhat more watery than russet Burbanks.

Low-starch: Red potatoes, or new potatoes. These are lovely steamed in their jackets and sliced for salads, since they do not fall apart. Use with the skins on when possible.

Potatoes can be sold graded or ungraded. If they are packaged or bagged they must be graded according to U.S. Department of Agriculture standards. Grades indicate size and shape, not quality. The highest grade, U.S. Fancy, indicates uniform size and carries a premium price. U.S. No. 1, the grade we see most, has varying sizes, the smallest of which is not less than 1⅞ inches.

To Store

Keep in a cool, dark place but do not refrigerate; below 40°, some of the starch turns to sugar, causing a queer sweetness and a darkening when cooked.

Sprouted potatoes become soft but are edible. Pick off the sprouts.

To Prepare

Just prior to cooking, wash in cool water and scrub well with a vegetable brush. Cut out any sprouting eyes, spots, and bruises. Potatoes retain maximum nutrients if cooked with the skin on, but if you are peeling them, do so with a swivel-bladed peeler, dropping them into a bowl of water as you finish each to prevent discoloration.

To Cook

Cooking times are approximate; a potato is tender when the tip of a sharp knife enters easily and comes out without flesh clinging to it.

Boiled unpeeled: This preserves the maximum amount of nutrients. Cover scrubbed potatoes with cold water, add 2 teaspoons salt per quart, bring to a boil,

and cook covered for 25 to 40 minutes, or until tender. Drain, cover with a folded tea towel, and shake pot over low heat to dry the skins.

Boiled peeled:
Cut peeled potatoes into equal-size halves, quarters, or chunks. Cover with cold water and add 1 teaspoon salt for each quart (a little milk added to the water will keep the potatoes very white and improve the flavor). Boil covered for 15 to 25 minutes, or until tender. Drain, return to pot, and shake over heat for a minute to dry.

Parboiled:
A preliminary step when potatoes are to be cooked with other faster-cooking ingredients. Boil peeled and halved potatoes for 10 minutes.

Parsleyed potatoes:
Melt 4 tablespoons butter in a saucepan, stir in ¼ cup minced parsley, and add boiled, dried potatoes—peeled or unpeeled. Turn them gently over low heat to coat.

Pommes Parisiennes:
Peel potatoes and cut out balls with the large side of a melon baller, dropping them into water. There is a lot of waste, so allow 2 potatoes per person. Dry well and put in a shallow baking dish with melted butter or suet. Bake at 375° for about ½ hour, turning them occasionally. Or sauté briefly in butter in a skillet. Cover the pan for 6 to 8 minutes. Remove cover and continue sautéeing, rolling them around until golden and tender. Use as a garnish for chicken or veal.

Steamed:
Peel and quarter potatoes lengthwise. With a sharp knife, pare the sharp edges of each piece, shaping them into uniform ovals. Since steamed potatoes have a tendency to break, first parboil them for 7 or 8 minutes. Drain, return to the pot in a colander over boiling water, press a piece of foil on top, and cook over low heat for 5 to 7 minutes until steamed through. To keep warm, leave covered over the hot water with the heat off. Do not attempt to reheat.

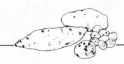

Mashed: Do not succumb to the popular notion that potatoes to be mashed will be creamier if they are cooked longer. This just makes them waterlogged and tasteless. Use all-purpose or baking potatoes; peel and boil just until tender. For added flavor I often put half an onion in the pot for each pound of potatoes. Discard before pureeing. Drain, return to the pot and shake dry briefly over heat. Mash with a hand masher or put through a ricer or food mill. (Don't use the food processor—you will end up with glue.) Stir in enough heated milk or cream to make the puree smooth but not too thin. Then beat in as much butter as your conscience allows, add salt and pepper (white, if you're a purist—I'm not) to taste. If not serving immediately, keep warm over boiling water.

Baked: Bake scrubbed potatoes in a preheated 400° oven right on the rack for about an hour. To shorten the time, use aluminum potato nails, which conduct the heat to the center more quickly. A thick metal skewer does the trick, too. If you are baking a number of potatoes, put them in a muffin tin to facilitate removal. Remove from the oven and pierce in several places with a fork to allow steam to escape, or slash an X in the top with a sharp knife. Wrapping them in foil is a nasty restaurant trick that makes a soggy potato and spoils the best part—the skin. Oiling the skin will give it an attractive sheen, though somewhat soften it. For a crisp, crusty skin, stretch aluminum foil over the floor of the oven, preheat to only 300°, and bake the potatoes on the foil. Turn halfway during cooking. This will take at least 1¾ hours.

Serve as is, with butter, sour cream with snipped chives or dill, or yogurt. For the calorie conscious, add only some dried or fresh basil, caraway or celery seed, chopped chives, dill or fresh thyme. A few toasted sesame seeds make an interesting crunch.

Stuffed baked: Cut a ½-inch lengthwise lid from a baked potato. Scoop out the flesh into a small bowl (take care not to break the skin) and prepare as

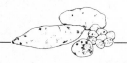

for mashed potatoes. Pile back into the skin, texture the surface with a fork, and top with a small piece of butter. Put under the broiler for 2 minutes or so until browned.

Stuffed baked potato with cheese:

Prepare for stuffing as directed; add 2 tablespoons sour cream, 2 teaspoons grated Romano or Parmesan cheese, a teaspoon of minced scallion, and 1 slice of crisply cooked bacon, drained and crumbled. Season and pile mixture back into the shell. Sprinkle top with an additional teaspoon of cheese and return to the top rack of the oven to heat and brown the top—about 10 minutes. Serve with a pat of butter on top and sprinkle with parsley, if desired. For a complete lunch or dinner, omit the butter and top with a fried egg. Omit the bacon for a vegetarian meal.

Oven-roasted: Preheat the oven to 350°. Parboil

peeled potatoes for 10 minutes. Pat dry; cut into quarters if large, or any desired size. Melt suet or a combination of butter and oil in a baking dish, add the potatoes, turn to coat, and sprinkle with the juice of half a lemon. Roast or, more correctly, bake, turning occasionally, until tender—about 45 minutes.

Pan-roasted: Peel new or old potatoes and dry

them. If using old potatoes, cut into quarters. Blanch in boiling water for 5 minutes; drain and dry well.

Melt butter in a sauté pan with a domed lid or in a shallow heatproof casserole and add the potatoes so all touch the bottom of the pan. Use two pans if necessary. Turn them to completely coat with butter. Cover tightly and cook over high heat for 15 or 20 minutes, until tender. (As the steam generated in the pan plays a large role in the cooking process, try not to uncover the pan during cooking. This will also keep the butter from burning.) Shake the pan occasionally to give all surfaces a chance to brown evenly. Season with salt and pepper and sprinkle with parsley.

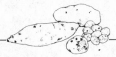

Potatoes roasted with meat or chicken:
Use halved or quartered parboiled potatoes, well dried. Add to the drippings in the roasting pan when the meat has about 1 hour to go. Turn occasionally with a wooden spoon. If pan drippings are scant, add a little oil or butter and let it heat before adding the potatoes. Season before serving.

Boiled new potatoes:
These present an exception to the rule of starting potatoes in cold water. Bring a large pot of salted water to the boil, add potatoes (try to choose ones of equal size), and simmer uncovered for 15 to 20 minutes. They are done when they feel firm yet can easily be pierced with a sharp knife. Drain, dry the pot, melt some butter in it, put the potatoes back and roll to coat. Season with salt and pepper. Sprinkle with a tablespoon or so of fresh finely chopped mint, if desired, and put in a serving dish decorated with a sprig of whole mint.

New potatoes and caviar:
This is about the best hors d'oeuvre I know. For 10 to 12 people, wash 24 tiny new potatoes, dry well, and lightly rub with vegetable oil. Put on a rimmed baking sheet and bake in a preheated 325° oven for 15 to 20 minutes. Make a cross on top of each with a paring knife and pinch slightly to open. Fill with half a teaspoon or so of caviar (black or red), top with a small dollop of sour cream and snippets of chives. Serve while warm.

Culls, or the tiny new potatoes left behind by the harvester, are perfect for this use.

French-fried Potatoes

I am so fond of these that when a French friend who is an excellent cook offered to make me something special for my birthday, I requested a mountain of her superb french fries and an entrecôte—a nostalgic reminder of Parisian student days. But the real gift was learning *why* the French *pommes frites* were so light, crisp, and greaseless: the classic double-fry or double-dip method.

In this technique a brief first blanching in hot oil seals the outer coating of the potato and keeps it from absorbing grease as it cooks to doneness. The flavor is further enhanced by the proportion of animal fat—beef suet or lard—in the cooking oil. (A tasty combination is one part melted beef suet to three parts oil. Chop suet roughly, place on a cookie sheet, and let melt in a slow oven. Strain before using.) This, by the way, is the secret of the good fries at McDonald's.

The double method is no harder than single-frying (in fact it's easier, because the first frying can be done hours ahead). It also does not smell up the house. I doubt you will ever make them any other way once you have tried this method.

Wash, peel, and cut any variety of firm, nonmealy potatoes lengthwise into strips ⅜ inch square by 2½ to 3 inches long. (This is the classic french fry size. If you use the french fry disk of a food processor you will get something a bit smaller, but this is not critical.)

Let the cut potatoes soak for at least an hour in cold water to cover. This is important, because the soaking removes some of the surface starch that could cause sticking. Drain well and dry before frying (use a spin-type salad dryer or an old Turkish towel kept for kitchen use), because—READ THIS TWICE—wet potatoes will splatter in hot fat and *water and hot fat can explode.* The potatoes also do not brown properly.

Heat about 6 cups of vegetable or corn oil or the suet-vegetable combination to a temperature of 350° (a cube of bread will brown in 60 seconds). Remember that at the first immersion, moisture being rapidly released from the potato can cause a certain amount of bubbling in the oil. If the fat bubbles up too quickly, remove the basket at once and lower again slowly.

First frying: Place a layer of potatoes in the basket (don't fill it more than half full—this is another precaution against sticking). Lower the basket into the fat and let the potatoes cook for 8 to 12 minutes, or until they just begin to turn golden. If there are several batches to go, drain and remove potatoes and repeat until all are done to this point. If the first frying is

done ahead, leave the potatoes in the basket propped on the side of the pan. (Deep fryers have a hook for this.) Turn the fryer heat off.

Second frying: This may be done immediately or hours later. Turn on or raise the heat of the oil to 375° (a cube of bread will brown in 20 seconds). Fill basket half full or less, lower potatoes, and cook about 5 minutes—until they are the desired golden brown. Shake the basket once or twice to discourage sticking. As each batch is done, drain on brown paper. There will be very little grease. When all are done, salt to taste and serve.

Hashed Brown Potatoes

6 **all-purpose potatoes, boiled and dried**	4 **tablespoons butter or margarine**

Cut the potatoes into ½-inch cubes. Heat the butter in a medium skillet, add the potatoes, and flatten slightly into a cake with a spatula. Shake pan gently from time to time to avoid sticking. When the underside has browned, turn and cook so that the second side browns. (Do this with the spatula or by sliding out onto a plate and flipping it over.) Check to see whether it is browned by gently lifting the edges of the cake. Serve immediately. Serves 4–6.

Note: A finely chopped onion may be added to the potatoes.

Baked Potato Skins

The crunch and hearty flavor make this one drink accompaniment that everyone is crazy about. And potato skins are good for you, besides. They can be prepared ahead and broiled just before serving.

6 **Idaho potatoes, baked**	**Salt and freshly ground**
3 **tablespoons butter, softened**	**pepper**

Cut the potatoes in half lengthwise and scoop out the

flesh, scraping the insides of the skins well. Save the flesh for another purpose—mashed potatoes, croquettes, or whatever. With a sharp knife or scissors, cut the skins into long strips about 1½ inches wide. Smear these well on the flesh side with softened butter and season with salt and pepper. Place on a foil broiling pan, and broil 6 or 7 inches from the heat source until brown and crisp—about 5 minutes. Watch that they do not burn. Serve hot. Can be stored in a tin and reheated. Makes about 24 strips. Allow at least 3 strips per person.

Straw Potato Nests

These are a charming conceit for a formal dinner, filled with tiny peas, sautéed cherry tomatoes, or tiny *haricots verts*. Once you get the hang of it, they are not at all hard to make. You do need a special tool called a bird's nest fryer, which consists of one small wire basket that gets clamped inside a larger one, but it is not terribly expensive.

6 firm boiling potatoes   **peanut oil for frying**
5–6 cups vegetable or

Peel and wash the potatoes. Using the large julienne or grating disk of a food processor or a mandoline, cut the potatoes into matchstick pieces. Soak them in ice water for 1 to 2 hours. Lay them on a Turkish towel and dry very well.

Heat the oil in a deep fryer to 375°. Make the first nest in the larger of the two baskets by laying the potato pieces close together, running them horizontally around the sides. Build the sides up high and make them thick, because they shrink when cooked. Clamp the inner basket in place and secure.

When the oil is ready (if you do not have a thermostatically controlled fryer, wait until the surface of the oil shows a faint wrinkle), slowly lower the basket into the oil. Fry for 2½ to 3 minutes, or until pale gold. Before unmolding the nest, cut away the odd pieces of potato that may be sticking out. When you

separate the baskets, the nest will adhere to the smaller one. Turn it over and rap the handle smartly on the counter to dislodge the basket. If it seems too pale, place on a skimmer and return to the oil for a few seconds. Drain on brown paper and proceed until all are made. Makes about 8.

Note: Nests may be made ahead and reheated on a cookie sheet in a 300° oven with the door ajar.

When working with a new bird's nest basket, it is necessary to season it as you would an omelet pan. Oil and place in a slow oven for an hour or so. To store, do not scrub with cleanser; merely wash, rub with clean oil, and wrap in foil.

Sugar-browned Potatoes

These are eaten throughout Scandinavia in varying degrees of sweetness and are very good with pot roast and poultry.

4 tablespoons butter	boiled and peeled
4 tablespoons sugar	Salt to taste
12 small red potatoes,	

Melt the butter in a heavy skillet. Stir in the sugar and let it turn light brown, but watch for scorching, which can occur very easily. Add the potatoes (do not crowd the pan; rather do them in two batches) and shake the pan constantly over medium heat until they are coated with the caramel on all sides. Serves 4.

Gratin Dauphinois

Slow baking allows the potatoes to absorb the garlic-perfumed milk or cream in this dish and is for me one of the glories of the French *cuisine de femme*— what we would call home cooking. Many different regions of France claim their version of potato gratin as the original, each saying the others contain some ingredient (usually cheese) that makes them inauthentic. The version called gratin savoyard, in which chicken

stock is used and thin slices of celery root are alternated with the potatoes, is also very good.

2½ pounds potatoes, Maine or Idaho	Freshly grated nutmeg
2½–3 tablespoons butter	Salt and freshly ground pepper
2–3 garlic cloves, peeled	1 cup grated Gruyère or Swiss cheese (about ¼ pound)
2 cups milk (or 1 cup milk, 1 cup cream)	

Preheat the oven to 375°.

Peel the potatoes and cut into slices somewhere between ⅛ and 1/16 inch thick. The slicing disk of a food processor does this rapidly. Drop the slices in cold water as you go. You should have 6 to 7 cups of slices.

Select a shallow baking dish (an oval gratin 8 × 14 × 2 inches is ideal) and grease it well with 1 tablespoon of the butter. Crush the garlic cloves and use one to rub the dish all around.

Put the milk in a saucepan, add all the garlic cloves, including the one used for the dish, and several gratings of nutmeg. Bring to a simmer. Meanwhile, drain the potatoes well and layer them in the prepared dish, seasoning each layer with salt and pepper. Strain the milk over, sprinkle with grated cheese, and dot with the remaining butter. Bake for about 1 hour, or until the milk is absorbed and the top is nicely browned. Remove from the oven and let set for 10 or 15 minutes before serving. Serves at least 8.

Note: Gratin Dauphinois is frequently made in a less rich version without the cheese topping. Just dot the top with 2 more tablespoons of butter so it browns nicely, or gild by passing briefly (watching all the time) under the broiler after it is cooked.

Serving suggestion: Superb with roast leg of lamb or veal, lamb chops, roast turkey, or broiled chicken. Good for feeding a lot of people—two gratins are little more trouble than one.

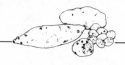

Roesti

This is served all over Switzerland as an accompaniment to meat or as a meatless meal. It is not for those with slimming in mind, but it certainly is delicious! A finely chopped onion is sometimes added to the potatoes.

1 pound medium potatoes (yellow waxy ones if possible)
Salt

3 tablespoons vegetable oil
3–5 tablespoons butter, in one piece

Boil the potatoes in their skins until tender on the outside but still underdone (about 10 minutes). Drain, cool, and chill thoroughly. (If possible, do this the night before or early in the day.) Peel and grate coarsely into matchstick strips, or use the grating disk of the food processor. Sprinkle with salt.

Butter a dinner plate and set it aside.

Heat the oil in a well-seasoned 9-inch skillet over high heat and, when it is quite hot, add the potatoes. Cook for about 2 minutes, then lower heat to medium and continue cooking, uncovered, about 8 minutes more. Take care they do not burn and keep loosening along the sides with a slotted spatula. From time to time, slide wafer-thin pats of butter down the side of the pan, lifting the potatoes slightly with the spatula so the butter can melt underneath. Keep gathering in the sides of the potato cake with the spatula to keep the cake compact. As the potatoes cook, keep loosening the bottom with your spatula—the whole cake should be able to slide around freely in the pan.

When nicely browned underneath, gently loosen the edges with the spatula, shake the skillet to make sure no potatoes are sticking, and slide out onto the buttered plate. Invert the skillet over the plate (thick potholders are a necessity here) and flip back, so cake is in skillet. Return the skillet to the stove. Remove the plate and continue cooking until the second side is brown, occasionally sliding bits of butter down the side as before, about 6 to 8 minutes. Slide onto a serving plate, first making sure no potatoes are sticking, and serve. Serves 4–6.

Serving suggestion: A popular lunch dish for skiers in Switzerland consists of nothing more than roesti topped with 1 or 2 fried eggs and liberally doused with fresh black pepper. The yolk is broken by the diner and drips deliciously down through the potatoes as one eats.

Berne-style Roesti:
Cover the second side of the roesti with ⅓ cup grated Gruyère or Emmental cheese a few minutes before the potatoes are finished cooking. When the cheese melts, top with a fried egg. Serve with a green salad.

Potato Pancakes
(Latkes)

No matter how many potato pancakes I make, there are never enough. The more you eat, the more you want!

2 pounds (about 8) medium-size old potatoes	potato flour, cracker meal, or matzo meal
2 medium onions, peeled	2 teaspoons baking powder
2 eggs, well beaten	1 teaspoon salt, or to taste
3–4 tablespoons flour,	Freshly ground pepper
	Vegetable oil for frying

Peel the potatoes and soak in a bowl of ice water for 2 or 3 hours.

Preheat oven to 250°.

Using the fine grating disk of a food processor or the finest side of a four-sided grater, grate the potatoes into a bowl. As you work, intermittently grate a little of onion with the potatoes, which will keep the potato mixture from darkening. You should have about 4½ cups of grated potato-onion mixture.

Drain the mixture through a large sieve set over a bowl. Using your hands, squeeze excess liquid from the potatoes; do not discard the liquid. Place the potato mixture in another bowl.

Add the eggs to the potatoes, enough flour or meal to thicken to the consistency of cooked cereal, the baking powder, salt, and a good amount of pepper.

Let the potato liquid settle for a few minutes; as it does, a starchy sediment will collect in the bottom.

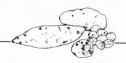

Carefully pour off the liquid and add the sediment to the potatoes.

Pour the vegetable oil into a large, heavy skillet to a depth of ½ inch and heat it. The oil must be very hot but not smoking. Scoop a heaping tablespoon of the potato mixture and lay it in the hot oil. Flatten it slightly. Fry about four of these at a time, over medium-high heat, until crisp and browned—2 to 3 minutes per side, turning once.

As potato cakes are finished, drain on absorbent paper and keep warm on a rack in a 250° oven. Makes about 24 pancakes, serving 6.

Note: The potato batter may be used to make 5 or 6 large single pancakes in a 10-inch skillet. Cook a little longer on each side, turning once.

Serving suggestion: These are the classic accompaniment to brisket of beef, but they can go with any roast meat or fowl. For a meatless meal, serve with apple sauce, sour cream, or yogurt. For another light entree, serve topped with crisp slices of bacon and a fennel and endive salad.

Italian New Potatoes with Rosemary

¼ cup olive oil
1 teaspoon salt, or to taste
2 pounds red-skinned new
potatoes

1 tablespoon minced fresh
rosemary, or 1 teaspoon
dried

Preheat the oven to 350°. Oil a 9 × 13-inch baking dish and set aside.

Combine the olive oil and salt in a shallow, medium-size bowl.

Scrub the potatoes and, without peeling, cut them into ¼-inch slices, dropping the slices into the bowl. When all are done, move them around in the bowl with two wooden spoons to coat them. Transfer to the prepared baking dish and spread slices out evenly. Sprinkle with the rosemary, cover with foil, and bake for ½ hour. Uncover, turn heat up to 400°, and bake

for an additional 10 to 15 minutes, or until tender. Do not let the potatoes overcook, as this makes them leathery and the rosemary bitter. Serves 6.

French Potato Salad

This warm potato salad depends on the absorbtion of broth and a vinaigrette dressing to heighten the flavor of the potatoes. It is classically paired with hot garlic sausage, but is superb with all kinds of cold meats and chicken as well as being an essential element of the hors d'oeuvre tray and salade niçoise. Critical to its success is cooking the potatoes just before they are to be used. If they are sliced and dressed while warm, they have a chance to absorb the broth and dressing flavors. The dish should be served at room temperature or even a little tepid—never refrigerate it.

5–6 medium boiling potatoes, about 2 pounds, or the same amount of new potatoes, scrubbed, skins left on
½ cup chicken broth
2 tablespoons minced shallots
½ cup mustard vinaigrette (p. 375)
2 tablespoons chopped parsley, or a mixture of parsley and chervil or snipped chives.

Boil the potatoes just until tender. Do not overcook or the salad will be mushy.

Take the potatoes out of the pot one by one with a slotted spoon and peel and cut into ¼-inch slices. Drop the slices into a serving bowl. Immediately pour the broth over the still-warm slices and toss gently with a wooden spoon. Let sit a few minutes so potatoes can absorb broth. Stir the shallots into the vinaigrette and add to the potatoes along with half the herbs; mix lightly, using wooden spoons. Garnish with balance of herbs. Serves 6.

New Potato Salad

2 pounds small
   red-skinned new
   potatoes, scrubbed and
   unpeeled
½ cup mayonnaise
½ cup sour cream
2 tablespoons lemon juice

1 tablespoon prepared
   mustard
2 tablespoons minced
   shallots
2 tablespoons minced
   parsley

Boil or steam the potatoes until tender. When they are cool enough to handle, cut into halves or thick slices and put in a bowl. Combine the remaining ingredients, pour over, and toss well. Refrigerate for 1 to 2 hours before serving. Serves 6.

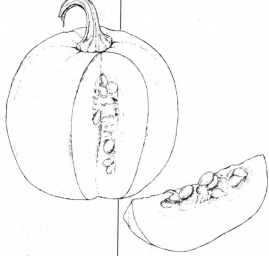

Pumpkin
(Cucurbita pepo)

Americans tend to think of pumpkin as belonging exclusively to this continent and are often surprised to learn others have found uses for it besides jack-o'-lanterns and pumpkin pie. The French make a very appealing soup of it, usually served right in the pumpkin; the Israelis stuff it with meat; and the Greeks fry slices in oil and eat it with the supergarlicky skordalia sauce. Pumpkin may be baked, boiled, or steamed and the puree used in any recipe calling for winter squash puree. Pumpkin bread is lovely with tea. And the toasted seeds make wonderful nibbles.

To Buy

Choose smaller (6–7 pounds or less), compact pumpkins; the flesh will be more tender. Look for the brightly colored sugar pumpkins, which are round rather than elongated. Avoid any that have mushy spots. To serve as a vegetable accompaniment, allow 1 pound per person. After peeling and trimming, you end up with about half this amount. A 6-pound pumpkin will yield about 4 cups of puree.

Pumpkin puree is also available canned.

To Store

Keep whole pumpkins in a cool place; they will last about a month. Refrigerate cut or peeled chunks in a plastic bag. These should last at least a week. The best long-term storage is to make puree and freeze it.

To Prepare

Cut off the top, scrape out seeds and strings with a thin-edged spoon, then peel. Pumpkin skin is tough, and you really have to slice it off. I prefer to work with small pumpkins; they are easier to handle. If the pumpkin does not sit firmly, cut off the bottom to make a flat surface. Then slice the skin from top to bottom all around. Don't worry if you lose some flesh. Cut into chunks, wedges, or cubes, depending on the way you intend to use it. Alternatively you can cut pumpkin into wedges or chunks first and peel each piece.

To Cook

Boiled: Add pumpkin cut into 3-inch chunks to boiling salted water, cover, and cook about 20 minutes from the second boil, or until tender.

Pureed: Put peeled chunks in a covered casserole over low heat with a little water to get them started.

Cook for 20 to 30 minutes, until soft. Uncover toward the end to cook off any excess moisture. Drain well, then mash or puree in a food processor. Use in pumpkin bread, pudding, or mousse. As a side dish, add butter, salt and pepper to taste, plus a little heavy cream and perhaps a grating of nutmeg.

Baked halves: Cut small pumpkins (2 pounds each) in half top to bottom, scrape out seeds and strings, and place cut side down on a rimmed cookie sheet with a little water. Bake in a 325° oven for 45 minutes, or until tender. Then turn cut side up and fill the cavity with butter, brown sugar, cinnamon, and, if you like, a splash of rum. Bake for another 15 minutes.

Gratin: Follow the recipe for Provençal Squash Gratin on page 296, substituting 2 pounds of diced pumpkin flesh from a young sugar pumpkin for the squash.

Pumpkin serving bowl: Choose a beautiful, unblemished, symmetrically round 6- to 8-pound pumpkin. Cut off the top with a sharp strong knife to make a lid; remove the seeds and fibers. Pour boiling water into the pumpkin and let stand for 10 minutes. Pour out water and repeat several times over an hour before using it. A cleaned 6-pound pumpkin should hold about a quart of stew or soup.

Toasted pumpkin seeds: Separate the seeds from the fibers (a slightly tedious operation) and discard the latter. Spread seeds out on a cookie sheet and toast in a slow oven (250°) for an hour. Turn the oven up to 350°. Mix with a bit of vegetable oil (about a scant tablespoon for each cup of seeds), spread again on the cookie sheet, salt lightly if desired with kosher salt, and roast for 15 minutes.

Pumpkin Soup

The Burgundian classic *potage au potiron* makes a stunning presentation for Thanksgiving or any fall meal when served in a "tureen" made of a real pumpkin. There are many versions, some involving Swiss cheese and quarts of cream. Mine is less rich; the bread is needed as a thickener. The flesh, when cooked, is simply scraped into the liquid and there's your soup. Choose an attractive, well-shaped, blemish-free pumpkin with a sturdy stem.

1 round pumpkin, about 6 pounds	2 cups diced French bread without crust
Salt and freshly ground pepper	1 quart well-flavored chicken stock, boiling
Vegetable oil	1 cup heavy cream
3 tablespoons butter	2 bay leaves
1 cup minced onion	Nutmeg

Preheat the oven to 375°. Cut around the top of the pumpkin with a strong sharp knife to make a lid. Scoop out the seeds and fibers. (Reserve the seeds for toasting). Season the inside with salt and pepper. Rub the outside of the pumpkin with vegetable oil, which will keep it from drying out and will impart a burnished sheen. Put it in a well-oiled baking dish.

Melt the butter in a saucepan and sauté the onions over low heat until soft. Mix in the bread and transfer to the pumpkin. Stir in the broth, cream, salt and pepper to taste, bay leaves, and several grinds of nutmeg. Replace the lid of the pumpkin. Bake for 2 hours; twice during cooking remove the top and stir everything with a long-handled spoon.

Remove the tureen from the oven and put it on a serving platter or sturdy tray with handles. Remove the lid (pry it up with a knife rather than pulling on the stem), check the seasoning and add more butter if you'd like it richer. Remove the bay leaves if you can. Serve in soup plates, scraping out some of the flesh with each portion. Serves at least 8.

Note: If you wish, the soup may be garnished with small fried bread croutons, chopped chives, or crumbled bacon.

Lamb and Pumpkin Stew

I am very fond of Armenian food and I particularly like this dish for its unusual combination of ingredients. Chicken broth can be used in place of water for a richer version.

1 pound peeled pumpkin flesh
1 pound boneless lamb, excess fat trimmed off, cut into 1-inch cubes
4 cups hot water
Salt to taste
3 garlic cloves, minced
2 large ripe tomatoes, peeled, seeded, and

chopped, or 1 cup canned
1 tablespoon tomato paste
2 tablespoons lemon juice
1 small green pepper, seeded, deribbed, and cut into 1-inch squares
1 tablespoon crushed dried mint leaves

Cut the pumpkin into 1-inch cubes and set aside. Combine the lamb, water, and salt in a heavy 6-quart pot. Bring to a boil and cook for 2 minutes, removing any scum that rises. Add the garlic, tomatoes, tomato paste, and lemon juice. Bring to the simmer, cover, and cook 1 hour. Add the pumpkin and green pepper and cook, covered, for another 45 minutes, until meat and pumpkin are fork tender. Stir in the mint leaves and correct seasoning. Serves 4.

Serving suggestion: Spoon over rice pilaf (p. 363) and accompany with Armenian Cucumber and Yogurt Salad (p. 116).

Pumpkin Custard

2 eggs plus 2 egg yolks
1 tablespoon flour
1½ cups pumpkin puree
½ cup sugar
1 teaspoon salt
¼ teaspoon ginger

½ teaspoon cinnamon
Several dashes nutmeg
1 teaspoon vanilla
1 cup heavy cream
1 cup milk

Preheat the oven to 350°. Butter 6 individual ramekins and place them in a large baking pan.
Combine the eggs, egg yolks, and flour in a bowl and beat briefly with a whisk just to blend. Beat in the

pumpkin puree, sugar, salt, ginger, cinnamon, and nutmeg. Stir in the vanilla, cream, and milk, mixing until well blended.

Ladle the custard mixture into the prepared dishes. Half fill the surrounding pan with boiling water. Bake for about 40 minutes, or until the custards are just barely set in the middle.

Remove the dishes from the water and let cool to room temperature (or chill if you prefer cold custard). Serve with lightly whipped unsweetened heavy cream. Serves 6.

Pumpkin Bread

Try this as a change of pace from pumpkin pie during the Thanksgiving season. It's nice with tea or coffee in the afternoon, too, and surprisingly good with vanilla ice cream.

4 extralarge eggs
1 cup vegetable oil
⅔ cup water
2 cups pumpkin puree
3½ cups sifted flour
2⅔ cups sugar
2 teaspoons baking soda
½ teaspoon baking powder

1 teaspoon salt
1 teaspoon cinnamon
½ teaspoon nutmeg
¼ teaspoon powdered cloves
⅔ cup chopped walnuts
⅔ cup coarsely chopped raisins

Preheat the oven to 350°. Butter two loaf pans (8½ × 4½ × 2½).

Beat the eggs lightly, then blend in the oil and water. Add and stir in the pumpkin puree. Mix together and sift the flour, sugar, baking soda, baking powder, salt, cinnamon, nutmeg, and cloves, then stir into the pumpkin mixture with a wire whisk. Add the nuts and raisins. Pour into the prepared loaf pans and bake for 55 to 60 minutes, or until the bread tests clean in the center. Cool on a rack in the pans; remove when cool.

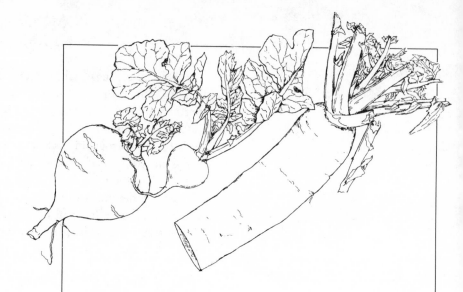

Radishes

(Raphanus sativus)

My Russian grandfather ate the most interesting things for breakfast. Sometimes tidbits of herring, sometimes soup. The most bizarre, in the eyes of someone to whom pancakes represented the outer limits of breakfast, was radishes. There might be grated white radish, bound with the tiniest bit of chicken fat, or buttered radishes, salted and eaten with thick slices of black bread and washed down with lashings of sweet tea. I thought this particularly Russian until I saw the French eat radishes with sweet butter and salt as an hors d'oeuvre.

There are four basic radishes: the common red; the white, also called icicle; the black radish, which looks like a sooty turnip and can range from mild and slightly musty to peppery; and the daikon, or Japanese white radish, which can grow to be a foot long and three inches thick.

To Buy

Red: Sold by the bunch, with the stems and leaves attached, or topped and bagged. Look for firm, uncracked, well-colored radishes; leaves, if present, should be bright green. Large ones can have a woody core; smaller ones are sweeter.

White (icicle): Usually sold in half-pound plastic bags.

Black: Appear in winter and early spring. Look for firm flesh, dark color.

Daikon: Those about an inch and a half in diameter are the sweetest. Larger ones can be flabby and pithy.

To Store

Store red, white, and black radishes in a plastic bag in the refrigerator. Refrigerate daikon unwrapped. Red radishes will keep for two to three weeks. White, black, and daikon radishes will keep for several weeks. Prepare just before using.

To Prepare

Red: Trim leaves and leave about an inch of stem. If required, gently scrape under water with a paring knife around the darkened area where stem joins flesh. Trim off taproot without cutting flesh. Wash and dry before using. Crisp by soaking in ice water for 30 minutes.

White: Scrape lightly with a paring knife.

Black: Wash well and peel with a swivel-bladed peeler.

Daikon: Trim and scrape before using.

To Cook

I do not find cooked radishes particularly rewarding, but they can be steamed in a tablespoon of butter and ¼ cup water for a bunch. This will take anywhere from 5 to 13 minutes, depending on size. Dress with a little additional butter and season to taste.

Oriental White Radish Salad

A pleasant accompaniment to Oriental-style marinated meats or grilled meats or chicken.

2 daikon, about 1¾ pounds total, scraped
3 scallions, white and green, finely sliced crosswise

Dressing:

3 tablespoons light soy sauce
1 tablespoon salad oil
2 teaspoons sesame oil (see note)
2 tablespoons mild vinegar
3 teaspoons sugar

1 tablespoon sesame seeds, toasted and crushed (p. 406)
½ fresh hot red chili pepper, seeded and finely chopped

Cut the radish into medium julienne strips by hand or with the appropriate disk of a food processor. You should have about 8 cups.

Mix the dressing ingredients, in the order listed, in the bowl in which you will serve the salad. Add the radish and scallions and toss, making sure the vegetables are well coated. Cover with plastic wrap and refrigerate for an hour. Serves 6–8.

Note: If you have hot sesame oil, which is merely regular sesame oil in which a hot pepper has been steeped, use it and substitute half a sweet red pepper for the chili pepper.

Chinese Smashed Radish Salad

30–36 small red radishes
1 teaspoon salt
2 tablespoons sesame oil

2 tablespoons vinegar
2 tablespoons soy sauce
2 teaspoons sugar

Trim tops and roots of radishes and wash and dry them. Crush the radishes slightly with the flat side of a knife or cleaver (not enough to break them apart). Sprinkle with the salt and let stand for 10 minutes. Add the oil, vinegar, soy sauce, and sugar. Toss and chill for 30 minutes. Serves 6.

Salad Greens

T hanks to great demand and improved shipping techniques, an awesome variety of lettuces, greens, and salad herbs is available all year. The combinations of texture and taste they afford are spectacular. The lettuces I like best are Boston, green and red curly leaf lettuce, and Romaine. Iceberg lettuce, the only salad green I knew as a child, isn't as tasty (it came into being as an invention of produce shippers looking for a lettuce that traveled well and was less perishable than ordinary lettuce), but it is good for shredding in tacos or as a base for certain Chinese dishes.

A Glossary of Salad Greens

Arugula: Also called roquette and rocket. Bright green and pungently peppery in flavor, it is a wonderful foil for endive or any other salad green and is delicious on its own. Sold with its roots, which are usually very sandy. Needs very careful washing in several waters. Wilts easily.

Bibb: A small-headed lettuce from Kentucky with a subtle, melting flavor, beautifully colored, very elegant, and usually priced to match. Also called Kentucky limestone. Nice combined with watercress or endive.

Boston: The archetypical lettuce, with loose floppy

leaves, a pale heart, and tender sweet flavor. Needs very careful washing. Serve alone or combine with any other green.

Chicory: Also called curly endive, of which family it is a member. Has a pleasant appearance and tartness that make it a good mixer.

Endive: Also called Belgian endive, a crisp, greenish white spear of tightly curled leaves, the *ne plus ultra* of salad bowl denizens and very pricey. Use the whole separated leaves, or cut the endive crosswise into rings or into julienne. Looks particularly beautiful slivered under a blizzard of chopped parsley.

Escarole: Crisp yellow-white leaves with a hearty flavor that can take a strong dressing. Wash carefully.

Iceberg: A tight ball of pale green leaves, low in vitamins, flavor, and appeal.

Leaf lettuce: Sometimes called curly lettuce. Has an attractive ruffly edge and pretty bright green color that enhances all salads. Use alone or in combinations.

Red leaf lettuce: A soft lettuce with a pretty maroon-red tinge at the end of the leaves. Nice to mix with other sturdier greens.

Romaine: A good keeper, also known as cos lettuce, thought to have originated on the Greek island of the same name. A large cylindrical head of oval leaves that can be tough when oversized. Has a nutty flavor that can take a strong garlicky dressing. Discard the outer leaves if very dark and leathery.

Watercress: Small, dark green, clover-shape leaves with a pleasant, clean, peppery taste. Cress mixed with julienned endive is a salad classic.

Endive

Some Unusual Greens:

Field lettuce or lamb's tongue: Called *mache* by the French, corn salad by the English, *feldsalat* in German, it has a subtle, nutty taste. Grows wild and is easily cultivated. Use alone or combine with cooked beets, dressed with a plain classic vinaigrette made with the best olive oil you can afford.

Nasturtium greens: Add a peppery note mixed with other greens.

Purslane: An herb, also known as portulaca, whose crisp leaves are eaten as a salad.

Radicchio: Also called red chicory and treviso, after the Italian town where it originates. A miniature, slightly bitter, ruby red winter lettuce recently imported from Italy and absolutely spectacular mixed with other greens. Expensive, but you need only one head to add color. Can take a strong dressing. There is also a loose-leaved variety.

Salad bowl: Also called oak leaf lettuce, because of the shape of its leaf. A favorite of home gardeners and sometimes seen at farm stands, it mixes well with red lettuce.

Sorrel: Also called sour grass, for its sharp, lemony taste. Use the leaves only, and mix sparingly with other greens.

Spinach: The traditional combination is with crumbled bacon and/or mushrooms. Sesame seed and soy dressing or sesame vinaigrette are more unusual and very good. Use the smallest, brightest leaves and wash very well. See Spinach.

Salads can also be garnished with edible petals, like those of nasturtiums, roses, and violets and some of the more unusual herbs like lovage and burnet.

To Buy

Weight is the key in selecting lettuce. Look for firm, heavy heads. A few outer leaves may appear wilted, but the inside should be firm and crisp. Avoid yellowed or large, leathery leaves and blackened stems. Use your judgment and your nose for other greens. Limp, yellowed leaves, a sourish smell, or lack of a characteristic smell are all signs of age.

To Prepare

Greens must be very well washed, because a gritty salad is unpleasant. Careful washing of each leaf is boring but necessary. I have often read that salad greens will turn brown and limp if washed too far ahead of time. Yet for years I have bought several kinds of lettuces at the beginning of the week, separated and washed them carefully (never soaked—this *does* make them limp), and dried them well in small batches in a salad spinner. Then I put them in plastic bags (not too many jammed together in one bag), expel the air at the top, and tie the bag closed. Refrigerated in the crisper drawer of the refrigerator, they last until Friday, if necessary. I think pressing the air out is the key, plus careful washing and drying so as not to bruise the leaves. Anyway, it works.

In assembling a salad, the greens must be very dry or the dressing will not cling uniformly to the leaves. If you don't have a salad spinner, use an old Turkish towel to dry the leaves. It is wasteful to use paper toweling, and dish towels are not absorbent enough. Don't use the French wire salad basket meant to be whirled about one's head in a demented fashion—it does more damage than good.

Dress the salad at the very last minute by pouring the dressing on the leaves, not the other way around. If the leaves seem too large, tear rather than cut them into bite-size pieces. Use a bowl large enough to allow a gently thorough tossing, and serve on flat salad plates, not in bowls, which are inelegant and make everything on the bottom soggy.

Salad Dressings

Once you find how easy it is to make vinaigrette dressing and how superior the fresh flavor is, you will not want to buy bottled dressings that are not only overpriced and full of chemicals, but invariably too vinegary. Vinaigrette is what the French dress salads with, but it is not that strange orange gluey stuff called French dressing in this country. Vinaigrette is nothing more than good oil and an acid (vinegar or lemon juice or a combination of the two), salt, pepper, and perhaps a bit of mustard. The classic proportions are three parts oil to one part acid, but these may be varied according to the degree of acidity of your vinegar. Since I like assertive vinegars, I find I like a four-to-one ratio best. There are countless permutations in which cream, herbs, garlic, and even cheese may be added, but they are all variations of the basic vinaigrette. Generally speaking, the strongly flavored greens can take a strongly flavored vinaigrette.

Always dissolve the salt in the vinegar before whisking in the oil. If mustard is used, it, too, is whisked in before the oil. You may also add further flavor with some herb or a teaspoon of chopped shallots. The flavor of garlic may be added either by smashing a clove and letting it steep in vinaigrette, or pounding it to a puree with the salt and adding to the vinegar.

Make your dressing in small batches; it is best when fresh. And make it as close to serving time as possible. Use the best olive oil you can afford, for its character cannot be matched by any "salad oil." Peanut, corn, and safflower oils keep well and have their place in cooking but lack character as salad oils. On the other hand, hazelnut and walnut oils add a special flavor to endive and beets. Experiment with lemon juice and flavored and plain vinegars until you find just the degree of tartness and kind of flavor that is pleasing to you. And no sugar, please.

Oils become rancid easily, so for long-term storage use the refrigerator, especially in summer. This may cloud the oils, but that is preferable to a stale taste, which can ruin the best salad or cooked food. Clarity will return with room temperature. Better still, buy your oil in small quantities.

Try several olive oils to understand the difference in types and flavors. The terms can be confusing, as they not only indicate the grade but the method of extraction, filtering, and refinement. The best oil comes from the first pressing; subsequent pressings usually yield an inferior and weaker oil, and this is reflected in the price.

The finest olive oil comes from Lucca, Italy, and has a nutty, sweet taste. Almost equally good is oil from Provence. Although I personally find the fruitiness of the French oil too intrusive, I am in the minority here. Spanish oil is too intense for me, as are Sicilian and Greek oils, which have a strong olive flavor.

Following are the common grade names given olive oil:

Extra virgin, or *extra extra,* is made from the first pressing. It is golden if made from ripe olives and has a green or greenish black cast if partly ripe fruit is used. It has the most pronounced olive flavor and aroma and is best used in salads where its aggressiveness is desirable. In cooking, the strong taste may overwhelm delicate flavors.

Virgin olive oil also comes directly from the fruit but may result from a second pressing. There is a nutty overtone.

Pure olive oil indicates the third pressing, extracted from the pulp after the first and second pressings are taken. It may contain solvents or have been made with a hot water process, both of which alter flavor and texture, making a greasy, rather flavorless oil.

Green Salad with Baked Marinated Goat Cheese

I first ate this delectable combination in one of the new *enoteques,* or wine restaurants, that have sprung up all over Paris. The idea is that one can try superb wines by the glass, with an appropriately enhancing food from a menu designated just for that purpose. The salad is incredibly easy and, though wonderful with a full-bodied Burgundy, just as good on its own.

2 small (about 2½ inches in diameter) round fresh goat cheeses, *not* those coated with wax	½ cup fine dry bread crumbs from home-style white bread
Several sprigs fresh thyme	Salad greens for 2 persons (see note)
¼ cup virgin olive oil	Vinaigrette dressing (p. 374)
½ teaspoon dried thyme	

Twelve to 24 hours in advance: Put the goat cheeses in a small dish with the fresh thyme, and pour the olive oil over them. If fresh thyme is not available, use a pinch of dried thyme for each cheese.

When ready to serve, preheat the oven to 450°.

Mix the dried thyme and bread crumbs. Dip each cheese in the crumbs, top and bottom. Place on a small oiled cookie sheet and bake for 10 minutes, until golden brown and slightly melted. Toss the greens with the vinaigrette and arrange on two plates. Remove the cheese with a spatula and place on top of salad in the center. Serve immediately with fresh French bread. Serves 2.

Note: Choose from or combine arugula, field lettuce, red or green leaf, Bibb, Boston.

Wilted Lettuce

The old Colonnade Restaurant in Philadelphia was a very elegant cafeteria that served such appealing vegetables I would often eat nothing else when taken there as a child—something quite unheard of in those days. Their wilted lettuce (they called it Dutch lettuce) was my favorite.

2 heads of Boston or any soft-leaf lettuce	¼ cup vinegar
4–5 strips bacon, diced	½ teaspoon salt
3–4 scallions, white and part of green, diced	1½ teaspoons sugar
	Freshly ground pepper

Heat the bowl you will serve the lettuce in by filling it with hot water. Separate, wash, and dry the lettuce leaves.

Slowly fry the bacon in a heavy skillet until half done. Add the scallions and continue cooking until bacon is crisp. Remove bacon and scallions with a slotted spoon and set aside. Discard all but 4 tablespoons of the fat.

Dry the serving bowl and in it combine and toss the lettuce, bacon, and scallions. Add the vinegar, salt, and sugar to the fat in the skillet. Bring to a boil, stirring, and when sugar is dissolved, add the lettuce. (It will accommodate as it wilts). Cover the pan with a lid or the inverted bowl until lettuce is warm and wilted. Put in the bowl, toss, and serve at once. Season with several grinds of pepper. Serves 4.

Vegetarian wilted lettuce: Omit bacon
and use 4 tablespoons vegetable oil to sauté the scallions, then proceed as directed. Add garlic-flavored fried croutons (p. 404) just before serving.

Mixed Salad of Greens with Lamb

Warmed salads are not a new idea, but nouvelle cuisine took the notion a step further by including meats of all kinds. I make the following salad with a lamb steak I cut off and save from a leg when I am roasting one, or with a lean duck breast. It makes a pleasant light lunch or an interesting first course. Be sure to use a very good vinegar.

1 Belgian endive, separated into leaves	lean raw lamb from the leg, in one piece
1 small head radicchio, washed and torn into bite-size pieces	1 tablespoon chopped shallots or white of scallions
1 head Bibb lettuce, washed and torn into bite-size pieces	¼ cup wine or sherry vinegar
1½–2 tablespoons olive oil	Salt and freshly ground pepper to taste
¾ pound (approximately)	

Arrange the endive leaves and the lettuces on four serving plates. Heat 1 tablespoon of the oil in a 10-inch skillet and, when quite hot, sauté the lamb and shallots just until the lamb is crisply brown on the outside (it should be quite rare). Remove and keep warm.

Deglaze the pan with the vinegar, scraping up any brown bits that cling to the bottom. Add and stir in a little more oil and salt and pepper to taste.

Slice the lamb thinly on the diagonal and lay the strips over the lettuce. Spoon the shallots over. Strain the warm vinaigrette and pour over each plate. Serve at once. Serves 4.

Note: The combination may be varied according to whim and availability. Red cabbage or watercress can be substituted for the radicchio, and thin slices of lean steak or a thinly sliced boned chicken breast may be used instead of the lamb.

Watercress Salad with Sesame Seeds

Trim away the coarse lower stems of two bunches of very fresh watercress. Add by the handful to a quart of rapidly boiling salted water, and boil uncovered for 4 minutes, until just tender. Drain in a colander and immediately run cold water over. Drain again and press out as much water as possible with the hands. Separate the sprigs on a towel.

Prepare the soy-sesame seed sauce in the recipe for spinach salad with sesame seeds on page 272, but substitute 2 tablespoons rice vinegar for the peanut oil.

Place the cress in a bowl and toss gently with the dressing. Divide and arrange attractively on four plates. Serve at room temperature. Serves 4.

Quick-sautéed Watercress

The slightly bitter, clean taste of this green as a vegetable accompaniment complements any Oriental food or Western-style meat. It must be prepared just before serving or it will become limp, but the cooking is so rapid that this is not a problem. If the amount of cress seems enormous, remember that it wilts and reduces considerably in volume. Also remember that it is so good everyone always wants seconds.

6 **bunches very fresh watercress**	2 **cloves garlic, peeled**
4 **tablespoons olive or peanut oil**	½ **teaspoon salt, or to taste**

Cut off the coarser bottom portion of the watercress stems; wash quickly and dry very well. This is important or you will have spattering.

Heat a heavy skillet or wok, add the oil, and heat; add the garlic and stir-fry over brisk heat for 30 seconds. Add the watercress and salt and stir-fry for 1 or 2 minutes, keeping the cress moving and turning constantly until it is wilted, bright green, and coated with oil. Transfer to a warm serving dish, or use to garnish a hot meat or poultry platter. Serves 8.

Variation: Reduce watercress to 2 bunches and combine with 1 pound well washed and dried spinach.

Watercress Soup

Many salad greens also make delicious soups. I first ate this one in the home of a French friend and had no idea what it was. When I found how easy it was to make, it became my most dependable first course.

4 **medium potatoes, peeled and cut into 1-inch cubes**	removed
	Salt and freshly ground pepper to taste
1 **medium onion, peeled and halved**	**Butter**
1 **bunch watercress, stems**	½ **to 1 cup cream**

Parboil the potatoes in 3 cups water (or half water and half chicken broth) for 10 minutes. Add the onion, place the watercress on top, and simmer, covered, 8 to 10 minutes more.

Let cool slightly, then puree in a food processor or blender until watercress is reduced to tiny green flecks. You may have to do this in two batches.

Add salt and pepper, stir in a good lump of butter, and add cream according to richness desired. Heat, but do not boil. If soup appears too thick, thin with some boiling water. This soup may be prepared entirely ahead and gently reheated at serving time. Serves 6.

Escarole and Rice Soup

The *minestre* of Italy, the thick vegetable soups that often constitute the evening meal, deserve to be better known. This one is light yet hearty, nourishing (the addition of cheese makes it nutritionally complete), and easy to make.

1 pound escarole
3 tablespoons olive oil
2 teaspoons finely chopped garlic
1 small onion, chopped
Salt to taste
5 cups chicken broth
⅓ cup raw Arborio rice, or ½ cup American long-grain rice
Freshly ground pepper
Freshly grated Parmesan cheese

Separate all the leaves of the escarole and discard any that are wilted or bruised. Soak in a basin of water and dunk up and down with your hands. Drain briefly, stack the leaves a bunch at a time, and cut crosswise into pieces about 1 inch wide. Set aside.

Heat the oil in a heavy soup kettle and sauté the garlic and onion until the onion is pale gold—about 3 minutes. Add the escarole, sprinkle lightly with salt, and cook 3 minutes more. Add 1 cup of the broth, cover, and cook over low heat until the escarole is quite tender—10 to 15 minutes, depending on how young the leaves are. Add the balance of the broth, bring to the boil, add the rice, cover, and simmer for about 12 minutes, or until the rice is tender but firm to the bite. Taste and correct seasoning; add several grinds of black pepper. Off the heat and just before serving, sprinkle with Parmesan cheese. Pass additional cheese at the table. Serves 6.

Note: You may substitute fresh spinach for the escarole, but be sure to wash it in several changes of water to remove any sand. This recipe may be prepared ahead, up to the point at which the rice is added.

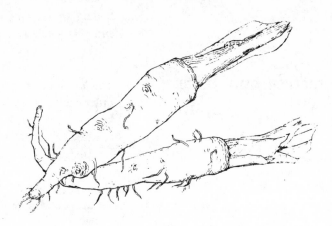

Salsify

(Trapopogon porrifoliuo)

Salsify, a member of the daisy family, was a very popular winter vegetable in nineteenth-century England and then seems to have fallen into relative obscurity. To my great joy, I have been served it recently in several restaurants and found it utterly delicious. I hope it will catch on. A root resembling a thinner parsnip, salsify is also called oyster plant or vegetable oyster for its subtle, faintly oyster flavor. Salsify has a distant, black-skinned relative called scorzonera, longer and more slender, with a similar flavor plus just a hint of coconut. They may be used interchangeably.

Salsify and scorzonera are given a preliminary cooking, then finished in various ways. They may be simply reheated in chicken or veal gravy and are particularly good with grilled meats, good when lightly sautéed in butter and sprinkled with herbs.

If you grow your own, you may have the bonus of using the young leaves in salad. Both salsify and scorzonera roots may be used in any carrot or parsnip preparation in which their more delicate flavor would not be overwhelmed.

To Buy

Salsify and scorzonera are rarely found in the average

market because of poor keeping quality and lack of general demand. They do appear in Italian or French markets, however.

Look for smallish, firm, unshriveled roots without scars. One pound, trimmed and peeled, will feed 3 people. One pound will give you a little over 1 cup pureed. Salsify is available canned, but it is short on flavor.

To Store

Unwashed, in an open plastic bag in the refrigerator. Salsify does not keep well; it lasts 3 days at most. Its flavor lessens each day, so try to use the day you buy it.

To Prepare

Scrub well, cut off the top and tail, and peel. Cut into 3- or 4-inch pieces. Use a stainless steel knife and immerse in acidulated water immediately; the flesh of both darkens on contact with air.

Both salsify and scorzonera may be cooked with the scrubbed skins on and peeled after cooking by slipping off the skins under cold running water.

To Cook

Blanched: Cook in boiling salted water to which lemon juice has been added, or *à blanc* (p. 17) for about 10 minutes.

Steamed: Bring ¾ inch of water to a boil in the bottom of a steamer. Steam peeled or unpeeled, for 12 to 15 minutes. Finish with butter. Steaming retains more nutrients but will darken the flesh a bit.

Sautéed: Melt 2 or 3 tablespoons of butter in a skillet and sauté blanched, cut-up salsify until lightly golden. Season to taste and sprinkle with finely chopped parsley and dill.

Pureed: Cook peeled salsify *à blanc* (p. 17) slightly longer than usual—about 20 minutes—then drain, puree in a food processor until smooth, and beat in butter and cream. Season with salt and white pepper and a few drops of lemon juice. Reheat in a double boiler.

Creamed: Turn blanched salsify in melted butter, but do not let the pieces take on any color. Season well with fresh pepper and a dash of lemon juice. Add ⅓ cup heavy cream or crème fraîche and stir over gentle heat until each piece is lightly coated and the sauce slightly reduced. Sprinkle with parsley and serve immediately.

Glazed: Turn blanched salsify in melted butter, sprinkle lightly with sugar, and cook, shaking pan, until glazed. Season with salt and pepper.

Sorrel
(Rumex)

Alternately praised and scorned for its acidic edge, sorrel is a perfect example of the fickleness of food trends. At the end of the seventies, this pungent little arrow-shape herb began to show up all over the place —in sauces accompanying fish and chicken, in both cold and hot soups—always presented as if it has just been discovered. Though sorrel has always been considered a classic accompaniment to fish in France, it has come into new focus in nouvelle cuisine as the perfect partner for sautéed scallops of salmon or any poached fish. My Russian grandmother frequently made a soup called schav, a blend of sorrel, eggs, sour cream, and lemon juice, which she said was "good for you." Like the ancients, she appreciated it as a diuretic. The Chinese believe it reduces fevers. In fact, another name for the classic French sorrel soup, potage germiny, is potage santé, or "health soup." Its slightly sour taste seems to stimulate the appetite.

Sorrel, which answers to lots of names—sourgrass, sourweed, herb patience, and patience dock—should be eaten young. Mature sorrel becomes unpleasantly acid. Like its relative rhubarb, sorrel is high in oxalic acid and can distress delicate kidneys.

To Buy

There are several strains of sorrel on the market; early varieties have pale green leaves, later ones have deeper green leaves. Avoid outright yellowish or limp leaves. Sorrel puree is also available in cans and is rather good. As sorrel wilts like spinach, allow 1 untrimmed pound per person.

To Store

Keep refrigerated in a plastic bag and use within a day or two. Freeze by making the very easy sorrel puree (recipe follows) and packing into plastic boxes.

To Prepare

Pick over the leaves, remove any roots, and wash well in two rinses of water. Remove the stem and rib by folding the leaf part in half and pulling the stem up and backward toward the leaf. Just-picked young sorrel needs no blanching at all. Older leaves should be plunged into boiling salted water, removed when the water returns to the boil, and drained.

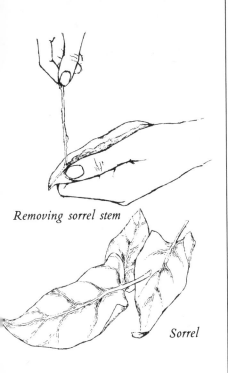

Removing sorrel stem

Sorrel

To Cook

Pureed: Blanch 2 pounds of washed, stemmed sorrel in an enamel-lined pot of boiling water for 3 minutes. Drain, scoop out by handfuls, press out excess water, and puree in a blender or food processor. Beat in ¼ cup heavy cream, and heat just until mixture thickens. Do not overcook or the tang will be lost. Season to taste with salt, pepper, a few drops of lemon juice, and, if desired, a grating of nutmeg. Use as a vegetable, a sauce for poached fish or hard-boiled eggs, or an omelet filling. Makes about 2 ½ cups.

To use canned sorrel puree: Melt 2 tablespoons butter and stir into the puree. Season to taste.

Potage germiny: Combine 1½ cups sorrel puree with 4 cups homemade chicken stock. Beat together 3 egg yolks and 1 cup cream. Add a little of the soup to warm the mixture, then add and blend with the balance of the soup. Season to taste with salt and pepper. Heat gently but do not boil. Diced cooked white chicken meat may also be added.

Hard-cooked eggs with sorrel: Halve 6 hard-cooked eggs and place in a buttered baking dish, cut side up. Pour 1 ½ cups puree over the eggs. Sprinkle with ¾ cup bread crumbs that have been quickly fried in butter, and bake in a 400 ° oven for about 15 minutes until the sauce browns lightly. Serves 4 as a first course.

Cold Sorrel Soup

4 tablespoons butter	and thinly sliced
1 large yellow onion, finely chopped	Salt to taste
½ pound young tender sorrel, cleaned and shredded	4 cups boiling water
	¾ cup heavy cream
	Freshly ground pepper
1 pound potatoes, peeled	Chopped chives

Melt 3 tablespoons of the butter in a heavy stainless-steel or enamel-lined 4-quart pot and stew the onion over gentle heat until soft but not brown—about 8 minutes. Add the sorrel, cook for a few minutes, stirring, until it wilts, then add the potatoes. Stir and cook together for a few minutes more. Add the salt and water, bring to the boil, lower heat, cover, and let simmer for 20 minutes. Uncover and cook for another 10 minutes, mashing the potatoes from time to time with a wooden spoon.

Remove from the fire and puree in a food processor or blender. Add the cream, the remaining tablespoon of butter, and pepper. Chill. If too thick, thin with a little cream or milk before serving. Garnish with chopped chives. Serves 4.

Spinach
(Spinacea oleracea)

Spinach," wrote the French gastronomic chronicler Grimod de la Reynière, "is susceptible of receiving all imprints: it is the virgin wax of the kitchen." I would call it downright gregarious, seeing how well spinach gets along with cream, butter, cheese, nutmeg, onions, mushrooms, crumbled bacon, and hard-boiled eggs. It also acts as a stuffing, beds down chicken breasts nicely, and takes particularly well to pastry, as in those delicious Middle Eastern rolls, triangles, squares, and pies that enclose spinach and sometimes cheese in filo leaves. Creamed spinach is splendid in crêpes, as a bed for poached eggs, and blended with ricotta cheese as a savory filling for hollow pastas, as well as with featherly light gnocchi. Many of these spinach dishes constitute a separate course or a light meal, so that those with eggs or cheese are especially good for vegetarian menus.

The botanically distinct New Zealand spinach, grown in home gardens for its heat-resisting properties, can be used like ordinary spinach.

Because that discriminating Florentine lady Catherine de Médicis was fond of spinach, florentine is the classic menu designation for any dish made with it.

To Buy

Look for dark green, bouncy leaves and crisp stems. If you have a choice, loose leaves are preferable to bagged spinach, which often contains some damaged leaves and thick, inedible stems. Pass over bagged spinach if it smells sour. One has to buy what seems a huge amount of spinach to feed even two, but bear in mind that the volume shrinks enormously in cooking. Allow 1 to 1¼ pounds for 2 persons; after cooking you will have only 1 cup. Spinach is also available frozen in whole-leaf and chopped forms. It is quite satisfactory for any use other than a salad or quick sauté.

To Store

Keep unwashed leaves in an open plastic bag in the refrigerator crisper drawer. Use within four days.

To Prepare

Sort over and discard coarse stems and damaged leaves. To remove tough stems from mature leaves, fold the leaf in half, right sides touching, and pull the stem back toward the leaf tip. It should come away in one piece along with any tough veins. Wash, swishing it around and lifting it with the hands, until no sand remains in the basin, and drain. Several changes of water may be necessary as the deeply convoluted leaves hold sand and dirt. Wash bagged spinach, too.

To Cook

Steamed:
If spinach is young and is to be just buttered, I steam-cook it this way. No liquid is needed other than the water clinging to the leaves. I also do this to avoid watery spinach that might spoil a dish like lasagne. Pile the spinach in an enamel-lined or stainless-steel pot (aluminum gives an off color and a metallic taste), cover, and put over a moderate fire for 2 to 4 minutes.

Blanched:
If I need to intensify the color of the whole leaf or cook a large quantity that is to be kept and finished later in the day, I blanch it, adding it by the handful to a large quantity of salted boiling water. Cook for about 3 minutes from the return to the boil. Run cold water in the pot to cool it quickly, then squeeze out the water. Finish and season as desired.

Winter spinach sometimes has a stronger flavor than the tender young leaves of summer. To offset the slightly acrid taste, add a pinch of sugar to the finished dish and use a fair amount of butter when finishing it.

Spinach absorbs an astonishing amount of butter, becoming more delicious as it does. There is a well-known story of Brillat-Savarin's recipe for the best spinach he had ever eaten, prepared by his friend the canon Chevrier. At first he was told it was simply cooked in butter. The recipe, which was finally pried from the abbé and is quoted in its enchanting entirety in Elizabeth David's *French Country Cooking,* calls for a first cooking on Wednesday, one-quarter pound of butter for each pound of spinach. On Thursday the spinach is cooked again for 10–15 minutes in 2 more tablespoons of butter, allowed to cool, and so on each day until the final cooking for Sunday dinner, by which time the spinach had absorbed three-quarters its own weight in butter!

Buttered chopped spinach: Blanch 2 to 2½ pounds spinach for 3 to 5 minutes and squeeze out water. Chop the spinach with a stainless steel knife. Melt 1 tablespoon butter in the pot, stir in the spinach, and add 3 more tablespoons butter cut into small pats, making each addition as the previous one is absorbed. Season to taste with salt, pepper, and a grating of nutmeg, if desired. Serve immediately. If you wish the spinach to be closer to a puree, process it, after blanching. Serves 4.

Creamed chopped spinach: Stir in 3 tablespoons of heavy cream, one at a time, after the butter.

Fresh spinach salad: Young tender leaves are best for eating raw. Mature leaves are hard to chew and can cause flatulence. Wash and dry the leaves well; chill. Use plain or combine with very fresh sliced raw mushrooms, hard-cooked egg quarters, and, if you like, crisp, crumbled bacon. Dress with mustard vinaigrette.

Poached eggs Florentine: Put 2 hot poached eggs for each person on a bed of buttered chopped spinach, cover with mornay sauce (p. 377) and a sprinkling of grated Parmesan cheese and run under the broiler to brown. Serve with toast points as a light lunch or supper.

Japanese Spinach Salad with Sesame Seeds

This salad came about because I misunderstood the directions for a Japanese dish called aemono, which calls for wilting the spinach first. The result was this salad that I serve often at an all-vegetable meal. It tastes simply marvelous, and the seeds make the meal nutritionally complete.

¼ cup soy sauce
2 teaspoons sugar
2 tablespoons peanut or
    vegetable oil

2 tablespoons sesame seeds
1½ pounds fresh young
    spinach, cleaned

Mix the soy sauce, sugar, and oil in a small saucepan and stir over gentle heat until the sugar dissolves. Let cool. Toast the sesame seeds in a dry frying pan over medium heat until they color and start to pop. Use a rolling pin to crush them between two pieces of wax paper and stir into the cooled sauce. Pour over spinach in a large bowl and toss very well. Serves 6.

Note: Half a pound of raw sliced mushrooms makes a heftier dish, suitable for lunch.

Sautéed Spinach

Karen Hubert, whose Hubert's restaurant serves some of the best vegetables garnishes in Manhattan, has very kindly shared with me the method for making this excellent spinach. You will be delighted with its appearance and taste, which even children like, and it is very simple and fast. (At the restaurant it is done at the last minute for each order.) It will seem impossible to make this quantity of spinach in one skillet, but remember that as it wilts it will be reduced to a quarter of its volume.

3–4 tablespoons butter
2 garlic cloves, peeled
1½ pounds fresh young

spinach leaves, cleaned
Salt and freshly ground
pepper to taste

Melt the butter in a 10-inch skillet without letting it brown. Put the garlic through a press into the butter, and immediately add about a quarter of the spinach. Keep the heat fairly brisk, and add more handfuls of spinach as it wilts. Keep large quantities of the spinach moving by giving it several scoops-and-turns with a pancake spatula (see note).

It is ready when the spinach is softened but still nicely green—a matter of 3 or 4 minutes. Serve immediately. Serves 4.

Note: At the restaurant, no utensil touches the spinach; it is kept moving with the upward-forward shake and wrist flip of the pans used by professionals. This is not advised at home, however, except for the most proficient. Under no circumstances should the garlic brown, which will give a bitter flavor.

Spinach with Raisins and Pine Nuts

The sweetness of the raisins counters any sharp edge the spinach might have, and the combination of textures is lovely. Especially nice with roast pork.

2 pounds loose spinach, or 2 ten-ounce bags, steamed and chopped	¼ cup pignoli nuts
	¼ cup olive oil
	2 garlic cloves, peeled
¼ cup raisins, plumped in warm water and drained	Salt and freshly ground pepper

Toss the spinach with the raisins and pignolis and set aside.

Heat the oil in a stainless-steel or enamel-lined skillet and sauté the garlic until light brown. Remove the garlic, add the spinach, toss well, cover, and simmer for 5 minutes. Uncover and raise heat if necessary to cook off any excess moisture. Season to taste with salt and several grindings of pepper. Serve at once. Serves 4.

Note: The Roman variation of this preparation consists of omitting the garlic and using bacon drippings or leaf lard in place of the olive oil. Swiss chard may also be used in this recipe in place of spinach.

Spinach Soufflé Roll

This elegant, light yet satisfying dish is composed of a savory spinach filling in a roll that is really a thin soufflé. For all its lightness, it is remarkably sturdy—it can be made ahead, refrigerated or frozen, and gently reheated. The leftovers are marvelous, too. It makes a lovely light supper or luncheon main course, and is an attractive buffet item combined with several vegetable salads.

The Roll:

4 tablespoons butter
½ cup flour
½ teaspoon salt
White pepper to taste

2 cups hot milk
5 large eggs at room
   temperature, separated

The Filling:

3 tablespoons butter
4 shallots, finely chopped
4 medium mushrooms,
   chopped
1 cup chopped cooked
   spinach (about 1 pound
   fresh, or 1 ten-ounce
   package)
1 cup chopped cooked
   ham, optional

1 tablespoon Dijon
   mustard
2 three-ounce packages
   cream cheese at room
   temperature, cut into 3
   pieces each
Salt and freshly ground
   pepper
Several gratings nutmeg

Preheat the oven to 400°. Have ready an 11- or 12-inch serving platter and a wire rack.

Grease a 15½ × 10½ × 1-inch jelly roll pan. Line it with wax paper (leaving a 1-inch overlap on each of the long ends for easy handling later). Grease the paper and dust lightly with flour, dumping out excess.

To prepare the roll, melt the butter in a heavy saucepan and stir in the flour, salt, and pepper. Cook for 2 minutes without letting the mixture take on color. Off heat, whisk in the milk. Return to the fire, bring to a boil, and cook for 2 minutes.

Beat the egg yolks lightly in a small bowl and heat by adding and stirring in a little of the hot white sauce; then add them to the sauce in the pan and cook over medium heat 1 minute longer, without letting the mixture boil. Let cool to room temperature, stirring occasionally.

Beat the egg whites until stiff but not dry. Stir a large dollop of them into the cooled sauce, then add the sauce to the whites and fold in. Spread the mixture evenly in the prepared pan, smoothing the top with a spatula.

Bake in the center of the oven for 25 to 30 minutes, until puffed and brown. Let the pan cool on a rack for 5 minutes. Have ready a clean dampened tea towel; turn roll out onto it. After about 10 minutes, carefully peel off the wax paper and trim the edges neatly.

While the roll bakes, prepare the filling. Melt the butter in a heavy 10-inch skillet and sauté the shallots until soft but not brown. Add the chopped mushrooms and cook until they give up their moisture and it evaporates—about 3 minutes. Add the spinach, ham, and mustard. Heat, stirring, then add the cream cheese and stir until well blended. Season to taste with salt, pepper, and nutmeg. Cover and keep warm if assembling now.

To assemble, unroll the roll, leaving it on the towel, and spread with the warm filling. Roll lengthwise. With the aid of the towel, slide the roll onto a serving platter so that the seam side is down. Garnish platter with sliced tomatoes moistened with vinaigrette and parsley clusters. Cut into slices. Serves 6–8 as a first course, 4–6 as a luncheon main course.

Preparation notes: Though it appears involved, this is not a difficult dish and goes very fast once started, so have all the ingredients ready before proceeding. The filling itself may be made ahead and gently reheated in a double boiler before assembling. The roll may be served piping hot from the oven or made a day ahead, refrigerated, well wrapped in aluminum foil, and gently reheated in a 325° oven for half an hour. Let roll come to room temperature first. It may also be frozen.

Spinach Quiche

Follow the directions for mushroom quiche (p. 177), but substitute 1¼ cups blanched, chopped spinach, or a 10-ounce package of frozen chopped spinach, defrosted, for the mushrooms. At the point of adding the vegetable to the shallots, stir over moderate heat, uncovered, to evaporate excess moisture. Add a dash of nutmeg to the seasoning.

Spinach Crêpes

Stuffed crêpes are a wonderfully pampering and satisfying dish. The crêpes themselves can be made ahead and refrigerated. The mornay sauce and the spinach filling may also be prepared ahead, so that the assembly and baking is all you have to do.

2 tablespoons butter
2 tablespoons minced shallots
1½ cups chopped cooked spinach
2½ cups mornay sauce (p. 377)
Salt and freshly ground pepper
Nutmeg
12 entree crêpes (recipe follows)
¼ cup grated Parmesan cheese

Heat a serving dish. Preheat the oven to 375° and arrange a rack in the highest position.

Melt the butter in an enamel-lined or stainless-steel skillet and sauté the shallots for 1 minute. Add the spinach and stir over fairly high heat for about 2 minutes to warm and cook off any moisture. Blend in ½ cup of the mornay sauce. Simmer, covered, for 7 or 8 minutes, stirring once or twice. Season to taste with salt, pepper, and a grating of nutmeg.

Lay a crêpe flat, wrong side showing. Put a big spoonful of filling on the bottom third and roll up. Lay crêpes side by side in the baking dish, seam sides down. Cover with the rest of the mornay sauce, sprinkle with the cheese, and bake in the upper third of the oven for 15 to 20 minutes. If the top needs more browning, run under the broiler for a few seconds, but watch carefully. Services 4–5.

Preparation notes: For a less rich version, omit the mornay sauce. Use 1 ½ cups creamed chopped spinach (p. 272), and spread 2 or 3 tablespoons of heavy cream on top of the crêpes before adding the cheese and baking.

Some chopped leftover ham or chicken may be folded into either of the spinach fillings.

Entrée Crêpes

⅔ cup milk	butter, melted and
¾ cup water	cooled, plus a little
3 large eggs	more to grease pan
3 tablespoons unsalted	1 cup all-purpose flour

Put all the ingredients in a blender or food processor and blend for 30 seconds. Scrape down with a spatula any flour that sticks to the side and blend again briefly. Cover batter, refrigerate, and let it rest for 2 hours before using.

Select a seasoned 7-inch French iron or Teflon crêpe pan. Heat until a drop of water sizzles and evaporates. Brush the bottom with a piece of paper toweling (see note) that has been dipped in melted butter. Spoon enough batter into the center of the pan to barely coat the bottom. (A small ladle with a ½-cup capacity is ideal for this.) Quickly tilt the pan this way and that to evenly coat the bottom; pour any excess batter back into the bowl. Cook over moderately high heat until the crêpe sets and the edges start to turn brown—about 30 seconds. Turn crêpe by flipping quickly with the fingertips or a flexible spatula. Cook on the second side briefly, without browning, for about 15 seconds. (This "wrong" side will be the side you fill.)

Turn crêpe out onto a piece of wax paper. Continue making crêpes until all the batter is used, stirring batter from time to time. After they have cooled a minute or two, stack crêpes on top of each other. It is not necessary to oil the pan after each crêpe. Makes about 20 crêpes.

To prepare crêpes ahead of time:

After crêpes have cooled, they may be stacked with wax paper between each, wrapped with aluminum foil, and refrigerated for several days. To freeze, place packages in a heavy plastic bag. In either case, bring to room temperature before using. To thaw quickly, place in a 300° oven, tightly covered in foil, for 15 minutes.

Note: Don't use a brush to grease the pan; bristles can come off and be cooked into the crêpes.

Spinach Soufflé

Spinach makes one of the best of the savory soufflés, very good to build a vegetarian meal around.

4 eggs at room temperature plus 1 additional egg white
4 tablespoons butter
1 tablespoon finely chopped shallots
¾ cup blanched chopped spinach (about 1 pound raw), or frozen chopped spinach
Salt
Nutmeg
2½ tablespoons flour
1 cup milk, heated
⅓ cup grated Parmesan cheese

Preheat the oven to 400°. Adjust the rack to center position and place a cookie sheet on it. Prepare a 1½-quart soufflé dish by buttering it well and sprinkling it with either fine bread crumbs or grated Parmesan and knocking out the excess. Separate the eggs carefully, putting the whites in a large, dry bowl. Add the extra white to them. Set aside.

Melt 1 tablespoon of the butter in a small saucepan. Add the shallots and cook for a minute. Add the spinach and cook, stirring, over high heat for several minutes to evaporate most of the moisture. Season with salt and several gratings of nutmeg and set aside. (All this may be done ahead.)

Melt the remaining 3 tablespoons butter in a heavy, enamel-lined saucepan. When the foam dies, stir in the flour with a wooden spoon. Cook over moderate heat, stirring constantly, until a bubbly, honeycomb pattern appears. Switch to a whisk and, off heat, pour in the milk all at once. Whisk rapidly until smooth. Beat in the egg yolks one by one and correct seasoning. Stir in all but 1 tablespoon of the cheese.

Add a pinch of salt to the egg whites and beat until stiff. Stir about one-fourth of them into the sauce base to lighten it. Using a large plastic spatula, scoop the rest of the whites onto the base and, using a down, up, and over motion, fold the whites carefully into the sauce. It is quite all right to have some patches of white remaining.

Pour into the prepared dish. Sprinkle remaining

cheese on top. Place in the preheated oven. Immediately turn the heat down to 375° and cook for 25 to 30 minutes (depending on how firm you like your soufflé), or until the top is brown and puffed. Serve immediately. In an emergency, it can wait in the turned-off oven for 5 minutes or so.

Services 4–6 as a first course, 3–4 as a main luncheon course.

Spinach with Potatoes Indian Style

A very filling and satisfying dish to serve as part of a vegetarian meal.

2 pounds potatoes, boiled
1 pound spinach, cleaned
¼ cup vegetable oil
1 cup chopped onion
1–2 garlic cloves, finely minced
1-inch piece fresh ginger, peeled and sliced in julienne
1 teaspoon mustard seeds
1 teaspoon ground cumin
1 teaspoon turmeric
½ teaspoon chili powder
1 teaspoon salt, or to taste

Cut the potatoes into cubes, and coarsely chop the spinach. Set aside.

Heat the oil in a heavy 10-inch saucepan and sauté the onion, garlic, and ginger. Combine the mustard seeds, cumin, turmeric and chili powder. Add to the saucepan, stir well, and cook the mixture over gentle heat until the onion is soft.

Add the potatoes and stir gently but thoroughly to coat. Add the spinach in handfuls; it may threaten to spill out of the pot but will reduce substantially in volume as it wilts. Add salt, stir again carefully but thoroughly, cover, and continue cooking for 3 minutes or so, until spinach is cooked down a bit. Serve at once. Serves 4.

Preparation notes: If the spices prove hard to come by, use a tablespoon or more of commercial curry powder, though the flavor will not be as interesting. The potatoes may be boiled and the spinach chopped early in the day, making the final cooking a matter of

10 minutes or so. Don't refrigerate the potatoes—it gives them an off taste.

Serving suggestions: A plate of raw vegetables such as quartered ripe tomatoes or ripe cherry tomatoes, slices of green and/or red pepper, celery, scallions, and carrots provide the perfect foil for this dish. Accompanied by yogurt-cucumber salad and a whole-grain bread, it provides a wonderfully satisfying and nutritionally complete vegetarian meal.

Wilted Spinach

This recipe always makes me think of the late Joan Crawford's description of the way she cooked spinach: "What I do is take boiling bacon grease and pour it over spinach until it *sags*" (in *My Way of Life*).

4–5 strips lean bacon, cut into 1-inch pieces
½ teaspoon dried oregano
3 tablespoons red wine vinegar
1 tablespoon olive oil
2 teaspoons sugar
1 teaspoon Dijon mustard
1 teaspoon Worcestershire sauce
10–12 ounces fresh spinach, cleaned and dried
Freshly ground pepper

Fry the bacon in a heavy nonmetallic skillet or casserole until crisp but not frazzled. Remove and drain on paper. Pour out and discard all but 1 tablespoon of the bacon fat. Crumble the oregano between your hands into the fat and stir in. Add the vinegar, oil, sugar, mustard, and Worcestershire and cook gently over moderate heat until the sugar is dissolved—about 2 minutes.

Off heat, add the spinach to the skillet and cover with a lid for about half a minute, or just until the leaves wilt from the heat. Season to taste with pepper. Crumble and add the reserved bacon and toss. Serves 2.

Note: If your skillet is small, put the spinach in a bowl, pour the hot dressing over, and cover with a lid to wilt it.

Spinach Lasagne

I came up with this tasty meatless lasagne once when I had to feed a number of teenagers, many of whom did not eat meat. Everybody, regardless of diet, loved it. Remember it for parties.

2 pounds fresh spinach, cleaned, or 2 ten-ounce boxes frozen chopped spinach
1 tablespoon salt
1 tablespoon oil
12 lasagne noodles, about 8 ounces (see note)
2 tablespoons butter
1 cup chopped onion
2–3 garlic cloves, finely chopped
3 tablespoons flour
1¼ cups milk
1 large egg
Salt, if desired

Freshly ground pepper
Nutmeg
1 pound ricotta or cottage cheese put through a strainer
12 ounces mozzarella cheese, coarsely grated
4 cups quick tomato sauce (p. 309)
2 eight-ounce cans tomato sauce
3 tablespoons fresh bread crumbs
⅔ cup freshly grated Parmesan cheese

If you are using fresh spinach, cook it for 2 minutes with only the water clinging to the leaves. Drain and chop finely. Squeeze out any excess water. If using frozen spinach, break up blocks and cook in an uncovered enamel-lined or stainless-steel skillet until it is soft and dry. Turn up heat if necessary to evaporate excess liquid. Set aside.

Bring about 4 quarts of water to a rapid boil. Add a tablespoon of salt and one of oil to the pot and add the lasagne pieces, 2 or 3 at a time. Cook uncovered for 10 to 12 minutes for dried lasagne, 10 seconds for fresh. Stir occasionally with a wooden spoon. Drain and separate the noodles and spread on a damp kitchen towel.

Preheat the oven to 375°. Butter a 13 × 9 × 2-inch baking pan or lasagne pan. Line a cookie sheet with foil.

To prepare the spinach filling, melt the butter in a heavy enamel-lined or stainless-steel 2-quart saucepan, add the onion and garlic and sauté until wilted.

Sprinkle with the flour, then cook for 2 minutes, or until the flour is pale gold. Off heat, add the milk all at once, return to the fire, bring to a boil and cook, stirring, until sauce thickens.

Add and stir in the spinach and let cool slightly. Add the egg, stir in well, then season with salt, to taste, liberal grindings of pepper, and several gratings of nutmeg. Add and blend in the ricotta.

Separately, combine the homemade and canned tomato sauces and blend well.

Put 3 or 4 spoonfuls of the tomato sauce in the bottom of the prepared pan and spread it out. Put down 4 noodles, letting them overlap by about half an inch. Over this make a layer of one-third of the spinach-ricotta mixture. Sprinkle with one-third of the mozzarella, then make another layer of the tomato sauce. Make two more layers like this, ending with the sauce.

Combine the bread crumbs and Parmesan and sprinkle over the top. Bake for 50 minutes on the cookie sheet in the upper third of the oven. The top should be attractively golden. If you would like it browner, raise the heat for the last 10 minutes. Let rest for 10 minutes before cutting. Serve very hot, with a green salad. Serves 12.

Preparation notes: You can use boxed curly edged lasagne noodles, but the dish is infinitely better with fresh pasta. From your own or a bought sheet, cut the noodles about 4½ inches wide by 11 inches long.

For an interesting taste and textural variation, add ½ cup or so raisins, plumped in hot water, and ½ cup pine nuts to the spinach.

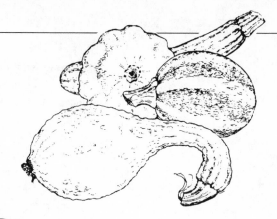

Squash
(Cucurbita)

Summer Squash

Squashes are generally divided into two broad classifications, summer and winter. Both groups are gourds, indigenous to the New World, and come in a varied array of sizes and shapes whose differences are perhaps more to the point than their seasons. The basic difference between the two groups is that summer squashes are picked and eaten while immature, while winter squashes are allowed to harden, thus developing resistant skins and mature seeds. Of the two, the summer squashes are more delicate in flavor, texture, and keeping quality.

The common summer squashes are zucchini, yellow straight-neck and crookneck, pattypan, and chayote, a more recent market arrival. Zucchini, because of its popularity, year-round availability, and the great number of ways it can be used, has a separate section in this book (see p. 322).

To Buy

Look for firm, nicely shaped squash with taut, unblemished skins. Four medium yellow squash weigh a little over 1 pound. Allow this amount for 3 people. Allow 1 medium pattypan or 1½-pound chayote squash per person.

To Store

Refrigerate all summer squashes in a loose plastic bag.

Use as soon as possible, within 4 days at the outside. Summer squash does not freeze well unless pureed. (Do this when they are at their height in mid-summer; by September yellow squash becomes too watery.)

To Prepare

Wash gently in cool water, drain, and cut off stem and blossom ends. Summer squashes are not usually peeled unless they are going to be pureed.

To Cook

See individual squash listings.

Sometimes called golden zucchini, both straight and crookneck varieties have their own delicate sweet flavor I find reminiscent of corn. Though "summer squash" is a squash category, many cooks use the term as a synonym for one of the two varieties of yellow squash. Either is incredibly good pureed and baked in the yellow squash casserole on page 289. Straight-neck yellow squash is ideal for stuffing; the seeds are usually concentrated in the broader end and are easily removed. It can also be prepared in any of the ways given for zucchini, though very aggressive seasoning will obliterate the delicate flavor.

I do not like to boil yellow squash—it becomes soggy. Steaming or steam-blanching, as recommended for zucchini, is preferable.

Broiled: Cut small, washed squash in half lengthwise, brush skin and cut side with oil flavored with garlic and thyme, and broil 6 inches from the heat.

Steamed: Bring ¾ inch water to a boil in the bottom of a steamer. Place squash in basket, cover, and steam until tender. Whole squash 1½ inches in diameter will steam in 7 minutes, ½-inch slices in 4 minutes. Finish with butter, salt and pepper, and/or a sprinkling of herbs.

Yellow Squash

Stuffed: Follow directions for stuffed zucchini (p. 331) but discard the scooped-out portion.

Greek-style fried summer squash: Cut squash into 1-inch slices. Shake gently in a paper bag containing flour seasoned to taste with salt and pepper. Fry in vegetable oil until golden on both sides. Serve with skordalia sauce (p. 200) as a separate course or as part of a vegetable dinner.

Pattypan Squash

Also called cymling, and known in England as custard marrow, this pale greenish white summer squash is shaped like a scalloped disk and ranges from 3 to 8 inches. Slices of pattypan may be treated like zucchini. Pattypan is also attractive stuffed.

Stuffed: Cut a slice off the rounded side of a 3- to 4-inch pattypan. With a teaspoon or a melon baller, scoop out the flesh and seeds. Drop the shells into boiling salted water for about 5 minutes to tenderize them. Drain, brush inside with melted butter, and season with salt and pepper. Chop the flesh, sauté in butter, add cream to bind, and season. Or combine the flesh with curried carrot stuffing for yellow squash (p. 288), grated sautéed zucchini (p. 325), or any other stuffing that appeals.

Steamed: Cut into 1-inch pieces and steam as for yellow squash slices, adding an extra minute.

Chayote

Known as mirliton or vegetable pear in the South, and as mango squash and christophene or cho-cho in the Caribbean, this pleasantly crunchy squash is about the size of a small avocado, with a pale yellow-green or white skin. The flavor is blander than yellow squash, and it needs some assertive seasoning. Mexico has a dark green, quite flavorsome variety.

Boiled: Put the whole chayotes in a saucepan with

water to cover, bring to a boil, cover, reduce heat, and simmer until tender when pierced with a fork—25 minutes to an hour, depending on size. Drain and cool. Cut in half and pry out the almondlike seed (it is edible). Put the shells upside down to drain for a few minutes, then scoop out the pulp carefully. Dice, dress with butter, and season with salt and pepper.

Steamed: Cut unpeeled squash into halves or quarters as above and steam over an inch of water until tender—about 20 minutes. Drain, peel, and dress with butter, salt, and pepper.

Fried: Boil whole chayotes and cut into ¼-inch slices. Dip into well-beaten egg, then coat with fine seasoned bread crumbs. Fry slowly in a mixture of butter and oil until crisp. Serve with highly seasoned tomato sauce as a separate course or with grilled meat.

Hungarian (Summer) Squash in Cream with Dill
(Tökfőzelék)

1¾ pounds small yellow summer squash or pattypan, cut into rounds
Salt
2 tablespoons vegetable oil
½ cup finely chopped onion
½ teaspoon vinegar
2 tablespoons flour
1 cup water or chicken broth
½ cup sour cream
2 tablespoons finely chopped fresh dill
Paprika

Place the squash in a bowl, lightly sprinkle with salt, and let stand for ½ hour.

Heat the oil in a skillet and sauté the onion until translucent.

Drain the squash and press out excess water with your hands. Add to the onion and sprinkle with the vinegar. Cook, stirring constantly, until the squash is limp—about 3 minutes.

Sprinkle the flour over and salt, if desired, and cook 2 minutes more, stirring gently so squash is evenly coated. Slowly add the water, stir in, and let simmer, covered, for 5 minutes. If any taste of flour remains, simmer a few minutes more. Remove from heat and let cool slightly.

Tip the pan and spoon out a tablespoon or so of sauce and stir into the sour cream. Return this mixture to the sauce and blend. Taste for seasoning, add the chopped dill, gently reheat but do not allow to boil, sprinkle with paprika and serve immediately. Serves 4.

Yellow Squash Stuffed with Curried Carrots

In this recipe, two rather ordinary vegetables are combined to make a very pretty and tasty side dish or pleasant element in a vegetarian meal.

4 medium yellow summer squash	carrot (about 2 large carrots)
Salt, if desired	1 tablespoon minced sweet red or green pepper
2 tablespoons butter	
2 tablespoons flour	Freshly ground pepper
½ teaspoon curry powder, or more to taste	2 tablespoons fine bread crumbs
1 cup milk	2 teaspoons grated Parmesan cheese
1 cup coarsely grated	

Preheat the oven to 375°.

Poach, drain, and refresh the squash as directed for zucchini on page 331. Cut in half, discard the pulp and seeds in the seed cavity, and turn upside down briefly to drain. Lightly butter a baking dish that will hold the halves, arrange them in it and salt lightly; set aside.

Melt the butter in a small saucepan and, when it looks like a honeycomb, add and stir in the flour and curry powder and cook for 2 minutes. Off heat, stir in the milk. Return to stove and cook for 2 minutes. Stir in the carrot and minced pepper, salt if desired and black pepper, and let simmer gently for 5 minutes. Spoon the mixture into the squash shells. (May be prepared ahead to this point.)

Combine the bread crumbs and cheese and sprinkle over each squash half. Bake in the upper third of the oven for 30 minutes. If a more golden top is desired, run under the broiler flame for 15 or 20 seconds. Serves 4–8.

Baked Summer Squash Casserole

This recipe evolved from an old Southern one that called for what seemed to me a bizarre quantity of Cheddar cheese. My cheeseless version was an instant hit at its inception and has been a great favorite in *The East Hampton Cookbook,* where it first appeared. It is so surprisingly substantial (and nutritionally complete) that it makes a delightful meatless meal, along with an herb-flavored baked rice and a green vegetable.

3 pounds yellow summer squash, cut into 1-inch pieces
¾ cup fresh bread crumbs
4 tablespoons melted butter
½ cup minced onion
2 eggs, lightly beaten
1 teaspoon salt
½ teaspoon freshly ground pepper
1 tablespoon sugar

Preheat the oven to 375°.

Cook the squash in boiling salted water, covered, for 10 minutes, or until tender. Drain and puree coarsely in a blender or food processor.

Combine the bread crumbs with the melted butter in a bowl. Set aside 4 tablespoons of buttered crumbs for the top. Add to the bowl the squash, onion, eggs, salt, pepper, and sugar. Pour into a greased 1½-quart baking dish, scatter reserved crumbs on top, and bake for 1 hour, until squash is puffed and crumbs are golden brown. Serves 6.

Stuffed Chayotes

2 large chayote squash, about 1 pound
2 tablespoons butter
1 medium onion, chopped
⅓ pound ground beef
Salt and freshly ground pepper
Nutmeg
Bread crumbs
Grated Parmesan cheese

Boil unpeeled chayotes for 10 minutes. Drain and run cold water over briefly. Drain again. Cut in half and remove seed. Using a spoon or melon baller, scoop out the pulp, chop, and reserve.

Preheat the oven to 425°. Lightly butter a baking dish.

Melt 1 tablespoon of the butter in a skillet and sauté the onion until wilted. Add the beef and cook, stirring, until it loses color. Add the reserved squash, and season with salt, pepper, and several gratings of nutmeg. Pile stuffing into shells, top with bread crumbs and cheese, and dot with the remaining tablespoon of butter. Bake for 15 to 20 minutes, until top is golden. Serves 2.

Squash Blossoms

Squash blossoms are considered a great delicacy by people as different as the Italians, the Provençal French, and the American Indians of the Southwest. Most blossoms picked for eating are zucchini blossoms, but I am told any kind of squash blossom, including pumpkin, is edible. While not easy to find in American markets (fancy Italian markets often have them in summer), they are abundantly available to anyone with squash in the garden.

Here is what you have to know when you pick your own: Leave the rounder, female blossoms on the plant, or you will have no vegetables; the males are the ones you want. These are on a long straight stem and are recognized by their elongated shape. Usually there are many more male flowers than are required to fertilize one plant. The zucchini is the stem of the female flower, which appears at the tip of the baby squash and eventually drops off. (In Italy, the baby squash, flower still attached, is picked and sold the same day and considered a great delicacy.)

Pick blossoms either in the early morning or late afternoon, when they will have their maximum moisture content and will not wilt easily. Check closely curled flowers for bugs and bees. Do not remove the stamens, which have an exquisite flavor. If the blossoms are not to be cooked right away, sprinkle them with some water and make a tent over them with plastic wrap in such a manner that it does not lay directly on them. Before cooking, rinse gently.

Ed Giobbi's Squash Flowers

2 eggs
1 tablespoon water
Salt and freshly ground
  pepper

16–24 zucchini or other
  squash flowers
Flour
Corn oil

Beat together the eggs, water, salt, and pepper to taste. Dip each flower in the batter, let excess drip off, then dust with flour.

Warm a serving dish.

Pour enough oil into a heavy skillet to come within about ¾ inch of the top, and heat until very hot. Test by flicking a bit of flour into the skillet—if the oil boils violently, it is hot enough. Add the flowers one at a time and cook until golden brown—about 1 minute. Remove with a slotted spoon to paper towels and keep warm. When all are cooked, transfer to the heated dish and serve immediately. Serves 4.

Spaghetti Squash

A novelty squash shaped like a yellow football, so called because the delicate flesh separates into gossamer threads that look more like yellow angelica to me than spaghetti. The delicate flavor borders on the bland and needs some enhancement like butter, salt, and pepper, or a zesty tomato sauce. Dieters love it, as the calorie count is negligible (66 calories per 8-ounce serving), though in no way is it as satisfying as pasta. Spaghetti squash may be boiled or baked, then dressed as desired.

To Cook

Boiled: Use a pot large enough to hold whole squash, fill with enough water to cover the squash, and bring to a boil. Drop in squash and cook, uncovered, for 20 to 30 minutes, according to size. Squash is done when a fork pierces it easily. Remove and let cool. When it is cool enough to handle, cut it in half lengthwise and scoop out seeds and strings. With a bowl handy, run a fork over the flesh from one end to the other; it will come away in strands like pasta. Finish in any of the ways suggested here.

Baked: Prick skin in several places with a fork and bake in a preheated 350° for about 1½ hours. Proceed as for boiled squash.

Spaghetti squash with cheese: Toss cooked strands with melted butter and 1 cup grated Cheddar or Parmesan.

Spaghetti squash with zucchini and tomato: To the strands from a large cooked half, add 1 cup grated zucchini, 1 cup tomato sauce, and salt and pepper to taste. Spoon back into the squash half, sprinkle with ½ cup grated Parmesan, and bake at 350° for 20 minutes.

Spaghetti squash with tomato sauce: Toss the squash with tomato sauce just as you would pasta.

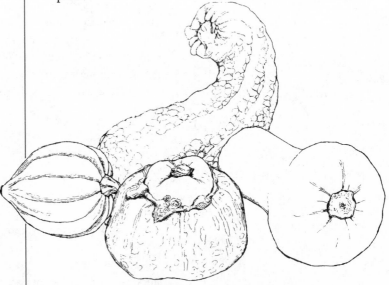

Winter Squash

The winter squashes are edible gourds, each with a special flavor and characteristic.

Acorn squash, probably the best known, is round and has a fluted, dark green skin lightly patched with orange. An all-green exterior indicates immaturity; if more than half is orange; it may be stringy. It is best cut in half and baked. Besides butter or margarine, complementary seasonings include cinnamon, ginger, nutmeg, brown sugar, honey, rum, maple syrup, sage, thyme, and orange peel.

Ripe acorn squash may also be quartered and steamed, or cut into rings, baked and glazed. Don't puree; it has too much moisture.

Buttercup is the squat, turban-shaped squash whose green-and-white striped skin and gray "hat" enclose mild yellow flesh that tastes something like a sweet potato. Choose medium-size ones, about 5 inches long. Prepare as for acorn squash.

Butternut, also called Waltham squash or African bell, looks like a large tan pear. Greenish patches around the end indicate immaturity and lack of flavor. Bake or boil. It is relatively moist, sweet, and dry, and is best pureed.

Hubbard can be as big as a basketball, and has a warty, ridged surface. It can be dark, green, orange, red-orange, blue, or gray. The flesh is deep orange, and can be used in any recipes calling for butternut.

Boston marrow is a thin-fleshed squash with a bright orange skin. Because the cavity is large, an 8-pounder may feed only 4 (they come up to 16 pounds). Boil or steam and puree the flesh for pies, or steam quarters and serve with lemon butter.

Turban squash comes in all sizes and color combinations ranging from orange-green to warty green. It is primarily decorative.

Pumpkin is a class of squash, treated separately in this book.

To Buy

Edible winter squashes are at their best when harvested fully mature. Select those that seem heavy for their size, with hard, unblemished skin. Acorn squashes store particularly well and so appear to have a long season, but actually they are past their prime by spring.

Yields are a bit difficult to calculate because squashes vary in water content and skin thickness from month to month. Allow ½ acorn squash per person; 1 pound of other squashes for 2 people. Three pounds whole squash will yield a little over 3 cups when cooked and pureed.

To Store

Winter squashes do not require refrigeration. Store at room temperature for up to a week, or for a month in a cool dark place. Winter squash puree freezes well.

To Prepare

For any winter variety, remove stem, cut in half, scoop out and discard seeds and strings. If you are planning to boil, steam, or fry it, cut into smaller sections and peel with a swivel-bladed peeler.

To cut a butternut or hubbard squash in half lengthwise, use a large knife steadied by both hands and rock the squash as you cut.

To halve an acorn squash, snap off the stem and work a heavy knife blade lengthwise into the flesh between two ridges. Strike the dull side of the knife near the handle with a mallet until squash splits.

To Cook

Boiled: I feel winter squash gets too waterlogged when boiled and always prefer baking it, but if time is a factor, here's how: peel, chunk, just barely cover with water, cover pot, bring to a boil, reduce heat and simmer until tender. Two-inch chunks will take about 8 minutes. Drain well.

Baked: Use this method for cooking and eating any winter squash "as is," or for cooking squash to make puree. Wash and dry squash, cut in half, and remove seeds and strings. Place cut side down on a rimmed cookie sheet, and add ¼ cup water so squash does not stick. Bake in a preheated 375° oven until squash is tender when pierced with a toothpick. Allow 1 hour, but start checking after 40 minutes.

Baked acorn squash: Use the method given, but set the oven at 325° and omit the water. Bake for 25 minutes, remove from oven, turn halves up, and sprinkle each with salt and pepper. Into each cavity put 1 tablespoon brown sugar, ½ tablespoon butter, a grating of nutmeg, and a tablespoon of rum. Bake cut side up for 15 to 20 minutes, or until flesh is tender and easily pierced with a toothpick.

Baked acorn squash with applesauce:

Bake as directed, but when you turn the halves up, fill with a well-flavored and spiced applesauce and dot with a little butter.

Pureed: Bake 3 to 4 pounds or more butternut or hubbard squash as directed. Peel and puree in a food processor or blender, but do not overprocess. Measure puree. For each cup, blend in 1 tablespoon butter, 1 teaspoon brown sugar, ½ teaspoon salt, a pinch of powdered ginger, and enough scalded cream to make the puree fluffy. Pour into a heated dish and serve.

Squash puree for pie or for freezing: Puree as directed, but omit the seasonings.

Squash Pie

I had never known of squash pie until the first Thanksgiving dinner with my new Rhode Island in-laws. It is much tastier and more delicate than pumpkin, and is now traditional in our house, too.

Squash Pie, continued

2 eggs
2 tablespoons flour
1 teaspoon salt
1½ teaspoons cinnamon
½ teaspoon nutmeg
½ teaspoon allspice
¼ teaspoon ginger
½ cup firmly packed dark brown sugar

½ cup granulated sugar
1 teaspoon vanilla extract
2 cups squash puree (p. 295)
1 cup milk or cream, or a mixture of both
1 partly baked 9-inch pie shell (p. 177)

Beat the eggs well, then beat in the flour, salt, cinnamon, nutmeg, allspice, ginger, sugars, and vanilla. Stir in the squash puree and the milk or cream and blend well.

Adjust oven rack to center position; place a cookie sheet on it, and preheat the oven to 425°.

Pour half the squash mixture into the pie shell. Pull out the oven rack slightly, set the shell on the cookie sheet, and carefully pour in the balance of the mixture. (This method avoids spills.) Bake for 10 minutes, then reduce oven heat to 350° and bake 45 minutes more, or until the pie tests clean. Cool on a rack. May be served warm, cold, or at room temperature, with whipped cream passed separately if desired. Serves 6–8.

Richard Olney's Provençal Squash Gratin

The large amount of garlic and parsley in this dish lends extraordinary flavor to the relatively bland squash. It is excellent with any meat or fowl.

2 pounds butternut or hubbard squash or pumpkin, halved, peeled, seeds and stringy flesh removed
7–8 garlic cloves, peeled and finely chopped

½ cup finely chopped parsley
Salt and freshly ground pepper
4 tablespoons flour
⅓ cup olive oil

Preheat the oven to 350°.

Cut the squash into ⅓-inch slices, and cut each slice into ⅓-inch strips. Cut firmly held bundles crosswise into tiny dice, and toss them in a mixing bowl with the

garlic and parsley, making sure that the cubes are well seasoned and coated. Add salt and pepper to taste. Sprinkle the flour over and toss the contents of the bowl repeatedly until each cube is evenly coated with flour (adding a bit more if necessary—excess flour will fall to the bottom of the bowl and may be discarded later).

Generously rub the bottom and sides of an 11 × 14-inch gratin dish with olive oil and fill with the squash mixture. Smooth the surface and dribble olive oil in a crisscross pattern over it. Cook for 2 to 2½ hours, or until a deep, rich brown crust forms. The squash beneath will have melted to a near-puree. Serves 4–6.

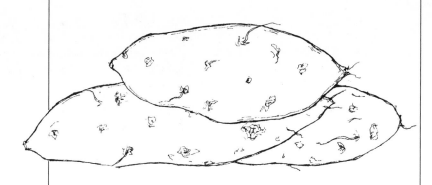

Sweet Potatoes and Yams

(Ipomoea batatas and *Dioscoreas)*

Besides being botanically distinct from white potatoes, sweet potatoes and yams are also two distinct plants in themselves. Though they are all tubers and frequently cooked in similar ways, the sweet potato belongs to *Ipomoa,* the morning glory family, while yams are a still different vining plant with a larger root and woody outer skin. Yams grow only in the tropics, while sweets grow almost all over the United States. The African slaves who ate sweet potatoes here called them *nyam,* because they reminded them of the tropical tuber they had known, hence came yam.

There are two basic types of sweet potato, one with pale yellow skin and flesh and another, sweeter and moister, with darker orange skin and flesh. This latter is the one erroneously called yam in the South.

To Buy

Look for medium-size sweets that are not gnarled or blemished. Three medium sweets weigh about a pound. Allow 1 per person. Yams can frequently be found in Latin-American markets.

To Store

Keep in a cool dry place, not the refrigerator. Sweets do not last as well as white potatoes.

To Prepare

Handle gently, because sweets crack easily. Scrub well, and remove any strings. For most purposes, do not peel until after cooking.

To Cook

Baked: Prick each scrubbed potato several times with a skewer and bake at 400° for about 40 minutes. You can oil the skins before baking if you like a softer skin. Serve with butter, or slit the jackets, scoop out the flesh, beat in some butter and seasoning, and serve as a puree. For this purpose, you can also simply boil them (in the skins—they're easier to peel after cooking).

Candied: Peel 4 sweet potatoes and cut in half lengthwise or into thick slices. Butter a 9 × 14-inch baking dish. Add the potatoes and sprinkle with about ½ cup firmly packed brown sugar, season lightly, and dot with 2 tablespoons butter. Bake in a 375° oven until tender and nicely glazed. Don't even think of debasing them with marshmallows.

Orange-glazed: Parboil and peel 4 sweet potatoes; cut in half. In a skillet large enough to hold the potatoes, mix 2 tablespoons butter and ½ cup packed dark brown sugar with ½ cup orange juice and 1 teaspoon or so of grated orange rind. Cook this gently until slightly syrupy. Add the potatoes and simmer, uncovered, for 15 to 20 minutes. Turn them frequently.

Maple-Glazed Sweet Potatoes and Apples

The perfect accompaniment to the Thanksgiving bird.

3 pounds sweet potatoes, baked	¼ cup firmly packed light brown sugar
2–3 apples, preferably Granny Smith or golden delicious	½ cup maple syrup
	2 tablespoons dark rum
¼ cup fresh lemon juice	½ teaspoon cinnamon
4 tablespoons butter	¼ teaspoon ground mace

Preheat the oven to 400°. Arrange an oven rack in the highest position. Butter a 14×9×2-inch gratin dish.

Let the potatoes cool slightly, then cut off the ends, pull off the peel with a dull knife, and cut on the diagonal into ¼-inch slices.

Peel and core the apples and cut lengthwise into eighths. Toss in a bowl with the lemon juice. Combine with the sliced potatoes in the gratin dish, making an arrangement of alternating slices if you have the patience.

In a stainless-steel or enamel-lined saucepan, combine the butter, sugar, maple syrup, rum, cinnamon, and mace, and stir over moderate heat until the sugar is dissolved. Pour slowly over the apple-potato mixture so that the top is uniformly moistened. Bake in the upper third of the oven, basting frequently, for 25 minutes, or until the apples are tender, the sweets have a nice glaze, and the edges of both are browned lightly. If this last does not happen, run under the broiler for 20 seconds. Serves 8.

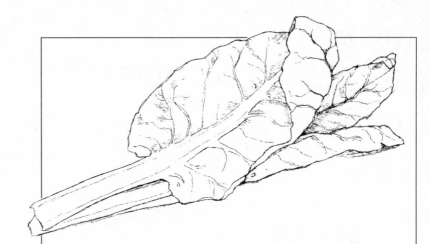

Swiss Chard

(Beta Vulgaris)

My first experience with Swiss chard was when a gardening neighbor offered me what I thought was hugely overgrown spinach. I felt intimidated by the weighty leaves and had a hard time believing they could be interesting to eat—until another neighbor, an Italian, set me straight.

The first thing I learned is that the stems, or ribs (which can be red or white, though they taste the same) can be treated virtually as a separate vegetable and are considered by many to be the best part. Steamed and served with melted butter, they taste rather like a cross between beets (of which family they are a member) and asparagus. Of course the very young leaves, whose flavor resembles spinach, may be cooked with ribs attached.

Chard—also called leaf chard, spinach beet, or sea kale—grows well in rather arid places and is quite popular in Mediterranean countries and in France. In Provence, a *tourte* is made of chard leaves with raisins, pine nuts, and apples.

Young chard leaves, blanched in water or a court bouillon, may be used in most spinach recipes in which chard's stronger taste would not interfere. Chard is too fibrous to eat raw.

To Buy

Chard is infrequently available at market as it ships and

stores poorly. If you do see it, look for crisp stalks and green leaves. Your likeliest source will be farm markets or home gardens. One pound of chard will give you ½ pound leaves and ½ pound ribs. A pound of ribs will serve 2 to 3, as will a pound of leaves.

To Store

Unwashed and loosely wrapped, chard may be refrigerated for 2 to 3 days.

To Prepare

Wash well in cold water. Separate leaves from stalks if the ribs are more than ½ inch in width. (They may be cooked separately but served together, as follows, or used on two different occasions.) If the ribs are thick and mature and have ribs of their own, peel them.

To Cook

Unless you are dealing with baby chard, which may be cooked whole, the leaves and ribs must be cooked separately or one will be over- or undercooked at the expense of the other.

Blanched Bring a large pot of water to the boil and add salt. To serve ribs and leaves together, slice the ribs into pieces roughly 1½ inches long. Add to the water and cook for 8 minutes after the second boil. Add the leaves and cook for 2 to 4 minutes after the boil, depending on age. Finish by sautéeing in butter over low heat, stirring constantly for 5 minutes or so. Season to taste. Or chop coarsely, stir to coat in olive oil in which 2 or 3 minced garlic cloves have been lightly sautéed. Finish with several squeezes of lemon juice.

Steamed: Bring an inch of water to a boil in the bottom of a steamer. Add the stems, cut into 1½-inch pieces, the leaves 5 minutes later. The stems will be

Separating chard leaf from stalk

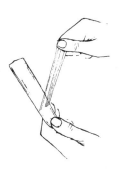

Peeling chard rib

tender in 9 to 12 minutes, the leaves in 4 to 6. Finish as for blanched chard.

Chard Ribs Parmigiana

This is a good way to treat mature stalks—those over an inch in width.

**Thick ribs of 2 pounds of
 Swiss chard, cut into
 4-inch lengths and
 blanched
Salt and freshly ground**

**pepper
½–⅔ cups grated
 Parmesan cheese
6 tablespoons butter,
 melted**

Preheat the oven to 400°.

Butter a 9×12-inch baking dish and make a single layer of drained chard stems. Season with salt and pepper and sprinkle with a third of the cheese and a drizzle of the butter. Make two more layers in this manner, saving enough cheese and butter to make a good top layer. Bake in the upper third of the oven for 20 minutes, or until the top is golden. Let sit for 10 minutes or so before serving. Serves 4.

Swiss Chard with Raisins and Pine Nuts

Follow the recipe for Spinach with Raisins and Pine Nuts on page 274, substituting 2 pounds of washed chard leaves for the spinach.

Tomatoes

(Lycopersicum esculentum)

The tomato is one of the world's most popular and versatile vegetables, existing in countless varieties, many bred to be resistant to the diseases the fragile fruit is prey to. Though for us the standard tomato is red, the ancestor of them all was a small yellow fruit (hence the Italian name *pomodoro,* from *pomo d'oro,* "golden apple").

Probably the most popular and best-known tomato in America is the beefsteak, big, thick, and meaty, with old-fashioned ridges. The tendency among breeders, however, is to seek round red globes, which is what we mostly see at market. Also popular are the miniature or cherry tomatoes, until recently the only ripe tomatoes available in winter. They are good for nibbling out of hand, for stuffing as hors d'oeuvres, and for color wherever you would use fresh tomatoes. The less common yellow tomatoes, probably related to the old original, are said to have the virtue of less acid (but they also have less taste). There are also yellow cherry tomatoes—a round variety and a pear-shaped variety good for salads and pickling.

Italian plum tomatoes, which have a thick skin, less liquid, smaller seeds, and a richer flavor than regular tomatoes, are best for sauces and stews. They are occasionally yellow, too. Green tomatoes, so abundant in every garden in early fall, are delicious when sliced and fried. Green tomato chutney, an old American standby for using the last tomatoes before frost hits, is delicious with meats.

The Mexican green tomato, called *tomatillo,* is not a tomato at all but a relative of the Cape gooseberry. It is used in Mexican sauces and must be cooked before it is eaten.

Sun-dried tomatoes, also called pumate, are tomatoes (plum or a combination of round and plum) that have been cut into strips, lightly salted, and dehydrated in the sun or under controlled outdoor conditions. They are usually sold put up in oil. Because it takes 10 pounds of tomatoes to make 1 pound of sun-dried, they are relatively expensive, though a little goes a long way because of the concentration of flavor. Use as a snack, spread on bread, serve with sliced mozzarella, offer on an antipasto tray, or sliver over cooked pasta, alone or with other vegetables.

To Buy

Tomatoes should be bright red and yield to the touch without being mushy. Green or yellow patches are sunburn and are not harmful, though they can taste bitter. Leathery dark patches indicate blossom-end rot and possibly a bitter tomato. Green tomatoes should be an intense green, with no traces of pink.

Avoid the flannel-textured pink globes euphemistically called firm slicing tomatoes; they are tomatoes picked absolutely green and treated to a dose of ethylene gas (the very same that the apple exudes naturally), which turns them a sickly pink. The flavor, like all unripe tomatoes, remains bitter, and the tomato itself so hard that, as Calvin Trillin once observed, you can't even throw them at politicians because you'd be arrested for murder.

Hothouse tomatoes are a slight improvement, as are those hydroponically grown, though both are still short on flavor. Shop carefully, and if in doubt, smell the tomato—if it has no smell at all, it probably won't have any taste, either.

I have had a good experience with Del Monte's canned sliced fresh tomatoes for those times when I needed the texture and color of the real thing. They are minimally processed. Otherwise I use the canned plum tomatoes and wait for summer.

Two large beefsteak tomatoes (about 3½ inches in diameter) weigh approximately 1 pound. Three medium tomatoes (about 2 inches in diameter) weigh approximately 1 pound. Seven or eight plum tomatoes weigh about 1 pound. A pound of tomatoes will give you about 1¼ cups pulp after seeding and peeling, less if you juice them hard. One 2-pound 3-ounce can, drained, will yield about 2 cups of pulp.

To Store

Tomatoes will rot if they are kept too warm and will deteriorate and be tasteless if kept too cold. Keep in a cool place out of the sun, but don't refrigerate. Blemished fruit should be used immediately. Canning is the best way to preserve them for long-term storage and the method requiring the most expertise. Consult the Ball Company's excellent book (see index). Simple tomato puree, sauce, or juice can be frozen.

To ripen tomatoes: Put them in a cool place in a brown paper bag with a ripe apple or a banana for a day or two. Don't set them on a windowsill in the sun.

To Prepare

For sandwiches: Slice tomatoes vertically; you get less jelly, more flesh, and a less soggy sandwich.

For salad: It's my view that tomatoes do not belong in a mixed green salad; I think they should be enjoyed on their own, sliced vertically. However, if you like the mixture, toss tomatoes with the dressing in a separate bowl, then, using a slotted spoon, scatter them over the top of the dressed greens. If the tomatoes are mixed with the greens, their juices will thin the dressing.

For stuffing: Hollow tomatoes by cutting off the stem cap and removing the core from the stem end.

Scoop out the pulp and seeds with a small spoon and discard. Drain tomatoes upside down for a few minutes, then salt insides lightly. Stuff with chicken salad, fish or crab salad, egg salad, or any bean salad, and serve as a first course or light lunch.

Tomato cups: Use these to garnish fish or meat. Cut a nice round tomato in half and lightly seed and juice it without breaking the skin. Use your thumbs to compress the inside flesh, then lightly season. Fill with salade russe, cucumber salad, or dry duxelles (or anything else that strikes your fancy).

To peel: Bring a pot of water to the boil. Lightly slash an *X* through the skin on the stem end. (For sauce making, also cut out and discard a cone-shaped plug from the stem end.) Using a slotted spoon or a Chinese frying basket, lower tomato into water for a count of 10. Cool on a rack for a couple of minutes until you can handle, then pull off the skin with a small knife.

To seed and juice: Unless they are being sliced for a sandwich or salad, tomatoes usually need to be rid of excess seeds and liquid, lest these thin and ruin a sauce. Cut tomato in half vertically, perpendicular to the stem, revealing a neat crescent of seeds. Squeeze each half gently over the sink to express seeds and juice.

To Cook

Tomato coulis: This is a neutral sauce of chopped or diced tomato flesh lightly cooked in butter with a minimum of seasoning. For 2½ cups of pulp (about 3 pounds fresh tomatoes that have been peeled, seeded, and juiced), melt 2 tablespoons butter in a heavy enamel-lined skillet and in it stir-fry 1 to 2 tablespoons minced shallot until it softens but does not take on any color. One small minced garlic clove may also be added. Add the tomatoes, a small pinch of sugar, salt and pepper to taste, and a small bouquet garni. Cover and cook over low heat for about 20 minutes. Put through a strainer or puree in a food processor. Use to garnish cooked fish or poached chicken, mix into rice, or as a base for shirred eggs.

A tomato fondue is a coulis that is highly reduced, stock being added during the reduction to heighten the flavor. Use to garnish poached eggs or in any recipe calling for tomato puree.

Fresh tomato pulp:
I use this often in the summer to garnish fish or vegetables. Peel, seed, and juice one or two ripe tomatoes, and chop roughly. Wilt 1 minced shallot in butter in a small skillet, add the tomato pulp, and stir for about 25 seconds until it is warmed. Season lightly.

Broiled:
Cut tomatoes in half, place in a foil baking pan, season with herbs of choice (fresh snipped basil, tarragon, oregano, etc.), dot with butter, lightly sprinkle with sugar, if desired, and broil 6 inches from heat source until lightly browned—8 to 10 minutes.

Stewed:
Peel and very lightly juice 4 pounds of tomatoes. Coarsely chop them. Soften ½ cup chopped onion in 2 tablespoons of butter, add the tomatoes and 2 more tablespoons of butter, and cook, covered, over low heat until the tomatoes break down—about 10 minutes. Add salt to taste, a teaspoon of sugar, and any herbs you like, and cook for another 10 minutes. If the tomatoes seem about to stick, add a little water. If you want the stew thicker, add a handful of white bread cubes, ideally from stale French bread. Correct seasoning. Use as a vegetable accompaniment.

Tomato juice:
Wash and core 5½ to 6 pounds very ripe tomatoes. This should give you about 2 quarts tomatoes. Simmer in an enamel-lined or stainless-steel pot for 20 minutes, or until very soft. Put through a food mill or fine-meshed sieve into a bowl. Let stand until light liquid rises to the top, and dip this out and discard. Chill and season as desired. Makes about 1 quart.

To freeze, let bowl cool in another bowl of ice cubes, then pour tomatoes into plastic containers, allowing plenty of head room. Don't spice or season until defrosted.

Sliced tomatoes with basil:
This is my favorite way to enjoy ripe tomatoes. Make vertical slices about ⅓-inch thick from as many tomatoes as you think you will need, and arrange them in an overlapping pattern on a serving dish. Sprinkle with salt and fresh black pepper. Drizzle an excellent olive oil over them. Refrigerate for about 20 minutes. About 5 minutes before serving, sprinkle with finely scissored basil leaves.

Sliced tomatoes and purple onion salad:
Alternate paper-thin slices of purple onion with the tomato and finish as for sliced tomatoes with basil.

Sliced tomatoes with mozzarella:
This is nice on a buffet or as a light snack. Lay the slices flat and top each with a thin slice of mozzarella. Top each with half an anchovy fillet, if desired, or make a mixture of half with anchovies, the other half without. Dress as for other sliced tomatoes.

Tomato breakfast muffin:
My favorite summer breakfast is simply a thick slice of tomato with a slice of mozzarella on a toasted and buttered English muffin.

Tomato and eggs rémoulade:
One of the easiest and tastiest luncheon dishes you'll ever come across. Arrange slices of ripe tomatoes, hard-cooked eggs, and green pepper rings attractively on a pretty platter, sprinkle with black pepper and dress with rémoulade sauce (p. 380). Garnish with sprigs of basil, and serve with crusty bread.

Cherry tomato and scallion salad:

This is wonderful when there are no ripe tomatoes available other than cherry tomatoes. It is very pretty, easy to make and quite delicious. Wash, dry, stem and cut in half two pint boxes of dead ripe cherry tomatoes. Chop five scallions, the white and a good portion of the green, and toss with the tomatoes. Sprinkle with a handful of chopped parsley, dress with Lemon Vinaigrette (p. 375) and toss well again.

Quick Tomato Sauce

This is useful to have in one's repertoire for all times when a recipe calls for tomato sauce. It is also good to cook shrimp in or to steam clams open.

3 tablespoons olive oil
¼ cup chopped onion
2 teaspoons chopped garlic
3 tablespoons chopped parsley
One 2-pound 3-ounce can Italian tomatoes, coarsely chopped, plus
their juice
2 teaspoons tomato paste
Twist of lemon peel, optional
Salt and freshly ground pepper
Cayenne

Heat the olive oil in a heavy saucepan and sauté the onion until it is transparent. Add the garlic and cook 2 minutes more. Stir in the parsley and add the tomatoes, their liquid, the tomato paste, and lemon peel. Season with salt, pepper, and cayenne to taste, reduce heat, and simmer uncovered over moderate heat for about 20 minutes. Stir occasionally. Should the sauce seem too thin for your purpose, raise heat a bit to evaporate some liquid. Makes about 2 cups.

Fresh Tomato Sauce

This is the ideal sauce to have in the freezer for the long tomato-less winter. You can use it wherever tomato sauce is called for, but my absolute favorite use is as an instant soup, which brightens a January day like nothing else. Simply defrost, heat, put through a food mill, and add chicken broth or water, milk or cream until you have a pleasing consistency.

9 pounds fresh ripe
  tomatoes
4 tablespoons butter
4 tablespoons olive oil
5 cups chopped onions
10 garlic cloves, minced
Salt and freshly ground

pepper
Cayenne
½ cup chopped basil
  leaves, 10 sprigs fresh
  thyme, or 5 teaspoons
  dried thyme

Peel, core, seed, and juice the tomatoes. Chop coarsely and let sit for 15 minutes. Drain well before using. You should have about 4 quarts.

Melt the butter in the olive oil in a large, deep enamel-lined or stainless-steel pot (you may have to use two). Sauté onions and garlic until transparent.

Add the tomatoes by handfuls, giving them a last squeeze as you do to divest them of more juice. Add salt to taste, a liberal amount of pepper, several dashes of cayenne, and the basil or thyme. Cook for 15 minutes partly covered. Let cool. Ladle into plastic containers, allowing an inch of head room. In each container bury a knob of butter and, if available, a fresh basil leaf. Yields about 3 quarts.

Preparation note: Since seasonings lose a lot of their strength in the freezer, plan to taste and season again when you defrost. Use as is, or strain and puree.

Salade Provençale à la Tapenade

For a change of pace during the tomato season, try this delightful dish as a first course, light lunch, or stunning addition to a buffet of salads (which is all one need offer luncheon guests on a summer day).

1 pound handsome ripe
  tomatoes
Salt
½ pound small red new
  potatoes
1–2 garlic cloves

½ cup fresh fennel tops or
  parsley leaves
¼ cup tapenade (see p.
  382)
Lettuce leaves

Wash and dry the tomatoes and slice in thick vertical slices. Flick the seeds out with the tip of a knife if you have the patience, then salt the slices and let them drain for 20 to 30 minutes on paper towels or on a cake rack set over a dish.

Boil the potatoes and, when they are cool enough to handle, peel them and cut into slices. Chop the garlic together with the fennel and gently mix in a serving bowl with the tapenade.

Add the tomato slices and potatoes and gently mix. Let sit for 20 minutes at room temperature before serving on lettuce leaves. Serves 6–8.

Marinara Sauce

Years ago, when the principal industry of Naples was fishing, boats would sometimes be gone for several days at a time. The fishermen took along a basket of tomatoes, some seasonings, and prepared a simple sauce to accompany fresh fish for their meals, which came to be known as marinara sauce. The basic combination was tomatoes, onions, garlic, and olive oil.

¼ cup olive oil
1½ cups coarsely chopped onion
2 garlic cloves, finely minced
One 2-pound 3-ounce can Italian plum tomatoes, or 3 pounds fresh ripe tomatoes, peeled, seeded, and lightly juiced
Salt and freshly ground pepper to taste
1 teaspoon dried oregano
1 tablespoon chopped fresh basil, if available, or parsley
2 tablespoons butter, optional

Heat the oil in a large heavy skillet, and sauté the onion and garlic until lightly colored. Add the tomatoes, salt, pepper, oregano, and basil, bring to the simmer, and cook partly covered for 15 minutes, stirring occasionally. Swirl in the butter, partly cover, and simmer 10 minutes longer. Makes 3–4 cups.

Serving note: Marinara sauce can be used on just about any pasta you can think of (my favorite is linguini) or with shellfish or fish of any kind.

Clams marinara: Soak and scrub 3 dozen littleneck clams. Add ½ cup white wine to the skillet after the onion and garlic are brown. Boil 1 minute, then proceed as directed. When the sauce is finished, add the clams, cover tightly, and cook over high heat for 5 minutes, or until the clams open.

Italian Stuffed Tomatoes

6 fresh ripe tomatoes, preferably beefsteak	2 cups hot chicken broth
½ cup olive oil	Salt and freshly ground pepper
2 garlic cloves, minced	Dash cinnamon
¼ cup chopped parsley	6 fresh basil leaves, chopped, optional
1 cup long-grain rice	

Cut off the top (the opposite of the stem end) of each tomato and reserve. Scoop out about 2 tablespoons of the pulp without breaking the shells. Squeeze the juice into a bowl and reserve. Lightly salt the whole tomato shells and turn them upside down on a rack to drain for 15 minutes or so.

Preheat the oven to 350°. Oil a shallow baking dish, put the tomatoes in and brush the skin of each with about 1 tablespoon of olive oil.

Heat most of the remaining olive oil in a heavy saucepan (reserve a small amount for drizzling later). Sauté the garlic and parsley over medium heat for 3 minutes. Add the rice and cook 3 minutes longer, stirring constantly. Add the chicken broth all at once, bring to the boil, cover, lower heat, and simmer for 10 minutes, until liquid is absorbed but rice is underdone. Remove from the heat and season to taste with salt, pepper, and cinnamon. Stir in the chopped basil. Fill tomatoes with the mixture and cover each with its own top. Drizzle a little additional oil over each. Pour the reserved tomato juice around the tomatoes to a depth of about ½ inch, adding water if necessary. Bake for 25 to 30 minutes, or until the rice is tender, basting occasionally. If the tomatoes show signs of drying out, add a little hot water to the pan. Serves 6.

Preparation note: The stuffing can be endlessly varied with herbs—2 tablespoons chopped mint (or 1 tablespoon dried) is delicious substituted for the basil. Currants and pine nuts may be added for texture and sweetness.

Serving suggestion: These tomatoes may be eaten warm as a vegetable accompaniment to a regular meal (they are very good with lamb of all kinds), or at room temperature with cold foods. In Italy, you always find them at picnics.

Tomato-Pesto Tart

This dish combines familiar ingredients in an elegant and unusual way that is also nutritionally complete for vegetarians. It is best made in the summer, when real tomatoes are available. Fresh plum tomatoes give a particularly handsome result.

6 small fresh ripe tomatoes of uniform size
Olive oil
1 recipe savory pâte brisée (p. 177)
2 eggs, one separated, one whole
1¾ cups ricotta cheese
¼ cup chopped parsley, **preferably flat-leaf**
1 tablespoon chopped fresh basil
1 teaspoon salt
½ teaspoon white pepper
Several dashes cayenne
½ cup pesto (p. 382), thinned with a little olive oil if very thick

Preheat the oven to 325°.

Halve the tomatoes vertically, and remove and discard seeds with a small spoon. Arrange the tomatoes cut side up in a baking dish, sprinkle with salt and pepper, brush with oil and bake for 20 minutes. Transfer to a rack, cut side down, and let drain for 20 minutes. Turn oven heat to 425°.

While tomatoes are baking, roll out the pâte brisée about ⅛ inch thick and fit into an 8-inch flan ring. Make a built-up decorative rim, prick bottom with a fork, and chill for 30 minutes. Line shell with wax paper and fill with rice or dried beans; bake in the lower third of the 425° oven for 10 minutes. Remove paper and rice. Beat the egg white lightly and brush over entire shell. Bake 10 minutes more. Transfer shell to a rack and let cool.

Set oven heat at 350°. Place cooled shell on a baking sheet.

Beat together the ricotta, egg yolk, whole egg, parsley, basil, salt, pepper, and cayenne. When the mixture is smooth, spread it in the shell, making 12 indentations with the back of a spoon. Arrange the tomato halves in the indentations. Bake in the middle of the oven for 30 minutes, or until cheese mixture is set. Remove from oven, transfer to a rack, and put 1 tablespoon (approximately) pesto in each tomato.

Let tart cool to lukewarm, and remove ring. Transfer to a serving plate and serve at room temperature. Serves 4–6.

Serving note: Preceded by cold cucumber soup (p. 117) and accompanied by a mixed green or arugula salad, this tart makes a wonderful summer lunch or light dinner. It could also precede a grilled fish and broiled summer squash.

Penne with Uncooked Tomato Sauce

A beautiful, incredibly simple, and filling dish to make when fresh tomatoes and fresh basil are at their peak. The Italians prefer it with penne, the quill-shaped pasta, but any tubular pasta can be used.

1½ pounds fresh ripe tomatoes, peeled, seeded, and cubed	1 cup fresh basil leaves, washed and dried (about 20 leaves)
⅔ cup fruity olive oil	Salt and freshly ground pepper
2 large garlic cloves, chopped	⅔ cup grated Parmesan or Romano cheese
8 ounces imported penne	

Put the cubed tomatoes in a bowl.

Heat ⅓ cup of the olive oil in a small skillet and

sauté the garlic for 30 seconds. Remove from the heat and let cool for 5 minutes. Add to the bowl with the tomatoes, add the rest of the olive oil, and let stand for 1 or 2 hours.

Put a large quantity of salted water to boil, and cook the pasta according to package directions until just tender.

While pasta cooks, warm a large bowl and serving dishes. Shred the basil coarsely and add to the tomatoes. Add salt to taste and a liberal grinding of black pepper.

Drain the pasta and put in the warmed bowl. Scoop a few tablespoons of the oil from the tomatoes, add to the pasta, and toss. Divide the pasta among the heated plates, top with the tomato mixture, and sprinkle with grated cheese. Serves 4 as a first course.

Preparation note: Most recipes for this dish do not require the garlic to be sautéed, assuming that it "cooks" by marinating in the oil and the acid of the tomatoes. But I find the uncooked garlic stays with the eater for too long afterward. Try it both ways and decide for yourself. If you do choose to sauté the garlic, remember to do it only for 30 seconds—once brown, it becomes bitter. The seemingly small amount of pasta is correct; tubular pasta goes a long way.

Tomato Soup

A very fresh-tasting soup that is easily made.

2 pounds fresh ripe
  tomatoes
2 tablespoons olive oil
2 garlic cloves
4 leaves basil, shredded, or
  ¼ teaspoon dried
  thyme

2 cups beef, chicken, or
  vegetable broth
Salt and freshly ground
  pepper
Pinch sugar
Chopped parsley

Peel, skin, core, and lightly seed the tomatoes. Heat the olive oil in a soup pot, add the tomatoes, and cook over moderate heat until they almost melt. Add the garlic and basil and cook 5 minutes longer. Add the stock or broth, salt and pepper to taste, and sugar. Simmer for another 5 minutes. Garnish with chopped parsley. Serves 4.

Serving suggestion: Serve hot with crostini, or cold with oven-toasted pita bread triangles.

Green Tomato Chutney

5 pounds green tomatoes, sliced
2 tart apples, peeled, cored, and finely chopped
2 large onions, sliced
1 cup firmly packed brown sugar
½ cup raisins
1 teaspoon salt, or to taste
2 chopped fresh green chilies, or ½ teaspoon cayenne
3 tablespoons mustard seed
2 tablespoons minced fresh ginger

Wash and sterilize three pint canning jars and closures.

Combine all the ingredients in a large enamel or stainless kettle, cover, and bring to the boil. Uncover and simmer for about 2½ hours, until the mixture has thickened. Ladle into sterilized jars, wipe rims, and seal tightly. Check seal when cool. Store in a cool dark place for at least 3 weeks before using. Makes about 3 pints.

Fried Green Tomatoes

1½ pounds green tomatoes
Salt and freshly ground pepper
1 large egg
2 tablespoons milk
2 tablespoons water
¾ cup cracker meal or corn meal
½ cup flour
Vegetable oil
1 tablespoon bacon fat, optional

Wash, core, and cut the tomatoes into ⅓-inch slices. Set aside the end slices for another use. Pat slices dry (this is important) and season on both sides with salt and pepper.

Beat the egg with the milk and water and season to taste. Put the cracker meal and flour on separate pieces of wax paper.

Pour vegetable oil into a 10-inch skillet to a depth of ¼ inch. Add the bacon fat and heat.

Lay each tomato slice on the flour, coating both sides; shake off excess, and use a fork to dip slices into the egg mixture, coating both sides. Let excess drip off, then dip into the cracker crumbs so both sides are coated. Fry the slices in the hot fat, a few at a time, for about 45 seconds on each side, or until golden. As slices are completed, remove with a slotted spatula and drain on paper towels set on a plate in a slow oven. Serve with scrambled eggs. Serves 4.

Turnips and Rutabagas

(Brassica rapa and *Brassica rapobrassica)*

I always associate turnips with a Chinese fable I read as a child in which a single turnip, the only food remaining in a snowbound, starving countryside, was found by a hungry but noble rabbit who gave it to a poor family. It was given to the ever more needy and eventually wound up on the rabbit's doorstep again; a cautionary tale about a gift given freely returning to the giver. Easy to grow and quick to mature in the same hostile soils that foster poverty, this cold-weather root crop has long been relied on by the poor and therefore scorned by everyone else. Turnips were said to be eaten by the poor in lean times and by the cattle of the poor in good times.

The turnips that nurtured this lowly view have little to do with young spring turnips, which are sweet as you please. Waverly Root, the late food historian, pointed out that his favorite Paris restaurant served the classic duck with turnips only during six weeks in April and May, turnips being deemed unfit to eat the rest of the time.

Now the young turnip has been rediscovered by nouvelle cuisine chefs, who admire its crispness and subtle sweetness and the ease with which it can be shaped or julienned. Its absorptive powers make it good in stews, its flavor actually enhanced as it absorbs fat.

The small, white, spherical root tinged with purple (sometimes called white turnip) and the large, waxy, yellow root (properly called a rutabaga) are not really the same vegetable, although they are related. Rutabaga, also known as the Swedish turnip or "swede," is a fairly recent food, seemingly unknown before the seventeenth century.

Turnips have two distinct edible parts—the root and the greens. The latter are a popular food in the South, where they are, unfortunately, cooked until all their considerable vitamin and mineral content is destroyed. Rutabaga tops are not eaten.

To Buy

Turnips are best when young and small, ideally no larger than 2 inches in diameter, without scarred or split skins. Greens, if attached, should be crisp and unwilted. Rutabagas should be smooth and without punctures. They should be heavy for their size, though size itself is not critical. Two pounds will serve 4.

To Store

Detach greens and store separately; use the greens within 2 to 4 days. Refrigerate turnips unwashed in a plastic bag for up to a week. After that they begin to shrivel. Store rutabagas unwashed and unrefrigerated. They may be kept for up to 2 months in a cool dry place. Turnip puree can be frozen.

To Prepare

White turnips should be peeled, unless they are very young. To preserve nutrients, peel just before use. Rutabagas are often dipped in paraffin and should therefore be peeled. Cut through and remove the stem end. Then cut off skin in circular strips about ¼ inch thick.

To Cook

Boiled: Drop into boiling salted water, bring again to the boil and cover. Whole small (about 1½ inches in diameter) white turnips will take about 20 minutes; 1½-inch ovals about 12 minutes. Rutabaga in ½-inch chunks takes about 30 minutes. Finish with butter.

Steamed: Bring ¾ inch water to a boil in the bottom of a steamer, add the turnips, and cover. Whole small white turnips will take about 25 minutes, turned turnips (see p. 387) considerably less. Rutabaga, cut into ½-inch chunks, takes about 25 minutes. Finish with butter.

Pureed: Boil as directed. Puree in a food processor or food mill, season with butter, salt, pepper, and, if you like, some heavy cream. Or combine with pureed carrot or mashed potato.

Roasted: Cut turnips or rutabagas into halves or quarters. Place around a roast, season, and baste often and turn in the drippings. Allow about 45 minutes; they are done when easily pierced with a fork, the outside a little browned.

Julienned: Both vegetables lend themselves to this treatment because of their size and texture. They also combine beautifully with any other vegetables you can treat the same way, like carrots, broccoli stems, and zucchini. Use the 3-mm-square julienne disk of a food processor, a mandoline, or cut by hand. Blanch for 1 to

2 minutes, depending on thickness of cut. Drain, dry, then finish in butter.

Information on cooking turnip greens is given in the section on greens.

Glazed Turnips and Carrots: see page 89.

For a change from potato gratin, try one with turnips.

Gratin des Navets

3 tablespoons butter
2 garlic cloves peeled
1½ pounds young turnips, scrubbed
Salt and freshly ground pepper
⅓ cup chopped fresh dill
¼–½ cup grated Gruyère cheese
½ cup heavy cream
½ cup fresh bread crumbs

Preheat the oven to 400°. Rub a 12 × 8-inch gratin dish or shallow baking dish with 1 tablespoon of the butter. Put the garlic through a press right into the dish and rub all over with the back of a spoon to blend with the butter.

Slice the turnips thinly, by hand or with the slicing disk of a food processor. Make a layer of slightly overlapping turnip slices, season with salt and pepper, and sprinkle with a third of the dill. Make two more such layers, top with the cheese, pour the cream over, sprinkle with the bread crumbs, and dot with the remaining butter. (May be prepared ahead to this point.)

Bake for 45 minutes, or until turnips are tender and top is golden. Serves 4.

Serving suggestion: This goes well with roast pork, with braised duck, or any roasted game bird.

Mousseline of Yellow Turnips

I hate to tell people they're eating rutabaga—it sounds so homely, especially at a company dinner. So I had to give this vegetable a fancy name. Whenever I serve it with roast chicken or pork, everyone asks for more.

3 large rutabagas	pepper
3 large boiling potatoes	Butter at room
1 teaspoon sugar	temperature
Salt, if desired	Heavy cream
Freshly ground white	

Peel the rutabagas and potatoes and cut into ½-inch cubes. Place in separate pots, cover with cold salted water, bring to the boil, and cook until tender—about 15 minutes for the potatoes, 25 to 30 minutes for the rutabaga. Drain well.

Combine the vegetables and puree in a food processor. Add the sugar, salt, pepper, and a large knob of butter, and process briefly. Add enough cream to make a satiny puree, and process briefly. Spoon into a heated serving dish, add another good lump of butter, and serve. Serves 8.

Note: May be prepared ahead and kept warm in the top of a double boiler over simmering water. Place a piece of plastic wrap directly on top of the puree.

Middle Eastern Pickled Turnips

(Torshi Left)

These are great favorites in the Middle East, where restaurants have huge jars of them on the serving counter to be dished out and placed on the table for patrons to nibble on while waiting for the food to arrive. They are low in calories and make a delicious counterpoint to any highly spiced food.

5 medium-size white	1¼ cups water
turnips	1 teaspoon salt
Salt	1–2 slices raw or cooked
1 cup white vinegar	beet for color, optional

Scrub the turnips and cut into quarters, or eighths if they are large. Sprinkle with salt and let stand in a nonmetallic bowl for 1½ hours. Discard the liquid, rinse the turnips, and put them in a clean 1-quart jar. Add the vinegar, water, salt, and beet slices. Add more water if necessary to cover the turnips and fill to the

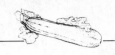

top of the jar. Cover and let stand for 3 or 4 days. If beet slices are used, upend the jar after 1 or 2 days to allow the color to permeate evenly. Makes about 1 quart.

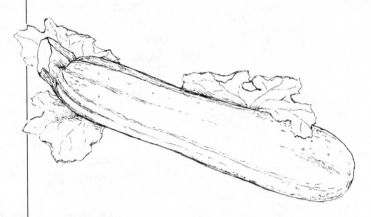

Zucchini

Zucchini is a vegetable that sort of crept up on us about fifteen years ago. Before that it was rarely seen outside Italian neighborhoods, and *New York Times* food writer Craig Claiborne, specifying it in a recipe as recently as the sixties, had to explain what it was. Although the name is Italian (meaning little squash) zucchini originated in America. The New England Indians introduced *askutasquash*—which means "eaten raw"—to the first settlers. Traders took the seeds back to Europe, where different varieties developed in different countries, and then the Italians brought it back to the United States. When American agricultural researchers developed hearty hybrids, it became a popular home garden vegetable, and with small wonder —it is extremely versatile, colorful, and, when young and fresh, has a delicate, sweet flavor not unlike young corn. It can be simply sliced, steamed, and dressed with butter or lemon; grated; or combined with other vegetables, the outstanding example of which is probably ratatouille. Small zucchini can be halved and stuffed with purees of other vegetables such as carrots.

Large ones stuffed with meat or rice mixtures become a meal in themselves.

When you see zucchini with white stripes and pale green skin, it is cocozelle, a similar summer squash. Use interchangeably with zucchini.

To Buy

Zucchini is marketed year-round, but is freshest, smallest, and most flavorsome in late spring and summer.

The youngest zucchini, 5 to 7 inches long, are the most tender and sweet. They should be firm, nicely proportioned pieces, heavy for their size, with vivid, taut green skin free of brown spots or cuts. Dull, pockmarked ones have been around too long. For stuffing, of course, buy large squash.

Allow 1 pound of zucchini for 3 people as a side dish.

One pound of zucchini, grated, yields approximately 2 cups after excess water is removed.

To Store

Keep in a loose plastic bag in the refrigerator. Use within 3 or 4 days at the outside.

Because of its high water content, zucchini does not freeze well. I do freeze grated zucchini with the excess liquid squeezed out, to use for pancakes, zucchini rapé, quiche, or baked zucchini and cheese.

To Prepare

Scrub gently with a soft brush to remove soil embedded in the skin. Drain well. Remove stem and blossom ends, but do not peel; the skin is tender and edible.

To Cook

Zucchini seems to benefit from a combination of steaming and blanching.

Steam-blanched: Bring ½ inch of salted water to the boil; add zucchini sliced into ¼- to ½-inch rounds. Cover-and cook over medium heat for 3 to 5 minutes from the second boil. Drain, dry briefly over heat, and dress with melted butter or lemon juice or both, season with salt and pepper to taste, and serve at once.

Steamed: Halve zucchini lengthwise. Place ¾ inch of water in the bottom of a steamer, bring to a boil, add the squash, cover, and steam until just tender—about 5 minutes. Finish as for steam-blanched zucchini.

Batter-fried: Cut zucchini into quarters lengthwise and then into fingers. Do not salt. Dip the zucchini into tempura batter (p. 346), and fry in an inch of vegetable oil in a skillet until golden—about 3 minutes a side. Salt, if desired, sprinkle with lemon juice, and serve hot.

Stuffed: This is especially good when you grow your own and have let some get large (zucchini can reach 18 inches in length). Scrub, halve, scoop out and discard the seeds, and stuff with any of the vegetable or vegetable-meat stuffings for eggplant or peppers to be found in this book. Bake at 350° for about 45 minutes, or until tender.

French-fried: Using the french-fry disk of a food processor or by hand, cut young unpeeled zucchini into narrow strips the size of thin french fries. Spread them on tea towels, sprinkle with salt, and let stand about 1 hour. Pat dry with paper towels. Place flour and some salt and pepper in a paper bag and shake the strips in it to coat them. Fry a small batch at a time in hot fat (375°) until golden. Drain strips on paper towels, sprinkle with additional salt, and keep them hot in the oven to retain crispness. Serve as a cocktail snack or an accompaniment to chicken or fish.

Zucchini Rapé

(Grated Zucchini)

This is a wonderful side dish because there is almost nothing it cannot accompany (it is particularly good with roast chicken or a simple broiled fish). A sauced dish, however, would compete with the zucchini's delicate flavor.

2½ pounds zucchini, scrubbed
1 teaspoon salt
2 tablespoons butter
2 tablespoons oil

Salt and freshly ground pepper
2 tablespoons chopped parsley, optional

Grate the zucchini on the largest hole of a four-sided grater or with the shredding disk of a food processor. Put into a colander or sieve set on a bowl, mix in the salt, and let sit for 30 minutes. Turn once or twice. Drain and squeeze out water (see note).

Heat the butter and oil in a large skillet (the larger the better, as this will allow additional moisture to evaporate). Sauté the zucchini quickly, tossing it about with a wooden spoon or spatula until it is hot but not soft. This should take 6 or 7 minutes. Season to taste, add the parsley, and serve immediately. Serves 6.

Note: For salt-free diets, rinse before squeezing.

Grated zucchini with shallots: Lightly sauté 2 or 3 chopped shallots in the pan before adding the zucchini. (A thinly sliced onion may also be used.)

Zucchini Provençal

4–5 medium zucchini, scrubbed
1 small onion, sliced
2 tablespoons olive oil
1 garlic clove, minced
2 fresh tomatoes, peeled,

seeded, and chopped
½ bay leaf
1 teaspoon dried oregano
1 teaspoon salt
Several grindings fresh pepper

Cut the zucchini into 1-inch rounds. Sauté the onion in the olive oil in a skillet until slightly brown. Stir in the garlic and tomatoes and cook 5 minutes longer over

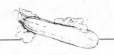

medium heat. Add the zucchini, bay leaf, oregano, salt, and pepper to taste. Cover and cook gently for 20 to 25 minutes, or until tender. (If after 15 minutes there is a great deal of liquid in the pan, remove the cover for the last 5 to 10 minutes of cooking.) Taste for seasoning, remove bay leaf, and serve. Serves 4.

Zucchini Gratin

Vegetables baked in a gratin can be flavored in such good ways I am always surprised they are not served more in this country. Here is a good case in point; not only is it tasty but it can be prepared ahead, as can most gratins, it can be easily doubled, and it can go from oven to table in its baking dish. The rosemary gives the zucchini a festive flavor.

**1¾ pounds young
   zucchini, scrubbed
⅓ cup olive or vegetable
   oil
Freshly ground pepper
Salt, if desired
2 slices home-style white
   bread**

**Several sprigs parsley
   without stems
1–2 garlic cloves
½ teaspoon dried
   rosemary
⅓ cup grated Parmesan
   cheese**

Preheat the oven to 400°. Oil a 12×7-inch oval baking dish.

Cut the zucchini slightly on the diagonal into ½-inch slices.

Heat the oil in a heavy skillet and sauté the zucchini until softened and slightly browned on both sides—5 to 8 minutes. Shake the pan and stir frequently. Remove the slices with a slotted spoon and arrange them in the prepared baking dish in an overlapping pattern. Season with liberal grinds of pepper and salt, if desired. Reserve the oil in the pan.

Trim the crusts off the bread, cut or tear into pieces, and process briefly in the food processor or blender; add the parsley and garlic and process with on-off turns until you have a homogeneous crumb mixture. Sprinkle the rosemary over the zucchini, then sprinkle the

crumbs over. Top with the cheese and drizzle over the reserved oil, adding a bit more if the top looks dry. (May be prepared an hour ahead to this point.) Bake for 20 minutes. Serves 4.

Serving suggestion: This is good with roast lamb or veal, with baked or broiled fish, or with broiled chicken. In summer, accompany with corn on the cob; in winter, with mashed potatoes.

Suzanne Hamlin's Zucchini Pizza

Suzanne's children are vegetarians and love all forms of pizza. So she invented this for them, really a giant zucchini pancake.

1½ pounds small zucchini, scrubbed
1 teaspoon salt
3 large eggs, lightly beaten
½ cup all-purpose unbleached flour
½ cup freshly grated Parmesan cheese

6 fresh basil leaves, finely chopped, or ½ teaspoon dried oregano
Freshly ground pepper and salt
1 tablespoon olive oil
1 cup tomato sauce
½–¾ cup shredded mozzarella

Grate the zucchini, using the shredding disk of a food processor or the large-hole side of a four-sided grater. You should have about 4 packed cups.

Mix in salt, let stand for 30 minutes in a colander to remove excess water, then squeeze the water out well with your hands; zucchini must be as dry as possible.

Preheat the oven to 350°, and grease well a 12-inch pizza tin. Combine the zucchini with the eggs, flour, Parmesan cheese, basil, and several good grinds of pepper. Taste for salt. Spread evenly on the prepared tin, smoothing out to the edges with a spatula. Pan will be only half-full.

Bake on the middle level of the oven for 25 to 30 minutes, or until the surface is firm and dry. Brush with the oil and run under a hot broiler 4 inches from the heat for 1½ to 2 minutes, or until lightly browned.

Spread with tomato sauce, sprinkle with mozzarella (the amount depending on how cheesy you like the top), and run under the broiler again for 1½ to 2 minutes, or until the cheese melts. Watch constantly, as broiler heat varies enormously. Serves 3–4.

Preparation notes: If I've no homemade tomato sauce on hand, I make this with Aunt Millie's Marinara Sauce, which I find the best all-purpose commercial brand, free from additives, thick, and delicious.

Frittata of Zucchini

A frittata is a flat omelet that is attractive and nourishing and makes a good first course or a splendid light meal with good bread and a salad. This Roman version, with zucchini punctuated by basil, is my favorite lunch and picnic staple in the summer, when both these ingredients are abundant.

¼ cup vegetable oil
1 cup thinly sliced onion
3 small or 2 medium
   zucchini, scrubbed
½ teaspoon salt, or to
   taste
5 extralarge eggs
⅔ cup grated Parmesan

cheese
Freshly ground pepper
6 large basil leaves,
   shredded, or 1
   tablespoon finely
   chopped parsley
3 tablespoons butter

Heat the oil in a heavy 10-inch skillet and cook the onion over low heat until completely wilted and golden but not brown.

Slice the zucchini into ¼-inch rounds. Add to the cooked onion, lightly salt, and cook over medium heat until softened and lightly browned. Stir frequently and gently. Put in a colander or large sieve set over a bowl and let drain and cool for 5 or 10 minutes. Discard the oil that drains off.

Break the eggs into another bowl and beat well. Stir in the cheese and the zucchini-onion mixture. Add several liberal grinds of black pepper, salt, if desired, and the basil. Let stand for 15 minutes or so if you

have time, so the eggs absorb the flavor of the herb.

Wipe the skillet in which the onions were sautéed and melt the butter in it over medium heat. When it begins to foam but not brown, add the egg mixture and turn the heat as low as possible. Gently push the vegetables away from the very edge lest they adhere. Do not stir or scramble; let the eggs cook until they are set and the top surface is just a little runny. This will take 12 to 15 minutes, but do stand by and watch constantly for burning.

If you are planning to serve the frittata immediately, warm a serving plate during this time.

Run the skillet under the broiler for 30 seconds to 1 minute to complete the top side of the frittata. It should be quite set but not browned on either side.

Loosen the edges with a spatula and slide onto the serving platter. (If it doesn't move easily, gently check with the spatula for a spot that may be sticking.) Cut into wedges like a pie and serve. Serves 4.

Serving suggestion: In Italy, a fritatta is frequently served as an evening meal, preceded by a light soup such as a consommé, when the main meal has been taken at midday. I like it as a lunch dish, served with good chewy country bread and butter and a salad of dead-ripe sliced tomatoes dressed with mustard vinaigrette, or a mixed green salad. The cold cucumber soup on page 117 makes a nice starter.

Tian of Zucchini and Tomatoes

A tian is a casserole, but that doesn't tell you the whole story. It is also a large, shallow, round earthenware terrine with slightly flaring sides, meant to cook a family dish in the local baker's wood-burning oven. The container gives its name to the dish, which is generally understood to be a gratin of green vegetables. There is tian of spinach, sometimes with chick-peas added, of Swiss chard, of onions, or of zucchini, all perfumed with garlic and one or another of the herbs of Provence, and of course made with good fruity olive oil. This succulent combination of zucchini and

tomatoes is adapted from a recipe of Roger Vergé. I can't think of anything nicer in the world to do with vegetables, which can then be eaten at any temperature and at any time.

1 large garlic clove
5 tablespoons olive oil
1 large onion, thinly sliced (about 2 cups)
3 medium very fresh zucchini, about 1¼ pounds, scrubbed

4–6 small, firm, ripe tomatoes, about 1½ pounds
Coarse salt and freshly ground pepper
½ teaspoon thyme leaves, fresh or dried

Preheat the oven to 475°. Select an oval or round shallow baking dish, about 10 inches in diameter. Put the garlic clove through a press and rub the mash all over the bottom and sides of the dish with the back of a spoon. Set aside.

Heat 2 tablespoons of the olive oil in a heavy skillet, and cook the onion until it is soft, with only the faintest suggestion of color. This will take about 10 minutes.

Using a vegetable peeler, remove lengthwise strips of skin from the zucchini at ⅜-inch intervals, leaving alternating bands of green and white. Slice the zucchini crosswise slightly on the diagonal into ⅛-inch pieces. Core the tomatoes and cut vertically into ¼-inch slices.

When the onions are done, put them in the baking dish and make an even layer on the bottom. Over this bed, arrange a row of overlapping zucchini slices, letting them lean at an angle against one side of the dish, so they are almost standing. Next to it, arrange a similar row of tomatoes; continue alternating rows in this manner until all ingredients are used. Don't be afraid to push the rows together to make room, as there will be some shrinkage during cooking.

Season with salt and pepper, scatter the thyme on top, and brush the vegetables with 2 more tablespoons of the oil.

Bake for 15 minutes; drizzle the remaining tablespoon of olive oil over and bake 5 minutes more.

Baste with the rendered vegetable juices (tilt the dish to catch them in a spoon), then bake 10 minutes more. At the end, the vegetables should be soft and lightly browned on top. Serves 4–6.

Preparation note: A mixture of grated Parmesan cheese and fine fresh bread crumbs may be sprinkled on top just before baking.

Zucchini and tomato tian with eggs:
When the tian is cooked, use a soup spoon to make depressions in the top for each diner. Break an egg into each, heat gently on top of the stove, then return to the still-hot oven and cook until the eggs are set but not hard. This makes a fine one-dish dinner for vegetarians.

Stuffed Zucchini

This is a surprisingly elegant and tasty dish for such a humble vegetable, and makes a pleasant and different accompaniment to fish or chicken. It may also be served as a first course, and is nutritionally complete enough to be the main course of a vegetarian dinner.

4 small zucchini, scrubbed
½ cup finely chopped onion
2 tablespoons butter
2 tablespoons olive oil
1 egg, lightly beaten
¼ cup grated Parmesan cheese
Generous pinch each of thyme, oregano, and rosemary
Salt and freshly ground pepper
¼ cup fine, dry homemade bread crumbs
2 tablespoons melted butter

Preheat the oven to 375°. Butter a baking dish large enough to hold *twice* the number of zucchini in a single layer and set aside.

Cut the zucchini in half lengthwise. Using a teaspoon or a melon ball cutter, carefully scoop out the inner meat and reserve it. Be careful not to pierce the skin. Bring a large pot of lightly salted water to the boil and

poach the zucchini shells for 5 minutes. Drain, run cold water over, and arrange the shells in the prepared baking dish. Set aside.

Chop the reserved zucchini flesh finely and mix together with the onion. Heat the butter and oil together in a large skillet, add the zucchini mixture, and cook for about 5 minutes, or until soft but not brown. Put the mixture in a bowl, let cool a few minutes, then add the egg, half the cheese, the herbs, salt, and pepper. Spoon into the zucchini shells. Combine the remaining cheese and the bread crumbs, sprinkle on top of each shell (may be prepared ahead to this point; bring to room temperature before completing), and drizzle melted butter over. Bake for 20 to 25 minutes in the upper third of the oven. If you wish the tops to be a little browner, run under the broiler for 30 seconds, watching them carefully. Serves 4.

Baked Zucchini and Cheese

This Armenian recipe illustrates the remarkable versatility of zucchini. Here it becomes quite forceful when combined with two cheeses and mint in a preparation that's great for vegetarians, and one I've used with great success as a buffet dish.

5–6 medium zucchini, about 2 pounds, scrubbed	chopped parsley
Salt	2 tablespoons finely chopped mint leaves
4 eggs, lightly beaten	6 scallions, the white and 2 inches of green, chopped
½ cup crumbled fresh feta cheese (about ¼ pound)	½ cup flour
1 cup freshly grated Gruyère cheese	Freshly ground pepper
2 tablespoons finely	Nutmeg
	6 tablespoons butter

Grate the zucchini coarsely. Measure, add ¼ teaspoon salt for each cup, mix, and let sit in a colander for 35 minutes. Press out and discard excess water. You should have about 4 packed cups grated zucchini.

Preheat the oven to 350°. Butter a 1½-quart

ovenproof casserole. Add the eggs, cheeses, parsley mint, scallions, and flour to the grated zucchini. Season to taste with salt, pepper, and a grating of nutmeg. Pour the mixture into the buttered baking dish. Dot the surface with butter and bake for 45 minutes, or until surface is golden and puffed. Serves 6–8.

Serving suggestion: Serve hot or at room temperature with poultry or meat. This recipe may easily be doubled for a buffet. Bake for the same time in a 2½-quart casserole.

Zucchini Salad with Tomato Dressing and Pine Nuts

When I can't face another green salad and have had my fill of sliced tomatoes, I find this salad makes a pleasant change. It's a great summer dish that can be prepared ahead of time.

2 pounds medium-small zucchini, scrubbed	¼ cup olive oil
2 pounds ripe tomatoes	2 tablespoons finely minced fresh chives
¾ teaspoon salt	3 tablespoons finely minced parsley, leaves only
1½ teaspoons sugar, or to taste	
¼ teaspoon pepper	½ cup toasted pine nuts (p. 406)
3 tablespoons red wine vinegar	

Drop the zucchini into a large kettle of boiling salted water. Boil 5 minutes, or until the squash are barely tender when pressed. Remove with tongs and place in a colander under cold running water until cooled through. Trim the ends and cut into pieces 2 inches long and ½ inch thick. Arrange pieces in a serving bowl, cover, and chill.

Drop the tomatoes into the same kettle of boiling water, return to the boil, then drain in a colander. Cool under cold running water for a moment, then skin and halve the tomatoes crosswise, squeeze out the seeds, and cut the flesh into ½-inch dice. Reserve.

Combine half the diced tomatoes in a food processor

or blender with the salt, sugar, pepper, and vinegar, and whirl until smooth. Add the olive oil and mix. In a bowl, combine the tomato puree mixture with half the remaining diced tomatoes. Add the chives and parsley and stir. Correct the seasoning and reserve until serving time.

Pour the dressing over the zucchini and garnish with the remaining diced tomatoes and the toasted pine nuts. Serves 6.

Serving Suggestion: Put this out on a summer buffet along with Conchiglie with Pesto, Red Peppers and Peas (p. 218), Corn and Pepper Salad (p. 109), and a cold poached fish with Consuelo's Green Sauce (p. 379). Or serve with anything made on the charcoal grill.

Gâteau of Zucchini and Rice

This is a delicious invention of one of the best cooks I know, Andrée Abramoff, who adapted it from gâteau financière for her vegetarian cooking classes. It is simple, can be made completely ahead, and is utterly delicious. Don't be confused by the fact that there is no liquid called for to cook the rice (it emerges from the vegetables) or that the crumb topping ends up on the bottom; this is intentional, to form a base for the gâteau. And be sure to wait until it reaches room temperature before unmolding.

1 tablespoon salt
2 tablespoons olive oil
2 tablespoons butter
1 large onion, chopped
2 pounds small zucchini, scrubbed and sliced into ¼-inch rounds
1 garlic clove, put through a press
Freshly ground pepper
1 pound fresh plum

tomatoes, peeled and chopped, or 2-pound 3-ounce can Italian plum tomatoes, drained and chopped
1 cup long-grain rice
2 tablespoons chopped parsley
½ cup grated Parmesan cheese
½ cup bread crumbs

Preheat the oven to 425°. Butter a 6-cup soufflé dish, a Pyrex loaf pan, or other similar size baking dish.

Heat the oil and butter in a large skillet and brown the onion. Add the zucchini and garlic and cook, tossing, for 3 minutes, until zucchini is barely tender. Season with several grindings of pepper.

Add the tomatoes and simmer gently, uncovered, until the mixture becomes a little dry—about 4 minutes. Stir in the rice, parsley, and ¼ cup of the Parmesan. Put in the prepared mold, sprinkle with the crumbs and remaining cheese. Bake for 30 to 35 minutes, or until the top is golden. Let come to room temperature before unmolding. Serves at least 6.

Serving suggestion: As an accompaniment to roast squab or chicken, or as a main dish for a vegetarian meal. Several of these gâteaus may be prepared completely ahead and used on a buffet.

Curried Cream of Zucchini Soup

1 pound small zucchini, scrubbed
2 tablespoons butter
2 tablespoons finely chopped shallots
1 garlic clove, minced
½ teaspoon curry powder, or to taste
Salt and freshly ground pepper to taste
1½ cups chicken broth
⅓–½ cup heavy cream
Chopped chives, optional

Slice the zucchini thinly. Reserve 4 slices.

Melt the butter in a heavy saucepan and add the zucchini, shallots, and garlic. Cover and cook over low heat for 5 minutes, shaking the pan frequently. Add the curry powder, salt, and pepper, and cook uncovered, stirring, for 30 seconds. Add the broth and bring to the boil.

Puree the soup in a food processor or blender. Add cream to the consistency you like, and additional broth if you like a thinner soup. Correct seasoning and chill.

Blanch the reserved slices of zucchini in boiling water for 1 minute. Float one on each bowl of soup, garnished with optional chives. Serves 4.

Fettuccine with Mushrooms and Zucchini

½ pound mushrooms,
  sliced paper thin
1 pound small zucchini,
  sliced paper thin
3 tablespoons butter
1 teaspoon minced garlic
½ teaspoon salt
3 ounces prosciutto ham,
  cut into 1-inch julienne

⅓ cup chopped parsley
1 teaspoon oregano
1 cup heavy cream
1 pound fresh fettuccine,
  cooked and drained
Freshly ground pepper
⅔ cup grated Parmesan
  cheese

Sauté the mushrooms and zucchini in the butter in a heavy skillet over high heat for 6 or 7 minutes, until they give forth liquid and it evaporates. After 3 or 4 minutes, add the garlic and the salt. Mix the ham with the parsley and oregano, and add to the vegetables. Sauté for another couple of minutes, stir in the cream, bring to a boil, and cook over high heat for 3 minutes, or until it reduces slightly. Add the fettuccine, toss well, remove from heat, taste for salt, and add a generous amount of pepper and the cheese. Toss again and serve at once. Serves 4–6.

Note: You can garnish each serving with a bit of fresh tomato pulp for color.

Zucchini Bread

Is there anyone who doesn't love zucchini bread? This is a particularly good version that freezes well (we are never without it) and is very easy to make. At Christmas, I make batches of miniature loaves and wrap them in red cellophane for little gifts.

3 eggs
1 cup vegetable oil
2 cups granulated sugar
2 cups grated zucchini,
  tightly packed, about ¾
  pound zucchini
1 teaspoon vanilla
3 cups all-purpose flour
1 teaspoon baking soda

1 teaspoon baking powder
½ teaspoon salt
1 teaspoon ground ginger
1 teaspoon ground
  cinnamon
½ teaspoon ground cloves
1 cup chopped walnuts
  (about 3 ounces)
½ cup raisins, optional

Preheat the oven to 325°. Butter two 5×8-inch loaf pans.

Combine the eggs, oil, and sugar in the bowl of an electric mixer. Stir in the zucchini and add the vanilla.

Sift together the dry ingredients and blend into mixture. Stir in the nuts and raisins (batter will be rather stiff), pour into the prepared pans, and bake for 1 hour. Cool for 20 minutes on a wire rack before removing from pan. Makes 2 loaves.

Preparation notes: You may also make 5 miniature loaves with this recipe: bake for 50 minutes at 325°. Either size freezes well.

Part Two

Mixed Vegetables

Crudités

It was pretty far out to serve raw vegetables a decade ago, but today the platter or basket of crudités is a must for cocktail parties. Crudités are low in calories and satisfy the need to nibble with drinks; the selection can be simple or elaborate, one vegetable alone or as many as you wish.

Among the most successful vegetables are zucchini and yellow squash spears, cucumbers, carrot and celery sticks, red and green pepper strips, small scallions plain or cut into brushes, paper-thin circles of peeled bulb fennel, and kohlrabi cut into slices. Very fresh white mushrooms may be used in thick slices.

The following vegetables may also be used, and are best quickly blanched (drop in boiling salted water, remove when the water returns to the boil, and refresh): broccoli and cauliflower flowerets, snow peas, string beans, and wax beans. Unless asparagus are pencil-thin, they should be blanched for 1 minute.

I like to serve cherry tomatoes separately with a little dish of coarse salt mixed with freshly ground pepper. For fancy cutting techniques, see vegetable garnishes, page 384.

To crisp the vegetables, cut them in the desired lengths and soak in a bowl of water and ice cubes in the refrigerator. Do not soak artichokes, cucumbers, or mushrooms.

Some good sauces for crudités are Consuelo's Green Sauce (p. 379), Tapenade (p. 382), and curried mayonnaise (p. 379).

To make a crudité basket: Use several
kinds of vegetables and balance the colors. First fill the basket almost to the brim with bunched tissue paper or a tea towel, and cover this base with a plain white napkin. Arrange clusters of like vegetables on end, and nestle a container with the dip in the middle. The dip container can also be a vegetable; try a hollowed-out purple or green cabbage or a giant cooked, hollowed-out artichoke. Then the leaves can be eaten, too.

Acar Campur

(Indonesian Cooked Vegetable Salad)

I first ate this pretty salad at a covered dish dinner at a food writers' symposium. It was the food that disappeared first. Since then, there is almost no time when it is not in my refrigerator, waiting to flesh out a lunch of leftovers, be added to a green salad as garnish, or just available for nibbles. The preparation of the vegetables is rather lengthy, but the dish itself is easy to make.

½ pound string beans
½ pound carrots (about 4)
1 cucumber
½ pound cauliflower
  (about ⅓ a small head)
1 green pepper
1 sweet red pepper,
  optional
1 red or green hot chili
  pepper
10 small white pickling
  onions
1 large shallot

2 garlic cloves
4 whole macadamia nuts
2 tablespoons vegetable oil
½ teaspoon turmeric
½ teaspoon ground ginger
4 tablespoons white
  vinegar
½ teaspoon salt, or to
  taste
1 cup water
1 tablespoon brown sugar
1 teaspoon dry mustard

Wash all the vegetables and set each aside separately as you prepare them. Top and tail the beans and cut each into 3 pieces. Peel the carrots and cucumber and remove the seeds of the cucumber if they are large. Cut both into strips of approximately the same size as the bean pieces. Separate the cauliflower into flowerets. Seed and derib the green and red pepper and cut into strips of a size compatible with the others. Remove the seeds from the hot chili pepper and cut it crosswise into 4 pieces. Pierce a shallow cross in the base of each onion, blanch them for 5 seconds, and slip off the skins.

Peel the shallot and garlic, chop coarsely, combine with the macadamia nuts, and crush to a paste in a mortar, a blender, or a food processor.

Heat the vegetable oil in a 3 or 4-quart stainless-steel or enamel-lined saucepan having a cover. Stir-fry the garlic paste for 1 minute. Add the turmeric, ginger, chili pepper, and white onions and cook, stirring, for a few seconds, then add the vinegar and salt. Cover and cook for 3 minutes.

Add the carrots, cauliflower, beans, green and red peppers, and the water. Stir to coat evenly, bring to a simmer, cover, and cook over moderate heat for 10 minutes.

Add the sugar, dry mustard, and cucumber, cover, and cook 3 minutes. Remove lid and continue cooking, stirring gently but continuously, for another 3 minutes. Transfer to a serving dish at once, and let come to room temperature. Will keep in a closed jar in the refrigerator for several weeks. Makes about 2 quarts.

Preparation note: As chili peppers vary greatly in their hotness, you may add a bit of cayenne pepper if a final tasting indicates the need.

Salade Niçoise

This makes a fine luncheon dish in summer. It must be assembled and dressed at the last minute, but much of the preparation can be done in advance. Although lettuce is not traditional in a salade niçoise, it makes it a more substantial dish.

1 pound slender green beans, blanched for 5 minutes, drained, at room temperature

1 cup mustard vinaigrette (page 375)

3 ripe tomatoes, quartered (see note)

1 head, Boston lettuce or romaine, separated and washed

2 cups cold French potato salad made without onions (p. 243)

7½-ounce can tuna,

packed in olive oil, drained

3 hard-cooked eggs, quartered

2-ounce tin flat anchovy fillets, drained

½ purple onion, cut into paper-thin rings

½ green pepper, cut into thin rings, optional

4 ounces small black olives, preferably cured in oil

Handful chopped basil and parsley

Toss the beans with several tablespoons of the dressing. Do the same with the tomatoes in a separate bowl.

Just before serving, toss the lettuce with about ¼ cup of the dressing; line a salad bowl with it. Mound the potato salad in the center of the bowl and make small clusters of the beans, tomatoes, tuna, and eggs around the potato salad. Garnish with the anchovies, purple onion rings, green pepper rings, and black olives. Spoon the remaining dressing over all and sprinkle with the basil-parsley mixture. Serves 4–6.

Note: If you have the patience, flick out the seeds of the tomatoes with the point of a knife.

Mixed Vegetables à la Grecque

Follow the recipe for mushrooms à la Grecque on page 178 using ¼ pound tiny white onions, peeled, with the root end pierced; ¼ pound mushrooms; half a small head of cauliflower separated into flowerets; 2 carrots, scraped, halved lengthwise, and cut into quarters; and 1 red or green pepper, seeded, deribbed, and cut into wide strips. Cook the onions for 10 to 15 minutes, depending on size; when 7 minutes of the cooking time remains, add the carrots; 2 minutes later, add the mushrooms, cauliflower, and peppers a handful at a time.

Aïoli

"Around an aïoli, well-perfumed and bright as a vein of gold, where are there men who would not recognise themselves as brothers?" wrote the poet Mistral of the dish that symbolizes Provence. Aïoli is a kind of garlic mayonnaise, served surrounded by a number of vegetables, all boiled separately. Snails, cockles, and a poached white fish like anglerfish are usually included, and at a grand aïoli, eaten on feast days, salt cod, beef, and lamb from a pot-au-feu as well.

Whether grand or small, aïoli is a lovely treat for your guests in summer. You can do all the vegetable preparation in advance.

Sauce Aïoli

8 garlic cloves, or to taste
2 large egg yolks, at room
    temperature
½ teaspoon salt
Juice of 1 lemon (about 3
    tablespoons)

Freshly ground white
    pepper
1½ cups olive oil, or half
    olive and half peanut
    oil, at room
    temperature

Puree the garlic in a food processor or blender. Beat
the egg yolks together with the salt and add to the
garlic. Add the lemon juice and pepper and blend to a
smooth puree. With the motor running, add the oil
very slowly in a steady stream, until you have a thick,
firm, shiny sauce. Cover with plastic wrap and
refrigerate until ready to use. Makes about 1¾ cups
sauce, enough for 6–8.

Serving suggestion: Serve the sauce in a small bowl
and the vegetables (and fish if you are using it)
attractively arranged in clusters on one or two large
platters. For 6 to 8, use as many of the following as are
available. Serve warm.

2 pounds boiled new potatoes in their jackets
1 young globe artichoke per person, trimmed, boiled,
    chokes removed
a few Jerusalem artichokes, boiled unpeeled
1½ pounds carrots, cut into 2-inch lengths, blanched
1½ pounds string beans, trimmed, blanched, and
    refreshed
1 small head cauliflower, separated into flowerets,
    blanched and refreshed
1 can cooked chick-peas, drained, or 1 cup dried
    chick-peas, cooked
1 hard-boiled egg per person, quartered
1½ pounds young zucchini, cut into thick diagonal
    slices, blanched
2½ pounds salt cod, poached, or a whole white fish,
    poached and skinned

Salade Russe

Carrots and a bean of some sort seem to be a given in this salad; some versions add diced potato, turnip, tongue, and even tomato. Sometimes I substitute fresh string beans, cut into 1-inch pieces, for the limas. Whatever you use, it is easily made at any time of the year and in any quantity.

2 ten-ounce boxes frozen peas, partly defrosted
2 ten-ounce boxes frozen baby lima beans, partly defrosted
2 tablespoons lemon juice
⅔ cup mayonnaise
1 teaspoon salt
¼ teaspoon white pepper
2 teaspoons sugar
4–6 carrots, scraped and cut into medium dice
¼ cup finely minced onion
Handful finely chopped dill

Bring 2 cups of salted water to a boil in a large pot; add the peas and limas, a box at a time, allowing the water to return to the boil each time. Cover, lower fire, and cook for 7 minutes. Drain in a colander and run cold water over. Allow vegetables to cool while you make the sauce.

Beat the lemon juice into the mayonnaise with salt, pepper, and sugar.

Put cooled peas and lima beans in a large mixing bowl. Add the diced carrots and onion. Pour sauce over vegetables and stir in gently. Add dill and mix again. Cover tightly with plastic wrap and refrigerate.

Serves 10–12.

Chinese Stir-Fried Vegetables

½ cup chicken broth
1 tablespoon soy sauce
½ teaspoon sugar
4 ounces snow peas
2 tablespoons vegetable or peanut oil
½ teaspoon salt
1 garlic clove, minced
¼ cup celery, sliced diagonally
4 ounces water chestnuts,
sliced
3 scallions, trimmed and sliced into 1-inch pieces
½ cup mushrooms, sliced, or 6 dried black mushrooms, soaked, drained, and shredded
1 cup bean sprouts, fresh or canned
Soy sauce to taste

Combine the broth, soy sauce, and sugar, and set aside.

Stem and string the snow peas; leave whole if tender; if not, cut in two. Blanch 1 minute, drain, and set aside.

Heat a wok or heavy skillet until a drop of water sizzles; add the oil and continue heating until it bubbles.

Add salt and garlic and stir-fry a few times. Add the celery, snow peas, and water chestnuts, and stir-fry for 2 minutes. Add the scallions, mushrooms, and bean sprouts, and stir-fry for 1 minute more, until heated through.

Add the broth-soy mixture and simmer for 1 minute. Serve immediately. Serves 2.

Curried Mixed Vegetables

You can curry any vegetables, alone or in combination, depending on seasonal availability. Just remember to adjust cooking times to the density of the vegetable.

2 tablespoons olive or
    vegetable oil
1 tablespoon butter
½ cup chopped onion
2 garlic cloves, minced
1 tablespoon grated ginger
    root
¼ teaspoon cayenne
    pepper, more or less
1 teaspoon ground
    coriander
1 teaspoon ground
    cardamom
1 teaspoon ground cumin
¼ teaspoon cinnamon
1 teaspoon turmeric
3 medium potatoes, peeled
    and cut into 1-inch
    cubes

2 tomatoes, roughly
    chopped
Salt to taste
½ head cauliflower,
    separated into flowerets
3 carrots, scraped and
    sliced into ½-inch
    rounds
½ pound okra, cut into
    1-inch pieces, optional
¼–½ pound string beans,
    cut into 2-inch lengths
2 cups chicken broth or
    water, or more to cover
2 tablespoons fresh
    coriander leaves

Heat the oil and butter in a heavy casserole and sauté the onion, garlic, and ginger until the onion is wilted. Do not let mixture brown.

Add the cayenne, coriander, cardamom, cumin, cinnamon, and turmeric, and cook, stirring, for a minute, until fragrant. Add the potatoes, 1 of the tomatoes, water and broth to cover, and salt. Bring to a boil, reduce heat to a simmer, and cook, covered, for 5 minutes; add the cauliflower and carrots, and simmer uncovered 5 minutes more. Add the okra, string beans, and the remaining tomatoes. Bring back to the boil and simmer for 5 minutes. The potatoes may break up a little bit at this point and will pleasantly thicken the sauce. The rest of the vegetables should be tender but not mushy. Serve hot over rice, garnished with fresh coriander. Serves 4–5.

Note: Any of the spices may be adjusted in amount or omitted according to taste; 1½ tablespoons prepared curry powder can be substituted for the separate spices.

Vegetable Tempura

Though the concept of fried, batter-coated food came to Japan with the Portuguese, who opened up trade with the Orient in the sixteenth century, tempura bears the unmistakable imprint of the Japanese. Unlike thick Western batters, the purposely thin tempura batter gives a gossamer coating to food, especially vegetables. Chilling the batter helps produce the characteristic crispness that is an essential part of the technique.

Good vegetables for tempura include trimmed asparagus spears, wedges of green or red pepper; quarter-inch-thick crosswise slices of peeled sweet potato, onion, or small eggplant (see note 1); string beans; and thick mushroom slices. You can use just one kind or a mixture, in which case vegetables with different cooking times must be cooked separately. Make sure like vegetables are of uniform thickness.

Tempura Batter:

1 large egg yolk
1¼ cups ice water
1¼ cups sifted all-purpose

flour
Peanut or vegetable oil
  for frying

Beat the egg yolk lightly in a bowl; slowly add the water, beating constantly. Mix in the flour. Do not overbeat; the batter will be lumpy. Chill for half an hour.

Heat the oil to 375°. Line a wire rack with paper towels. Using chopsticks or tongs, dip vegetables into batter, let excess drip back into the bowl, and lower into the oil. Fry small batches at a time, 2 or 3 minutes a side, until the batter is lightly golden and crisp (see note 2). Drain on the paper towels and serve immediately with dipping sauce. Makes about 2 cups batter.

Tempura Dipping Sauce

¼ cup soy sauce
4 tablespoons Mirin or
   sherry (see note 3)
1 teaspoon sugar
4 tablespoons grated white
   radish (daikon), or 2
   tablespoons peeled fresh
   ginger, or a
   combination
1 cup beef broth

Combine all the ingredients and serve in individual bowls as a dipping sauce for tempura.

Notes: (1) Eggplant slices should be dusted with flour before dipping in batter.

(2) Skim oil of any loose particles of batter, which will burn and give an off taste to the oil. Use a wire skimmer or a slotted spoon.

(3) Mirin is a sweet wine available in Oriental stores.

Greek-Style Roasted Mixed Summer Vegetables

(Tourlou)

Paula Wolfert discovered *tourlou*—or *briami,* as it is called in some parts of Greece—when she was doing a magazine story on the food of the island of Corfu. Paula, whose adaptation for the American kitchen appears here, explains that in Greece this dish is made with different ingredients at different times of the year; other combinations might be peas, artichokes, squash blossoms, and fava beans; or tomatoes, green peppers, and eggplant.

1½ pounds fresh ripe
   tomatoes, peeled, cored,
   and thinly sliced
Pinch sugar
1½ pounds medium
   boiling potatoes, peeled
   and cut into wedges
1 pound medium red or
   yellow onions, each cut
   into 6 wedges
1 pound zucchini,
   trimmed, rinsed, and
   cut into 1¼-inch
   chunks

2 ribs celery, trimmed and
   cut into 1¼-inch
   lengths
⅓ cup finely chopped
   parsley
1½ tablespoons finely
   chopped fresh dill
1 teaspoon finely chopped
   fresh mint
2 teaspoons finely chopped
   garlic
Salt and freshly ground
   pepper
¼ cup fruity olive oil

Place oven rack in upper third of oven and heat to
400°. Oil a large shallow baking dish, approximately 11
× 13 × 2 inches.

Sprinkle the tomatoes with a pinch of sugar and
spread half of them on the bottom of the baking dish.
Scatter the potatoes, onions, zucchini, and celery on top.
Arrange the remaining tomatoes on top. Sprinkle with
parsley, dill, mint, garlic, salt, and pepper to taste.
Drizzle top with oil.

Bake for 30 minutes, remove from oven, stir
carefully to redistribute the vegetables, then bake for
another 30 to 40 minutes. Serve hot or lukewarm.
Serves 6–8.

Serving suggestion: Serve as an accompaniment to
any meat, fish, or chicken, or as a vegetarian meal
accompanied by feta cheese and Italian bread.

Spaghetti Primavera Le Cirque

As soon as this vegetable-bejeweled pasta appeared at
New York's Le Cirque restaurant seven years ago, it
became a runaway success, spawning a host of imitations
and approximations around the country—few as good
as the original. Based on the concept of the Risotto
Primavera found in Venice, it should be made only
with the freshest vegetables. The most important
element is the sauce that coats the strands of pasta and

makes a homogeneous mixture of noodle and vegetable. It is not difficult to make, though it does call for a fair amount of preparation and cooking pots.

½ bunch broccoli
2 small zucchini
4 slender asparagus, optional
¼ pound fresh string beans, cut into 1-inch lengths
½ cup fresh or frozen green peas
½ cup fresh or frozen snow peas, optional
1 tablespoon vegetable oil
1 cup thinly sliced mushrooms
2 teaspoons finely minced garlic
Salt and freshly ground pepper
1 tablespoon finely chopped fresh hot chilies (red or green), or ½ teaspoon dried

red pepper flakes
¼ cup finely chopped parsley
6 tablespoons olive oil
1 cup ripe tomatoes, peeled and cut into 1-inch cubes, or halved cherry tomatoes
6 fresh basil leaves, if available, or 1 teaspoon dried oregano
1 pound spaghetti
4 tablespoons butter
½ cup heavy cream (more or less)
⅔ cup grated Parmesan cheese
2 tablespoons chicken broth
⅓ cup toasted pine nuts (p. 406)

Prepare the vegetables as follows, setting each aside in a separate pile as you do: Trim the broccoli, remove the stalks, and cut into bite-size flowerets. Reserve the stems for another use. Trim the zucchini ends, cut each into quarters and then into pieces 1 inch by ½ inch. You will have about 1½ cups. Break off and discard the tough ends of the asparagus and cut each spear on the diagonal into 3 pieces.

Have a bowl of ice water ready. In a saucepan, bring a cup of salted water to the boil and cook the broccoli for 3 minutes. Drain, run cold water over, plunge into the ice water, drain again, and place in a large bowl. Repeat this procedure separately with the zucchini, asparagus, and beans (you may want to have two or three pots going at the same time if you can handle this). Refresh each as directed, and add to the bowl.

Cook the peas for 3 minutes, drain, and add to the bowl. If you are using fresh snow peas, trim and string them and cook for 1 minute. If using frozen snow peas, cook for 30 seconds. Refresh as directed in cold water, and add to the bowl.

Heat the vegetable oil in a skillet, add the mushrooms and half the garlic, and cook for 2 minutes, stirring and shaking the skillet all the while. Season to taste with salt and pepper, and add to the vegetables in the bowl. Add also the chopped chilies or pepper flakes and parsley. (May be prepared ahead to this point.)

Bring a large pot of salted water to the boil for the pasta. Heat shallow soup plates or bowls.

Heat half the olive oil in a saucepan, add the remaining garlic and the tomatoes, and cook only until the tomatoes are heated through, stirring gently so as not to mash them. Add the basil and set aside.

Add the remaining olive oil to a large skillet, heat, and add the vegetable mixture. Cook, stirring gently, just to heat through. Set aside.

Cook the spaghetti in the boiling salted water until al dente, drain well, and return to the pot.

Put the butter in a pot large enough to hold the spaghetti and all the vegetables. Melt it, add the cream and the cheese, and stir well. Stir in the broth. Cook gently, stirring, lifting the pot off the fire every few seconds until the sauce is smooth. Add the spaghetti and half the vegetables, and toss well over very low heat. Add the remaining vegetables and toss; if the mixture seems on the dry side, add ¼ cup more cream. The dish should be moist but not soupy. Add the pine nuts and give one final toss.

Spoon into hot bowls. Spoon some of the reserved tomato mixture over each. Pass with additional grated cheese and a pepper mill. Serves 4 as a main course, 6–8 as an appetizer.

Dierdre's Summer Squash Pot

Some of the best dishes are invented by home cooks who want to use what is abundant, with a minimum of fuss. My friend Dierdre David came up with this one-pot dinner, seasoned like chili, that takes advantage of an August vegetable garden. Amounts can vary according to what's available—a little more of one or less of another vegetable won't matter a bit.

3 young yellow squash
3 young zucchini
2 green peppers
3–4 ears fresh corn
¼ cup vegetable oil
2 medium onions, chopped (about 1¾ cups)
3 garlic cloves, minced
1 pound ground beef round

½ teaspoon oregano
½ teaspoon ground cumin
4 fresh tomatoes, lightly seeded and coarsely chopped
8-ounce can tomato sauce
Salt and freshly ground pepper to taste
2 tablespoons good chili powder

Preheat the oven to 375°.

Wash, trim, and cut the yellow squash and zucchini into ½-inch slices.

Seed and derib the green peppers, cut into 1-inch strips, and blanch for 5 minutes; drain. Cut the corn off the cob. Set vegetables aside.

Heat the oil in a Dutch oven and sauté the onion for 2 or 3 minutes—until the onion is limp. Add the garlic and the meat and cook, stirring, until the meat loses color. Stir in the oregano and cumin, and cook for 30 seconds more, stirring.

Add the green peppers, squash, zucchini, corn, tomatoes, tomato sauce, salt, pepper, and chili powder. Cover and bake for 30 minutes. Serves 5–6.

Vegetable Pizza

Pizza, the ultimate transformation of bread, can be made with many savory vegetable combinations that are surprisingly hearty, needing only a salad as accompaniment. It is difficult for the home cook to achieve the same crispy crust as commercial pizzas, though a high-gluten flour (and a pizza stone, if you have one) will give you pretty good results. The dough may be made the day before and refrigerated.

Pizza Dough:

1 package granular yeast	high-gluten flour, such
¾ cup warm water (105°	as Hecker's
–115° F)	½ teaspoon salt
1½ cups unbleached	1½ tablespoons olive oil

Combine the yeast with ¼ cup of the water in a small bowl, and cover. Let sit for 10 minutes or so, until doubled in volume. If mixture does not rise, discard and repeat, using a fresh packet of yeast.

Combine the flour and salt on a work surface and make a well in the center. Add the yeast mixture, olive oil, and remaining water. Gradually add the flour to the well, working in with a wooden spoon. When very stiff, knead for 8 to 10 minutes, until smooth and shiny. Add a little more flour if dough seems sticky.

Place dough in a mixing bowl, cover with a damp towel, and let rise in a warm place for 1 hour, or until doubled in bulk. Punch down, sprinkle with flour, knead very briefly, and let rise again for 1 hour.

Oil a 12-inch pizza tin (if you are using a pizza stone, follow the manufacturer's directions). Flatten the dough with a floured pin or your hands. Transfer to the pan and, with oiled fingers, stretch the dough to the pan rim; trim any overhanging dough to ½ inch and fold inward. (Except for edge, dough should not be more than ½ inch thick.) Let sit for 10 minutes before filling and baking.

Topping:

1 medium-large eggplant, about ¾ pound	1 teaspoon garlic, minced
	½ teaspoon oregano
1 green pepper	¼ teaspoon thyme
1 red pepper	Salt and freshly ground
4 tablespoons extra virgin olive oil	pepper to taste
	¾ pound mozzarella in
⅓ cup chopped onion	thin slices
35-ounce can whole Italian plum tomatoes, drained and chopped	Vegetable or peanut oil
	Flour for dredging

Cut the eggplant into ¼-inch slices, sprinkle with salt, and let sit for 20 to 30 minutes to draw off excess liquid.

Preheat the oven to 425°.

Slice the peppers in half lengthwise, seed and derib them, then cut in half again through the middle and cut into ½-inch strips. Heat 1 tablespoon of the olive oil in a medium skillet and cook the peppers for 1 minute, or until just wilted. Remove with a slotted spoon and set aside.

Heat 2 tablespoons of the olive oil in the same skillet and cook the onion until softened. Add the tomatoes, garlic, oregano, and thyme. Cook, uncovered, at a gentle simmer for 20 minutes, stirring occasionally. Season to taste with salt and pepper. Let cool before using.

Pat the eggplant slices dry with paper towels. Add vegetable oil to a heavy skillet to a depth of ¼ inch. Dredge the eggplant lightly with flour, shake off excess, and fry the slices over medium-high heat until golden —about 1 minute on each side. Do not crowd the pan. Drain on brown paper.

Brush the dough with olive oil. Sprinkle lightly with salt. Spread the tomato sauce over it, arrange the mozzarella slices on top, then the eggplant slices in a pretty pattern, overlapping them slightly if necessary. Scatter the peppers over the top. Drizzle with the remaining oil and bake on a rack at the lowest level for 25 to 30 minutes. Serves 4–6.

Note: If you are preparing the dough ahead, punch down after the first rising and refrigerate with a weight on it to prevent the second rising. Dough may also be frozen at this point, well wrapped in plastic.

Pizza with olives: Substitute dried rosemary for the oregano, and add ½ cup sliced, pitted black olives to the top.

Pizza with artichoke hearts: Omit the peppers and eggplant. On top of the cheese, arrange a

package of frozen artichoke hearts that have been defrosted, cut into halves, and placed facedown on the cheese. Drizzle with the remaining olive oil.

"Plain" pizza: Omit the eggplant and peppers. Grate or cube the mozzarella instead of slicing it. Bake the pizza for 15 minutes, add the cheese, sprinkle with the oil, and bake 10 minutes longer, or until cheese melts. If fresh basil is available, omit the oregano and thyme from the tomato sauce and decorate the top with a few shredded basil leaves.

Mushroom pizza: Sauté 2 cups sliced mushrooms in 2 tablespoons of the oil until they have wilted and the excess moisture evaporates. Season well with salt and pepper. Arrange mozzarella over the tomato sauce, spread mushrooms over, and sprinkle with the remaining oil.

Julienne of Mixed Vegetables

I am very fond of a mixed vegetable julienne, because it allows me to use small amounts of vegetables, no one of which would be enough for dinner. The result is often quite pretty.

A julienne is nothing more than vegetables cut into matchstick size. This can be done by hand with a sharp knife or cleaver, on a mandoline, or in one of the newer food processors that have 2-centimeter and 3-centimeter julienne disks.

Vegetables that can be successfully julienned are turnips, rutabaga, carrots, broccoli stems, fresh snow peas, zucchini, yellow squash, leek, salsify, and parsnip. Leek, because it shreds easily, is best done by hand. Cut vegetables into thick julienne (¼ inch) to serve as a side dish, thin julienne (⅛ to 1/16 inch) when they are to garnish the top of some other food. They can be 1 to 2 inches long.

To cut vegetables for julienne, first prepare them as necessary, scraping carrots, cutting ends off zucchini, and so on. Cut lengthwise slices in the thickness you prefer. Stack the slices and cut lengths of the same thickness.

Then cut the lengths crosswise into the desired length. If you are using more than one vegetable, keep the piles separate until the end.

Blanch hard vegetables like turnip, carrot, and broccoli cut into thick julienne for 30 to 90 seconds.

With a very thin julienne, and one of soft vegetables, melt butter in a skillet, add the vegetables, cover, and cook over moderate heat for 2 minutes, or just until they soften slightly.

A very thin, threadlike julienne of carrots need not be blanched. In fact, a small amount makes a lovely garnish for a hot clear soup and will soften just the right amount in the heat of the liquid.

Raw mushrooms in an inch-long fine julienne are a lovely touch in a salad of green beans in shallot vinaigrette. If you are feeling flush, add a julienned truffle as well.

Thick or thin julienned vegetables may also be stir-fried in peanut oil.

Mother's Vegetable Soup

3½ pounds shin of beef
1 beef knuckle bone, cracked
4 quarts water
2½ cups (20-ounce can) tomatoes
3 garlic cloves, minced
1 tablespoon salt
¼ teaspoon peppercorns
1 dried hot pepper (or substitute several dashes cayenne)
1 bay leaf

½ teaspoon dried thyme
4 parsley sprigs
2 cups chopped onion
2 cups diced celery
2 cups diced carrots
½ cup diced parsnip
1 medium potato, cubed
1 sweet potato, cubed
½ package frozen baby lima beans
1 small can whole-kernel corn

Place the shin and knuckle bone in a large kettle. Add the water, tomatoes, garlic, and salt, and bring to a boil. Make a bouquet garni by tying the peppercorns, hot pepper, bay leaf, thyme, and parsley in a piece of cheesecloth. Add to the pot, bring again to the boil, lower heat, cover, and let simmer for 3 hours or longer, until meat falls from the bones.

Remove bones and bouquet garni. Return the broth

to boiling and add all the vegetables. Simmer gently, covered, for about 40 minutes, or until vegetables are tender. Taste for seasoning.

Cool a bit and skim off excess fat. If desired, add the meat from the shin. Reheat and serve hot in large bowls, along with garlic bread. Serves 8.

Minestrone alla Milanese

Each section of Italy has its own version of minestrone, which is basically a vegetable soup bolstered with beans, pasta, rice, potatoes, or even bread. Some use salt pork or prosciutto to flavor the broth, or hot consommé can be substituted for part of the water requirement.

In this version, the vegetable stock is water-based, making it an ideal dish for vegetarian meals. It will feed at least 12, but any leftover can be frozen.

1½ cups dried kidney beans
3 tablespoons butter
¼ cup olive oil
1½ cups finely chopped onion
1 cup finely chopped celery
3 garlic cloves, minced
2 tablespoons salt
½ teaspoon black pepper
2 medium leeks, sliced, white and part of the green
2 carrots, scraped and sliced into ½-inch rounds
1–1½ cups string beans cut into 1-inch pieces
2-pound 3-ounce can tomatoes
½ cup finely chopped parsley
1 teaspoon dried oregano
1 teaspoon dried basil
3 medium zucchini, cut into ½-inch rounds
2 cups finely shredded cabbage, preferably Savoy (about ½ head)
½ cup long-grain rice, preferably Arborio, or 8 ounce ditalini or elbow macaroni
1 cup grated Parmesan cheese

Soak the kidney beans overnight in cold water to cover, adding more water if necessary. Drain and put in a very large, heavy soup pot with 3½ quarts water. Cover, bring to a boil, adjust heat so liquid simmers, and let cook partly covered for 40 to 60 minutes, or until tender.

Melt the butter in the olive oil in a skillet, and sauté the onion and celery until the onion is soft but not brown. Add the garlic and cook 2 minutes more. Add this mixture to the cooked beans, along with 1 tablespoon of the salt and the pepper.

Add the leeks, carrots, string beans, tomatoes and their juice, half the parsley, the oregano, and the basil. Simmer for 20 minutes. Add the zucchini, cabbage, rice, and remaining 1 tablespoon salt, and simmer for another 20 minutes. If the soup becomes too thick, add a little more water—up to a cup, as needed.

Serve steaming hot, sprinkled with the remaining parsley. Add an additional knob of butter if desired. Stir in the cheese or pass it and let the diners help themselves. Serve with a good crusty bread and butter. Serves 12.

Serving suggestion: This soup is virtually a vegetable stew and can easily constitute an entire meal. Follow with a salad of mixed greens and a dessert of apples, walnut halves, and a firm cheese.

Philippine Vegetable Soup

In the Philippines this soup is often eaten when one is indisposed or needs a rest from heartier fare. Sometimes milk is added, but the addition of cream makes it elegant enough for a company dinner.

3 tablespoons vegetable oil
1 large onion, chopped
½ small head broccoli, washed, separated into flowerets and stems, stems cut into 1-inch pieces
2 medium carrots, scraped and cut into chunks
2 stalks celery
1 zucchini, washed and sliced
¼ cup frozen or fresh shelled peas
3 cups chicken broth or water to cover
1 teaspoon salt, or to taste
Freshly ground pepper
½ cup milk or heavy cream, optional

Heat the oil in a large heavy soup pot and sauté the onion until it is wilted. Add the broccoli, carrots, and celery, and, over fairly brisk heat, stir-fry until the broccoli turns bright green—about 3 minutes.

Cover, lower heat, and cook for 3 minutes without adding any liquid.

Add the zucchini, peas, broth, salt, and pepper. Raise the heat, bring to a boil, cover, reduce heat, and simmer for 20 minutes. Let cool slightly and puree in a food processor or blender. For an extra-silky texture, put through a sieve or a food mill. Add the milk or cream, check seasoning, and reheat, but do not boil. Serves 6.

Note: If puree seems too thick, thin to a pleasing consistency with milk, broth, or water.

Gazpacho

Gazpacho originated in Spain during the Moorish occupation and, like many firmly entrenched regional classics, has many versions. One is almost a puree, another has oil-soaked bread as its base. Sometimes the vegetables are marinated first. The soup itself is fairly bland, relying for its flavor on the garniture, a reprise of the ingredients. In Spain the garniture often includes raw onions.

This particular version, easily made with a food processor or blender, came from the late Charles Masson of La Grenouille restaurant.

1 cucumber, peeled and seeded if large
2 medium green peppers, seeded and deribbed
1 medium-large onion, peeled
2 garlic cloves
Good handful parsley, leaves only
⅓ cup mild wine vinegar
⅔ cup olive oil
Salt and white pepper
Cayenne
2 cups tomato juice
1 egg yolk

Garnish:

2 tablespoons each finely chopped parsley, green pepper, cucumber, and peeled, seeded, and juiced tomato

Cut the cucumber, peppers, and onion so they can be conveniently processed in a food processor or blender. Combine with the garlic and parsley and process until finely chopped. Add the vinegar and oil and process until smooth. Add salt and pepper to taste, a dash or two of cayenne, 1 cup of the tomato juice, and the egg yolk. Blend very briefly.

Place in a bowl, stir in the remaining cup of tomato juice, and chill. Serve in individual bowls, topped with a garnishing mixture. Serves 4.

Two Accompaniments for Vegetable Soups

Crostini: Melt a stick of sweet butter and saturate 1¼-inch-thick slices of good Italian bread with it. Lay on a cookie sheet and cover with a good layer of grated Parmesan cheese. Bake in a preheated 350° oven until the cheese melts and the bread is crisp—10 to 15 minutes.

Herbed pita crisps: Split 3 regular-size pita breads into 2 rounds and spread with any of the herb butters, softened, given in the section on Culinary Herbs. Cut each round into 4 triangles with kitchen scissors. Bake in a preheated 300° oven for ½ hour, or until golden brown and crisp. Makes 24.

Soupe au Pistou

(Basil Soup)

This lovely French vegetable soup of Genoese origin is given delicious authority by the addition of the pistou at the end, the magical flavor mixture of fresh basil and garlic. The hot soup is poured over it, releasing a heavenly aromatic cloud of basil. With its pasta, beans, and cheese, it is a complete vegetarian meal in itself. The vegetable assortment here works well but is in no way a strict formula; proportions and amounts are strictly up to you and your garden. Just remember to have one green vegetable, tomatoes, potatoes, and one or more kinds of fresh beans with the other vegetables.

¼ cup olive oil

2–3 medium onions, coarsely chopped

2 carrots, scraped and cut into thin rounds

2 center ribs celery, sliced

2–3 potatoes, peeled and cut into ¾-inch dice

2–3 small zucchini, cut into rounds

2–3 fat garlic cloves

½–¾ pound string beans, cut into 2-inch pieces

2–3 peeled tomatoes, seeded and coarsely chopped, or the contents of a 1-pound can (reserve liquid)

Salt and pepper to taste

Several dashes cayenne

2–3 handfuls vermicelli noodles

1 cup fava beans, cooked navy beans, or canned cannelini beans, drained

Pistou:

3 large garlic cloves, peeled

Pinch salt

1 cup tightly packed fresh basil leaves, washed and dried

2 tablespoons grated Parmesan cheese and ¼ cup grated Gruyère cheese, mixed

4–6 tablespoons olive oil

Heat the oil in a large soup kettle and sauté the onions, carrots, and celery until softened but not brown —about 3 minutes. Add the potatoes and zucchini; add the garlic through a press and cover with boiling water by about 2 inches. Cover, bring to a boil, lower heat, and simmer for 15 minutes. Add the string beans, tomatoes, salt, pepper, and cayenne, and cook 5 minutes longer; add the vermicelli and beans and cook, covered, 10 minutes longer, until the pasta is tender.

While the soup cooks, prepare the pistou. Put the garlic, salt, and basil in a food processor or blender and process until finely chopped but not liquid. Add the cheese and 2 tablespoons of oil and process with on-off turns until mixture is a creamy pale green and thick. Add an additional 2 tablespoons of oil while the motor is running. Mixture should be almost of pouring consistency; if it appears too dry, add up to 2 more tablespoons of oil, incorporating with on-off turns.

Correct seasoning of soup (remember that you will

have the additional flavor of the pistou). Put the pistou in a heated soup tureen and mix into it a ladleful of broth. Add the balance of the soup, stirring. Serve at once along with a bowl of additional grated cheese and hot crusty bread. Serves 6–8, with seconds.

Preparation and serving notes: The pistou may be prepared an hour or so ahead, and the soup up to the point of adding the pasta and beans. Cover the pistou with plastic wrap; it will darken a bit, but this will not affect the flavor. Stir it before serving time.

If you don't have a large tureen, add a spoonful of pistou to each hot soup plate, mix in some broth, then carefully ladle in the soup.

Pureed Vegetables

Purees can add contrast to a meal in which everything else has a firm texture, and combining different vegetables is a fine way to use leftovers, as long as their blending doesn't produce an unappetizing mud color. Try mixing carrots and parsnips, turnips and carrots, potatoes and celery root, fennel and rice. When fresh vegetables are scarce, puree frozen peas and watercress that have been cooked together. The mixture produces a stunning green and is delicious.

Freezing purees is a good way to store a vegetable you have in excess. They can be turned into flavorful soups to fill out a meal for unexpected guests; defrost and add stock, cream, and butter in proportions that please you, and season to taste. Purees can also be used to sauce pastas; broccoli puree, with a few red pepper flakes added, is especially good. Broccoli or cauliflower puree can be used as the base for a soufflé.

To make a puree, simply boil the vegetable until tender and put through a food mill or food processor. If the vegetable you are using has a fibrous stalk or woody core, and you've pureed it in a processor, pass it through a food mill or sieve. (To check for fibers, taste or rub some puree between your fingers.)

Before serving, if you find a puree too watery, give it a brief sojourn over heat, stirring all the time until it

Combination
Salads

is just at the point of sticking. You'll also find a discreet addition of cream and/or butter will heighten the flavor. Season pale-colored purees with white pepper.

You can combine many foods in a salad, but generally it is a good idea to avoid too many bits and pieces. When quantities are small or the look needs perking up, rely on a bed of greens and garnishes like hard-cooked eggs, tomato or avocado slices, canned artichoke hearts, rings of purple onion and strips of red pimento.

Almost any vegetable that can be served hot can be lightly blanched, cooled and dressed for a salad. It is a good idea to dress them while they are still slightly warm, so they absorb some of the flavor (though you shouldn't do this with a mayonnaise-type dressing). For example, potatoes should be cooked with jackets on and peeled while warm. Turning them in some white wine or a vinaigrette at this point and letting them steep will greatly improve the taste of the finished dish.

I like cold vegetable salads nearer room temperature rather than really cold. They offer great flexibility in terms of color, texture, and taste, and have the advantage of being able to be prepared ahead. Then you can set out a fine lunch just by putting out an assortment, like the "cold tables" at great European resorts.

Rice and
Other
Grains

I serve a lot of rice and often cook an extra amount which can either be reheated by steaming in foil or used cold in rice salads like the one on page 369.

I make plain boiled rice to accompany a dish with a sauce, and pilaf if I feel the meal calls for rice with a definite flavor of its own. I use long-grain Carolina rice; it is drier and fluffier than the medium-grain varieties, and the short-grain kind comes out too sticky.

There are a couple of exceptions. The fat, oval-grained Italian Arborio rice is a must for making a proper risotto because of its special chewy texture and the way it absorbs flavorings. With curried vegetables, I sometimes use basmati rice with its unique nutlike flavor and elegant silky texture.

The most common problems in cooking rice are that it sticks, is heavy and gluey, or turns out mushy. Chinese cooks recommend washing the starch off thoroughly before cooking. I have never washed rice and it is always light and fluffy. The method here, taught me by a Turkish cook many years ago, is foolproof.

Boiled: Measure your rice (allow ¼ to ⅓ cup per person). Put double the amount of water on to boil. Melt 1 tablespoon butter for each cup of rice (you can also use any cooking oil) in a heavy pot that has a good lid. Add the rice and stir it with a wooden spoon over low heat just to coat the grains. They should not brown, though some will become slightly opaque. Add the boiling liquid. It will sputter furiously for a moment, then calm down. Add ½ teaspoon salt, or to taste, stir, bring to the boil, cover, turn down the heat, and cook for 18 minutes. Do not stir again. (Stirring releases starch, which makes the rice sticky.)

Remove the lid, place a clean folded tea towel on top of the pot, and put the lid back on. Let it sit for 5 minutes or so. The rice will not get cold, and the steam it contains will be absorbed by the cloth instead of condensing inside the lid and falling back onto the rice, which can make it gummy. (I also keep rice hot this way, with the towel and lid on top, in a very slow oven, for up to half an hour.) Then fluff with two forks and serve as is, or tossed with a knob of butter.

Pilaf: Substitute chicken broth for the water. You can also use a little more butter and sauté half a small minced onion in it before adding the rice.

Herbed rice: Make pilaf and add any sweet herb you like along with the raw rice, giving the dish a different character in each case. Adding a cooked

legume like peas, chick-peas, or lentils makes a valuable addition to a vegetarian meal.

Saffron rice: Soften half a small onion, minced, in the butter before adding the rice. Dissolve a pinch of powdered saffron in a tablespoon of hot water and stir into the onion, then proceed as directed.

Brown rice: Use the same proportions and method, but cook for 35 to 40 minutes, or until all the liquid is absorbed.

Risotto: For the basic method, which applies to making risotti of all kinds, see risotto of mushrooms, page 171.

Wild rice: This is not rice at all but the seed of a water grass native to Minnesota. It is handsome, tasty, expensive, and has twice the protein of white rice. Try mixing the two to accompany poultry or game. Cook according to package directions.

Baked Rice

This tasty form of rice with its gentle inflections of herbs plays along nicely with any chicken dish and functions well as part of an all-vegetable meal. The baking method is good to remember if your oven is going to be on anyway; if you make it in an oven-to-table casserole, it simplifies things further. This rice can be kept in a warm oven for up to an hour without drying out. The degree of richness can be varied according to how much butter you stir in at the end.

3–5 tablespoons butter	Several sprigs parsley
3 tablespoons finely chopped onion	1 sprig fresh thyme or rosemary, or ¼ teaspoon dried
1 garlic clove, minced	1 small bay leaf
1½ cups long-grain rice	Salt and freshly ground pepper to taste
2¼ cups chicken or vegetable broth	

Preheat the oven to 400°.

Melt 2 tablespoons of the butter in an oven-to-table

casserole, add the onion and garlic and cook, stirring, just until the onion is wilted. Add the rice and, over low heat, stir to coat with the mixture.

Add the broth, parsley, thyme, bay leaf, salt, and pepper. Bring to a boil on top of the stove, then cover and bake for 17 minutes. Pick out and discard the parsley, herb sprigs, and bay leaf. Stir in the balance of the butter. Cover pot with a folded towel and the pot lid, and keep in a low oven until ready to serve. Serves 6.

Armenian Rice Pilaf with Vermicelli

8 tablespoons (1 stick) butter
1 cup very fine egg noodles (vermicelli) broken into 1-inch pieces
2 cups long-grain rice
4 cups chicken or beef broth
Salt and freshly ground pepper to taste

Melt the butter in a heavy saucepan or casserole over moderate heat. Add the vermicelli and sauté gently until lightly browned.

Add the rice and stir so the grains are thoroughly coated with butter but not browned. Pour in the broth, add salt and several grindings of pepper, and bring to a boil, stirring. Cover the pan tightly, lower the flame, and simmer for about 20 minutes, or until all the liquid has been absorbed and the rice is tender but still firm. Gently fluff with a fork and spoon onto a heated serving platter. Serves 8.

Serving suggestion: Pilaf is the traditional accompaniment for any lamb dish with Middle Eastern overtones and can be used whenever it is desirable to have a rice dish that can stand on its own instead of being merely the underpinning for a sauce. It is especially good with roasted peppers, vegetable or other kebabs, or one or more vegetable salads.

Indian Baked Spiced Rice

Fragrant spiced rice with local variations can be found all over India. I have adapted a recipe of Madhur

Jaffrey's in trying to reproduce the version served at our local Indian restaurant. It's so satisfying I find it makes a complete dinner with a few tasty vegetables dishes. It is not meant to be hot, though I like it that way, Adjust the chili or cayenne to your taste.

4 tablespoons vegetable oil
1 medium onion, peeled, cut in half lengthwise, and sliced into paper-thin rings
2 cups long-grain or Indian basmati rice
2 garlic cloves, minced
1 teaspoon grated fresh ginger
1-inch piece fresh hot green chili, minced, or several dashes cayenne pepper
¾ teaspoon garam masala (see note)
1 cup shelled fresh peas, or frozen peas, defrosted
1 teaspoon salt, or to taste
3 cups hot vegetable or chicken broth

Preheat the oven to 325°.

Heat the oil in a heavy 2-quart pot, add the onion slices, and fry them for 2 or 3 minutes, until the edges turn brown. Add the rice, garlic, ginger, green chili, garam masala, peas, and salt. Lower heat slightly, and stir and fry the rice for 7 minutes, or until it turns translucent. Add the heated broth, and keep stirring and cooking for another 5 minutes. When the top of the rice begins to look dry, cover tightly (if lid is loose, use aluminum foil in addition), and bake for 20 to 25 minutes, or until rice is tender. Remove from the oven and let sit in a warm place for 10 minutes. Fluff with two forks before serving. Serves 6–8.

Note: Garam masala is an aromatic spice mixture used to flavor Indian dishes. There are many variations, but generally it consists of cloves, cardamon, cinnamon, cumin, nutmeg, and black peppercorns, all ground together. It is available in specialty food stores.

Spanish Rice

You'll never find rice like this in Spain, but throughout the Southwest, it is served under this name. It goes with everything.

¼ cup olive oil
1 medium onion, chopped
½ green pepper, seeded, deribbed, and chopped
2 garlic cloves, minced
4 canned plum tomatoes, drained and coarsely chopped
1 teaspoon chili powder
1 cup long-grain rice
2 cups water
Salt and freshly ground pepper to taste

Heat the oil in a heavy saucepan. Sauté the onion, pepper, and garlic until the onion is transparent. Add the tomatoes, chili powder, rice, water, and salt and pepper to taste. Bring to a boil and simmer, tightly covered, over very low heat for 20 minutes. Let sit with a folded towel under the lid for 10 minutes. Fluff with two forks before serving. Serves 4–6.

Fried Rice

This is one of those wonderful concoctions that has the virtues of economy, nutrition, and good taste, and can be endlessly varied. Like all stir-fry cookery, the dish is made very quickly, so read the recipe carefully, decide on your ingredients, and have them all at hand. A heavy seasoned skillet or a wok is a virtual necessity; after that, you may improvise to your heart's content.

3–4 cups cold cooked rice
15–18 very small raw shrimp (defrosted, if frozen)
½ teaspoon baking soda
½ teaspoon salt
3 tablespoons peanut or corn oil
½–¾ cup cooked diced chicken, lean pork, or ham
2 eggs, beaten
⅓–½ cup fresh or frozen peas
2 tablespoons oyster sauce (see note)
½–¾ cup bean sprouts
3 scallions, white and part of the green, minced

Loosen the rice with wet hands, breaking up any big lumps so that all grains are separate. Set aside.

Shell, devein, and butterfly the shrimp, by deepening the deveining cut so shrimp is half open, like a book. Toss with the baking soda and salt in a small bowl. Let stand for 15 minutes, then drain, rinse under cold water, and pat dry.

Heat the oil in a wok or large heavy skillet until smoking; add the shrimp and stir-fry for about 30 seconds. Remove with a slotted spoon to a dish and set aside.

Add the chicken or meat to the pan and stir-fry quickly just to coat with oil. Add the rice and cook while stirring rapidly so that it is heated through but not browned.

Make an indentation in the center of the rice and pour in the eggs with one hand, stirring them constantly with the other. Keep eggs moving until they are all scrambled and no white shows. Quickly and deftly begin blending the rice into the eggs until they appear completely absorbed. When the blending is complete, add the peas and oyster sauce, stirring. Add the cooked shrimp, incorporating everything with a circular stir and toss motion. Add the bean sprouts, put in a hot serving dish, garnish with the minced scallions, and serve. Serves 4–6 as a main course, 6–8 as part of a Chinese meal.

Note: Oyster sauce, available in Oriental markets, is a rich brown seasoning liquid that intensifies flavors without adding any of its own. If it is unavailable, mix together 2 tablespoons soy sauce, ½ teaspoon each sugar and salt, and 1 teaspoon dry sherry and use instead.

Preparation notes: To prepare a vegetarian version, double the amount of bean sprouts, and stir-fry 1½ cups mixed vegetables in place of the shrimp and meat. Combine any number of the following: blanched chopped celery; sliced fresh mushrooms or dried black mushrooms; minced green pepper; sliced water chestnuts; sliced bamboo shoots; sliced onions. Also consider a handful of slivered almonds or walnut halves.

If the rice seems very dry, moisten it with 2 or 3 tablespoons chicken or vegetable broth when you add the oyster sauce.

Finally, if you want your fried rice to be brown, as

it is in restaurants, add some brown gravy made with a concentrate like Maggi.

Lemon Rice with Grapes

(a cold dish)

2 cups long-grain rice
Juice of 2 lemons (about ½ cup)
Grated zest of 2 lemons

2 cups fresh green grapes, sliced in half lengthwise

Boil the rice (p. 363), cover with a tea towel, replace the lid, and let pot sit for 20 minutes.

Fluff rice with two forks, put in a bowl, and again cover with a towel for 30 minutes. Combine ¼ cup of lemon juice with the grapes and let sit for the same time.

Add the balance of the lemon juice to the rice and toss; add the lemon zest and grapes and toss again. Add salt, if desired. Serves 12 as part of a cold buffet.

Middle Eastern Rice Salad

Tasty, attractive, filling, and sturdy—the same qualities that make this a wonderful picnic or outdoor lunch dish make it a reliable city-to-country traveler. The only company it needs is a cold roast chicken, crusty bread, and some white wine.

1½ cups long-grain rice
1 large cucumber, peeled, seeded, and cubed
2 ripe tomatoes, diced, or 8 cherry tomatoes, sliced in half
5–6 scallions, white and pale green parts, thinly sliced
½ teaspoon dried red pepper flakes, or to taste
3 tablespoons finely

chopped parsley
3 tablespoons finely chopped fresh mint, or 1 teaspoon crushed dried mint
3 tablespoons olive oil
2 tablespoons fresh lemon juice
Salt and freshly ground pepper to taste
Dash cayenne pepper, optional
Black olives, optional

Boil the rice (p. 363), cover with a tea towel, replace the lid, and let sit for 20 minutes. Put in a mixing bowl and fluff with two forks.

While the rice is cooking, salt the cucumber slices and let them sit in a colander for ½ hour to get rid of some excess water.

While the rice is still warm, add the drained cucumbers, tomatoes, scallions, pepper flakes, parsley, mint, olive oil, and lemon juice. Toss well. Season to taste with salt, pepper, and cayenne. Garnish with black olives. Serves 6.

Note: If you wish to serve the salad as part of a buffet, it is very easy to mold: pack it into a smallish, round-bottomed bowl and press rice down firmly with your knuckles. Weight with a plate that fits inside the rim, and let sit for 30 minutes. Replace the plate with a serving platter, invert the whole works carefully, and garnish pleasingly.

Bulgur

Bulgur is parched cracked wheat from which some of the bran has been removed, made by boiling wheat kernels and spreading them in the sun to dry. It is then boiled, like rice, or soaked in water with no further cooking. The unrefined wheat is highly nutritious, has superb keeping qualities (you can keep it in the refrigerator indefinitely), and combines with any desired flavorings. Bulgur is available in three degrees of coarseness; the finest, #1, is usually available only in markets specializing in Middle Eastern foods. Most commercially boxed bulgur is #3, generally suitable for all purposes. Cook it exactly as you would rice, or make tabbouleh.

Tabbouleh

(Middle Eastern Cracked Wheat Salad)

When I'm in the mood for light food, this earthy salad is my favorite thing to eat, especially in summer. It's beautiful to look at, extremely tasty, and easy to make in quantities. Don't skimp on the amount of parsley—it is a vital characteristic of this dish.

1 cup bulgur, preferably
    fine (#1)
1 small onion, chopped
1 bunch scallions, chopped
1 cup minced parsley,
    preferably Italian
    flat-leaved
¼ cup crushed dried mint

leaves, or ½ cup
    chopped fresh mint
Salt and freshly ground
    pepper to taste
¼ cup lemon juice
¼ cup olive oil
Romaine lettuce leaves
Black olives
Cherry tomatoes

Mix the bulgur with 2 cups cold water, and let stand for ½ hour at room temperature. Drain thoroughly. The wheat will have expanded quite a bit.

Put it in a bowl and add the onion. Squeeze the wheat and the onion together so the onion juices penetrate the wheat. Fluff with a fork, and add the scallions, parsley, and mint; toss to mix. Add salt and pepper. Beat the lemon juice and olive oil together, add, and toss. Taste for seasoning. Refrigerate for at least 1 hour, uncovered.

Arrange the lettuce leaves decoratively on a shallow platter to form a bed for the salad, and mound it in the center. Decorate with the black olives and cherry tomatoes. (Other garnishes that may be used include unpeeled cucumber batons, strips of sweet red pepper, and carrot curls.) Serves 6–8.

Note: In the Middle East, tabbouleh is often eaten by scooping it up on the lettuce leaf. Grape leaves and the tender inner leaves of green cabbage may also be used.

Kasha

Kasha is the name of the dish made from braising buckwheat groats, a species of grain (not related to wheat) that originated in Siberia and is the staple grain food in Russia. It has a hearty, strong flavor and is useful to vary the grain requirement in vegetarian diets.

To Cook

Mix 1 cup buckwheat groats with 1 lightly beaten egg. Heat a large, heavy skillet, add the mixture, and stir constantly over fairly high heat until the grains are separate and dry but not brown. Add 2 cups boiling chicken broth or water, 2 tablespoons butter, salt to taste, and pepper. Cover tightly and simmer for 15 minutes, or until the liquid is absorbed and the grains tender. Makes 2½ cups, serving 3 to 4 people.

Barley

Barley is a cereal grain that is as simple as rice to cook but takes longer. The kind most commonly available in packages is "medium pearl" barley, *pearl* meaning that the grain is husked and polished, *medium* connoting the cooking time. Also available is a presteamed, quick-cooking variety, and whole barley, which takes longer than medium to cook and remains rather chewy but is more nutritious. Whole barley is found in health food stores.

Barley adds another grain source to vegetarian meals. It combines particularly well with mushrooms and can be served in a pilaf or used to give body and nourishment to vegetable broth or soup.

Cook pearl and precooked barley according to package directions. Use 3 cups water for 1 cup whole barley; cook for 75 minutes. One cup uncooked whole barley yields 3½ cups cooked.

Stocks

There is nothing wrong with using water to make any soup or to cook grains, but a well-flavored stock or broth adds both nourishment and another flavor dimension that cannot be discounted. I use defatted chicken stock for many grains and vegetables that are to be cooked in liquid, and always have it frozen in one- and two-cup containers.

When space is a problem, I reduce stock by boiling and freeze in an ice-cube tray, then pop out the cubes and keep them in a plastic bag. They facilitate sauce making, and one or two cubes with a like amount of water give you enough liquid in which to cook a vegetable.

Basic Vegetable Stock

Vegetable stock can be made many ways, and need be based on nothing more than the trimmings from vegetables—carrot ends, pea pods, spinach stems, mushroom peelings—combined with aromatic vegetables, such as sautéed onions or celery, and herbs of your choice. Avoid members of the *Brassica,* or cabbage, family, which can add a sulfurous note when boiled for a long time.

The following is a good basic stock that you may play with and vary to your whim. Fresh tomatoes might be added for color, or potatoes, or slivered, blanched snow peas, if you wanted to serve it as a soup on its own. Tamari, a strong soy sauce popular with vegetarians, adds a distinctive rich flavor and color but a definite Oriental note that may or may not be in keeping with the way you cook. Marmite, a yeast extract imported from England and loaded with vitamins, is a preferable addition. The so-called vegetarian bouillon cubes are composed chiefly of salt and MSG, which no one needs.

2 medium onions, quartered
2 carrots, washed and coarsely chopped
2 celery ribs, coarsely chopped
2 leeks, well washed, white and all the green, or leek greens only
1 parsnip, optional

5 garlic cloves, peeled
5 sprigs parsley, stems only
1 bay leaf
¼ teaspoon thyme
2 cloves
6–8 whole black peppercorns
2 teaspoons Marmite

Combine all the ingredients in a large heavy stock pot with about 1½ quarts cold water. Bring slowly to a boil, then adjust heat and simmer, partly covered, for 1 hour. Strain through a fine-mesh sieve, pressing down on the vegetables to release all the juices. Discard vegetables and spices. If the flavor seems weak, reduce to your liking. Correct seasoning. Makes about 10 cups.

Basic Chicken Stock

All chicken carcasses, giblets, necks, backs, and other scraps get saved in my freezer in labeled plastic bags, and occasionally a chicken farmer provides me with feet, which are the devil to clean but make the best stock of all. Packages of wings, available in most supermarkets, can also be used.

4 pounds miscellaneous
  chicken bones and bits
2½ quarts water
Salt to taste
1 large onion, quartered
2 carrots, scraped and cut
  into thirds

1–2 celery ribs
½ cup chopped celery
  leaves
4 parsley sprigs
1 bay leaf
Large pinch thyme

Put the chicken scraps in a large, heavy soup pot. Add the water and salt to taste, and bring to the simmer. Cook for a few minutes, skimming off any scum that rises. Add the balance of the ingredients, partly cover the pot, reduce heat, and simmer gently for 1 hour. Let cool slightly, strain off liquid, discarding solids, strain again through a sieve lined with cheesecloth or paper towels. Chill and degrease. Refrigerate or freeze. Makes about 6 cups.

Sauces
Basic Vinaigrette

2 tablespoons wine vinegar
¼ teaspoon salt
½ teaspoon Dijon

mustard, optional
8 tablespoons olive oil
Freshly ground pepper

Put the vinegar in a small bowl and whisk in the salt and the mustard. Add the oil, whisking vigorously until you have a nice smooth emulsion. Grind in pepper to taste. Makes about ⅔ cup.

Mustard vinaigrette: Increase the mustard to 1 teaspoon, or 2 if you like the bite.

Lemon vinaigrette: Substitute strained fresh lemon juice for all or part of the vinegar.

Garlic vinaigrette: Smash a peeled garlic clove with the side of a knife and let it steep in the vinaigrette for 10 to 30 minutes. Remove before serving.

Other variations: Sherry wine vinegar gives a gentle, distinctive flavor to vinaigrettes, especially in combination with walnut oil in place of olive oil. Various herbal notes may be introduced, either by adding the fresh herbs themselves, or steeping them in your vinegar. A finely chopped hard-cooked egg can also be added. And, to make a less expensive dressing, substitute vegetable oil for half the olive oil.

Sesame Vinaigrette

2 tablespoons wine vinegar
1½ teaspoons light soy
    sauce
Salt and freshly ground
    pepper
¼ cup peanut or vegetable
    oil
¼ teaspoon Oriental
    sesame oil

Whisk together the vinegar, soy sauce, salt, and pepper in a small bowl. Combine the oils and add, whisking. Beat again just before serving. Makes a scant ½ cup.

Herbed Vinaigrette

This is my children's favorite dressing for cold artichokes and asparagus, and they sometimes dress salad greens with it as well. It keeps, refrigerated, for at least a week.

Don't be put off by how unappetizing it looks in the making—everything comes together nicely after it's shaken.

1 tablespoon coarse salt

Several grindings black pepper

½ teaspoon sugar

½ teaspoon dry mustard

1 teaspoon Dijon mustard

1 teaspoon lemon juice

1 garlic clove, pressed

5 tablespoons vinegar

2 tablespoons olive oil

10 tablespoons vegetable oil

1 raw egg

¼ cup milk

¼ cup heavy cream

1 tablespoon parsley

1 tablespoon drained capers

In a screw-top pint jar, combine everything except the parsley and capers. Shake well, add the parsley and capers, and shake again. Makes about 1⅔ cups.

Béchamel Sauce

Vegetables in white sauce were something I used to turn my nose up at. It was regarded in my house as a salvage technique for overcooked or inferior ingredients. Only when I grew up did I begin to perceive the usefulness of béchamel, or white sauce, with its many permutations—mornay, velouté, and as a base for soufflés.

According to the way it will be used, béchamel may be made thick or thin by varying the proportion of flour to butter. Nutmeg is sometimes added sparingly, and cream may be added as well, to enrich the sauce.

4 tablespoons butter

4 tablespoons flour

1½ cups milk, at room temperature

Salt and freshly ground pepper

Nutmeg

Melt the butter in a heavy-bottomed saucepan. Add the flour and stir with a wooden spoon until smooth. Cook over low heat, stirring constantly, for 2 minutes, but do not let the mixture become more than pale tan. Remove from the fire, switch to a whisk, and pour in all the milk, whisking. Return to moderate heat and stir until the sauce reaches a simmer. Simmer gently for 8 to 10 minutes, stirring constantly. Season to taste with salt, pepper, and a grating of nutmeg, if desired. Makes about 2 cups.

Note: The liquid is added after removing the sauce from the heat to prevent lumps from forming. If lumps do occur, strain the mixture, whisk it, and put back to cook.

Mornay Sauce

This is simply a béchamel with cheese, very useful for gratinéed vegetables.

2 tablespoons butter
3 tablespoons flour
2 cups milk
Salt and freshly ground
  pepper
½ cup grated Gruyère or

Swiss cheese, or a
combination of Swiss
and Parmesan
Several gratings nutmeg
Dash cayenne, optional

Melt the butter in a saucepan and add the flour, stirring with a wire whisk. Add the milk, whisking rapidly. Season to taste.

Remove from the heat, add the cheese, and let it melt. Bring mixture to a boil; add the nutmeg and cayenne. Makes about 2½ cups.

Note: A richer sauce can be obtained by whisking in a tablespoon or two of softened butter at the end. This would be appropriate for a binding sauce but not one to be used for gratinées.

Hollandaise Sauce

Hollandaise is really a hot mayonnaise, superb with vegetables. Serve it with asparagus, broccoli, or a mixed selection of blanched or steamed vegetables. It is not difficult to make but is tricky; it must be made over enough heat to allow the eggs to emulsify, but not so much that the eggs actually cook, which results in a curdled sauce. Temperature is the key and *tepid* the operative word. Also, if the butter is added too quickly, the sauce may not thicken, or may separate. Take these precautions: Have the egg yolks and butter at room temperature; add the butter slowly; use a double boiler, and make sure the water in the bottom does not boil.

3 **egg yolks**	**pats**
2 **teaspoons water**	**Salt**
1½ **sticks butter (6**	**Cayenne pepper**
ounces), cut into small	**Lemon juice**

Combine the egg yolks and the water in the top of a double boiler. Whisk the eggs until they are slightly thickened. Set over the lower pot half filled with hot water. Put the double boiler over moderate heat and whisk in the butter gradually.

Make sure the water does not boil. Keep whisking until the sauce is thick and smooth, like custard. Season to taste with salt, a dash of cayenne, and a squeeze or two of lemon juice. May be kept over hot, not boiling, water for 15 minutes. Makes 1–1½ cups.

Notes: If sauce begins to curdle: immediately whisk in by droplets a tablespoon of hot water from the bottom pan.

If the sauce does not thicken: put a teaspoon of lemon juice in a large clean bowl. Add a tablespoon of the sauce and whisk together. Add and beat in the rest of the sauce a dribble at a time, letting the sauce in the bowl thicken before the next addition. Then return to the top of the boiler and continue.

If sauce gets lumpy: push through a strainer.

Sauce Mousseline: Whip ½ cup of heavy cream stiffly and fold into the hollandaise just before serving.

Sauce Béarnaise: Put ¼ cup white or red wine vinegar and ¼ cup dry white wine in a heavy saucepan. Add 1 tablespoon finely chopped shallots, 2 teaspoons chopped fresh tarragon (or 1 teaspoon dried), and a pinch of salt. Boil down until the shallots are as soft as puree and about 2 tablespoons vinegar remain in the pan. Strain and let cool. Make a hollandaise sauce and use this reduction in place of the lemon juice requirement.

Sauce Maltaise: Maltaise is a hollandaise flavored with orange instead of lemon. Follow the recipe for hollandaise, substituting ¼ cup orange juice and a teaspoon of grated orange zest. Especially good with fresh asparagus.

Mayonnaise

The blender and food processor have made a snap of the once-tedious job of making mayonnaise. It takes all of two minutes, and the taste and consistency are far superior to store-bought. This method requires a whole egg in addition to the usual yolks.

1 egg, at room temperature	1 tablespoon fresh lemon juice
2 egg yolks, at room temperature	1¼ cups vegetable oil, or half olive, half vegetable
½ teaspoon salt	
½ teaspoon Dijon mustard	White pepper

Put the egg, yolks, salt, mustard, and lemon juice in the container of a blender or food processor. Blend for 20 seconds, until lightly fluffy. With motor running, slowly drizzle the oil through the feed tube or blender top until mixture has the consistency of heavy cream; then add balance of oil in a slow, steady stream.

Add pepper, taste and adjust seasoning. Refrigerate, covered, for up to 5 days. Makes 1¾ cups.

Curried Mayonnaise:
To 1 cup Mayonnaise add 2 teaspoons curry powder (or more to taste), 1 teaspoon turmeric, several dashes cayenne, and a good squeeze of lemon juice.

Consuelo's Green Sauce

(Green Mayonnaise)

I have eaten *sauce verte,* or green mayonnaise, with poached bass or salmon at countless dinner parties, but this is the best I've ever had. My hostess very nicely let me talk to her Spanish cook, who supplied the following recipe.

Taramasalata

Consuelo's Green Sauce, continued

3 dill pickles, cut up, about ⅔ cup	3–4 branches watercress
1 bunch scallions, roots and last 2 inches removed	1½ cups homemade mayonnaise
1 good handful parsley	Salt
	Lemon juice

Place pickles, scallions, parsley, and watercress in the food processor. Process until fine. Add the mayonnaise and process again until sauce is pale green—about 10 seconds. Sauce should have some texture. Add salt and lemon juice to taste, and process briefly to blend. Makes about 2½ cups.

This fish roe dip is served in Greek restaurants with warmed pita bread. I love it as a dip for crudités and as a sauce for steamed vegetables. Leftovers can be used as a dressing for salad.

4–5 slices home-style white bread, crusts removed	1 small onion, chopped
4 ounces tarama (see note)	1¼ cups olive oil
	⅓ cup lemon juice, or more to taste

Crumble the bread in a bowl and soak in a small amount of water. Put tarama and onion in a blender jar or the bowl of a food processor, and blend until pureed but not liquid. Squeeze excess water from bread and blend in. Add oil with motor running, pouring in a slow, steady stream, then add and blend in lemon juice to taste. Should consistency be too thin, add another slice of crustless bread, blending until it is completely absorbed. Makes about 2½ cups.

Note: Tarama (Greek salted codfish roe) is available in jars in many supermarkets and specialty food shops.

Rémoulade Sauce

Use this to dress sliced tomatoes, hard-cooked eggs, or cold shellfish.

1½ cups homemade
   mayonnaise
2 tablespoons minced
   drained capers
¼ cup grated onion
1 garlic clove, finely

minced, optional
2 teaspoons each chopped
   parsley, tarragon, and
   chives
Dab of anchovy paste
Lemon juice to taste

Mix all the ingredients and refrigerate the sauce for 1 hour. Makes about 1¾ cups.

Note: If not using on tomatoes, a bit of diced tomato may be added to the sauce.

Garlic Yogurt Sauce

This delicious sauce completes the protein picture with any cooked vegetables at a meatless meal and is especially good with fried eggplant or zucchini.

1 cup unflavored yogurt
1 garlic clove pushed
   through a press
¼ teaspoon salt
Several grinds fresh black
   pepper

2 teaspoons fruity olive oil
1 teaspoon crushed dried
   mint or
1 tablespoon minced fresh
   mint, optional

Put the yogurt in a bowl and whisk with a fork to lighten. Mash the garlic and salt together and beat in the mint. Cover and chill for several hours. Makes 1 cup.

Noisette Butter

A simple brown butter sauce, this is excellent over many vegetables. Though it is also called *beurre noir,* it must never be really black or contain burned, black specks, because these make it bitter. Since it is the butter solids that burn most easily, it should be made with clarified butter. For 1½ sticks butter, clarified (see p. 404): set the butter over moderate heat and, when the foam dies down, it will turn nut brown. Remove immediately from heat, pour into another pan, and add a small handful chopped parsley. Deglaze the pan in which butter was melted with ¼ cup lemon juice or wine vinegar, boil, and reduce to 1 tablespoon. Stir into the browned butter.

Noisette butter with capers: Add a tablespoon of capers to the butter along with the parsley.

Tapenade

This tangy sauce with its fragrant mixture of black olives, capers, and anchovies is virtually synonymous with Provence. It is essential to use good quality, oil-cured black olives to obtain the proper taste; bland, watery California olives will not do.

¼ cup capers
2–ounce can anchovies
7–ounce can tuna
15 Italian black olives, pitted

Juice of 1 large lemon (about ¼ cup), or more to taste
¼ cup olive oil

Place all the ingredients except the olive oil in a blender or food processor and blend until pureed. With the machine running, add the olive oil in droplets until the mixture is thick and creamy. Makes about 1½ cups.

Serving suggestions: Use as a dip for raw vegetables; spread on thin, buttered rounds of toasted French bread as an hors d'oeuvre; serve with goat cheese on French bread as a snack; or use as a filling for hollowed-out cherry tomatoes.

Pesto Sauce

Basil, pine nuts, garlic, and oil are the base of the famous Genoese sauce that Elizabeth David calls "the best sauce yet invented for pasta." (It is also heavenly with gnocchi.) *Pistou,* which adds its uniquely delicious aroma to Provençal soups, has the same origin. Traditionally it is made in a mortar with a pestle (hence the name), or chopped on a wooden board in the Tuscan version. The food processor or blender takes the labor out of making it, though care must be taken not to overprocess.

Since fresh basil is unavailable in winter, I make a whole year's supply of pesto in the summer and freeze it in appropriately sized portions to defrost as needed, preferably overnight in the refrigerator. For freezing, I omit the cheeses and butter and add these just before using. Pesto can also be stored in a glass jar in the refrigerator (again omitting the cheese until ready to use), adding enough olive oil to cover by about ½ inch. The oil will preserve it indefinitely. In either case, let it come to room temperature before serving.

I have found many delicious uses for pesto besides saucing pasta: Try stirring it into freshly made tomato soup or into a plain omelet before rolling it; dress a new potato salad with half a cup of mayonnaise mixed with 2 tablespoons pesto; add 2 tablespoons pesto to ¼ cup vinaigrette and spoon it over sliced dead-ripe tomatoes and slices of mozzarella cheese. Pesto-flavored mayonnaise is also a great way to spark leftover cold chicken or fish.

**2 tightly packed cups
     fresh basil**
½ cup olive oil
3 garlic cloves
3 tablespoons pine nuts
Salt to taste

**½ cup freshly grated
     Parmesan cheese**
**2 tablespoons freshly
     grated Romano cheese**
**2 tablespoons softened
     butter**

Put the basil, oil, garlic, pine nuts, and salt in a blender or food processor; blend until smooth, stopping to scrape down the sides of the bowl as needed. Add the cheeses and the butter, and blend into a smooth paste. Makes enough for 1 pound of pasta.

Note: A handful of parsley may be used along with the basil leaves. A lighter, less sharp pesto may be had by blending in 3 tablespoons of ricotta cheese. This is especially good with gnocchi.

Pasta with pesto sauce: Pesto can be served

on a number of pastas, the most popular being linguini and the spiral shapes.

Put the pasta on to cook. Warm a large pottery bowl and put the pesto sauce in it. When the pasta is done, fork it directly into the bowl and toss with the sauce. Add 3 or 4 tablespoons of the hot pasta water and toss again.

Vegetable Garnishes

Because of the great variety of their colors and textures, vegetables can be turned into some very attractive decorative garnishes—some meant to be eaten, others merely to be admired. All you need is a good idea of what you're after and a sharp paring knife. Large, firm, fresh vegetables are the easiest to work with.

Radish rose: Trim off the stem and root ends. Holding the radish vertically and working halfway up, make a slightly curved cut on each of four sides; make a second row of cuts inside the first row. Where the tip was removed, pierce a shallow cross. Soak in ice water so the petals open. Use parsley or a dill frond for the green.

Radish fan: This is particularly pretty when you have fresh radishes that still have nice green leaves attached. Cut off the tip and lay the radish on its side. Make a series of close thin cuts, each to within ⅛ inch of the root base. Spread the fan by flattening the radish slightly with your fingers. If you are using radishes without leaves, you can soak them in salted water for a few minutes, which will make the spreading easier. The salted water would, however, make the leaves wilt.

Radish mum: Cut off a good-size piece from the stem end and, holding the radish vertically, make a close series of parallel cuts three-quarters down through the radish. Make a second series of cuts at right angles

to the first. Drop into ice water to open, then use with
an appropriate green.

Tomato rose:
These are a pretty garnish for
entrée platters, trays of hors d'oeuvres, sandwiches—just
about anything you can think of. Use a firm red
tomato; choke up on your knife blade and, starting at
the stem end, use the forward part of the blade to
detach a continuous strip of skin ½ to ¾ inch wide.
(Twist the knife slightly as you go, to give a scalloped
edge to the strip.) Holding the peel skin-side down,
make a small center spiral at one end; wrap the strip
around and around on itself, using the fingers to keep
the center from popping out. Spread out slightly on a
flat surface in the form of a rose. Put into place with
two small, pale green leaves from the heart of a head of
soft-leaved lettuce, watercress, or any other greenery
that appeals to you.

Tomato cups:
These can be used as a simple
garnish, or hollowed and filled with a macedoine of
vegetables, salade russe, and the like, as part of an
elaborate garnish for fish or meat platters on a buffet.
Insert the tip of a small, sharp paring knife on the
diagonal into the midsection of a firm, ripe, well-shaped
tomato, going through to the center. Turn your knife
and make an adjacent cut on the opposing diagonal, so
you now have an upside-down *V*. Keep repeating these
cuts all the way around, going through to the center
each time, until you have sawtoothed your way around
the entire tomato, at which point you should be able to
separate the two halves easily. Use as is, or scoop out
the flesh with a spoon to make a cup.

Cucumber water lily:
Cut off a 2-inch piece
from the end of a rather good-size cucumber. Remove
the seeds from the center with a sharp knife or a melon
baller. Cut a sawtooth pattern around the cucumber,
cutting down to within ½ inch or so from the bottom.
You should get around nine points. Then make a
second series of cuts to separate the skin from the meat,

and soak in ice water for 20 minutes so that the flower opens. Fill the center with chopped parsley.

Cucumber twists: Wash and dry a medium-size cucumber. Score with tines of a fork or peel so white and green alternate. Cut in half and slice off a thin round. On it make one cut from center to edge, like one hand of a clock. Grasp a side of the cut in each hand and pull gently in opposite directions and twist into an S-shape curve. Set atop a cooked fish or a sandwich, curved side up.

Carrot curls: Select a fairly large, nicely shaped carrot. Cut off a shallow lengthwise section from one side, so it will lie flat. Repeat on the remaining curved side, so you have a long, flat surface to work with. Detach a thin strip with a swivel-bladed peeler or a very sharp knife. Repeat, making as many slices as you need. Strips will curl of their own accord in a bowl of ice water.

A garnish can also be the actual vegetable accompaniment whose basic form has been improved, like julienned vegetables and those that are turned. *Turning* means paring the sharp edges of a root vegetable so it resembles a large olive in shape. This latter is purely an esthetic measure to give a pleasant shape to vegetables, which would otherwise be in odd-shaped chunks. The facets of turned carrots, potatoes, and turnips, glistening with the burnished sauce of a *navarin,* add a jewellike quality and great sophistication to what is basically lamb stew.

The technique is not difficult to master and requires only a good, sharp paring knife and a steady hand. Save the parings for use in soups, or cook and puree them to use as sauce thickeners.

Turned carrots: Turning carrots is good practice and useful to master, since this colorful root is called for in so many dishes and is available all year. Turned

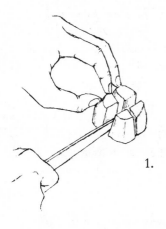

1.

2.

3.

Turned potatoes

carrots may be glazed and served alone, or in combination with glazed turnips as a separate vegetable dish (p. 89).

Select carrots that are straight, not gnarled, and young. Otherwise you will have nothing but the woody core of an old carrot when you finish cutting. Do not peel. Cut into pieces 1¾ to 2 inches long; hold the piece of carrot as shown in the drawing and cut off a thin lengthwise strip, cutting in deeper at each end. Turn the carrot and, immediately adjacent, make another cut like the first. Keep turning and cutting until you have completed the carrot. The perfect turned carrot has seven sides, but don't be concerned about this at the beginning. Now make a second series of little edge cuts, if required, to perfect the oval form.

Turned potatoes:

Use boiling potatoes. Since potatoes vary widely in shape, cut a peeled potato as shown in drawing 1, and turn each of the four sides you remove (drawing 2). Then cut two or three pieces from the center, depending on size, and turn those. Be sure to drop the ovals into water as you work so they do not turn brown.

Turned turnips:

Use small white turnips and cut as directed for turned potatoes.

Turned mushrooms:

Select large, firm, very white, well-shaped mushrooms. With a very sharp paring knife, cut off the stems close to the caps and remove a thin layer of peel by a continuous cut-and-turn motion, as if you were peeling an apple. Then choke up on the blade and, starting at the center of the cap, make a double-cut groove on an angle to the edge. Continue in this manner until the entire cap appears fluted with spiral grooves. As each mushroom is completed, place it in a saucepan in a simple broth made of water with a tablespoon or two of butter, some lemon juice, and a dash of salt. When all are completed, cover the pot and cook for 3 minutes. Drain (the broth can be added to soup or a sauce) and, if not using immediately, lay a piece of buttered paper right on the caps. (Good cooks never waste anything and, in the case of mushrooms stems and peelings, these are saved to go into soups and stocks. The same holds true for the peelings that result from turning other vegetables.)

Chiseled mushrooms:
Similar to turned mushrooms but considerably easier, the mushroom is simply peeled and a decorative pattern is pressed into it all over with the point of a sharp knife.

Scallion brushes:
Use whenever you need a cool dash of green and white. Have a bowl of ice water handy before you begin. Remove the roots from as many nice firm scallions as you wish to use. Cut off most of the green, leaving a section approximately 3 inches long that is mostly white. Lay the scallion on its side and make a series of cuts with the point of a small sharp paring knife to within ¾ inch of the base. Place cut scallion in ice water.

The Culinary Herbs

Herbs are the fragrant leaves and sometimes nonwoody stems of plants, fresh or dried, such as parsley, basil, dill, savory, sage, and tarragon. Spices are pungent barks, roots, or seeds, such as cinnamon, ginger, and nutmeg. They may also be berries, like pepper and juniper, or flower parts, like saffron and capers.

The French also designate certain vegetables as *herbes potagères* (potherbs), those we would call soup greens, like leek, turnip, and carrot. Further, the French use the term *aromates* to indicate a category of cookery ingredients that includes herbs, spices, and such other things as might be added to food to enhance its flavor, like citrus zest.

Bunching the herb

Coarse chopping

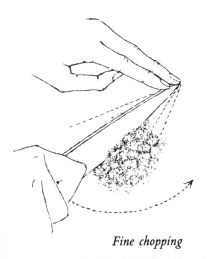

Fine chopping

I don't think anyone has to be convinced that fresh herbs are the best, but they are not always available, especially in winter. Many, however, can be grown rather easily indoors, either from seed or as small annual plants, which usually come on sale in early spring. A number of the perennial herbs, like oregano, thyme, sage, rosemary, and mint, will last through the winter on a sunny windowsill, though eventually they will grow rather leggy and puny of leaf. If you are fortunate enough to have a garden, pot your herbs and bring them in when the weather turns cool. If they remain vigorous until the following year, you can put them out again. If not, throw them away and buy new ones for outdoors, knowing that a winter's pleasure from herbs is easily worth trice the number of summers.

Most dried herbs, if they are in good condition, are two to three times as strong as an equal amount of minced fresh herbs, so that a tablespoon of fresh herbs would equal a teaspoon of the dried. (See notes on bay leaf for an exception.)

A bouquet garni, fundamental to French and especially Provençal cooking, is a method of flavoring long-cooked dishes. It consists of fresh or dried herbs and spices tied in a cheesecloth bag. The usual combination is parsley, thyme, and bay leaf, with black peppercorns or cloves sometimes added. Occasionally a recipe will specify other herbs.

The purpose of the cheesecloth bag is to facilitate removal of the herbs and spices when the flavor has been cooked out; the dark bits and pieces swimming around in a sauce are less than attractive, and can be, in the case of a clove or bay leaf, downright unpleasant to bite down on.

To Buy

Fresh herbs: look for bright green color and a fresh, strong smell. A sour smell means rot is beginning.

Dried herbs: Don't be taken in by fancy presentations; what you want are herbs that are not stale. If you are buying commercially put up herbs (and spices), stick with a brand you trust, such as Spice Islands. Jars are generally better than cellophane packets for retaining freshness. If buying from bulk storage, go to a dealer with a high turnover.

To Store

Fresh herbs: Try not to buy more than you will use in a few days. If necessary, a minigreenhouse storage method will keep parsley for at least ten days, and other herbs like dill and coriander for at least five. To do this, wash, shake off excess water, and place the stems in about an inch of water in a glass jar. Put a plastic bag loosely over the top and store on the highest shelf in the refrigerator. (Cut the stems a bit if height is a problem.) Change the water every three days.

Dried herbs: Glass jars with screw tops make the best containers. Keep them away from heat, light, and moisture. If you like a few herbs and spices at hand in the open, keep them out of direct sunlight. Sniff them from time to time and, if they smell dull and grassy, replace them; they'll do nothing for your food.

To dry fresh herbs: Place leaves and small sprigs of a single herb variety on brown paper and put in an oven set at about 150°. When dry, strip from stems, seal in airtight glass containers, and label.

To freeze: Frozen herbs lack crispness and good color, but certain of them can be frozen to use for flavor. I freeze chopped chives in a plastic box and tarragon leaves, which have been washed and dried, frozen on a cookie sheet, and then stored in a plastic bag.

Basil

A pungent, clove-scented member of the mint family whose English name is derived from the Greek word for *king,* it is superbly complementary to tomatoes and the basic ingredient of Genoese pesto, a sauce made by pounding its leaves together with garlic. It is used widely in France, especially in Provence. Basil is the specific flavor of the liquor chartreuse, and, in England, the traditional flavoring for turtle soup.

There are several dozen basil species; the one we use is sweet basil, *ocimum basilicum*. There is also a purple basil, used chiefly as an ornamental herb.

Basil is a very easy herb to grow and is abundant in spring and summer. One way to preserve it is to layer the washed and dried leaves in a clean jar, add some coarse salt, more leaves, and continue this layering until the jar is full. Fill the jar to the brim with olive oil. When a leaf is needed, remove, blot on a paper towel, and use as desired. The oil itself may be used for cooking when the leaves are gone, and will be permeated with their delicious scent. Handle basil gently; it discolors easily.

Commercially dried basil has none of the pungency of the fresh leaf and will do nothing for your food. If I don't have fresh basil, I simply omit it when a recipe calls for it or use parsley, which at least gives a fresh taste.

Bay

The aromatic leaf of the evergreen sweet bay tree (the true laurel), a native of the Mediterranean and Asia Minor, is used fresh or dried to impart its characteristic flavor to stews, marinades, and tomato sauces. It is thought to be one of the oldest flavoring additives in culinary history. The ancient Greeks and Romans believed that wearing it warded off lightning, and they made wreaths of it to laud the achievements of athletes, scholars, and the like, hence *poet laureate, winning your laurels,* and so on. The belief persisted, for herbalist William Culpeper wrote in the seventeenth century that "neither witch nor devil, thunder nor lightening will hurt a man where a bay tree is."

The true bay leaf—the *Laura nobilis,* or Mediterranean bay—is a wide, silver-gray leaf quite distinct from the California bay laurel, a slender, dark green leaf offered as bay in the average spice line. The latter is more bitter, with less of a spicy overtone. The Mediterranean bay is stronger but sweeter.

Bay is an exception to the rule that dried herbs are stronger than fresh; fresh bay is twice as strong as dried. If you are using dried bay leaves, it is important that they be pungent and not old, or the point of using them is lost. Best results are gotten when bay is crumbled before adding it to the dish being cooked. Because it is quite strong, usually only one or two leaves are needed.

Though it grows slowly, bay can be grown in tubs and is quite hardy. To dry, pick early in the morning and place in a warm, shady place spread out in thin layers until dried but not brittle. Store in glass jars.

Chervil

(Anthriscus cerefolium)

A delicate herb rather like parsley combined with tarragon, chervil is little used in this country but very popular in France, where it is a standard ingredient in many recipes and a component of *fines herbs*. Dried chervil tastes like grass and is of no use whatever. Use the fresh liberally in omelets and vegetable soups and with white fish; add at the last minute, as cooking destroys the gentle flavor. The leaves may also be added to a green salad.

Chives

(Allium schoenoprasum)

The mildest member of the onion family, chives doubly enhance vegetables, soups, and sauces: They lend a delicate onion flavor and a green garnish as well. Chives have an affinity for mild creamy foods like cottage cheese, yogurt, and sour cream. Sprinkle on creamed soups, sliced tomatoes, and broiled fish, and add to omelets. Because the flavor is destroyed by cooking, add at the last minute.

Chives are a hardy perennial, as anyone who has them in the garden will attest. Potted chives are available at many greengrocers for windowsill use. They want frequent watering, sunshine, and repotting if they appear crowded in the pot. To use, snip off a number of whole blades about half an inch above the soil, then snip or cut with a knife into tiny pieces. Like other onions, chives begin to develop a harsh flavor after being cut and exposed to the air, so cut, chop, or snip just before use.

Chive butter: Follow the recipe for tarragon butter on page 397, substituting 2 tablespoons chopped chives. Use with broiled or baked fish.

Coriander

(Coriandrum sativum)

Coriander, also known as Chinese parsley, is a contradictory plant belonging to the carrot family. It is both spice and herb (one of the earliest used); it has two kinds of leaves, two kinds of flowers, and two usable parts. Some herbalists thought it smelled awful (one sixteenth-century writer said coriander smelled so bad it made other plants smell better) and others thought it delightful, likening it to lemon peel. It was introduced into the New World by the Spaniards and is now a characteristic flavor of Mexican and South American dishes. Whole or chopped leaves are used to garnish and flavor many Oriental dishes.

Coriander seeds: The dried seeds, which are pungent and slightly sweet, are used in many countries as a spice. They flavor pickles, coffee, and mulled wine, and are an ingredient of the Indian seasoning garam masala. Crushed, the seed flavors Scandinavian baked goods and puddings and American hot dogs.

Coriander seeds are not a substitute for the leaf and have a different taste. Commercially ground coriander seeds rarely have the pungency of those ground at home, unless they come from a Middle Eastern market where they grind their own in small quantities.

To roast and grind coriander seeds:
Put the seeds in an ungreased skillet, set over heat, and toast lightly. Grind in a spice mill or with a mortar and pestle.

Dill Weed
(Anethum graveolens)

D ill is widely used in Scandinavian and Central European cookery; its feathery leaves complement mild foods like sour cream, cottage cheese, and cream sauces. Mixed into yogurt, dill is a delightful topping for a baked potato. It is also good with poached fish, as a flavoring in soups, and marries well with cucumbers, carrots, potatoes, and cauliflower. The seeds give their name and flavor to dill pickles. Dried dill weed is virtually flavorless compared with the fresh.

Wash fresh dill well; the complex leaves hold dirt.

Dill butter: Substitute 4 tablespoons chopped dill in the recipe for tarragon butter (p. 397) and add an extra ½ teaspoon of lemon juice. Use with broiled fish and vegetables.

Fennel
(Foeniculum Vulgare)

F ennel seeds are produced when the feathery tops of the bulb go into flower. They have a pungent anise taste and are used by the Italians to flavor sausages and figs and, in Sweden, together with the leaves, to make fennel sauce. They can also be used with carrots, beets, and parsnips.

Lovage
(Levisticum officinale)

T his splendid member of the parsley family is available mostly to gardeners, who prize it because it is the first perennial to come back in spring. The taste is a cross between parsley and celery, a sprightly note in green salads, potato salad, and various slaws. Long cooking in stews and soups heightens the flavor. Lovage seeds can be used like celery seeds.

Marjoram

S weet marjoram is really a sweeter, less bitter version of oregano, which was very popular in the Middle Ages for scenting baths, perfumes, and strewing about rush floors. A fresh sprig can be used in meat stock or a sauce, or with any green vegetable or bean dish. In its most common dried form, however, the taste isn't that different from regular oregano.

Mint

Oregano

(Origanum vulgare)

Parsley

(Petroselinum crispum)

Mint can do a lot more for food than subdue a muttony leg of lamb. It is lovely with peas, zucchini, new potatoes, green beans, carrots, and eggplant, and indispensable in many Middle Eastern and Moroccan dishes. Try it chopped in a green salad.

Related to marjoram, but stronger in flavor, *Origanum vulgare* is an indispensable flavor for Italian-style tomato sauces and useful in basting sauces and marinades. Oregano is very pungent in its dried form, and is almost always used that way. Any Mediterranean-style recipes involving eggplant, zucchini, or tomatoes do well with oregano.

There are two major varieties of this most popular herb, the curly-leaved ornamental and the Italian flat-leaved type, which is not as pretty but is more strongly flavored. There is virtually no vegetable that is not enhanced by a sprinkling of chopped parsley. To keep a quantity of chopped parsley fresh for at least two days, wring out the excess moisture in a kitchen towel and refrigerate in a plastic container.

Parsley butter: Follow the directions for tarragon butter (p. 397), substituting 3 tablespoons finely minced parsley. Use on broiled meats or fish or any vegetable.

Maître d'hôtel butter: Make parsley butter with 2 tablespoons parsley and 2 tablespoons finely chopped shallots or chives. Use with broiled meats.

Snail butter (buerre d'escargot): Cream 1 stick of unsalted butter, then beat in 2 tablespoons very finely minced shallots, 2 or 3 cloves garlic put through a press, 2 tablespoons finely minced parsley, and salt and pepper to taste.

Rosemary

(Rosemarinus officinalis)

Sage

(Salvia officinalis)

Rosemary has a great variety of uses and is loved nowhere as well as in the north of Italy, where butchers automatically include a sprig of rosemary and one of sage along with your meat order.

The name derives from the latin *ros marinum,* meaning "dew of the sea." Rosemary was introduced into England by the Romans, and by medieval times, no garden was without its rosemary bush.

Dried rosemary is intense and resinous, and a little goes a long way. It is splendid rubbed into pork, lamb, or veal, and enhances fish, poultry, baby goat, and many bean dishes. Try marinating a goat cheese in a fruity olive oil into which dried or fresh rosemary has been crumbled. Also add to the cooking liquid of turnips and broccoli.

Rosemary butter: Follow the directions for tarragon butter (p. 397), but substitute 2 teaspoons dried or 3 tablespoons fresh crumbled rosemary. Use on broiled pork chops.

Sage was used medicinally by the ancient Greeks and Romans, as a calmative and to ward off the symptoms of senility, hence its Latin name—*salvia* from *salvare,* to heal. The American Indians used it as a primitive dentifrice. In cooking, it is a popular taste for poultry stuffings, but it is not used here with as much variety as in Italy. Deep-fried fresh sage makes a delightful garnish for meat and chicken dishes. There are several types of sage; the most common has a lemony camphor flavor, but others are reminiscent of mint, lilac, and pineapple.

Deep-fried sage: Heat oil in a deep fryer to 350°. Dredge large, unblemished fresh sage leaves with flour, shake off excess in a strainer, and fry in hot oil for 1 or 2 minutes. Remove with a slotted spoon and drain on brown paper. Sprinkle with salt to taste.

Savory

Tarragon

(Artemisia dracunculus)

Thyme

(Thymus vulgaris)

All members of the cabbage family marry well with this herb, whose peppery piquancy is useful in sodium-restricted diets. It enhances soups containing beans and other dried legumes, and beans flavored with savory are an institution in Germany. There is a winter and summer variety, the latter being the most popular.

A pretty perennial herb with slender, shiny green leaves and a distinctive anise flavor, tarragon is widely used in French cooking and is indispensable in béarnaise sauce. It is also extremely popular as a flavoring for vinegar. It is especially good tucked into a chicken to be roasted, and in veal stews and cream sauces. Tarragon butter is marvelous with broiled fish or lobster.

There is nothing like the taste of fresh tarragon, but, unless you grow it yourself, it is hard to come by. What is available fresh at market is often hot-house grown and lacking in taste. Dried tarragon sometimes tastes like fermenting hay and unless used sparingly lends a bitter taste to food. Fresh tarragon is powerful and should also be used sparingly.

Tarragon vinegar: Put a handful of fresh tarragon leaves or two full branches into a quart of red or white vinegar. Cork well and let stand in the sun for ten days, turning occasionally. Strain, rebottle, and seal well.

Tarragon butter: Cream 1 stick of unsalted butter and beat in 1 tablespoon lemon juice a bit at a time. Blend in 3 tablespoons chopped fresh tarragon and salt and pepper to taste. Refrigerate or freeze in a sausage-shape roll, cutting off pieces to garnish fish or meat as needed.

Thyme is an extremely useful herb because it retains so much flavor when dried. It can always be used in combination with bay and has a special affinity for garlicky tomato and eggplant dishes. The herb is splendid in marinades, stews, and rubbed on roasts, especially lamb. Mixed with a crumb topping and dotted with butter, it complements gratins of turnips, potatoes, and zucchini. Thyme butter can be used like tarragon butter.

Thyme is a powerful herb and should be used sparingly; the dried form is always stronger than the fresh. Powdered thyme exists but seems pointless.

Fresh thyme is hard to find in this country unless you grow your own. *Thymus vulgaris,* ordinary cultivated thyme, or any subvarieties like lemon or mint thyme, can be planted in the cracks between flagstones of a walk—trodden underfoot, they release their delightful aroma. The Swedish botanist Linnaeus thought thyme a cure for hangovers, and Culpeper, the English herbalist, recommended thyme tea at bedtime to thwart nightmares.

Thyme butter: Follow the directions for tarragon butter (p. 397), substituting 2 teaspoons dried thyme or 3 tablespoons fresh.

Appendix
Pasta

I often think how fortunate I am to be living in the Pasta Age. When I was a child, *pasta* meant spaghetti, you ate it with meatballs or meat sauce or clam sauce and that was about it. Now, new and exciting combinations (some of them actually old ones, resurrected) appear on restaurant menus every day and quickly find their way into the home. And by far the most exciting are those that include vegetables. I find that when I serve something like ziti and sweet peppers or eggplant, or linguini with pesto, everyone is so satisfied they never miss meat or chicken, and my vegetarian friends have taught me that the addition of the usual grated Parmesan gives you adequate and complete protein.

Pasta has an undeserved reputation for being fattening, due in part to the American custom of making a whole meal of it, something none but the poorest Italians would think of doing. Except as a light-hearted, slightly makeshift meal (what is called in Rome a *spaghettata,* where friends convene on the spur of the moment, say after a cocktail party, and someone makes pasta), pasta is meant to be a course to whet the appetite, filling you up just a little bit. A 3- or 4-ounce portion (no seconds!) with a light vegetable sauce made with a moderate amount of oil does not have more than 350 to 400 calories. Eaten this way, pasta can be consumed frequently without being fattening, a fact always marveled at by Americans traveling in Italy.

The relationship between pasta shape and length and the accompanying sauce is a subtle one, since there are more than a hundred shapes to choose from. Size, texture, and ease of eating must all be taken into account; shapes popular at the moment do not necessarily go with the sauce currently in vogue. As a general rule, the thicker pastas like spaghetti, linguini, and tagliarini are used with tomato or butter-based sauces. Delicate pastas like angel's hair tend to mat into an unappealing mass when served with heavy sauces. Tubular pastas and shells are meant to be used with a sauce thin enough to be easily conveyed to the mouth; otherwise they are dry and boring. Well-seasoned vegetable purees, which make wonderful sauces for pasta, are particularly effective here.

Once you've experienced the tasty tender velvet of the fresh noodle, you'll find it hard to go back to packaged dried pasta, though the latter has its place. If fresh pasta is not feasible, the best dried kind to buy is an Italian import like De Cecco, made from durum wheat and semolina flour. Look for the words *durum* or *grano duro* on the package.

Fresh pasta should be eaten as soon as possible, though it will keep well for 2 or 3 days in the refrigerator or longer, well-wrapped, in the freezer. Since it cooks much more rapidly than dried, have your sauce ready, cheese grated, and bowls and dishes warmed.

The cooking method for fresh and dried is the same:

Bring a large amount of water to a boil, ideally a quart for each 4 ounces of pasta. When the water hits a rolling boil, add 2 or 3 tablespoons of salt and a dollop of oil, then the pasta a bit at a time. Push it down so it is uniformly submerged, and cook uncovered. Even if frozen, fresh noodles will be al dente in 50 seconds to 3 minutes, depending on thickness (spinach noodles take a little longer; cooking time for dried pasta is usually on the box but start checking several minutes before the suggested time). The tooth is the ultimate test, so bite a strand if you're not sure; it should be slightly chewy yet not taste of flour.

If you are going to use what the Italians call the *segreto* (secret) method of cooking the pasta in with the sauce for 2 or 3 minutes before serving, then undercook it for that amount of time.

Use a wooden fork for stirring. Drain quickly in a big colander and don't rinse it, which can make it sticky and horrid unless it is to stop the cooking instantly for the *segreto* method.

Some professionals like to fork pasta directly from the pot into a warmed pottery bowl, letting the water drain off each forkful back into the pot, the idea being that this keeps the pasta hotter and more receptive to the sauce.

There are some wonderful suggestions for pasta and vegetable combinations in the two books on Italian cooking by Marcella Hazan. Some of my favorites are fettuccini with fried zucchini or simply with butter and rosemary; tonnarelli, a thin noodle, with sautéed porcini mushrooms; and shells with a broccoli-anchovy sauce. In this book, I especially recommend the fettuccini with zucchini and mushrooms and the shells with sweet peppers, peas, and pesto sauce. The pesto sauce is also great with cheese-filled tortellini, which you can now buy frozen.

Planning Vegetarian Meals

I am not a vegetarian; I eat very little red meat because I find I feel better and am better able to maintain my weight without it. I serve chicken and fish frequently, veal occasionally, and at least two meatless meals weekly, which are usually built around a hearty soup or several substantial vegetable dishes served in two or even three courses. To provide adequate protein on these occasions, we have cheese with our salad and a dessert made with dairy products, like a soufflé or a flan.

Today more than ever there are several persuasive arguments for the vegetarian diet, or at least for a diet in which vegetables dominate. Vegetables contain little or no fat. In the opinion of many nutritionists fat is the greatest single cause of poor health. The latest research shows a correlation between a low-fat diet and a reduced risk of coronary heart disease, the country's leading killer. Cholesterol and blood pressure levels, both of which play a major role in heart disease, are lower among vegetarians than among people who eat meat. In addition, the American Cancer Society recommends the daily consumption of dark-green leafy vegetables and deep yellow vegetables, both good sources of beta carotene, a substance associated with reduced risk of cancer of the breast, lung, bladder, and skin. The society also recommends eating daily certain vegetables in the cabbage family, such as broccoli, cauliflower, kale, and brussels sprouts, thought to contain other cancer-inhibiting agents.

The vegetarian diet not only replaces undesirable fatty foods but is also helpful in weight control. A diet composed primarily of vegetables and grains is bulky and filling, making it hard to overeat. And calorie for calorie, vegetables as a food group have more nutrients than other natural foods.

There are three main types of vegetarians: *lactovegetarians,* who obtain protein from milk, cheese, and other dairy products but not eggs; *ovolactovegetarians,* who obtain protein from eggs, milk, cheese, and other dairy products; and *strict vegetarians,* sometimes called vegans, who obtain all their protein from plant sources and eat no food of animal origin.

The major hazard of the strict vegetarian diet has always been obtaining a sufficient amount of complete protein. For the first two groups of vegetarians, and for part-time vegetarians and quasi-vegetarians who eat fish, this is not a problem. But to understand how to eat wisely on a vegetarian diet, one must understand protein and how it functions. Amino acids, about twenty of them, are the chemical building blocks of protein, which is needed to make muscle and organ tissue and vital enzymes. The human body can manufacture all but eight of these amino acids from any food containing plant as well as animal protein. These eight, called essential amino acids, must be supplied ready-made in our food. All eight must be present in the same meal in order for the body to use dietary protein to manufacture body protein. Animal products, such as meat, eggs, and dairy products, contain all eight, and therefore the protein they yield is complete. The protein in plants is incomplete, but combining one plant food with another so that each supplies the amino acid deficient in the other yields protein as complete as that derived from animal products. The body does not distinguish the source as long as the protein it receives is complete. This combining of nonmeat foods to make a nutritionally complete meal is called vegetable *complementarity*. Legumes (beans and peas) combined with grains, peas and rice, for example, yield complete protein. So do legumes combined with nuts or seeds. So does any plant food combined with a dairy product such as cheese, milk, or eggs. In addition to supplying protein, legumes, nuts, and other seeds are sources of iron and B vitamins; grains contribute thiamine, iron, and trace minerals.

Committed vegetarians who already know how to make efficient use of plant protein through careful meal planning will find many ways to use the recipes in this book to create nutritious meals. I have noted those recipes that are nutritionally complete in themselves or that lend themselves particularly well to vegetarian meal planning. Readers who wish to learn more about vegetarianism should consult one of the several good books on the subject. One I like especially is *The Vegetarian Handbook* by Rodger Doyle (Crown, 1979).

For quick planning, remember that the ideal vegetarian diet should draw every day from the following four food groups: grains, legumes, nuts, and seeds; vegetables; fruit; and dairy products. In the last group, two glasses of lowfat milk for adults and three or more for children are recommended. Other dairy products or one egg may be used to meet this requirement. Allow up to four eggs a week.

Vegetarians need a wide selection of tasty, interesting foods that fit their dietary needs. With fewer food groups to choose from, they need variety sufficient to ensure that they will not be deficient in any one nutrient.

My vegetarian friends also advise against the trap of looking for substitutions in the standard meal planning format. Don't think about the "entrée" or "the main course," but concentrate instead on several equally important courses, as in a Chinese-type meal with several harmonious dishes.

Glossary

Acidulated Water: Water to which lemon juice or vinegar has been added (about 1 tablespoon to 1 quart) to prevent air from darkening the cut surface of certain pale vegetables.

Blanc à Légumes: Some pale vegetables darken unattractively when cooked. This technique, also also called cooking *à blanc,* may be used with globe artichoke hearts, Jerusalem artichokes, salsify, Swiss chard stalks, and celeriac. To make a blanc, see p. 17.

Beurre Manié: A blend of equal amounts of flour and butter used to thicken soups, sauces, and stews. Blend with the fingers in a bowl, add to the liquid in small balls, and whisk in, or plunge the whisk with the mixture adhering into the liquid and blend.

Capers: The pickled unopened buds of a trailing shrub *capparis spinosa,* which grows wild in Mediterranean countries. Their piquancy gives a lift to eggs, fatty fish, meat, and sauces. The best are the tiny *nonpareilles* that come from the Var in France. Very large capers are usually nasturtium buds, which give the look if not the true caper flavor.

Chiffonade: Shredded greens, most frequently lettuce and sorrel. To cut leaves *en chiffonade,* roll each into a cigar shape, and then, using a stainless steel knife, cut each cigar crosswise into roughly half-inch slices that, when unfolded, will fall into ribbons. Use as a base for vegetables or other food, in salads or in soups.

Clarified Butter: Butter from which the milk solids are removed so that it can be heated to high temperatures without burning. Ghee, frequently called for in Indian cookery, is clarified butter. To make, cut unsalted butter into small pats and melt it over low heat. Remove from heat, let stand for 3 minutes, then skim the froth from the top and discard. Let stand until the milky solids have settled to the bottom. Pour off the clear liquid, which is clarified butter, and store covered in the refrigerator, where it will keep indefinitely. Discard the milky solids. Alternatively, you can strain the butter after skimming through a sieve lined with a rinsed cheesecloth. Two sticks of butter will make about ¾ cup.

Croutons: Bread pieces that are toasted in one of several ways.

Brush a required number of slices of good-quality French or Italian bread with olive oil and run them under the broiler until golden brown on one side, then turn and repeat the process. Each crouton is then rubbed with a cut piece of garlic. Or trim the crusts from slices of slightly stale bread and cut into ½ inch squares. Fry them in a skillet in a mixture of butter and oil, or all oil, until golden brown. You can also deep-fry them, if you want to go to the trouble, or oven-fry them by buttering the bread with softened butter before cutting, and spreading them out on an ungreased cookie sheet in a slow oven for about 20 to 25 minutes, turning each one once during the baking. You can mix a pressed clove of garlic into the butter, or a choice of herbs or Parmesan cheese. For a low-calorie version, cube the bread, spread on a cookie sheet, and bake in a 325° oven, stirring occasionally, for 15 minutes, until crisp and light brown. Store in an airtight container.

Commercially packaged croutons always seem to be rancid.

Crème Fraîche: A partly fermented cream with a minimum of 30 percent butterfat and a distinctive nutty flavor, widely used in French cooking because it does not curdle or separate when boiled. Unpasteurized cream with a high butterfat content will thicken naturally as it ferments. But pasteurized cream needs the addition of buttermilk or yogurt to ferment.

To make crème fraîche, stir a tablespoon of buttermilk (it gives the best flavor) into a cup of heavy cream. Heat gently to just under body temperature, then let sit covered in a warm spot for 7 to 10 hours, or until thick. Refrigerate covered.

Crème fraîche is now sold commercially in food specialty shops, as is a powdered starter of the lactic ferments (see Shop by Mail).

Garam Masala: An aromatic spice mixture used to flavor many Indian dishes. There are many variations, but generally it consists of cloves, cardamom, cinnamon, cumin, nutmeg, and black peppercorns, all ground together.

Mirepoix: A classic flavoring composed of finely chopped carrots, celery, and onions in equal amounts. It may be seasoned with parsley, bay or thyme, and salt to taste. A mirepoix is often used as a preliminary step in braising to enrich the braising liquid. Use about 3 tablespoons butter for each cup of vegetables, and sauté over low heat in a heavy skillet, stirring frequently, until vegetables are soft but not brown. This will take 20 to 25 minutes.

The same vegetables, roughly chopped, add immense

flavor to the final sauce when added to the pan in which chicken or meat is being roasted. After the meat is done, simmer the pan juices and vegetables on top of the stove, then push them through a fine-meshed sieve to extract their final essence before discarding.

Pignoli: Pine nut kernels, also called pine nuts and piñon nuts. Frequently used in Italian cookery, pine nuts were popular in medieval England.

To toast: Preheat oven to 300°. Spread pine nuts on a rimmed baking sheet and bake for 20 minutes, stirring several times, until they are lightly golden. Do not let them become brown. Cool before using.

Provençal Herbs: an extremely fragrant herb mixture, to be used sparingly. Mix together 1 tablespoon each dried thyme, tarragon, marjoram, and chervil and 1 teaspoon each dried organo, rosemary, summer savory, and 2 Mediterranean bay leaves, well crushed. Store in a tightly sealed glass jar.

Sesame Oil: An aromatic cooking oil that imparts the splendid nutty sesame seed flavor to cooked foods and salads. Do not use the colorless kind; look for the brownish sesame oil found in Oriental markets.

Sesame Paste: Also called tahini. Ground roasted sesame seeds, available in jars in many supermarkets and specialty food stores.

Sesame Seeds: The seeds of a small annual plant grown in the Far East, India, and the Balkans, used in baking and in many Oriental dishes. Available in jars in the spice section of most markets and by weight in bulk in Indian and Oriental stores, they are an excellent source of protein.

To toast: Place sesame seeds in a small, heavy, dry skillet over medium heat until they begin to color slightly and one or two pop. Remove to a piece of wax paper, place another on top, and crush with a rolling pin to release the flavorsome oil.

Sofrito: A cooking base used in Spanish cooking in the same way a mirepoix functions in French cookery. A basic sofrito consists of chopped onions and tomatoes; frequent additions, depending on the use and depth of flavor desired, are minced garlic, minced green peppers, diced ham, or chopped sausage. To make a basic sofrito, sauté finely chopped onions in olive oil until pale gold. Add peeled, seeded, and chopped tomatoes, salt mixture lightly, and cook over moderate heat, uncovered, for 15 minutes, or until thickened and saucelike.

Tahini: See sesame paste.

Shop by Mail

Chinese Foods

The Chinese Grocer
209 Post St.
San Francisco, CA 94108

Shing Chong & Co.
800 Grant Ave,
San Francisco, CA 94108

Wing Chong Lung Co.
800 7th St NW
Washington, D.C. 20001

Wing Wing Imported
Groceries
79 Harrison Ave.
Boston, MA 02111

Asia House Grocery
2433 St. Paul St.
Baltimore, MD 02111

King's Trading
3736 Broadway
Kansas City, MO 64111

Wing Fat Co.
33–35 Mott St.
New York, N.Y. 10013

Kam Man Food Products
200 Canal St.
New York, N.Y. 10013

Wing On
1005 Race St.
Philadelphia, PA 19107

Harmony Oriental
247 Atwood St.
Pittsburgh, PA 14213

Oriental Import-Export
Co.
2009 Polk St.
Houston, TX 77003

Indian Specialties

Bazaar of India
11341 University Avenue
Berkeley, CA 94702

Bezjian Grocery
4725 Santa Monica Blvd.
Los Angeles, CA 90029

American Tea, Coffee &
Spice Co.
1511 Champa St.
Denver, CO 80202

Spices & Foods
Unlimited
2018A Florida NW
Washington, D.C. 20009

Cambridge Coffee Tea
and Spice House
1765 Massachusetts Ave.
Cambridge, MA 02138

Annapurna
127 East 28th St.
New York, N.Y. 10016

Middle Eastern Foods

Haig's Delicacies
441 Clewment St.
San Francisco, CA 94118

Bezjian Groceries
4725 Santa Monica Blvd.
Los Angeles, CA 90029

Skenderis Greek Import
1612 20th St
Washington, DC 20009

Athens Imported Food
City Market 84–85
Indianapolis, IN 46204

Central Grocery Store
923 Decatur St.
New Orleans, LA 70116

Syrian Grocery Import
Co.
270 Shawmut Ave.
Boston, MA 02118

K. Kalustyan
123 Lexington Ave.
New York, N.Y. 10016

Sahadi Importing Co.
187 Atlantic Ave,
Brooklyn, N.Y. 11202

Chinamart Trading Co.
210 Spadina Ave.
Toronto, Ontario
Canada

Japanese and Other Oriental Foods

Asia Food Market
2000 Judah St.
San Francisco, CA 94122

Debashi Co.
240 East Jackson St.
San Jose, CA 95112

Ai Hoa Market
860 North Hill Street
Los Angeles, CA 90012

Pacific Mercantile
Grocery
1925 Lawrence St.
Denver, CO 80202

Asian Supermarket
2581 Piedmont Rd.
Atlanta, GA 30324

Far East Trading Co.
2837 North Western
Ave.
Chicago, IL 60618

Jung's Oriental Food
Store
913 East University Ave.
Des Moines, IA 50316

Sun Sun Co.
34 Oxford St.
Boston, MA 02139

Oriental Food Store
18919 West Seven Mile
Rd.
Detroit, MI 48219

Japan Imported Foods
808 N.W 6th St.
Oklahoma City, OK
73106

Asia Products Corp.
226 N. 10th St.
Philadelphia, PA 19107

Eastern Foods
8626½ Long Point
Houston, TX 77053

Iwaki Japanese Food
Store
2627 Yonge St.
Toronto, Ontario
Canada M4P 2J6

Spanish Groceries:
dried chilies and canned
jalapeño and serrano
chilies

El Mercado
First Avenue & Lorenzo
Los Angeles, CA 90063

Casa Estiero
2719 West Division St.
Chicago, IL 60622

Mexican Kitchen
Box 213
Brownsville, TX 78520

Italian groceries:
dried mushrooms,
imported macaroni,
Arborio rice, cheese, etc.

Todaro Brothers
555 Second Ave.
New York, NY 10016

Balducci's
424 Sixth Ave.
New York, NY 10011

Il Conte di Savoia
555 West Roosevelt Rd.
Chicago, IL 60607

Specialty items:

Mushrooms: fresh shiitakes may be ordered by overnight express mail from

Elix Corp.
Route 1
Arvonia, VA 23004

Oakville Grocery
1555 Pacific Ave.
San Francisco, CA 94109

Vidalia onions: for a list of mail order sources write to

Vidalia Chamber of Commerce
P.O. Box 306
Vidalia, GA 30474

Sun-dried tomatoes: order from

Dean & Deluca
560 Broadway
New York, NY 10012

Christopher Stephens, Importer
P.O. Box 114
Carversville, PA 18913

Spices, dried herbs:

The Complete Cook
405 Lake Cook Plaza
Deerfield, IL 60015

Aphrodisia
282 Bleecker St.
New York, NY 10012

Hard-to-find herb plants, seeds, etc.

Jardin du Gourmet
West Danville, VT 05873

Fox Hill Farm
440 West Michigan Ave.
Parma, MI 49269

Seeds for a wide variety of chili peppers and cilantro:

Horticultural Enterprises
P.O. Box 34082
Dallas, TX 75234

Crème fraîche starter:

Freeze-dried solait starter is available from

Williams-Sonoma
Mail Order Dept.
PO Box 7456
San Francisco, CA 94120

Canning Information

For the famous Ball step-by-step canning

booklet with useful charts and tables, write to

Ball Blue Book
Box 2005
Muncie, IND

Olive oils

The olive oils I use are Callisto Francesconi for general cooking and Badia a Coltibuono for salads and dishes where a fruity oil is indicated. The Badia oil is available by mail from Dean & Deluca (560 Broadway, New York, NY 10012), the Francesconi from Balducci's (424 Sixth Ave., New York, NY 10011).

Works Consulted

Anderson, Jean, and Elaine Hanna. *The Doubleday Cookbook.* New York: Doubleday and Co., 1975.

Apicius, Coelius. *De Re Coquinaria.* Edited by Jacques André, titled *l'Art Culinaire,* Paris: 1965.

Beard, James. *James Beard's American Cookery.* New York: Little Brown & Co., 1972.

Bertholle, Louisette. *French Cuisine for All.* New York: Doubleday & Co., 1980.

Bocuse, Paul, *French Cooking.* New York: Pantheon, 1977.

Boni, Ada. *The Talisman Italian Cook Book.* Translated by La Rosa. New York: Crown, 1950.

Brown, Dale. *The Cooking of Scandinavia.* Foods of the World. New York: Time-Life, 1968.

Bugialli, Guiliano. *The Fine Art of Italian Cooking.* New York: Times Book Co., 1977.

Cameron, S. M. "The Best from New Mexico Kitchens." *New Mexico Magazine* (1978).

Chamberlain, Samuel. *Bouquet de France.* New York: Gourmet Dist. Corp., 1966.

Child, Julia. *From Julia Child's Kitchen.* New York: Knopf, 1975.

Child, Julia. *Mastering the Art of French Cooking.* New York: Knopf, 1965.

Claiborne, Craig. *Cooking with Herbs and Spices.* New York: Bantam Books, 1981.

David, Elizabeth. *Mediterranean Food, French Country Cooking, Summer Cooking.* New York: Knopf, 1980.

Deonna, W., and M. Renard. *Croyances et Superstitions de Table dans le Rome Antique.* Brussels: 1961.

Diat, Louis. *Gourmet's Basic French Cookbook.* New York: Gourmet Dist. Corp., 1961.

Doyle, R. *The Vegetarian Handbook.* New York: Crown, 1979.

Fitzgibbon, Theodora. *The Food of the Western World.* New York: Quadrangle/NY Times Book Co., 1976.

Gerard, John. *Gerard's Herball* 1636. Reprint. London: Minerva, 1974

Gewanter, Vera. *A Passion for Vegetables.* New York: Viking, 1980.

Giobbi, Ed. *Italian Family Cooking.* New York: Vintage, 1971.

Grigson, Jane. *The Mushroom Feast.* England, Penguin Books.

Hale, William Harlan, and eds. *The Horizon Cookbook and Illustrated History of Eating and Drinking through the Ages.* New York: American Heritage, 1968.

Hambro, Natalie. *Particular Delights.* London: Jill Norman and Hobhouse, 1981.

Hazan, Marcella. *The Classic Italian Cook Book.* New York: Harper's Magazine Press, 1973.

Hazelton, Nika S. *The Regional Italian Kitchen.* New York: M. Evans, 1978.

Helsel, Jane. Article on radishes. *Cuisine* Magazine, September 1981.

Hendrickson, R. *The Great American Tomato Book.* New York: Doubleday, 1977.

Hillman, Howard. *The Cook's Book.* New York: Avon, 1981.

Jaffrey, Madhur. *World of the East Vegetarian Cooking.* New York: Knopf, 1981.

Jones, Evan. *American Food: The Gastronomic Story.* New York: Dutton, 1975.

Kennedy, Diana. *The Cuisines of Mexico.* New York: Harper & Row, 1972.

Kluger, Marilyn. Article on fiddlehead ferns. *Gourmet,* May 1982.

Machlin, Edda Servi. *The Classic Cuisine of the Italian Jews.* New York: Everest House, 1981.

Marcus, George and Nancy. *Forbidden Fruits and Forgotten Vegetables.* New York: St. Martin's Press, 1982.

Medecin, Jacques. *La Cuisine de Comte de Nice.* Juilliard, 1972. Trans. published by Penguin Books, Ltd, London.

Miller, Gloria Bley. *The Thousand Recipe Chinese Cookbook.* New York: Atheneum, 1966.

Montagne, Prosper. *Larousse Gastronomique.* New York: Crown, 1963.

Olney, Richard. *Simple French Food.* New York: Atheneum, 1974.

Ortiz, Elizabeth Lambert. *Caribbean Cooking.* London: Penguin Books, Ltd., 1977.

Owen, Sri. *The Home Book of Indonesian Cookery.* London: Faber & Faber, 1979.

Papashvily, Helen and George. *Russian Cooking.* Foods of the World. New York: Time-Life, 1969.

Pepin, Jacques. *La Technique.* New York: Pocket Books, 1978.

Pohren, D. E. *Adventures in Taste: the Wines and Folk Food of Spain.* Moron de la Frontera, Spain: Society of Spanish Studies, 1972.

Pullar, Philippa. *Consuming Passions.* Boston: Little, Brown, 1970.

Reilly, Harriet. "Amazing Fried Foods." *Cooks Magazine* 3 (1982).

Robertson, Laurel, Carol Flinders, and Godfrey Bronwen. *Laurel's Kitchen.* Berkeley, Cal.: Nilgiri Press.

Roden, Claudia. *A Book of Middle Eastern Food.* New York: Knopf, 1972.

Root, Waverly. *Food.* New York: Simon & Schuster, 1980.

Ross, Janet, and Michael Waterfield. *Leaves from Our Tuscan Kitchen.* New York: Atheneum, 1974.

Thomas, Anna. *The Vegetarian Epicure.* New York: Vintage, 1972.

Urvater, Michele, and David Liederman. *Cooking the Nouvelle Cuisine in America.* New York: Workman, 1979.

Uvezian, Sonia. *The Cuisine of Armenia.* New York: Harper & Row, 1974.

Verge, Roger. *Roger Verge's Cuisine of the South of France.* Translated by Smoler. New York: William Morrow, 1980.

Waldron, Maggie. *Fire & Smoke.* San Francisco: 101 Productions, 1978.

Index